D1234168

DEATH ZONES AND DARLING SPIES

....

STUDIES IN WAR, SOCIETY, AND THE MILITARY
....

What's a nice girl like Beverly Deepe

doing in a dirty war like this?

Covering it for the Herald Tribune.

TIME Magazine called Beverly Deepe "Saigon's prettiest Western correspondent." She's not only the prettiest, but one of the best informed. As TIME further stated: "What she does not know she can usually get from her two Vietnamese assistants, both wise in the labyrinthine ways of the country's politics."

Beverly Deepe's inside information and perceptive insights make her new series one you won't want to miss. In six articles, starting Sunday, she puts the whole Viet Nam situation into perspective:

1) What makes the Communists fight so hard (one of the war's biggest and most perplexing problems)

2) U.S. political mistakes in Viet Nam during the past 10 years

3) Today's hottest issue: corruption

4) Problems of strategic hamlets and political reform

5) Land reform programs

6) What have we done *right?*

Read Beverly Deepe's vital series on Viet Nam starting in Sunday's Herald Tribune

Death Zones and Darling Spies

SEVEN YEARS
OF VIETNAM WAR
REPORTING

Beverly Deepe Keever

UNIVERSITY OF NEBRASKA PRESS | LINCOLN AND LONDON

© 2013 by the Board of Regents
of the University of Nebraska

Acknowledgments for the use of
copyrighted material appear on
page 325, which constitutes an
extension of the copyright page.

Frontispiece: From the *New York Herald
Tribune*, May 28, 1965. © 1965 by the *New
York Times*. All rights reserved. Used
by permission and protected by the
Copyright Laws of the United States.
The printing, copying, redistribution, or
retransmission of the Material without
express written permission is prohibited.

All rights reserved
Manufactured in the United
States of America

♾

Publication of this volume was assisted
by a grant from the Friends of the
University of Nebraska Press.

Library of Congress
Cataloging-in-Publication Data
Keever, Beverly Deepe.
Death zones and darling spies:
seven years of Vietnam War reporting /
Beverly Deepe Keever.
p. cm. — (Studies in war, society,
and the military)
Includes bibliographical
references and index.
ISBN 978-0-8032-2261-8 (pbk.: alk. paper)
1. Vietnam War, 1961–1975 — Press
coverage — United States. 2. Vietnam
War, 1961–1975 — Journalists.
3. Vietnam War, 1961–1975 — Personal
narratives, American. 4. Keever,
Beverly Deepe — Travel — Vietnam.
5. Women war correspondents — Vietnam.
I. Title. II. Series: Studies in war,
society, and the military.
DS559.46.K44 2013
070.4'499597043 — dc23   2012041230

Set in Arno by Laura Wellington.
Designed by Nathan Putens.

CONTENTS

ILLUSTRATIONS

MAPS

Preface

History, despite its wrenching pain, cannot be unlived, but
if faced with courage, need not be lived again.

Maya Angelou, at Clinton presidential inauguration, 1993

November 8, 1960. Brisk gusts descended with the twilight hour as Sam
Lubell and I entered Rockefeller Center in Midtown Manhattan, headed
for the news studio of the National Broadcasting Company (NBC). We
were geared up to assess the soon-to-arrive ballots cast in the presidential
election between Democrats Senator John Kennedy and his running mate,
Lyndon Johnson, versus Republicans Vice President Richard Nixon and
Henry Cabot Lodge.

I cradled a dog-eared cardboard box of notes Sam and I had handwritten during the campaign to record his pioneering doorbell-ringing
technique of interviewing voters. My one-time professor at Columbia's
Graduate School of Journalism and now my boss, Sam was a big name
in political journalism, thanks to his syndicated newspaper columns and
award-winning book.[1] His reputation prompted NBC to contract him to
predict accurately the winner of what proved to be the nation's closest
presidential race up to that time and to do so ahead of the computers
pitted against him by the other two network stations.

Throughout the night I answered phone calls bringing us latest results
of voting in selected precincts where we had earlier conducted interviews.
By matching the phoned-in results with our earlier statistics, Sam beat
the other networks' computers to project accurately that Kennedy would
win the popular vote. Not in my wildest dreams did I then imagine that
these four politicians would influence so profoundly what would happen in Vietnam — or even that I would be in Vietnam. Yet Kennedy was

president when I arrived there, Nixon was when I left, and Lyndon B. Johnson was sandwiched between them, with Henry Cabot Lodge twice serving as U.S. ambassador to Saigon.

May 2001. I was one of some four dozen combat correspondents whose work had been selected for an exhibit designed to trace 148 years of war reporting starting with the Crimean conflict of 1853. Displayed at the Freedom Forum's Newseum in Washington DC, these "War Stories" illustrated "how correspondents deal with the challenge of reporting the facts of war accurately," especially when their coverage contradicts official pronouncements (as mine had done). I was also among those included because of my seven continuous years of reporting on the Vietnam War, from 1962 to 1969, longer than any other Western journalist up to that time.

In addition, based on my series of dispatches from and about the siege of the beleaguered Khe Sanh outpost, the *Christian Science Monitor* in 1969 had nominated me for the Pulitzer Prize in International Reporting. I remember chuckling as I read the nomination letter. "Most of Beverly Deepe's readers presume she is a man — for her beat in Vietnam is rough, tough and dangerous," *Monitor* managing editor Courtney R. Sheldon told the Pulitzer Prize committee. "Yet Miss Beverly Ann Deepe, who hails from little Carleton, Nebraska, has been reporting the war and political developments from Saigon and military outposts such as Khe Sanh for seven years now. She holds her own with hosts of masculine correspondents — and asks no favors."[2]

The "War Stories" exhibit, accompanied by photographs and a North Vietnamese trenching tool I had sent, was organized by experts selected by the Freedom Forum.[3] The exhibit was on display from May to November 2001, bracketing the cataclysmic hijacking of four airliners on September 11 that resulted in the leveling of the Twin Towers of the World Trade Center, destruction of parts of the Pentagon just miles from the Newseum, and the deaths of nearly three thousand civilians. Those horrifying attacks set in motion a chain of global events that ultimately prompted me to write these memoirs.

I began to write these memoirs forty-some years after leaving Vietnam and three years after retiring from teaching and researching journalism and communications. I was spurred by sensing that the U.S reaction to 9/11 had begun to degenerate in Afghanistan, Iraq, and the neighboring countries into another bloody, agonizing Vietnam-like experience. I became painfully aware that many shortcomings in U.S. policy and actions that I had noted in my reporting from Vietnam were arising again nearly a half century later in another part of the world. Not only was the Vietnam War a failure for the United States, but it was also a humiliation because U.S. government leaders failed for decades to study this defeat and to learn from it. Instead, they replayed its strategic shortcomings.

Nor was I alone in beginning to make this brutal assertion about the United States having squandering time, blood, treasury, and legitimacy after Vietnam. When they faced a growing insurgency in Iraq, some U.S. officials recognized the essence of U.S. failures in Vietnam found in my seven years of reporting. In 2006, for example, former vice chief of staff of the army Gen. Jack Keane explained on national television that in Iraq "we put an Army on the battlefield that . . . doesn't have any doctrine, nor was it educated and trained, to deal with an insurgency. . . . After the Vietnam War, we purged ourselves of everything that had to do with irregular warfare or insurgency, because it had to do with how we lost that war."[4]

On the nonmilitary side, too, U.S. civilian leaders failed to assess and dampen grievances against U.S. policies abroad and may have even inflamed outrages by invading Iraq in 2003. In January 2005, when rebuilding Afghanistan and Iraq was deemed critical, national security advisor Condoleezza Rice told Congress: "We didn't have the right skills, the right capacity to deal with a reconstruction effort of this kind."[5]

My memoirs may be more relevant now than at any time during the last forty years as Vietnam's shadow is cast more starkly over the United States' current so-called war on terror centered in Afghanistan, Pakistan, and the Middle East.

Fast-Forward Forty-Plus Years: New U.S. Counterinsurgency Policy

Upon completing the first draft of my memoirs, I discovered that the U.S. government had issued in two parts a new counterinsurgency policy. First, it released the *U.S. Army/Marine Corps Counterinsurgency Field Manual* on December 15, 2006, while "our Soldiers and Marines [were] fighting insurgents in Afghanistan and Iraq."[6] Second, in 2009 it released a civilian interagency *Counterinsurgency Guide*, which it described as "the first serious U.S. effort at creating a national counterinsurgency framework in over 40 years."[7]

I was taken aback when I studied the new policy because it admits to four specific U.S. failures. First, the new policy recognizes that an insurgency is foremost a political struggle, unlike the premise four decades earlier in which most U.S. resources and efforts in Vietnam focused on conventional military operations and activities. Second, it establishes the fallacy of relying on the body count of deceased persons, which was used so extensively in Vietnam, as a measure of progress. Third, it criticizes the U.S. Army's building, training, and equipping of Vietnamese soldiers "in the U.S. military's image."[8] Last, it notes the U.S. "sustainment failure" in Vietnam, explaining, "South Vietnam's agrarian-based economy could not sustain the high-technology equipment and computer-based systems established by U.S. forces and contractors."[9]

In my dispatches I had described some of these failures. In 1968, for example, after covering the citywide destruction of the one-time imperial capital of Hue, I criticized Gen. William Westmoreland's concentration on search-and-destroy operations conducted in the remote jungles instead of adopting what I dubbed a "people-perimeter" strategy.[10] Nearly forty years later I was surprised to read that my "people-perimeter" strategy had morphed into what the new policy calls a "population-centric approach,"[11] designed to address the political nature of the insurgency.

In one dispatch I remember well, I quoted a Western diplomat's alert: "Westy [General Westmoreland] obviously cannot command a machine he doesn't have. And he doesn't have the political-economic-military counterinsurgency machine he needs to wage this war." I added my own perspective: "At a higher level, this was not simply General Westmoreland's dilemma in Vietnam; it would be an American dilemma in other underdeveloped countries for the next decade."[12] The policy also maps out tomorrow's conflicts, warning of the "near certainty" that the United States will engage in counterinsurgencies "during the decades to come."[13]

My Vietnam Reporting Trove of Forty Years

For these memoirs I rely mainly not on memory but on a collection of materials I systematically amassed in my Vietnam War reporting and shipped out of Saigon when I departed in 1969. This trove consists of three separate chunks. Most important were copies of the full-page broadsheets of most of my articles published by the *New York Herald Tribune* and the *Christian Science Monitor*. In Saigon I had these copies bound in one volume that was covered in royal blue satin embossed with golden phoenixes and lotus blossoms like that worn by Vietnamese on special occasions. On the black spine of this volume I had imprinted in gold ink, "To my parents with love and thanks."

The second chunk consists of fifteen bound volumes of flimsy tissue carbon copies of dispatches I had written (my scoops, my rejections, my cables scolding and being scolded by my editors, suggestions to and from them for stories, some memos of my random thoughts). These looseleaf flimsies were sent to a local bindery and bound in buckram-colored leather. The result: two volumes contain "rejected articles"; two contain dispatches and correspondence to and from *Newsweek* from Vietnam and Laos (September 1962–February 1964); six contain my dispatches and correspondence with the *New York Herald Tribune* (1964–mid-1966, when that newspaper ceased publication); four contain my carbons, memos, and letters to and from the *Christian Science Monitor* (May 1967–January 1969); one contains carbons of my dispatches and correspondence to and from the *Economist, London Daily* and *Sunday Express, North American Newspaper Alliance,* and the *Pittsburgh Gazette* (1961–68).[14]

For the third chunk I encased in plastic bags the remaining bulky documents, appropriately labeled, and tied them with heavy string.

These included my notebooks, copies of the Vietnamese government's English-language versions of *Vietnam Press*, the British Information Service translations of Vietnamese newspapers, U.S. and South Vietnamese military and civilian communiqués and organizational charts, old French maps, annual reports from U.S. and Vietnamese agencies, and a bundle containing excerpts of Mao Tse-tung's choicest writings. I discovered that I had some 54.8 linear feet of these documents that were packed in 170 plastic, dirt-, bug-, and water-proof packets. Upon opening these packets in 2008, I found that they were completely intact, despite several relocations, some forty years of storage, and water that flooded a room where they were stashed. This trove of documents was then painstakingly compiled by my husband, Chuck Keever, into databases that proved essential for guiding me through these primary materials (see appendix 1).

A Unique, Lipsticked Panoramic Perspective

From this treasure trove I selected for these memoirs vignettes and episodes that provide microcosms of larger issues or paint slice-of-life portraits of key aspects of the war, that freeze-frame events and thinking as they occurred *at the time*, and that give immediacy, intensity or veracity to my observations and experiences. Extensive quotes from participants I interviewed *at the time* and my eyewitness descriptions are taken from my notes written with some shorthand that I had learned in a correspondence course in high school or using my own abbreviations and typed up soon afterward as news dispatches or drafts. Far more than I could remember after forty years, these wafer-thin papers preserve an accurate chronicle of what I witnessed and experienced, thus permanently recording a lipsticked reporter's perspective about a man-made and male-conducted war reported mostly by newsmen.

I was as a twenty-six-year-old freelance reporter when I arrived in Vietnam in February 1962. For the first seven months I freelanced and so did not face the burden of covering daily events on deadline that beset the eight Western reporters tied down in Saigon. I set out to explore the life, emotions, feelings, and problems of South Vietnam's rural villagers, who constituted about 75 percent of the country's estimated 16.1 million population.[15] These early reporting odysseys gave me a panoramic perspective and unique baseline to eyewitness the war while it was being led, governed, largely fought, and suffered by the Vietnamese. This period was the most critical of the war as well as the least examined in the thousands of books about U.S. involvement written since.[16]

With 1962 as a baseline, I am able to use a unique, personalized, topical approach in the opening chapters of this book to begin telling the story of key segments of the Vietnam War that I covered. I then discuss the evolution of that topic during my seven years of reporting. Instead of being an exhaustive account of all that I covered or adhering to a day-to-day chronology, these memoirs flow from one defining topic to another.

By preserving on paper or film what I observed, analyzed, and was told *at the time*, I have chosen not to reconstruct quotes and events years after the fact, to create composite persons, to indulge in the luxury of hindsight, to crawl inside people's heads or hearts to second-guess motivation and feelings or to include fictionalized materials. I kept in mind that memoirs are commonly defined as a record of events about matters coming "within the personal knowledge of the writer, or are obtained from particular sources of information,"[17] and as such they usually emphasize "what is remembered rather than who is remembering."[18]

But these memoirs are more than just my re-reporting of the Vietnam War or my instant replay of the history that I witnessed. Instead, in split-screen fashion I also incorporate information that was classified at the time but has since been made public about how, at the highest levels of the U.S. government, officials made critical decisions about Vietnam that reporters in the field did not, and could not, have known. I often include information from official documents and analyses that are contained in the forty-three top secret volumes known as the *Pentagon Papers*. Described as "a history based solely on documents,"[19] the unprecedented, highly classified *Papers* were leaked in 1971 to selected newspapers, which analyzed them, and were released in full to the public by Senator Mike Gravel of Alaska. The *Papers* pulled back an opaque curtain of secrecy to stun the public — and me — by exposing the inner workings of U.S. decision making within Washington, between Washington and Saigon officials, and between U.S. officials in Saigon and the Vietnamese. As Gravel observed at the time, the *Papers* reveal that U.S. decision makers at the highest levels of the executive branch gave little consideration to the costs of their policies that would be borne by the Vietnamese — "the very people we claimed to be helping" — and they treated the U.S. public in contempt by forcing it "to subsist on a diet of half-truths or deliberate deceit." He concluded, "No greater argument against unchecked secrecy in government can be found in the annals of American history."[20]

Along with my horizontal, on-the-ground reporting, I move vertically to incorporate high-level policymakers' once secret, but now revealed, decisions, which provide the backstory for events I describe unfolding in Vietnam. These memoirs hinge together bottom-up and top-down narratives. Readers can view online or on DVD many personalities, places, and battles that I describe.

A Treasury of Acknowledgments

In writing these memoirs, I alone am responsible for errors of omission or commission. Yet these memoirs would not have been made possible without the direct or indirect help of countless Vietnamese and Americans who served, suffered, or died in Vietnam. For editing and structural assistance I thank Bridget Barry, Elizabeth Gratch, and Heather Lundine of the University of Nebraska Press, Carolyn Martindale, and two anonymous reviewers. I am grateful to James Pickerell, a photographer I teamed up with years earlier in Vietnam and Washington DC, for permitting me to hold and study dozens of his personal wartime photos; he currently publishes www.Selling-Stock.com, which deals with issues related to the marketing of stock photography. I also appreciate the scanning and restoration by Ed Roever, of Hawaii Pacific Photo (www.hppdigital.com), of the photographs in my personal collection published in this volume.

I am indebted for the love, support, and sacrifices bestowed upon me by my late father, my mother, and my sister. Last, this volume would not have happened at all without the support and help of my husband — moving around dust-encrusted boxes, compiling two databases, and divining the past with me. He is the joy I serendipitously encountered forty-plus years ago in the midst of that joyless war.

Beverly Deepe Keever, PhD, MLIS, MSJ

DEATH ZONES AND DARLING SPIES

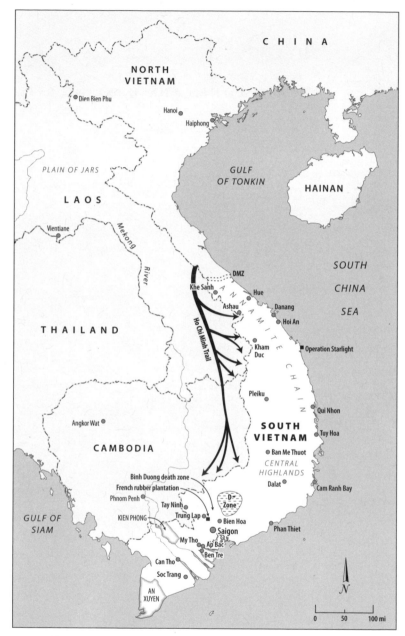

Map 1. Places in Laos and South Vietnam discussed by author. (Map by Erin Greb, copyright Beverly Deepe Keever)

Introduction

From Midwest Dustbowl to Mystical Vietnam

The past is never dead. It's not even past.

William Faulkner, 1950

The past isn't dead and buried. In fact, it isn't even past.

Barack Obama, 2008

The farmhouse still had that lived-in look, although it had been uninhabited for eleven years. All the windows in the house were intact, adorned with stiffly starched, sand-colored curtains. At the beginning of the graveled driveway leading to the house stood a red metal mailbox holding a crimped-up tin plate bearing the name of the owner: Martin Deepe, my father.

Dad had wanted a son to carry on the family farm. Instead, my parents got me, on June 1, 1935, after they were barely able to reach the Hebron hospital by crossing a decrepit bridge submerged by a flash flood. Twenty months later came another daughter, Joan, their last child. Without sons to take over the family farm and with their two daughters leaving to pursue other livelihoods, my parents eventually rented their land, barn, and bins and moved in 1996 to the Thayer County seat of Hebron, leaving empty buildings to deteriorate until this fateful day.

The farmhouse was hardly aware of the violent death awaiting it on that Monday, July 2, 2007. It had been a wrenching decision for my mom, Doris Deepe, "to put the house down," she said, using the euphemism usually reserved for putting to sleep ailing farm horses and pets. "This is the only place that was really home," she told me. Because Mom could not bear to witness the end of the house, garage, outhouse, cellar, and even the mailbox that held so many memories for her, I was the sole family member to attend this death knell. A hulking Komatsu with dinosaur-like jaws first smashed the upstairs bedroom and within twenty minutes had transformed the once-upon-a-time home into a heap of rubble. Five minutes later the sun broke through the haze and puffs of dust. A breeze fanned wild, gold-tipped bromegrass so that it resembled prairies of the past.

That evening Mom and I drove to the burial site of the home where she had lived for forty-three years. Mom was ninety-two — in age and probably in weight. She was much frailer than she had been as a young bride beginning seventy-one years of marriage. Her hands, folded in her lap in the passenger's seat, evidenced bumps from a broken wrist, arthritis in her knuckles, and crippled fingers from years of watering chickens, hoeing gardens, canning produce, cooking, laundering, and even helping Dad hack weeds in the fields or lay out irrigation tubing. I turned the car off the graveled county road, headed up the driveway, and swung the car around so that its nose faced the U-shaped void framed by two rows of centuries-old evergreens on the north and west. Mom and I peered at the gently rounded mound bigger than a tennis court where the house and other structures were buried. The mound was much bigger than the one that had covered Dad's coffin only fifteen months earlier. Stillness permeated the evening coolness. "Amazing grace," Mom whispered. "It's eerie."

A solitude and serenity hung over the spot. A dove cooed in the distance, momentarily breaking the silence. "It's better than it was," Mom said. "It wasn't a home anymore." She summed up: "The house is at peace."

From an Old Frontier to a New One

The buried farmhouse had been built around 1890 and witnessed the settling of the rolling hills and flatlands of southeast Nebraska after Pony Express riders and pioneers in covered wagons plied the Oregon Trail only a dozen or so miles away. Some pioneers stopped to homestead on free or cheap government-dispensed land, depleting "the timber, grass and game of the Pawnee, Sioux, Cheyenne, Shoshoni, and other tribes."[1] Bloody encounters between whites and the "painted devils of the plain" were described at the time in the *Hebron Journal*, established in 1871. Today Hebron (pop. 1,565) claims to stake out the geographic center of the United States; lamppost banners lining its main street proclaim it the "capital of the Oregon Trail."

These banners and newspaper accounts ignore the dispossession and despair of the native peoples that loom large in the more sweeping perspective provided by historian of the West Patricia Limerick. "All the cultural understanding and tolerance in the world would not have changed the crucial fact that Indians possessed the land and that Euro-Americans wanted it," Limerick notes.[2] This crucial fact gave rise to what she calls the "legacy of conquest." She asserts, "Conquest forms the historical bedrock of the whole nation."[3]

The dependency of the United States on expansionism — or blocking the perceived expansionism of its enemies — came to be stretched across the Pacific Ocean in the 1960s to involvement in South Vietnam. The legacy and imagery of that conquest across the American continent was used by John F. Kennedy to proclaim a "New Frontier" that helped to underpin his policy to deny communism to South Vietnam. In his nomination acceptance speech on July 15, 1960, Kennedy told Democratic convention delegates: "We stand today on the edge of a New Frontier. . . . The harsh facts of the matter are that we stand on this frontier at a turning-point in history."[4]

From "the Knob" and Country School

Mom and Dad were married on August 28, 1934, the driest year recorded in the High Plains. The next year, when I was born, the drought was even worse.[5] My parents moved onto the heavily mortgaged, 160-acre farm of Dad's parents, John and Anna Deepe, before I was born. Grandpa Deepe had emigrated from Germany in 1887 at the age of sixteen, attending high school until he was twenty-four so that he could be proficient in English and arithmetic. He lived alone in a sod house for a while and, after marrying Anna from Austria, purchased and moved in 1912 to his own farm.

Mom and Dad had a bleak existence. Dad cultivated the gumbo-like soil with horses, but the drought and poor farm prices produced little income. The wooden house was so thin walled and isolated that Mom named it "the Knob" and routinely described it as "unfit to live in." There was no telephone, no electricity, and for some time no battery-powered radio. During the Dust Bowl days of the 1930s Mom crimped wet towels around the windowsills to catch the red earth swirling about. Winter winds were so frigid that Mom often had to keep Joan and me warm by dressing us in our little blue snowsuits and placing us on the oven door of the cook stove. Oblivious to my parents' hardships, Joan and I had immense fun. We played with Old Shep, helped water the chickens and hoe the garden, rode our spunky Shetland pony, and herded in the cattle grazing on prairie pastureland.

I started my education at home. Mom, who had taught in a country school before her marriage, drilled my sister and me on spelling and phonetics. For my first Christmas, when I was only six months old, Mom gave me a book; Dad laughed at her, scoffing, "This kid can't read!" Mom retorted that I deserved a book, thus jumpstarting my love of reading and writing. Mom was also a saver. To this day she has preserved our first curls after they were shorn, our toddler booties and bonnets, and later on boxes of clippings of my magazine and newspaper articles from Vietnam, marking some things, including Christmas issues of women's magazines: "Save forever!" Years later, in Vietnam, I often thought of her as I wrote my dispatches, hoping that she would understand them.

In 1941, when I was six, I began my eight years of education at Coon Ridge School, which Dad had attended for eight years a generation before me. Organized in 1871,[6] the school was named in honor of the raccoons that prowled the playground and neighboring farm buildings. Dad often drove me there over the five miles of dirt road. But during decent weather Joan and I walked home, stopping along the roadside to pick a bouquet of wildflowers for Mom.

The one-room country school was small and spartan, but the no-nonsense teachers were excellent. During my years there no more than a dozen pupils were enrolled in any one year. On warm days the meadowlark's songs and farm-fresh breezes wafted in, but in the winter so did the frigid blasts that sent us huddling around the coal-burning stove in our coats and scarves. Without electricity lighting was poor, and I soon needed eyeglasses. An outhouse was a necessary fixture, rain, snow, or shine. During recess we played hide-and-seek on prairie grass once trod by buffalo and American Indians.

In the one room I could hear lessons discussed in the upper classes. I was intrigued to hear the geography studies of advanced students, and these lessons stirred my desire to travel the world, not to write travel articles but to witness for myself how other peoples lived and worked. Here I first read Pearl Buck's *The Good Earth*, which sparked my dream of seeing China. I also learned geography from V-mail, those tissue-thin, reduced-size letters that Mom's four brothers sent home from overseas during World War II. *Guadalcanal, Iwo Jima, Okinawa*, and *the Solomon Islands* became household words as V-grams arrived and we tracked news from Pacific combat zones. After finishing the eighth grade, I took my four years of high school in nearby Belvidere.

I graduated from high school in 1953 and enrolled at the University of Nebraska at Lincoln, spurred by receiving a Regents Scholarship and by Mom's insistence that I get the college education she had been denied by the Depression. I double-majored in political science and journalism, took a number of courses in Asian Studies, and graduated in 1957, having been selected as a Phi Beta Kappa for academic excellence and Mortar Board for campus leadership. That same year Mom and Dad bought the farmhouse, other buildings, and a quarter section near the Coon Ridge School, living there for the next forty-three years in the home that I saw "put down." At last Dad was his own boss on his own land; he was not a tenant farmer like many in the area, having to shell out rent money to landlords. The hard life of these tenant farmers stuck with me years later in Vietnam when I reported on the war fought in rice paddies owned by big landowners and rented out to dissatisfied peasants.

After graduation I landed a summer job in the regional bureau of the Associated Press (AP) in Des Moines, thanks to key assistance from the head of the university's journalism school. That fall I was admitted into the Columbia University Graduate School of Journalism with the substantial help of a scholarship from the New York Newspaper Women's Club. While at Columbia, I worked part-time for one of my professors, Samuel Lubell, who had parlayed his pioneering public opinion polling into syndicated columns and an award-winning book. After graduating in mid-1958, I was selected by the Young Women's Christian Association as one of forty U.S. students nationwide to visit the Soviet Union for forty days as part of the first student exchange initiated by the two governments. That trip became my launching pad for Asia. I wrote a five-part series on Soviet life for Associated Press Newsfeatures and then told the head of the office that I would return in two years with a proposal to write articles for him from and about Asia. I had formed a pact with two young women I met on my Soviet trip, vowing that we would save our money and then take off for Asia.

Upon returning from the Soviet Union, I worked as Lubell's assistant in New York for two years. He and I analyzed voting returns of precincts across the country to select those barometer precincts that mirrored the nation and then, practicing journalism from the bottom up, we rang doorbells in those areas to ask voters how they were going to cast their ballots in key 1958 congressional and 1960 presidential races.

Working for Lubell did not pay much. But I often worked weekends, traveled a lot on an expense account, and built up a nest egg of funds. I became used to traveling light, fast, and on a moment's notice over the eastern half of the nation. When I left New York after the 1960 election, I mentally carried with me Sam's grassroots interviewing approach and his note-taking and filing system. I was ready to leave for Asia, but my two girlfriends who were to go with me backed out. With my nest egg in hand, I decided to go alone. I returned to AP Newsfeatures with my proposal to write from and about Asia and was given a list of suggestions for articles and letters of introduction to AP bureau chiefs in Asia.

I was twenty-six when in April 1961 I eagerly took off for my dream trip around the world, allotting just two weeks for a tourist's stop in South Vietnam. I was mainly hoping to see China, although the Communist country was then closed to U.S. citizens. I succeeded in visiting the port of Shanghai on a Polish steamer but was not given permission to disembark. I wrote a feature story that AP Newsfeatures requested on the ship-side view of Shanghai, based on what I could see from the deck and hear from Polish sailors. I also made a quick study of other parts of Asia. I lived with and taught English to Japanese students, hired interpreters to talk with South Koreans about the 1961 military coup d'état that I witnessed outside of Seoul, interviewed prostitutes in Hong Kong and Macau, visited opium dens in Singapore, and traveled by tramp steamer to talk to descendants of headhunters in British-held Borneo. AP bought some of my airmailed or teletyped dispatches and distributed them to newspapers worldwide.[7]

"Things Are Really Heating Up in Vietnam"

By the time I reached Hong Kong, AP's bureau chief there, Roy Essoyan, had just returned from South Vietnam and suggested I go there. He had covered the offloading of the first U.S. banana-shaped H-21 Shawnee helicopters, but when the first of them crashed due to mechanical failure, Roy wrote a wire story that embarrassed the Pentagon. It then barred correspondents from future rides on U.S. helicopters manned by U.S. crews—and Roy wrote another wire story exposing the U.S. government's withholding information from American taxpayers, despite their funding of the war. The story caused more negative publicity for the Pentagon, so it relented and again allowed accredited journalists to ride aboard U.S. aircraft, space permitting. This authorization gave journalists unparalleled mobility throughout the course of the war to swoop into battlefields, even during the fighting, or into isolated outposts and villages. Roy advised me to head to Saigon, adding, "Things are really heating up in Vietnam."

Even as Roy was briefing me, President Kennedy, on February 7, 1962, was affirming to journalists in Washington his policy to help protect an independent South Vietnam from "a subterranean war, a guerrilla war of increasing ferocity," which he painted as one of aggression directed by Communist North Vietnam, rather than a civil war waged by homegrown insurgents against a heavy-handed South Vietnamese government.[8] Kennedy's rationale for involvement was continuing the "domino theory," the belief that Communism would spread by toppling one non-Communist regime after another. Kennedy also saw in Vietnam the necessity to defeat a war of national liberation model of warfare, like that which had enabled Mao Tse-tung to seize control of China in 1949 and which was now being trumpeted outside its borders.[9]

A day after Kennedy spoke in Washington, the United States established in Saigon its Military Assistance Command, Vietnam (MACV), headed by Gen. Paul D. Harkins, as it tried to exert more influence on South Vietnam's anti-Communist military efforts. But in escalating the U.S. military presence in Vietnam, Kennedy brushed aside the prophetic warning given to him in 1962 by French general Charles de Gaulle: "You will, step by step, be sucked into a bottomless military and political quagmire."[10]

I followed Roy's advice. Instead of staying in South Vietnam for two weeks, as my globetrotting schedule called for, I served as a correspondent there for seven years. I never imagined that I would witness and report on the rise and stalemate of U.S. power there and the ghastly destruction of such a mystical country and many of its people. As then secretary of defense Robert McNamara, a key architect of Kennedy's policy, wrote later, the Vietnam War was to become "among the bloodiest in all of human history."[11] Vietnam was also to become the United States' longest war. As Gen. Bruce Palmer Jr. noted in 1984, "Exactly twenty-five years from 1 May 1950 — the day President Truman authorized the first U.S. military assistance to Indochina — Saigon and the South Vietnamese government fell to the communist regime of North Vietnam, on 30 April 1975. Thus ended the longest conflict in American history." And, he added, it would end as "the first clear failure in our history."[12]

Paris-like with Unknown Tomorrows

I departed Hong Kong on a small passenger-cargo steamer bound for Vietnam, which is shaped like a verdant boot forming the outer, seaside rim of a peninsula jutting out from the great Asian land mass. Vietnam was divided in 1954 by international agreement. Being about the size of

1. I wore civilian clothes when I first traveled to the Central Highlands and interviewed these highlanders. (B. Deepe Collection)

Washington state, U.S.-backed South Vietnam was slightly larger than Communist-ruled North Vietnam; the population of each was estimated at about sixteen million — roughly double the size of New York City.

My steamer lazily glided from the South China Sea about fifty miles inland up the Saigon River, past huge fronds of a seemingly unending mangrove swamp. The lush greenery trapped the breezes so that the air hung oppressively under the blazing sun. I arrived on February 14, 1962, as a freelancer with my Olivetti Lettera 22 portable typewriter, a Yashica camera, and one suitcase; my dresses with hemlines reaching midcalf seemed frumpy as other Western women began donning miniskirts. I wore these frumpies for travel and reporting until I could buy a military outfit on Saigon's black market. Without a regular paycheck I existed on my nest egg and erratic income earned from selling articles and photographs, with my loving parents covering overdrafts of my Nebraska bank account. As a fellow correspondent later wrote, "Beverly Deepe, one of the first young vagabonds to land in the tiny Saigon press corps, was the girl next door, a symbol of the rapidly fading apple-pie fifties."[13]

I disembarked near the foot of one of Saigon's main boulevards, where U.S. helicopters had only months earlier arrived on the flat top of an American ship while throngs of skeptical Vietnamese watched. When, on December 11, 1961, thirty-three Shawnee helicopters manned by four hundred ground and air crewmen arose from the deck of the aircraft carrier and fluttered toward the airport, the crowd roared, a Vietnamese friend later told me. Helicopters went on to become the war's iconic images, creating signature bookends of the beginning and the ending of the United States in Vietnam, as CH-46 Chinook helicopters desperately rescued panic-stricken Americans and Vietnamese fleeing North Vietnamese troops and tanks from a Saigon rooftop on April 30, 1975.

The arrival of these Shawnees symbolized a new phase of public knowledge of the U.S. war in South Vietnam. President Kennedy dispatched entire U.S. combat support units to operate or handle helicopters, aircraft, rivercraft, intelligence, and logistics to reinforce Saigon government forces, which were already being advised by individual U.S. officers and GIs. It would be the fourth time in history that the United States established a wartime advisory and training mission of such size.[14]

These newcomers expanded the number of U.S. military in South Vietnam to about 6,000. The number was nearly tenfold the limit of 685 U.S. military advisors allowed in South Vietnam under international accords agreed upon on July 21, 1954, at the end of the French Indochina War. Seven months before the Saigon arrival of these helicopters and other combat support units, on May 11, 1961, Kennedy had secretly ordered 400 U.S. Green Beret soldiers and 100 other military advisors to South Vietnam. As the *Pentagon Papers* revealed in 1971, this increase "signaled a willingness to go beyond the 685-man limit on the size of the

2. I relied on cyclo pedalers like these to skirt me through Saigon's hurly-burly traffic. (B. Deepe Collection)

U.S. [military] mission in Saigon, which, if it were done openly, would be the first formal breach of the Geneva agreement."[15] Also, as the American public was to learn years later, breaching this international agreement was Kennedy's secret order initiating covert operations against North Vietnam and Laos conducted by U.S. Special Forces and by South Vietnamese units trained and paid by the U.S. Central Intelligence Agency.[16] I later was able to describe these kinds of covert operations in connection with the Tonkin Gulf incidents that catapulted the United States into a massive air war against North Vietnam and a buildup of its troop strength in the South.

3. My walk-up apartment with a mirrored bookcase would a year later be shot up and looted during the first of many coup d'états. (B. Deepe Collection)

Upon my arrival I was enchanted with Saigon. Its wide boulevards were lined with majestic trees that reminded me of France and garnered it the nickname the "Paris of the Orient." Main government buildings, the opera house on the city square, and the high-steepled Catholic cathedral at the head of a main avenue carried the imprint of the French colonialists. More than Paris, however, Saigon exuded a relaxed pace necessitated by muggy days that made a midday siesta a must. The streets were teeming with bicycles pedaled by lithe women in flowing *ao dai*, the national dress fashioned with a Mao-styled collar and nipped-in waist from which flowed to the ankles two sheer panels that fluttered over pantaloons. For transport I hailed pedicabs powered by emaciated Vietnamese men or nabbed rickety blue-and-white taxis.

I was lucky to find an apartment to rent in the heart of the city just blocks from the central market and the palace of President Ngo Dinh Diem. The apartment was on the second floor above an automobile repair shop fronting a major one-way street leading from the airport. My walk-up apartment, No. 5 at 101 Cong Ly Street, was austere. The floors were of concrete. The bamboo sofa and chairs were covered in crumpled cotton slipcovers. Housekeeping chores were time-consuming, and to do them, I hired a young Vietnamese woman, who then moved in to share my apartment. There was no stove; instead, charcoal was burned in a ceramic hibachi for cooking and for boiling the city's water, which was unsafe to drink, even in Saigon's best hotels. There was no refrigerator, so the maid shopped at the nearby central market daily to buy pineapples and live chickens that she killed and plucked in the kitchen. From my second-floor living room window, I could peer down into a Hindu temple that was alive with worshippers, incense, flowers, and tinkling bells.

But below this surface nonchalance Saigon was electric with an air of uncertainty mixed with danger. I chatted with American GIs in mess halls or at airports who nervously wondered how they would fare during their one-year tour of duty. Pro-Communist guerrillas were launching 120 attacks a week, and, as the *Pentagon Papers* reveal, U.S. officials feared insurgents would soon be able to establish a "liberated area" somewhere in the country. Sidewalk cafés that had once provided a relaxed ambience were banned by the Vietnamese government in the wake of a grenade explosion at one Saigon establishment that had been aimed at Americans but wounded two Germans instead.[17] Saigon became a floating life of fleeting acquaintances, hidden dangers, and unknown tomorrows.

On February 27, two weeks after my arrival in Saigon, I heard the bombing of the Presidential Palace just blocks up the street from my apartment. Dissident Vietnamese government pilots in low-flying fighters were strafing it. Upon hearing gunfire that day, Mert Perry of *Time* magazine was the only reporter to get the news to the outside world before the Vietnamese government cut telegraph communications connecting Saigon to the outside world. The quick-thinking reporter had picked up the telephone even before he knew who was strafing the palace. His example taught me that it was not enough to gather the news; one also had to get it out of the country. Later I instinctively grabbed my Olivetti to cover Saigon's recurring coups d'états, quasi-coups, and false coups and rushed to the post-telegraph office before it was shuttered. To my astonishment my advisory to editors in London of my mad dash to the cable office was published in 1964 as the lead story on the foreign page before I could even identify the coup makers.[18]

Reporting without Deadlines

During my first seven and a half months in Saigon I freelanced stories gathered by traveling to the surrounding countryside. I was struck by the beauty of Vietnam and its mystical, magical fusion of cultures from both China and India. Vietnam's landscapes often reminded me of the mist-covered mountains and straggly evergreens I had viewed in scrolls of the countryside of ancient China.

Freelancing was a laborious, unlucrative, time-consuming process. I mailed story ideas from the antiquated Vietnamese post office to news media outlets or sent completed articles on speculation, gambling I would be paid for them. But not having to meet regular deadlines permitted me to travel for extended periods to cover the two-track war of insurgency and infiltration. I visited locations where U.S. combat support units were being stationed; I hitched rides by helicopters, aircraft, jeeps, and riverboats; I even rode an elephant.

Almost everywhere I visited, great changes were taking place. U.S. junior officers were arriving in all of the forty-some province capitals to advise and assist South Vietnamese military officers administratively and logistically. I searched out and interviewed women performing extraordinary duties, such as Patricia Smith, a doctor sent from Seattle by a Catholic organization who was treating dozens of frail mountain tribes inhabitants in a pink dispensary in the highlands city of Kontum, and an intelligence officer, Maj. Anne Doering, who had been born in

4. I rode an elephant in 1962 before these beasts became casualties of the war. (B. Deepe Collection)

Haiphong and was the only Women's Army Corps representative in Vietnam. These and my other dispatches, distributed by AP Newsfeatures to subscribing newspapers nationwide, painted a lipsticked, though not rosy, portrait of Vietnam.[19]

Saigon's All-Male Press Corps, Mostly Male War, and Me

My freelancing gave me little chance to mingle with other correspondents. Upon arriving in Saigon, I found the resident Western press corps consisted of eight other journalists, four of whom worked for wire services: Agence France-Presse, AP, Reuters, and United Press International.[20] All were Caucasian. All were male. When I left Vietnam seven years later, I had outlasted all of them.

These journalists working for the U.S. media were young. The youngest, age twenty-four, was Michel Renard, a Belgian freelancer for Columbia Broadcasting System. Neil Sheehan, who covered for United Press International, and I were twenty-six. The oldest, at thirty-three, were *Time-Life*'s Mert Perry and *Newsweek*'s François Sully. Malcolm Browne, age thirty-two, was a lanky, blond chemist-turned-correspondent who filled me in on newsy developments as I read the incoming and outgoing wire copy in AP's spartan office on Rue Pasteur. Shortly after my arrival, David Halberstam, then twenty-nine, took over the *New York Times*'s coverage from Homer Bigart, fifty-four, a two-time Pulitzer Prize winner whom the Saigon government came close to expelling for his critical articles. Halberstam continued the *Times*'s criticism of the government, but he left five weeks after it was toppled on November 1, 1963,[21] telling friends that covering the war had become too risky.[22]

From this original group of eight correspondents, the U.S. government accredited a peak number of 645 journalists by the end of March 1968, prompting Maj. Gen. Winant Sidle, the chief U.S. military information officer from 1967 to 1969, to assert, "That's far too many, especially when most of them stayed in Saigon." Sidle estimated that only about 75 to 80 correspondents regularly went into the field but added that "young reporters who stayed a year or longer eventually became quite good." The top U.S. commander for much of the war, Gen. William Westmoreland, observed that with the "constant turnover" in reporters, "providing the press with background and perspective was like trying to paint a moving train."[23]

I had hand-carried to Saigon letters from news media outlets that permitted me to become accredited by both U.S. and Vietnamese officialdoms. Journalists reporting from Vietnam needed to be accredited by U.S. and Vietnamese governments, which required documentation that the journalist was writing for a media outlet. Accreditation gave journalists access to military transportation, quarters, and rations, if available, and allowed them to accompany military operations. "It was

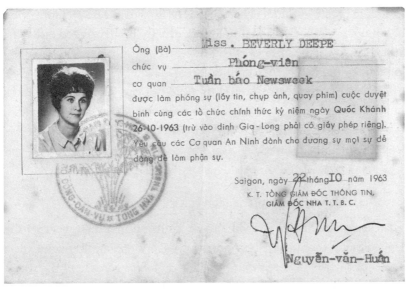

5. The South Vietnamese government issued my accreditation card for *Newsweek* just before it was toppled in the November 1963 coup d'état. (B. Deepe Collection)

the first war in which reporters were routinely accredited to accompany military forces yet not subject to censorship," a media historian notes, thus giving them "extraordinary freedom."[24]

In 1965, when the U.S. buildup of troops was under way, Westmoreland did consider ordering press censorship but decided it was too complicated to censor television stories and written articles created by non-U.S. journalists and sent to their home countries. Besides, correspondents would then only smuggle their copy to neighboring cities to be sent (as I had done during the 1963–64 crises that blocked or delayed the Vietnamese government's telegraph operation). Westmoreland indicated the ultimate decision was up to President Johnson, who confided in 1972 at the LBJ Ranch a few months before his death that during the early days of the war he felt he should have imposed press censorship, despite the obstacles.[25]

After U.S. combat troops arrived in South Vietnam in mid-1965, journalists who were accredited by the U.S. military command had to agree to adhere to fifteen voluntary guidelines relating to release of information about upcoming operations, adequacy of supplies in isolated outposts, and accuracy of incoming shells.[26] Several correspondents violated the guidelines and had their accreditation revoked.[27]

Like most other correspondents, I did not carry a weapon and was not embedded with any one unit for long periods of time, as was the case in earlier, conventional wars. In another revolutionary change news from the first uncensored U.S. war was delivered into living rooms, and viewers worldwide experienced history while it was happening.

Reporters' "Declarations of Independence"

I had arrived in Saigon without any preconceptions about whether the United States should have become involved in Vietnam, although I knew some journalists believed that the United States had to fight the war.[28] Vietnam was not discussed at all during the 1960 presidential campaign, for which I had done political polling, and after the election I was too preoccupied with my upcoming travels to hear the soaring rhetoric of Kennedy that captivated some U.S. journalists.[29] Besides, I had been drilled in my journalism schools to remain a disinterested observer, to avoid taking sides or becoming emotionally involved, to concentrate on accuracy and fairness, and to use brainpower to explain complexity. So, I focused on gathering the best evidence of what was happening in Vietnam and what it meant.

I was one of a group of Saigon-based journalists who was credited with spearheading an era in which reporters wrote new "Declarations of Independence" by rising up "to challenge — and change — the rules of the game." Journalists were no longer willing to accept statements by the U.S. government at face value and disseminate them uncritically.[30] I was so absorbed with my work during these early years that I was unaware of the landmark U.S. Supreme Court case that constitutionally protected the public's right to challenge the government and its officials. In writing for the Court's 9–0 decision in March 1964, Justice Brennan stated, "We consider . . . a profound national commitment to the principle that debate on public issues should be uninhibited, robust, and wide-open, and that it may well include vehement, caustic, and sometimes unpleasantly sharp attacks on government and public officials."[31]

Even so, press coverage of the war continues to be debated by scholars, policy makers, and top brass. As one professor observed in 1990, "Questions about the role of the news media during the Vietnam era are as common as questions about the war itself."[32] Some accused us of producing antiwar coverage that caused the U.S. defeat. President Nixon declared in 1971, "Our worst enemy seems to be the press!"[33] At the other extreme some accused us of being little more than a propaganda arm of the U.S. and South Vietnamese governments.[34] Yet a scholar commissioned by the army to study U.S. information policy and press performance during my seven years in Vietnam concluded, "It is undeniable . . . that press reports were still often more accurate than the public statements of the administration in portraying the situation in Vietnam."[35] The *Pentagon Papers* note that even the U.S. Embassy was often caught by surprise by developments in Vietnam and "had no effective system, either through overt or covert contacts, for finding out what was going on." During the 1963 political protests leading to the overthrow of the Diem government, the *Papers* state, "the U.S. press corps was reporting a far different view of both the war and the Buddhist crisis, one which was, in retrospect, nearer the reality."[36] Writer Michael Herr aptly described the Vietnam press corps of 1968: "We all had roughly the same position on the war: we were in it, and that was our position."[37]

Continuous (Often Lipsticked) Perspective

During my seven continuous years of reporting in Vietnam, I acquired an institutional memory and an array of valuable local sources that few other Americans had, giving me a unique perspective.

During those seven years the top levels of the government and the armed forces of South Vietnam changed eight times, and these changes trickled down to the countryside, leading to further instability. In March 1964 thirty-five of the forty-one province chiefs at work three months earlier had been replaced, with nine provinces having three new province chiefs and one province having four.[38] Besides the Vietnamese revolving door, the U.S. ambassador in Saigon changed five times, the top U.S. general three times, and the U.S. Mission, which coordinated all American agencies, had been reorganized three times. By 1967, the *Pentagon Papers* reveal, officials in Washington were secretly assessing that the U.S. Mission in Saigon was "badly organized to conduct almost any kind of large and complex operation, let alone a war."[39]

In contrast, throughout the entire war the United States confronted a core leadership of battle-tested Vietnamese Communists. They were led by revered president Ho Chi Minh and his masterful general Vo Nguyen Giap, who had teamed up decades earlier to fight the Japanese during World War II and then the French colonialists. All the top brass of the North Vietnamese army who accepted the surrender of South Vietnam in Saigon's Independence Palace in 1975 had fought twenty-one years earlier as junior officers at the defeat of the French at Dien Bien Phu.[40] To these North Vietnamese and to the insurgents fighting the Saigon government in the South, the war came to symbolize U.S. imperialism linked to their old French colonial masters.

My gender afforded me a distinct perspective in a war zone dominated by male soldiers, officials, and reporters. It enabled me to go beyond traditional battlefield coverage and male-focused controversies to report much-needed stories about the views of Vietnamese women and others on how the war impacted their lives, about the political, economic, and historical factors underlying the conflict, and about why the pro-Communist guerrillas and cadre fought so vigorously.

The U.S. command accredited 467 women as correspondents from 1965 to 1973, when U.S. combat troops withdrew. Of this number 267 were American. Most arrived in or after 1965, when U.S. combat troops arrived. The war killed two, and disease killed a third; Vietnamese Communists captured two in Cambodia.[41]

With more women reporting the Vietnam War than any previous conflict, a media scholar concludes, it was "a turning point — to some extent a watershed — for American women as war correspondents." Another media scholar argues that women correspondents in Vietnam were "revolutionaries before the feminist revolution of the 1960s formally began." My arrival in 1962 was four years before the establishment of the National Organization for Women and a decade before the founding of *Ms.* magazine. Female journalists in Vietnam established themselves as equal to their male peers, one scholar observes, and "in doing so, they staked out a lasting place for their gender on the landscape of war."[42]

Sixty-six Journalists Killed Reporting the Vietnam War

During my seven years I volunteered to write one exceptionally sad story and mailed it to the Overseas Press Club newsletter in Washington DC. It was the obituary of famed photographer-writer Dickey Chapelle, the only American woman ever killed while covering a combat operation.[43] She had covered seven wars and conflicts around the world, including trudging with U.S. Marines during the battles for Iwo Jima and Okinawa in World War II. Twenty years later, patrolling with a new generation of marines on November 4, 1965, she was killed by an exploding land mine. AP photographer Henri Huet captured on film her trim body crumbled in blood. Six years later Huet himself perished when North Vietnamese antiaircraft weapons shot down the helicopter in which he was riding. In all at least sixty-six journalists were killed in South Vietnam from 1955 to 1975, almost equal to those killed in the four years of World War II.[44] "Civilians suffered almost as greatly as soldiers in the Vietnam War," one researcher wrote. "Most American civilian casualties were media people."[45]

In a *National Geographic* article published six months after her death, Dickey Chapelle described the most bewildering, still inadequately answered enigma of the conflict: "As I fell into the hypnotic rhythm of the patrol — we were moving between trees and cane fields, stepping high so we would not trip and clatter on the uneven ground — I was obsessed by a question that had plagued me on other walks in other wars: Why?"[46]

6. Famed photographer-writer Dickey Chapelle was struck down by an exploding mine and received last rites from Chaplain John McNamara on November 4, 1965, thus becoming the only U.S. woman killed in action covering a combat operation. (AP Photo/Henri Huet)

1

The People's War

Know the enemy and know yourself; in a hundred battles
you will never be in peril. When you are ignorant of the
enemy but know yourself, your chances of winning and
losing are equal. If ignorant both of your enemy and of
yourself, you are certain in every battle to be in peril.

Sun Tzu, *The Art of War*, about 400 BCE

Our army is a *people's army* because it defends the
fundamental interests of the people, in the first place those
of the toiling people, workers and peasants.

North Vietnamese general Vo Nguyen Giap, 1959

The two-ton truck jostled me from side to side as it lumbered down the
cinnamon-colored road, swooshing puffs of dust through the window
and engulfing the armed escort vehicles behind us. The daredevil Vietnamese military driver and I were headed toward D-Zone, a vast jungled
area controlled for decades by the Communist-led guerrillas fighting the
U.S.-backed government of President Ngo Dinh Diem. Within a month
of arriving in Saigon in February 1962, I arranged for my first patrol in
South Vietnam to report on Diem's government forces and their American
advisors. I also caught my first glimpse into what the guerrillas called
their "liberated zone."

7. A Viet Cong provincial committee and Buddhist priest gaze silently in this photograph printed from a roll of film taken from a dead pro-Communist soldier in the mid-1960s. (Courtesy of James Pickerell)

I fiercely clutched my Yashica camera and a few other belongings, as we drew closer to D-Zone. Huge craters pockmarked the road that had been dug up by the guerrillas or their supporters from the surrounding villages. The craters served as a visible, jagged line showing that we were entering into the liberated zone where the guerrillas and their cadres governed. Liberated areas such as D-Zone served as essential safe havens for the guerrillas to rest, train, build up their forces, and conduct operations. A 1962 Communist document reminded its political cadres and armed guerrillas that a liberated area "is neither a temporary station nor a retreat . . . but is permanent, a flag flying for the Revolution."[1]

The Communist-led Viet Cong, shorthand for Viet Nam Cong-San,

8. These youths, probably recruited by the Viet Cong, are shown in a photograph printed from a roll of film taken from a dead pro-Communist fighter in the mid-1960s. (Courtesy of James Pickerell)

which means "Vietnamese Communist,"[2] were unlike fighters in conventional wars. These elusive guerrillas wore no distinctive uniforms, rarely carried their arms openly, and often commingled or even lived with civilians, making them hard to distinguish from friendly faces. They were, as a youthful Senator John F. Kennedy told Congress in 1954, after his visit to French Indochina, "an enemy which is everywhere and at the same time nowhere."[3]

Our destination was Trung Lap, a Vietnamese government training camp only thirty-five miles northwest of Saigon, which housed Vietnamese Ranger units and thirteen U.S. Army advisors headed by Maj. Fred K. Cleary. Barbed wire encircled Trung Lap, which was in turn encircled by the Viet Cong liberated zone. A dozen wooden buildings including a mess hall, an open-air water tower, about ten tents for four 140-man companies of Vietnamese Rangers in training, and a bar (where I slept) dotted the barren land. Not a tree was growing near the buildings, and with the sun's reflection off the parched rice land, the temperature was higher than in Saigon. I felt I had landed in the Sahara.[4]

I had asked for this patrol to gain a firsthand view of how U.S. advisors were working with South Vietnamese government troops. The U.S. military office that had accredited me had arranged it. To prepare for the patrol, I bought a canteen and military boots, helmet, and fatigues from the open-air, black market not far from my apartment. I had already decided against carrying any type of weapon that might misidentify me as a combatant. Besides, I sensed that U.S. GIs expected femininity in the field and decided it was always more important to wear lipstick than a pistol.[5] The patrol also gave me a snapshot of a microcosm of the war: on one side, U.S. soldiers training elite Vietnamese troops to fight organized, armed enemy units in a conventional war; on the other side, an unconventional people's war of national liberation.

The Viet Cong's people's war was a Vietnamized version of Mao Tse-tung's memorable strategy-by-analogy: "The people are like water and the army is like fish."[6] North Vietnamese general Vo Nguyen Giap had honed that strategy into a people's army that succeeded in defeating French colonialists in 1954. A one-time law school student, high school teacher, and journalist, in 1937 Giap analyzed the feudal and colonial conditions repressing Vietnam's peasants. He learned that reducing land rent and taxes was fundamental for winning support of the peasant masses, who created their own local defense forces and gradually built up regular units.[7] "An army structured in this way could not be destroyed," Giap prophesized. "The regular units were constantly replenished from below with combat veterans."[8]

"You Never Hear the Bullet That Gets You"

Shortly after twilight I left the Trung Lap Training Center with the Vietnamese government Rangers and their handful of U.S. advisors. They were planning to coordinate with another Ranger company to set up an all-night ambush in a jungled area amid fifty or so hamlet houses. We trudged silently for several hours along a road and paddies. Gunfire from nearby government forces boomed sporadically through the night, but unlike me, none of the Rangers seemed to notice. The Rangers also shrugged off sniper shots five hundred yards up the road. As the ambush area was being established, the Ranger in front of me was walking gingerly over a heavily thicketed area — and suddenly disappeared. He had fallen into a well-camouflaged mantrap with six bamboo spikes jabbed into a five-foot pit. One spike gouged such a deep wound in the back joint of his right knee that he had to be carried by two men. Besides mantraps, the thorny shrubs and thickets also hid the openings of tunnels that were cleverly dug with underground zigzags so that they could not be destroyed by grenades. When we stopped to rest, I relaxed in a Viet Cong fighting hole carved and smoothed like a contour chair with a comfortable sloping curve for my backside.

As we moved to stake out suspected guerrilla movements, strong moonlight cast eerie shadows around the edge of the jungled canopy interspersed with banana trees. Every twig snap made me jittery. I hugged the shadows of dense thickets and bamboo groves, trying to avoid being a target. A U.S. advisor whispered: "Don't worry. You never hear the bullet that gets you." This uncomforting advice stayed with me through my years in Vietnam, and I never again worried about being killed.

The next morning, as our patrol headed back to Trung Lap, we meandered through the hamlets of the Viet Cong's liberated zone. An early morning fog hovered over the bamboo-and-wood huts with straw roofs and gave a nip to the moist air. Children ran along the roadside; parched rice paddy land was waiting for the rainy season, when the whole area would be transformed into a sea of mud. Women in pajama-like clothes made of rough cotton watched us with great curiosity from their doorways, straw broom in hand or cradling a toddler.

Hand-scrawled Viet Cong signs had been tacked on the trees along the pathways. The Vietnamese Rangers jerked them down and flung them on the ground. One sign contained the most famous slogan created by Ho Chi Minh to exhort his people: "Khong Gi Quy Hon Duc Lap" (Nothing Is More Precious than Independence and Liberty).[9] Ho had written these words as he endured prison life in the 1940s. (They are

9. A village woman in pajama-styled clothes like this one scrutinized U.S. advisors, Vietnamese Rangers, and me as we ended our night patrol in 1962. (B. Deepe Collection)

inscribed in gold letters at the entrance to his mausoleum in Hanoi.)[10] These signs carried the core Viet Cong messages that sought to woo support and sympathy from the rural population. The first message called on the Vietnamese and U.S. governments to respect the provision of the 1954 Geneva Accords providing for free elections, which these two governments had rejected.

I later interviewed a U.S. official who told me that of more than two hundred Viet Cong prisoners and defectors he had interviewed by 1965, not one mentioned anything about Marxist-Leninism, atheism, or collective farms. Instead, the Viet Cong preached about freedom and democracy. "The Communists have swiped the American ideals," a Western diplomat told me in 1965, by "promising the peasants a New, Fair, Square Deal — land reform, democratic elections, land courts for justice."[11]

During my patrol the Vietnamese Rangers could not or did not address the Viet Cong's messages that undergirded the people's war. The United States had trained, equipped, and funded the Rangers only for the military side of the war, and their American advisors could not translate and understand the hand-scrawled signs.

This patrol gave me valuable insights about a liberated zone secured by using Giap's people's war strategy. I became intrigued to learn why villagers were joining the Viet Cong and what drove these do-or-die guerrillas to battle a global superpower. Over the next seven years I probed as much as possible, consulting my Vietnamese assistants and numerous other sources, dissecting translations of captured documents, and writing dispatches based on interviews with Viet Cong who had defected and guerrilla fighters who had been captured.

The Viet Cong's "New Reality"

I learned that the Viet Cong leaders had developed several effective ways of appealing to the rural population to gain its support. Undergirding their methods, however, was the nationalist charisma gleaned from the anti-French fighters that coalesced later into xenophobia aimed at Americans, a major factor U.S. officials rarely discussed in public and failed to recognize in their decision making. Ambassador Maxwell Taylor, a French-speaking retired general, recognized this xenophobia, however, when he argued unsuccessfully in February 1965 against introducing U.S. Marine combat units into Vietnam, prophesying that the United States — like France — would fail. "The 'white-faced' soldier cannot be assimilated by the population," Taylor warned. "He cannot distinguish between friendly and unfriendly Vietnamese."[12]

Channeling this xenophobia, the Communist-led Viet Cong promised villagers a better way of life. In November 1965 I learned of their visionary appeal from Mrs. Nguyen Van Long, a one-time nurse who had received three months of medical training from the Viet Cong. When I asked her why she had joined the Viet Cong, her eyes sparkled as though she had spun into a new and exciting world.[13]

"The Viet Cong from the village executive committee gave me the propaganda line that this is a feudal society — that we had to stand up and have a new society; we had to liberate the country and so on. I was so happy. I wasn't afraid. There were so many people like me — it was fun." The Viet Cong shouted their exhortations to the gatherings of villagers,[14] rather than relying on mass media messages like Saigon and U.S. leaders did. Mrs. Long was captivated by the Viet Cong as they heaved skyward their demonstration banners reading "down with" and "long live."

In 1960 the Viet Cong village committeeman persuaded Mrs. Long to "struggle." This was the Communist Party's key social movement technique used to galvanize villagers into enlisting their support to undermine the Saigon government. As Giap explained it, "Armed struggle has developed on the basis of political struggle brought to a higher level; these two forms of struggle develop simultaneously in a vigorous manner and stimulate each other"; both are "fundamental and decisive."[15] Thousands of demonstrations and other struggle events were held throughout the South during the war.[16] Mrs. Long's struggle involved seven or eight villages — "if everyone from all these villages converged at one time there would be 7,000 to 8,000 people."

The Viet Cong had a riveting appeal for village youth. As a source detailed for me in May 1965: "The Viet Cong promise them fun — that life will be gay. Many who join believe they get this." Even if a young man had been dragooned into joining the Viet Cong, a highly effective indoctrination session immediately began to mold him into an enthusiastic, well-disciplined fighter. One youthful guerrilla, who had been recruited at gunpoint by the Viet Cong, told an American official enthusiastically, "If I told you what I thought about out there in the jungle, you'd think I was crazy. The Viet Cong create a new reality; you feel you are in the world and not out of it."[17]

I learned how the Viet Cong whipped up this sense of a "new reality" when I interviewed Neil Jamieson. Jamieson, a Vietnamese-speaking province representative from Gloucester City, New Jersey, had spoken with newly arrived Viet Cong defectors and had translated a number of their songs. These young southerners were led and mentored by some of the thousands of Communist-led veterans of the French Indochina War who had remained in the South in 1954 instead of migrating to Communist North Vietnam.[18] Many of the recruits' songs centered on victory, Jamieson told me, in contrast to the melancholy lyrics reverberating in the government-held areas. Viet Cong songs bound the soldiers with the peasants, he continued, "fighting oppression not only against the foreigners but also the upper classes within society. The troops accept — in fact, glorify — the hardship because it identifies them with the people. It's almost like old Christianity. It's like little kids' Sunday school hymns — the idea of picking up the Cross for Jesus, but instead of a cross, it's a pack."

Mobilizing the People for the People's War

Beyond songs and words Viet Cong cadres used a clandestine process to seize power in the embattled countryside and to mobilize the rural population. In June 1967 I learned about this process from a Vietnamese elder who had survived it by fleeing from a Communist-controlled village situated near U.S. troop camps.

Stroking his straggly gray beard, he told me that within three weeks — and without troops — the Viet Cong could seize control of a village.[19] "Even with only armed secret cells of men still working in the underground," he explained, "they can organize the population into associations and seize control without even the government village chief knowing it. So how can we expect American troops to know it — or stop it?"

He went on to detail the effective way the Viet Cong organize a village. "First they have cells of a few men. Then they try to organize associations. They have associations for the youth, for the women, for the old people, for the peasants. So everyone becomes a member of at least one organization." Specially trained agitation-propaganda cadres used these associations to build social organizations (like Boy Scouts or churches do) as their primary vehicle to communicate their ideas, facts, data, and value judgments to the rural population. These associations were the foundation of the Communist-led support structure and "the keys to revolutionary social transformation."[20]

Viet Cong control was so rigid that villagers needed Viet Cong permission to travel even short distances. "Who do the people have to present their papers to?" the elder asked me without expecting an answer. "The children," he answered himself. "The Communists even organize the little children as guards to check the papers. Even the little children spy on where the people go and whom they talk to and report everything to the Communists."

Once the people were organized, the Viet Cong cadres exhorted them with cries of social injustice, denouncing poverty. "Then a tenant turns against the landowner and a servant against his master and the poor against the rich," the elder continued. The Viet Cong's most effective weapon is to sow suspicion among the inhabitants so that "even people in the same family distrust each other." He likened the predicament to a bowl of rice filled with ants so that one could not separate the ants from the rice. "Maybe," he concluded, "the only way is to destroy both the rice and the ants."

When I interviewed this frail village elder in mid-1967, South Vietnam was a battlefield of not only warring military forces but also two warring governments. Throughout much of the countryside it was the Communist-run "shadow" government that functioned in reality. This shadow government had its own province chiefs to parallel those of the Saigon government. It operated its own schools, erected bridges and hamlet defenses, collected taxes, maintained first-aid wards, broadcast from a clandestine radio station, and organized a press agency.

The boundaries of the shadow government were fluid. The German journalist Hugo Portisch asked a U.S. advisor in the mid-1960s, are there no maps, clearly marking Viet Cong territory? "There are plenty of maps, new ones are drawn every day," was the answer. "But three or four such maps would have to be published daily to keep up to date. Territorial control changes hour by hour. There are always at least two maps: one to show who held what during the night and the same for the day."[21]

Land for the Landless

Key promises made by the Communist cadres were for land redistribution and rent reduction to the poorest farmers. To produce their revolution from the bottom up, the Communists gave top priority to recruiting and promoting the lowest economic level — that is, to those most excluded from the Saigon government's social power structure. Most cadres, Communist Party members, and military commanders were peasants, so that if the Saigon government resumed control, "the peasants would return to their former status as slaves," a former Viet Cong concluded. "Consequently they must fight to preserve their interests and their lives, as well as their political power."[22]

Based on their classic premise of class warfare, the Communists divided Vietnam's rural society into five categories, punishing the big landowners at the top and rewarding the many at the bottom. Yet the peasants had not been told that with a Communist victory any land given to them by the Viet Cong would be taken from them and collectivized. Nor were they told that in 1954, when the Communists established their nation in North Vietnam, the Party instituted such a harsh land reform program that numbers of those killed ranged from more than ten thousand to fifty thousand people.[23]

As a South Vietnamese government officer, Lt. Col. Nguyen Be, bluntly told his American colleague, the question for the U.S. government was not "How do we get the people on our side?" but, instead, "How do we get on the people's side?"[24]

Some U.S. technicians and Vietnamese province officials had long urged implementation of an effective land reform program, but none was successfully carried out on a meaningful scale. "The Viet Cong are gaining a lot of points with the peasants by simply issuing land titles — and it costs them nothing. They take the land from the landowner and give it away," a U.S. technician told me in 1965. "Nothing we give to the peasants — like pigs, pesticides, fertilizer — is as important as land."[25]

The rural population's dissatisfaction with the Saigon government also made recruitment for the Viet Cong easier, not because the Communist cadres were so exceptional, but as one of them explained, "the people they talked to were ready for rebellion. The people were like a mound of straw, ready to be ignited."[26]

The Viet Cong also selectively and effectively used terror, coercion, and other strong-arm tactics to gain and maintain domination over the rural population. As U.S. officials so often told the American public, the Viet Cong executed or kidnapped hundreds of Saigon government personnel and sympathizers. For two and a half years beginning in 1958, for example, 1,206 civilians were assassinated, and 861 were kidnapped.[27] But as one scholar observes, the Viet Cong used terror against the Vietnamese population "judiciously, selectively, and sparingly," carefully explaining to villagers why a person was targeted.[28]

I was told one sensational example of their terror-torture technique. Describing it as the "goriest account ever," a Western counterinsurgency expert detailed how the Viet Cong had snuck into a government-controlled hamlet, grabbing the village chief and his family. "They forced the chief to watch as they cut off the legs of his five children then bayoneted out the abdomen of his wife," he detailed. "And then they emasculated him, leaving them all to die as slowly as possible." The profound impact served their deliberate political purposes. "That story will spread like wildfire through Binh Dinh Province," he elaborated. "Every government village chief knows if he takes an active stand against the Communists, the same thing will happen to him and his family."[29]

Yet more decisive than the use of terror and violence, one researcher argues, was the social revolution promised by the Viet Cong to the lower classes. "Violence may explain the cooperation of a few individuals," he continues, "but it can not explain the cooperation of a whole social class."[30]

U.S. Imperialists' "Disguised Colonial Regime"

By December 1960 within South Vietnam, the National Liberation Front (NLF) was officially announced as an umbrella organization for groups and individuals dissatisfied with the Diem regime. In its manifesto the NLF emphasized social justice and nationalistic goals, but to attract a wide net of dissidents, it made no mention of Marxist-Leninism or communism.[31] The NLF emerged from the efforts of secret, southern-born Communist Party members who were being hunted down during the Saigon government's repressions. Soon Hanoi's leaders supported them.[32] Both groups were decidedly anti-American. The NLF declared, "American imperialists who had in the past helped the French colonialists massacre our people have now replaced the French in subjugating the southern part of our country through a disguised colonial regime."[33]

Despite efforts of U.S. officials to portray the conflict to the world as a response to armed aggression from North Vietnam, a classified U.S. study made in 1965 indicated that almost all of the seventy-three NLF leaders had been born in South Vietnam. Additionally, the *Pentagon Papers* reveal, almost all were highly educated, with histories of anti-French political activity or identification with religious movements.[34] Significantly, despite U.S. claims that Communist bloc countries were supplying and equipping the Viet Cong, I reported in late 1963 that only 2 percent of their arms were from outside sources and that the best supplier of Viet Cong weapons was the U.S.-backed forces, not the Chinese or Soviets.[35] I also notified *Newsweek* that with a high level of homegrown support in the South, for every Viet Cong killed, another could be recruited.

The NLF drive for a nation free of foreign domination was launched decades earlier by Ho Chi Minh, a founder of the Communist Party in Indochina, France, and Vietnam.[36] Shortly before his death in 1969, Ho was described by a veteran French journalist-writer as a "small man, with a face the color of tea, a beard the color of rice." "This is a man so fragile that he seems to survive only by the sheer force of his imagination in the midst of a battle fought by a people as frail, as frugal and as stoic as he."[37]

Ho was the son of a scholar who had earned a degree in the Chinese classics. In Paris at the end of World War I, he made unsuccessful pleas for support for Vietnam's independence to President Woodrow Wilson and leaders of other Western democracies. Ho also traveled to Boston, where he worked as a pastry chef in the bakery of the elegant Parker House, which bills itself as "America's oldest continuously operating hotel." The table that Ho worked on from 1911 to 1913 is still in the bakery, near Boston's Freedom Trail of sixteen historic sites that sparked the American Revolution.[38]

When World War II began, Ho established war zones for his straggly guerrilla bands to fight Japanese Imperial forces. I interviewed a Saigon businessman who had fought with Ho and his guerrillas as American aircrews parachuted supplies into hidden jungle bases in return for anti-Japanese intelligence information and rescue of downed U.S. fliers.

On September 2, 1945, just four days before the atom bombing of Hiroshima and the expected defeat of Japan, Ho established the Democratic Republic of Vietnam and announced its "Declaration of Independence." He had penned it based on the one written by American patriots in 1776. Ho then appealed directly to President Truman to support Vietnam's independence from France, sending at least eight letters within three months, from October 1945 to February 1946. His letters went unanswered.[39]

After 1949, when the Soviets had broken the American monopoly of the atomic bomb and when China's "war of national liberation" led to the Communist government headed by Mao Tse-tung, the United States began increasing aid and supplies to French colonialists fighting to recapture Indochina from Ho's guerrillas. In 1954 these guerrillas defeated the garrison of the French colonialists and what Ho described as the "U.S. interventionists."[40] With this description Ho tied the Americans to a new form of colonialism that for many Vietnamese influenced their next generation's war, fueling the formation of the NLF and the Viet Cong insurgency. In the 1960s a Vietnamese teenager recounted the Viet Cong's explanation of U.S. intervention: "We were taught that Vietnam was *con rong chau tien* — a sovereign nation which had been held in thrall by Western imperialists for over a century."[41]

Clashing Worldviews of War

On January 29, 1961, a month after the formation of the NLF, Hanoi Radio gave it international publicity via its English-language broadcasts to Asia and Europe.[42] A day earlier in Washington and eight days after being inaugurated, President Kennedy had approved a new counter-insurgency plan for South Vietnam that added $42 million to bolster Saigon's armed forces, a significant increase to his annual $220 million aid package.[43] Thus, at about the same moment both the U.S. and the Communist sides took decisive steps toward what became an unimaginably destructive regional war.

But the two sides were fighting very different wars. In his New Frontier initiative Kennedy funneled in more military aid to a shaky, unpopular political regime, but he slighted the socioeconomic and political aspects of the war.[44] In so doing, the president ignored the warning of a top State Department official offered in 1961: "The Communist operation starts from the lowest social level — the villages. The battle must be joined and won at this point."[45]

The NLF was preparing for a socioeconomic, political, military confrontation, scholar Douglas Pike noted in 1986, "for which *there is no known proven counterstrategy.*" By wooing, cajoling, exciting, or terrorizing the Vietnamese rural population, he observes, the NLF's cadres "put armed conflict into the context of political dissidence" and galvanized "the people as an instrument of war." This war "represented something new on the world scene," Pike adds, and creates a paradox: "It was possible to lose the war by losing battles, but winning battles did not mean victory."[46] Which of these clashing worldviews of war would prevail became the question that riveted my attention — and that of the world — in the coming years.

2

Rice-Roots Reporting

Our lives are at the mercy of the gods!

Farmer I interviewed in a Mekong Delta hamlet, 1962

Counterinsurgency, the way I figure it, is mostly
being nice to the goddam people.

U.S. advisor, 1960s

A rice farmer grumbles that he is too afraid to leave his home in a government-held zone in the Mekong Delta and cross over to his paddy land controlled by the Viet Cong. A riverboat peddler of rice, fruit, and textiles grimaces that the war has reduced the waterways that he can safely travel to earn his living. A saintly looking villager tells me people in his Dong Nhi hamlet are too terrified to go out at night. "The government soldiers think we are Viet Cong and will shoot us," he laments. "The population is caught in the crossfire." A sickly man bitterly exclaims: "There are two vermin in the country—the government and the Viet Cong. They are the same."

These voices of fear and helplessness introduced me to the plight of Vietnam's rural families when in the spring of 1962 I first visited the Mekong Delta province of Kien Phong, abutting the Cambodian border southwest of Saigon. Stopping in the shade of trees or their thatch-roofed homes, these villagers also revealed some early problems besetting the

10. The United States, hoping to win the hearts and minds of the people, heavily funded the South Vietnamese government's strategic program that fortified hamlets with barbed wire, bamboo-spiked trenches, and watchtowers like this one. (B. Deepe Collection)

Saigon government's fledgling efforts to pacify them. The Mekong Delta was home to about six million, or 46 percent of South Vietnam's rural population,[1] and produced a surplus of the country's rice and other agricultural necessities. The Viet Cong concentrated their attacks in this rice bowl area, controlling great swathes of land and those on it with an estimated fifty thousand fighters of all kinds — hardcore, province guerrillas, saboteurs. These fighters faced off with eighty thousand government army, civil guard, self-defense corps, and village militia.

I decided that villagers in such a pivotal region would be ideal for interviews using the grassroots, public opinion polling approach I had learned in New York. Four years after I initiated my project, U.S. government officials began polling Vietnamese nationwide about their attitudes toward the war and the United States, but the White House stopped the project when negative results became public.[2]

I selected Kien Phong Province for my interviews so that I could visit some "strategic hamlets" that the South Vietnamese government had launched to counter the homegrown Communist-led insurgency. Proclaiming 1962 as the "Year of the Strategic Hamlet," President Ngo Dinh Diem launched his ambitious program to provide security in the countryside by encircling hamlets with U.S.-supplied barbed wire and building watchtowers and then to uplift the area with social and economic developments.[3] The United States heavily funded the program, envisioning it as a dramatic way to win the hearts and minds of the people.[4]

Diem developed his program to counter Mao's fish-in-the-water strategy. As one counterinsurgency expert advised Diem, his program had to "get all the 'little fishes' out of the 'water' and keep them out; then they die."[5] At first Diem's program alarmed the Viet Cong. They feared that it would cut their connections to villagers, or as one wrote, the guerrillas would become "fish on the chopping block."[6]

To fly to Kien Phong, I squeezed into the seat behind the pilot of a two-seater L-20 aircraft at Saigon's Tan Son Nhut Airport. Within five minutes we were soaring above the vast lushness of the Mekong Delta, a chaotic spiderweb of canals, rivers, and streams.

Along the delta's waterways were scattered some of South Vietnam's 16,398 hamlets, where rural families lived in a cluster of houses surrounded by rice paddies or thick vegetation, rather than being isolated from each other like families were in my native Nebraska. Each hamlet ranged in population from four to seventeen thousand villagers, with half containing a population of only five hundred or fewer.[7] Three to five hamlets in turn made up each of South Vietnam's three thousand or so villages, which was the most basic traditional unit of Vietnamese society.

From the plane I saw farmers the size of mechanical toys in black pajama-like outfits and conical hats prodding water buffalo to plow rice paddies as their ancestors had done for centuries. Brown-skinned children bathed in streams of the same color. Perched at the water's edge, a white-bearded man sucked in the cooling breeze and watched the red-and-blue taxi boat, the small fishing houseboats, and the unpainted, canoe-shaped sampans quietly skimming home from market. It appeared to be a serene day.[8]

Despite the appearance of serenity, I soon learned, this countryside was the traumatic front line in the war of no front lines. It was here that the Communist-led Viet Cong were cajoling, caressing, wooing, promising, or terrorizing villagers in an invisible yet dynamic scheme to conquer South Vietnam. In response the U.S.-backed Diem government had launched its much-touted Strategic Hamlet Program.

Fish-in-the-Water Interviews

I found that interviewing villagers was risky for them and for me. Traveling by jeep, helicopter, and speedboat, I visited five hamlets that were all supposedly government-secured strategic hamlets. But to my surprise, provincial officials insisted I would need to have additional military protection. Government forces swept through the area and set up a company command post before I visited hamlets to speak with inhabitants. These precautions were in response to ongoing dangers in the region. In Tan-An, the first strategic hamlet I visited, the local chief had been killed two months earlier when he opened his desk drawer and a grenade exploded in his face. In Binh Long Thuan, which had earlier been 100 percent Viet Cong controlled, guerrilla bands still sauntered outside the bamboo fences in the banana groves five hundred yards away and had launched grenades into the hamlet the day before I arrived.

As expected, some of my questions were too sensitive to ask or answer. Fear of identifying themselves with either side prevented villagers from freely discussing politics, government policies, or local Viet Cong tactics. "Please don't ask us to say which side is best," one farm laborer pleaded with me. "If I answer the Viet Cong is best, the government will put me in prison. If I say the government is best, the VC will kill me." A government soldier volunteered to me in broken English, "If I talk politics, my head leaves my neck."

In Dong Nhi, site of three major government operations in one month, I talked through a Vietnamese government interpreter with Mrs. Nguyen Thi The and made numerous notes. The wife of a thirty-one-year-old rice paddy farmer, Mrs. The told me she had never seen a movie. Although one was shown the night before in the neighboring hamlet three hundred yards away, she was too afraid of the Viet Cong to attend. She said she had never heard a radio in her hamlet. She could not read or write. She had neither telephone nor electricity. She did not know the name of the U.S. president and was unaware that U.S. military advisors were based only seven miles away. She said she was delighted with my visit and my request to photograph her, explaining, "It's the first time since I was born I've seen an American or myself in a picture."

She invited me into her thatch-roofed house, spread a reed mat on a low table that served as a nighttime bed and daytime chairs, and asked me to sit down. Her house, like about half of those I peered into here and on patrols in other parts of the country, had deep holes dug in the floor — the primitive equivalent of a Cold War fallout shelter. Mrs. The pointed to her floor hole under the low table I was sitting on. Her sister-in-law, eavesdropping on our conversation, explained she had to stay near the house to rush her own children into floor holes whenever gunfire started to sound; another man told me he nose-dived into his floor hole upon first hearing U.S. helicopters buzz overhead. In soft-spoken words Mrs. The summed up the villagers' helplessness. "The government soldiers came, and we wanted to throw them out, but they had guns," she volunteered. "Then the Viet Cong came; we wanted to toss them out, but they also had guns."

Then there was the voice of hopelessness. A mother complained that her ten-year-old son had no opportunity for schooling and needed to drive water buffalo. "When he grows up, there will be no future here," she explained. "We live for today. Tomorrow will be like today."

Some were emboldened to voice economic grievances. With astonishment I watched an irate forty-five-year-old woman scold the official in charge of civic improvements intended to win the villagers' sympathy. She complained that the eight-foot-wide road being built for the strategic hamlet would cut a piece off her rice land and would require her to chop down her favorite orange tree. "I had planted it as a baby," she grimaced, "and now I can sell the fruit for five hundred piastres. A piastre is very big here." (It was worth the equivalent of about seven-tenths of a U.S. penny.) She pleaded that the road construction not force her to move her wooden house. Her father chimed in: "Every person must build the road in front of his house. But I am sick. How can I do it?" Family members said officials had promised to pay them for their work in rice allotments, but these payments had not arrived.

The travails of building strategic hamlets added to hardships caused by the war. Villagers whom I talked with said the most widespread effect of the war was its systematic drain on their livelihood. The increase in taxes and inflation coupled with constrictions on the economy devastated an already poor rural population. Only families with draft-age sons said the war was a more serious problem than the economy.

Some told me they were attempting to protect themselves no matter which side won. After World War II Kien Phong Province had been controlled by the pro-Communist Viet Minh, who had fought both the French colonialists and the Japanese invaders, and then by the Viet Cong after the 1954 Geneva agreements ended French rule. The Communists issued certificates of paddy and garden ownership to landless farmers and thus gained much popular sympathy. Much later, in 1958, President Diem also issued land certificates to begin his less radical land reform program. Farmers swapped the certificates among themselves until each had documents from both sides for a plot of land. The U.S.-Diem government side was failing to mount a rousing counter to the Communists' promises of land and power to the rural poor.

Although hardly an extensive study, my interviews revealed that the Strategic Hamlet Program was off to an exceedingly shaky start. There was no assurance a strategic hamlet could withstand a well-planned Viet Cong attack, and lacking that assurance on a sustained basis, villagers would not be safe from Viet Cong coercion, intimidation, or recruitment.

There was no guarantee the Viet Cong had not infiltrated the hamlet or had not lived inside it all along.

My interviews also indicated that villagers felt they were being forced by the Saigon government to work without sufficient benefit or without the rice and services that they had been promised. Thus, in my first rice-roots reporting I detected that Diem's Strategic Hamlet Program, backed with U.S. encouragement and funding, was on the road to failure unless it overcame significant security, administrative, and socioeconomic shortcomings.

"Operation Sunrise" and the Dawn of "Death Zones"

Unlike the efforts under way in the Mekong Delta region, the government was forcibly relocating the rural population in the Viet Cong–controlled area of D-Zone, the jungled area northwest of Saigon not far from my Trung Lap patrol. I visited Ben Tuong, the first hamlet being constructed for relocated villagers after the Vietnamese government launched "Operation Sunrise" on March 22, 1962, in Binh Duong Province, containing the strategic highway running northwest of Saigon into Cambodia. The Viet Cong infested the area; only ten of forty-six villages were under government control. U.S. officials lamented that Sunrise "got off to a bad start,"[9] as dramatically detailed in news reports, including mine.

To launch Operation Sunrise, Vietnamese government airplanes air-dropped thousands of leaflets and used airborne loudspeakers to blare instructions urging the population to move out to secured areas. Then a massive contingent of Vietnamese regular and elite units swooped in, but the Viet Cong had already faded away. When the disastrous relocation of villagers began, only 70 families volunteered for resettlement. The 135 other families "were herded forcibly from their homes," the Pentagon Papers report. Some came with their meager belongings, others with little but the clothes on their backs. "Then their old dwellings — and many of their possessions — were burned behind them." Vietnamese officials refused to distribute much of the U.S.-supplied three hundred thousand dollars in local currency essential for economic development until uprooted Vietnamese indicated they would not bolt their new resettlement hamlet.[10]

I interviewed Maj. Tran Van Minh, the government's province chief. He told me that villagers not vacating their homes within an announced time limit would be presumed to be Viet Cong sympathizers and would "be shot on sight." Then U.S. and government forces would treat the forty-square-mile Viet Cong–held stronghold as a "death zone" and massively bomb it. I focused on this new, chilling death zone strategy in an article distributed worldwide by the Associated Press and published in the *Manila Times*.[11]

The gripping *death zones* term would soon become sanitized into the label of *free-fire zones*. The name change also signaled an increase in the number of allied air strikes and artillery bombardments designed to keep the Viet Cong on the run, spur or force Vietnamese peasants to move to safer areas, and substitute firepower for allied casualties but which often created civilian casualties or refugees. In May 1965 strategic B-52s from Guam began above-the-clouds saturation bombardments of death zones considered to be Viet Cong enclaves. By 1968, as President Lyndon Johnson began peace negotiations, death zones gave way to the realization, one scholar explains, that "further applications of massive American firepower across South Vietnam seemed likely to annihilate all too well the country the Americans had come to save."[12]

To demonstrate the economic development phase that followed Operation Sunrise, the Saigon government announced a flow of resources pouring into Binh Duong Province. Vietnamese government workers distributed U.S.-funded fertilizer and medical equipment, were building a new dispensary, issued plastic identity cards to 128,786 persons out of the 176,572 population, and constructed five new hamlets along a major highway for more than 6,000 persons in 1,104 families.[13]

Yet security remained tenuous. A guerrilla who had hidden in a crowd of strategic hamlet workers assassinated a village official. Two years after Diem launched Operation Sunrise, Secretary McNamara told President Johnson that the Viet Cong still controlled 90 percent of the territory of the province and that "the hamlet militia were disarmed because of suspected disloyalty."[14]

By destroying hamlets, forcing relocation of the inhabitants, and bombarding the surrounding area, a scholar notes, the government over time seemed cruel, created rootless elements in the countryside, and "drove many potential supporters of the Saigon government into the arms of the enemy."[15]

Following the Sea Swallow Story

After Operation Sunrise's "bad start," the Vietnamese government launched a showpiece strategic hamlet operation code-named "Hai Yen," or Sea Swallow. To cover that operation, I traveled to Phu Yen Province, situated halfway up the coast from Saigon to the 17th parallel.[16] In the province a ribbon of verdant rice paddies snuggle along the South China Sea and National Highway No. 1. Interior regions lie between mountains that form the Annamite chain, mountains that spectacularly dominate the northern third of the country. Perched on a hillside overlooking the provincial capital of Tuy Hoa was an exquisitely ornate temple tower of richly carved sandstone. It alerted me to the ancient, India-influenced Champa civilization that first rose up against Chinese domination in 192 CE, established an independent nation for the next six centuries, and then was conquered by the Vietnamese moving down from the north in the tenth or eleventh centuries.[17]

Like many other sections of South Vietnam, Phu Yen Province had seen two decades of fighting during World War II and the French Indochina War. Traces of these conflicts were scattered across the region. The cement skeleton of a bridge blown up by Allied bombers rose from the murky waters. In late 1961 such heavy fighting erupted in the countryside and province capital that U.S. military advisors feared they were about to be overrun. Civilian life had come to a standstill.

Then, on May 8, 1962, the South Vietnamese government launched Operation Sea Swallow, an integrated civilian-military venture. Within weeks Sea Swallow's first two phases — securing the capital area and then moving into the more VC-influenced areas — were successful, allowing the government to create 222 strategic hamlets by erecting defensive barbed wire fences, training defenders and civilian workers, and issuing ID cards.

Diem also used substantial outlays of U.S. funds and materials to push vigorously for economic development. He intended the province to showcase high-impact programs for fast rural development that might serve as successful prototypes in other provinces. Through these projects U.S. and Vietnamese planners recognized that the Viet Cong must not only be eliminated militarily but also be countered economically by improving the lives of the local population. "If you have the people with you, you can defeat the Communist guerrilla," one U.S. official involved in the counterinsurgency program told me. "If not, it doesn't matter how much military action you have, you can never win a guerrilla war."

The government took dramatic steps to spur economic improvement. Rural development workers distributed rat poison as a means to preserve stored grain; farmers chopped off three hundred thousand rat tails so they could document success in using the poison. Other workers parceled out medical kits, two-way radios to improve defense, farm tools, seeds, fertilizer, fishing equipment, and funds for paying a bounty for captured weapons.

One high-impact program I dubbed a "Three-Little-Pigs Project" designed for a war zone. In it the United States imported six hundred Yorkshire hybrid hogs, "which grow twice as big twice as fast" as the centuries-old Vietnamese inbreeds, and distributed them to two hundred families in Phu Yen. First, each family received on credit two feeder pigs and one breeder sow. Then, within eight months the farmer was able to sell the two feeder pigs, earning enough money to repay his initial debt, the cost of feed, and the building of pigsty and compost pit, where manure was stored until it could be used as fertilizer to increase food production. Then, when the sow bore pigs, the farmer began earning profits.

The pigs hit Phu Yen Province like a Sahara sandstorm. I learned that one man tore down half of his house to provide land to build a pigsty. Pigsties made of cement floors and walls and tile roofs were often more elaborate than the owners' homes of hard-packed dirt floors, thatched roofs, and bamboo siding. Some farmers washed their pigs daily, a blessing that not all Vietnamese children received. In hamlet meetings and street corner gatherings, farmers discussed the weight gain of the pigs and their feeding schedules as other farmers eagerly watched to determine whether they should seek pigs next year. The pigs had clearly become the status symbol of Phu Yen and a boost for the United States' image abroad.

But such a glowing pig project also obscured a problem that was to loom a year later as a national crisis for the Diem government. I found that those receiving U.S.-supplied pigs were the elite, primarily Catholics, the religion of Diem, who was once described as "a blend of East and West, a Roman Catholic with Confucian ethics ruling a Buddhist country."[18] The Vietnamese agricultural union, which had a key membership of Catholics, selected the lucky recipients. Yet most people in Vietnam were not Catholic, and they were the ones the government was trying to sway against atheistic communism.

Sea Swallow's initial results in the province were encouraging for the government. The civilian population again began to venture into the towns for marketing and socializing. Stores began to remain open until 10 p.m. The number of civilian vehicles on roads increased. In just three months intelligence information from the people almost quadrupled, one U.S. advisor working closely with the project told me, and it came from people who had not cooperated before. "One good example of the people's support was some villagers who stopped a convoy and told us the Viet Cong had set up an ambush along the roadside," he explained. Within four months Viet Cong defections had increased fivefold. "If we can continue to win the people," he exuded, "the Viet Cong can't operate."

Despite some successes, problems plagued the Strategic Hamlet Program, causing it ultimately to bog down. Administrative and technical ability and initiative of the hamlet personnel were limited, and the military draft siphoned off potential civilian talents needed at all levels. A hamlet medical cadre told me that he had not been paid for six months, although the United States had supplied the necessary funds to the province. I heard so many other examples that a U.S. major working with strategic hamlets nationwide told me, "Without honest local leadership at the rice-roots level, you're really hurting." One Vietnamese official I talked with doubted that, even with good leadership, guerrillas and their sympathizers could be won over to the U.S.-supported side. "A Viet Cong is a Viet Cong," he said. "He'll take your money and still be a Viet Cong."

Others maintained that the most pressing demand still was airtight security to counter the Viet Cong's strategy to "attack from the outside; infiltrate the inside." Viet Cong "sleepers" lived inside some hamlets, spying on government operations. Many villagers had had close contacts or relatives in North Vietnam or within the Viet Cong.

A U.S. scholar noted a more fundamental flaw. The Saigon government failed to elevate the socioeconomic and political status of most villagers and to promise as much or more than the Viet Cong. "What use is the fertilizer you just bought with the government loan, when the landlord takes half the crop and the district chief refuses to prosecute him?" he notes. "What use is the farmers' association when the poor always have been and always will be treated like trash?"[19]

Diem, galvanized by his brother Nhu, vigorously pushed his strategic hamlet initiative.[20] By mid-1963 Diem was set to complete 10,500 strategic hamlets throughout the country — or covering 90 percent of the rural population — at an estimated cost of eighty-five million dollars in U.S. funds and much more from the Vietnamese budget. But by then the top Australian counterinsurgency expert in Vietnam, Col. Ted Serong, told me he was worried Diem was pushing the program too fast over too big an area. "We're a sailing ship with sails flapping in the wind," he explained, "but not going anywhere."[21]

The End of Diem and His Strategic Hamlets

On November 1, 1963, military generals overthrew the government of Ngo Dinh Diem and murdered him. His Strategic Hamlet Program died with him.[22] Instability followed. A merry-go-round of Vietnamese generals who sought, gained, and lost power resulted in six major changes of the Saigon government within eighteen months.[23] More and bigger Communist-directed attacks on strategic hamlets and government outposts led a U.S. advisor to tell me: "This used to be cowboys-and-Indians type stuff. Now one of our battalions may meet one of theirs toe to toe like World War II."[24]

As the Viet Cong were dismantling Diem's strategic hamlets, I interviewed U.S. military planners trying without much luck to resurrect the
program in the provinces ringing Saigon, naming their plan "Operation
Hop Tac." But Vietnamese leaders balked at supporting it. They viewed
it as the "American plan," resented U.S. advisors' presence at the district
and village levels,[25] and within eleven months changed twenty-four out
of thirty-one district chiefs and five out of seven province chiefs in the
area.[26]

A year later I saw firsthand the deterioration in the Hop Tac area lying
only ten miles from Saigon's Presidential Palace. Arriving in a commercial
taxi and surveying the blackened ruins, I was shaken upon learning what
had happened. A five-hundred-man Viet Cong battalion had attacked
and overrun Tan Buu outpost, using U.S.-made .57 mm recoilless rifles
and .75 mm Chinese Communist–made recoilless rifles. Before retreat-
ing in January 1965, the Viet Cong raided the premises, stealing all the
weapons from the armory and so much ammunition they could not
paddle it all down the river. They even commandeered the Vietnamese
company commander's boots and uniforms. "The Viet Cong now have
the same weapons that we have," a U.S. advisor told me. "It appears we
are equipping both sides, but we are giving advice to only one side."[27] I
was hardly surprised when I saw the *Pentagon Papers* conclude that Hop
Tac had been "faultily conceived and clumsily executed."[28]

McNamara: Five Years of Failed U.S. Pacification Efforts

The demise of Diem's Strategic Hamlet Program meant U.S. officials
needed a new label to define their efforts to win the hearts and minds of
the people. The Americans adopted the term *pacification*, despite warnings that the French had used it to describe their domineering colonial
and military approach to the villagers.[29]

In 1966 McNamara made a two-week trip to Vietnam and returned to
give President Johnson grim news about pacification. When I first read
the report by McNamara, I was struck by how markedly his language
seemed to echo villagers' problems that I had heard four years earlier in
doing my rice-roots reporting. But McNamara's assessment was even

more negative and sweeping than mine. McNamara told Johnson the most difficult policy recommendation to implement "is perhaps the most important one — enlivening the pacification program." He warned the odds of success are less than fifty-fifty "because we have failed so consistently since 1961 to make a dent in the problem."[30]

My time in Vietnam, talking to its people and seeing the war firsthand, made me share McNamara's pessimism. In May 1967 I chronicled the failures of the pacification program. A Vietnamese official told me that it was failing and that some Vietnamese government's cadres were ineffective. "They are supposed to be revolutionaries, but they are only draft dodgers," he said, and even then the government had trouble recruiting enough to meet its quotas. "We need a new strategy of how to secure the countryside and to win over the peasant," he continued. "But no American or Vietnamese leader has even started to think of that yet."[31]

A week after my May 1967 interview, the U.S. pacification effort was turned over to the Military Assistance Command.[32] By then, the *Pentagon Papers* observe, progress on pacification in the field "was not only not satisfactory, it was, according to many observers, nonexistent."[33]

Tet 1968: "A Severe Setback" for Pacification

Within seven months I was hectically covering how the U.S.-Saigon pacification efforts had suffered a monumental blow. Pro-Communist main force units and saboteurs slashed through the countryside during the Tet Lunar New Year holiday in late January 1968 and attacked numerous province capitals and urban centers, including the U.S Embassy in Saigon.

Having reported and analyzed what I could from Saigon, I knew that the *Christian Science Monitor* needed coverage about Tet from the countryside. I hired a taxi for a solo journey to the provincial capital of Bien Hoa, twenty miles northwest of Saigon, traveling on the country's only paved, four-lane superhighway. With Saigon still being shelled and with little traffic on the road, I was jittery about the journey, but it proved uneventful as we lumbered past rice paddies that glistened in the midmorning sun, heading for the sprawling complex of installations of strategic importance around Bien Hoa. These included a jet-length runway and airbase facilities, the U.S. Army's Long Binh post, where more than thirty thousand Americans worked and the headquarters for the U.S. and Vietnamese commands of the eleven provinces forming the Third Corps.

Arriving in Bien Hoa, I was appalled to learn of the ferocity of the fighting that had occurred there. One U.S. veteran officer living on the gigantic base recounted, "This is the worst battlefield I have ever seen — and this is my second war." Several villagers told me of finding clumps of five to fifteen Viet Cong near their homes and gardens. About two thousand Communist dead littered the greater Bien Hoa area within the first forty-eight hours of fighting.

I soon learned that the pacification effort had been hit hard. A U.S. official confided to me that in eleven provinces it had been set back "a minimum of six months." A Vietnamese source agreed, saying, "The whole pacification program has been blown skyhigh."[34] The *Monitor* headlined this grim news on page 1. A month later a secret "Intelligence Memorandum" revealed that my dispatch had been too mild. While the Johnson administration was publicly criticizing the press for negative coverage of Tet, the CIA memo dated March 19, 1968, stated, "The pacification program unquestionably suffered a very severe, and perhaps disastrous setback in some of the most important areas of III Corps."[35]

I then flew to the northernmost provinces, while the U.S. Marines and elite South Vietnamese units were still battling to recapture Hue (pronounced *whey*). Command staff and civilian officials told me the pacification program in the five northernmost provinces had suffered a "disastrous defeat" and a "tremendous shellacking."[36] My dispatch for the *Monitor* was nearly as pessimistic as a secret Pentagon report being made at the time. It said the Tet Offensive appeared to have killed off the pacification program "once and for all" and exemplified "a bleak picture of American failure in Vietnam."[37] That failure ultimately continued, a historian notes, so that by the time Saigon fell to North Vietnamese army units in April 1975, "the CIA and the U.S. government were no closer to 'pacifying' the countryside than they had been when the effort began almost two decades earlier."[38]

The gunshots and crossfire terrifying the villagers I talked to in 1962 escalated drastically through the years. The intensified violence caused the pacification program to degenerate into depopulation of the countryside. By early 1965, when the first U.S. combat units began arriving, pacification was turning more into an effort "increasingly devoted to refugee centers and relief."[39]

Military might befitting the world's superpower intensified the dangers and destruction in Vietnam's countryside as the pro-Communist forces also increased their numbers and use of more deadly weaponry. Incoming U.S. units, as well as Saigon's forces, relied heavily on artillery or airpower to help repel Viet Cong, who often caused higher casualties of civilians by intermingling with them. Even without the enemy, U.S.-Vietnamese forces increasingly used airpower and artillery to bombard hundreds of "death zones" that I first described in 1962. Destruction from round-the-clock bombardments in Long An Province in 1968 prompted one official to describe large areas as looking "like the face of the moon."[40]

Allied firepower also devastated the lives and livelihoods of the rural population. "The property of the people, such as gardens and fruit trees and their houses, were flattened by bombs," a villager in Dinh Tuong Province complained. "You could say they are all gone. Because of B52s there is nothing left."[41]

Hundreds fled the countryside, finding safety in squalid shantytowns that one U.S. official dubbed as "fields of shit."[42] Many became beggars or refugees, prompting a researcher to observe, "Depopulation of the countryside proved to be the most effective, if brutal and indiscriminate, method of pacification."[43]

I was disheartened to see the impact of the war transform Saigon. Beggars, black marketers, and destitute women selling themselves increasingly cluttered the streets, creating a slum-like sprawl that overshadowed the captivating, Frenchified city I first visited in 1962. U.S. servicemen paid minimal wages to hundreds of maids and laundrywomen, some probably sympathizing with or spying for the very opponents the Americans were sent to defeat. A waif peddled elegant jet ink–on–silk sketches of Saigon in its vanishing heyday. Huddled outside swank hotels were ragamuffin children called *bui dui* — "dust of life." By 1969 about one-quarter or more of South Vietnam's sixteen million people over the seven-year span of the war had become refugees or displaced in their own homeland, victims of relocation policies, the ground fighting, shellings, and bombings.[44]

Just how counterproductive U.S. firepower was becoming to the pacification effort — and to American prestige and purposes — was being secretly communicated to U.S. officials. Hamlet residents along a river in Ba Xuyen and Chuong Thien Provinces were increasingly reluctant to travel the waterways after U.S. Navy boats began patrolling the area, one American in the field learned in 1966, thanks to U.S. polling of Vietnamese nationwide. From the province the American alerted Saigon of a developing problem: "U.S. presence equals the kiss of death."[45] Ultimately, air strikes, gunfire, and forced relocations led some to conclude, "The United States has made more 'Viet Cong' than it has killed."[46]

3

"The World's First Helicopter War"

Cavalry, and I don't mean horses!

Gen. James Gavin, 1954

No sound or image is as evocative of Vietnam as the helicopter.

British historian Alasdair Spark, 1989

The first American helicopter unit started moving into the Mekong Delta on April 9, 1962, and I went to visit it soon afterward. I was eager to cover the first contact between these newcomers and the delta's population. To arrange the visit, I met with the commander of Marine Squadron 362, Col. John Franklin Carey, a forty-six-year-old Minnesota-born, cigar-chomping veteran of World War II and Korea. Carey entered the stuffy public information office of the U.S. military advisor's command in Vietnam, limping slightly, a reminder of the Battle of Midway.

"This is no place for a woman," he warned me.

"Well, I adjust quickly," I responded.

Then he kindly suggested that I exchange my blue sports dress for a pair of fatigues. "Marines don't allow women with legs down there," he told me. I borrowed oversized fatigues from an information officer until I could buy my own.

U.S. generals thought helicopters were the wingless airborne wonders that were key to defeating their elusive enemy by being able to ascend vertically, fly upward or backward, hover, and skim the rice fields or treetops. Helicopters would thus provide more mobility for ferrying Vietnamese soldiers into remote battle zones or for rapidly reinforcing isolated forts and villages under attack. One U.S. captain ending his eighteen-month tour in Vietnam was so exuberant about the mobility provided by helicopters that he exclaimed: "The Viet Cong are everywhere and nowhere, and so are we, everywhere and nowhere."[1]

My trip to the marine squadron provided my first glimpse of what I would later describe as the "world's first helicopter war."[2] The American military had used helicopters for medical evacuations in the Korean War but, fearing their vulnerabilities, resisted developing them for combat—until 1961, when President Kennedy fast-tracked them to Vietnam to launch his New Frontier counterinsurgency initiatives. Kennedy learned from the ideas of Gen. James Gavin, who touted helicopters after the Korean War in a magazine article headlined, "Cavalry, and I Don't Mean Horses."[3]

Helicopters became instant symbols of the United States' technological approach to fighting a people's war. This approach was epitomized by Robert McNamara's reliance on statistics and computers. But North Vietnamese general Vo Nguyen Giap warned, the Americans "don't reckon on the spirit of a people fighting for what they know is right, to save their country from invaders."[4]

"First World Suburbia and Third World Death"

I traveled south by chopper with Colonel Carey to the Mekong Delta, where our destination was Soc Trang, a province capital of thirty thousand population, eighty-five air miles south of Saigon.[5] The first of the four-hundred-man marine unit arriving there on April 9 started to develop a self-contained enclave encased in barbed wire, and a week later the full unit moved in. The marines had transformed swampland, weeds, debris, and six structures into a city of tents, wooden frame toilets ("You don't have to flush them; they're the latest kind"), a flimsy canvas shower hall

("You have hot water if the sun's still shining"), their own water purifying system, a fuel field, a seventy-five-kilowatt electric plant, and a thousand-foot, all-weather runway, equipped with portable lights. "This is just a typical marine operation," Carey said offhandedly. "It's our business to come into a new site." Yet this spartan site illustrated the time-consuming and expensive logistics of moving entire U.S. support units to Vietnam, where, in contrast, the Communist-led guerrillas relied on living-off-the-land operations or backpacking their own supplies.

This base camp was the home for the twenty-four helicopters, fifty-six plane commanders, forty-eight crew chiefs, plus maintenance mechanics, and support personnel of the squadron of HUS, shorthand for Helicopter Utility Sikorsky, the manufacturer. Army soldiers joked that HUS was shorthand for *Hussies*.

Upon landing inside the enclave, I was shown my private "room," ordinarily reserved for generals. It was a small tent containing a mosquito-netted bed, a five-gallon water can, a wooden plank desk, two tin chairs, a stand for a washbasin; thankfully, it stood near a little-used latrine like the one I had used in my country school days. The tent grew oven-hot as the late afternoon heat percolated within its screened canvas sides. When leaving on all-day missions, I learned to stash my typewriter and suitcase on the bed in the middle of the room, for although it was supposedly rainproof, the tent had big holes in places. Half of the day was torrid, half was torrential, but the nights were nippy.

Besides missions and briefings, I took careful note of the humdrum camp activities so that I could make vivid the scene and conditions for readers half a world away. During the day the PX was open for drugstore items from 9 to 6, the post office from 7:30 a.m. on. Holes were being dug for a frame chapel near the mess hall, which served breakfasts of ham, eggs, and pancakes and dinners of mashed potatoes and meats. Repairs were being made on a stucco building that would be a lounge and medical center. A violent windstorm had a week earlier blown down the sides of the dispensary. Officers and enlisted men lived in crowded, hot conditions, ten cots to a long tent. The "fog machine" rolled through spewing antimalarial spray to kill mosquitoes and chiggers. Around the camp roamed gasoline tankers, water carriers, jeeps, cargo transports, and two live curry-colored Brahma bulls given to the colonel by the province chief as a token of appreciation.

My visit and walk-through included talking to a California marine who operated the electric Laundromat and dryer ("Vietnam is all right if you have to be here"). Nearby two pots-and-pans washers were scrubbing away. I toured the shop where one third of the squadron's personnel maintained the helicopters ("We have to work four-man hours for every hour of flying time"). Despite the in-the-rough living, the contrast between this camp supplying "transplanted portions of America" and the war outside the perimeter provided what one writer described as "instant transitions between first world suburbia and third world death."[6]

Soc Trang: Off-Limits, Except for the Trash Run

I was surprised to learn that contact between the marines and Soc Trang residents was limited. The garbage dump swamp was one of the few places where several marines regularly met Vietnamese; Soc Trang was off-limits. Going to the trash run gave me a snapshot of the stark poverty of the people. At 1:15 p.m., shortly after our lunch of roast pork, lima beans, mashed potatoes and gravy, and fruit tart, I started out in a two-and-a-half-ton truck driven by Chicago-born PFC Neil Glenn Jaeger. We drove through the sleepy town of Soc Trang, passing a quarter-mile line of busses and Lambretta scooters that had been stopped by the Vietnamese military for searching.

As we drove, Jaeger explained that on their first trash runs people were milling around the road and were under the canvas grabbing boxes and cans before the truck even stopped. "I'd get on the back of the truck with my weapon to keep the kids off," he explained. "The only thing we could try to do was to roll the tarp back so it wouldn't get messed up." Until half of the truck was unloaded, the situation was completely out of hand, "like an old-fashioned American stampede."

PFC E. V. Strickland Jr. of Goldsboro, North Carolina, interrupted, "Once I threw a tin can out in the middle of that stagnant water and

11. Impatient youngsters await the regular trash run made by U.S. Marines in the Mekong Delta town of Soc Trang in April 1962. (B. Deepe Collection)

ten people were after it." I asked why. "I hope it's for their pigs," Jaeger answered. "But you wonder — they fight for it so much."

Strickland added, "They'd get our old beer bottles and use them for other things or sell them." At first youngsters scooped up the trash of bottles, cans, or metals and sold them to the Viet Cong, who used it for making gasoline bombs that were packed full of TNT powder, stones, and homemade fuses, Jaeger explained, and those weapons caused casualties. So the marines began stashing these materials inside their base camp.

As we approached the swampy dumpsite fifty yards from a long row of

12. Youngsters dive into the marines' garbage containers to scoop up scraps before they could be dumped in Soc Trang in April 1962. (B. Deepe Collection)

houses, a small boy began running to outdistance us. People sprang from houses and the bus stop across the street. Even before Jaeger could leave the driver's seat, about twenty of the one hundred villagers were already doing his job for him — rolling back the tarp and unloading the trash. One small boy plopped his hand in the middle of the large garbage can filled with slushy semiliquid. A few lima beans swam on top. Six other boys pulled out hunks of food and stuffed them into pails and bamboo baskets. Strickland exclaimed, "The people in the States don't know how lucky they are 'til you see something like this."

13. An unidentified crew chief and I—in oversized fatigues borrowed from a U.S. information officer—wait at the U.S. Marine base at Soc Trang before lifting off in a helicopter in April 1962. (AP Photo)

Fluttering Away in the Dragonflies

In my one week with the squadron I accompanied the marines on five of their combat support missions, which included ferrying Vietnamese troops into an area where only hours before two U.S. Army advisors had been killed. For these missions I adopted the marines' routine: up before dawn, hot breakfast in the mess hall, a ride to the flight line, where clusters of Vietnamese troops were already huddled. As first light peeked through the fog, the helicopters cranked up, their rotor blades creating whirlpools of debris and a symphony of *whump-whump-whump*. I usually jumped in to sit beside the machine gun–toting crew chief, his football-like helmet contrasting with my bandana. Then a dozen Vietnamese troops piled in.

The HUS took off one by one but soon were fluttering amid the clouds in a precise formation, like a gaggle of hungry geese headed south. Upon approaching the assigned landing zone to unload the soldiers, each pilot hovered his vehicle so that one rear tire slumped into the mud and its two front wheels quivered a few feet above the ground. While the Vietnamese leaped into unfamiliar terrain, the HUS hovered for its half minute of maximum vulnerability. "Those 30 seconds seem like an eternity," one pilot told me.

The helicopters initially posed "some fearful moments" for Communist-led fighters, as one North Vietnamese veteran, Bui Tin, recalled. "Sometimes dozens would appear, all crackling noisily, the sound of their engines mingling with the rattle of machine-gun fire. The wind caused by their blades raised such a storm of dust. They could descend right on top of you or surround you."[7]

Helicopters also bewildered unsuspecting villagers, as recounted by Le Ly when she first encountered the *may bay chuong-chuong* — or dragonfly. As a sixteen-year-old tending her water buffalo near her village in central Vietnam, she heard a noise sounding like a tiger's growl that crescendoed into a roar. Her water buffalo fled to the trees. Two helicopters fluttered downward, whipping her clothes and sun hat. A giant American alighted to survey momentarily the landscape with binoculars and then climbed into the machine. "As if plucked by the hand of god," Le Ly recalls, "the enormous green machine tiptoed on its skids and swooped away, climbing steadily toward the treetops, the second craft behind it." Another sound arose behind her. "Bay Ly — are you all right?" her father shouted. She exclaimed, "The *may bay chuong-chuong* — the dragonflies — weren't they wonderful!" Angered, he scoffed, "Wonderful? Hah! They were *Americans*. You risked your life hanging around here while they landed. Even our buffalo has more sense than you!"[8]

"These Big Sweeps Are Useless"

Seven months after flying with the marine helicopters, I covered one of the biggest heliborne-ground operations as of that time, code-named "Morning Star." I traveled to the Vietnamese government division command post in the province of Tay Ninh, which translates as "Peaceful West." The province sits on that misshapen side of Cambodian territory that protrudes into Vietnam in an odd geographical layout that resembles, and was usually called, the "Parrot's Beak."

On October 11, 1962, U.S. helicopters began ferrying about five thousand Vietnamese government forces to launch the first phase of a search-and-destroy operation that fanned out in a multi-province arc west of Saigon over the next eight days. For it the United States introduced four HU-1 Iroquois costing $280,000 each. They became the world's first "offensive" whirlybirds to launch gunship strikes.[9]

In the second phase twenty U.S. H-21 Shawnees worth nearly one million dollars were shuttling in 2,500 crack Vietnamese airborne and marines; thirty coal-colored M-113 armored personnel carriers worth a million dollars each floundered in the knee-deep rice paddies; thirty naval landing craft totaling nearly two million dollars patrolled rivers and canals; ten fighter planes costing millions strafed troop-landing zones and swooped onto Viet Cong sampans.

The troops were sweeping through a Viet Cong liberated zone with its own intervillage postal system, propaganda signs above arched village entrances, and a homemade defense system consisting of fifteen-foot antihelicopter poles and bamboo stakes that could and did pierce combat boots. This system added to a tunnel and cave complex, built in the 1950s by anti-French fighters, that could withstand bombardments from air or artillery.[10]

But despite this multimillion-dollar extravaganza, I ventured the results were "far from record-breaking." At the end of the eight days sixty-one Viet Cong lay dead, thirty-three were captured, and eighty-two persons were held as suspects. Vietnamese government casualties were three killed and twenty-seven wounded; no U.S. casualties. Vietnamese troops had destroyed sixty sampans, twenty-five buildings, ten information centers, and heaps of rice. A high-ranking Vietnamese officer emphasized to me that any operation was useful because it disorganized the Viet Cong by disrupting their logistics.

But I called the monster operation a "fabulous fizzle." Vietnamese and U.S. military officials offered me a variety of explanations. Plans might have been leaked to the Viet Cong, or reconnaissance flights may have tipped them off. Or the guerrillas had hidden in the jungle or completely submerged themselves in rice paddy water and breathed through reeds. Or Vietnamese ground troops had avoided combing the area by tiptoe-ing along rice paddy dikes and marching in single-file columns through narrow jungle trails.

The U.S. and the Vietnamese military sources did agree, however, that the Viet Cong would move back into the area once government forces had withdrawn. "These big sweeps are useless," one advisor told me. "You'd think they were planned so we did not engage the Viet Cong."

I ended my visit with a peek into the future: more Morning Star–styled search-and-destroy sweeps that, once conventionalized government forces had moved on, would leave villagers vulnerable to Viet Cong recruitment, intimidation, and pressure. Morning Star could have, but did not, serve as a flashing light to warn U.S. and South Vietnamese generals to reassess their search-and-destroy strategy.

Helicopters proved "a fatal fascination for military commanders," according to Sir Robert Thompson, the counterinsurgency guru who had garnered successes during the victorious British counterinsurgency in Malaya (now Malaysia) and who was then advising President Diem. Without the helicopter search-and-destroy sweeps like Morning Star would probably not have been possible. He concludes, "In this sense, the helicopter was one of the major contributions to the failure of strategy."[11]

Ap Bac: "Biggest Clobbering in U.S. Helicopter Warfare"

Not all search-and-destroy operations were a fabulous fizzle like Morning Star. A year after the first H-21 Shawnees arrived and nine months after I left Soc Trang, I saw firsthand the vulnerabilities of helicopters when they suffered what one battle-weary U.S. pilot described to me as "the biggest clobbering in U.S. helicopter warfare." I was taken aback by his exclaiming, "When else in history have we lost five choppers in one day in one landing zone!" The Viet Cong shot down five U.S. helicopters and damaged fourteen of the participating fifteen. That "clobbering" occurred on January 2, 1963, at an obscure hamlet called Ap Bac (Northern Village), nestled among a V-shaped cluster of coconut trees, foliage, and paddy dikes.

To rush to the battle scene, I took a commercial taxi to Tan Hiep, the command post of the Vietnamese Seventh Division, situated only thirty-five miles southwest of Saigon, rather than waiting for the luck of hitching a safer, faster helicopter ride. Traveling along a two-lane highway in any direction out of Saigon was not the smartest way to get around because of the dangers of surprise ambushes or snipers, but it was a risk I took to get to the scene. After a jostled ride down pockmarked Highway 4, past coconut fronds waving lazily in the tepid breeze, the nervous taxi driver dropped me at the dusty command post, where I set about interviewing helicopter pilots and other participants.[12] I also sent, via a Saigon-bound colleague, rolls of film I had taken, including one grisly shot that *Newsweek* published showing a U.S. casualty lying on the floor near the open doorway of a grounded helicopter.[13] Ap Bac became such a big news story that I ended up cabling *Newsweek* more than twenty pages of text, updates, advisories, reaction of U.S. top brass, and background on relations between U.S. advisors and their Vietnamese counterparts.

The operation began peacefully. At 6:50 a.m. ten H-21 Shawnee helicopters, escorted by five more powerful and armed HU-1 Iroquois gunships, dropped off without incident the first wave of Vietnamese Seventh Division regular troops. But then ground-hugging fog delayed liftoff of the next two waves of troops until 9:50 a.m., when the Shawnees, escorted by the Iroquois, ferried in the remaining two loads of troops. Suddenly the lead Shawnee took heavy crossfire from the tree line and was shot down, leaving its four-man crew in danger on the ground. A second chopper, badly disabled, crashed five hundred yards away, but its crew was picked up. Another chopper received automatic weapons fire. "It was damn near suicide," a crewmember told me. "It was a sheet of fire in there."

Then in a dramatic but disastrous attempt to rescue the four-man crew of the first downed Shawnee, another Shawnee was shot down, its gunner killed in action, and its crew chief and pilot wounded. "The first time we didn't like our approach to the area," copilot CWO Richard G. Watlack explained about the rescue attempt. So the chopper circled again and was ready to set down. "But we never got in," he continued. "We were hit. The rotor blades flew off, and the chopper flopped over on the right side." The first thing he saw was the face of pilot Lt. James E. Stone in the mud. "I told him to get his head out of the water," Watlack whispered to me, "and then I realized he was knocked out." A Korean War combat medic, Watlack then turned and saw his crew chief, Sgt. William L. Deal, strapped in his seat. "I knew that when a colored boy turned white and had a helmet-ful of blood, I couldn't do anything for him."

An hour and a half later, as three Iroquois strafed the tree line, one Shawnee landed for another rescue try. "Zap! In thirty seconds they'd had it," a pilot told me. The crew chief had leaped out of the craft to help the wounded, but the Shawnee received such heavy fire, it quickly pulled out, leaving the crew chief on the ground and crashing out of the battle zone. The Viet Cong were still entrenched in heavy foliage lining the canal side hamlets. "After napalm bombs, machine-gunning, and artillery bombardment, the Viet Cong came right back out of their holes and continued firing," Capt. Joel R. Steine, the Iroquois platoon commander, exclaimed to me.

Shortly before nightfall a battalion of experienced Vietnamese para-troopers was airdropped onto the west side of Ap Bac, contrary to the pleas made to the commanding general by Lt. Col. John Paul Vann, senior military advisor to the Seventh Division. Vann wanted the paratroopers landed east of Ap Bac so as to block the Viet Cong's most likely escape route. The Vietnamese general refused — and his enemy faded into the night. Fuming that the Vietnamese general "chose to reinforce defeat,"[14]

Vann was easily recognized as the reporters' source who had described the battle as "a miserable damned performance."[15]

Vann's widely publicized criticism exposed a complex military organization that was subject to political pressures. Political loyalty to President Diem often counted as more significant than military competence, some U.S. field advisors complained. They indicated this lack of will-to-win leadership was based on Vietnamese commanders' fear of reprimands by Diem if they suffered many casualties or weapons lost even though they might inflict heavy Viet Cong losses.

Diem denied this view, yet it trickled down to the field, as revealed in a conversation I had with a U.S. advisor. "I used to sit in battalion headquarters every day and look out and see the Viet Cong harvesting their rice," the American captain told me. "When this had insulted government troops enough, the commander ordered out his troops, who fired at them 'til they ran away. This happened every day. But we never got them — the commander did not want anyone killed or to lose a weapon."

Vann and the Vietnamese field commanders were shocked. Expecting to face off with 120 Viet Cong guerrillas, they instead encountered 350 fighters of the Viet Cong's 261st Battalion,[16] the largest, crack main force unit in the area.[17] When the final figures were in, the "clobbering" consisted of 3 Americans killed, 10 wounded; Saigon forces suffered 80 killed and 100-plus wounded, compared to the Viet Cong's 18 killed and 39 wounded.[18]

Within a month after Ap Bac top U.S. military leaders issued public statements defending the valor of Vietnamese fighting troops and commanders and calling the battle an allied victory. In contrast, the Communists came to view Ap Bac as a victory that had "important historical significance," one scholar notes. It "opened the way for the bankrupting of the 'helicopter mobility' and 'armoured vehicle mobility' tactics," which served as the "trump cards" of the anti-Communists.[19]

Forty years later Ap Bac still served as a case study at West Point, the nation's institution for training future army thinkers. The U.S. leaders' inflated victory claims led a military historian there to call the Battle of Ap Bac an "interesting historical paradox" because "its greatest importance lies in the perceived unimportance by American policymakers," who missed "the warning signs of a flawed policy in Southeast Asia."[20]

Rewinding History: Hitching JFK's New Frontier to the Old West

On June 27, 1964, I attended a simple ceremony that retired all of the famed slow-moving H-21 Shawnees from service in Vietnam. During their two and a half years in Vietnam GIs and journalists often called them "banana boats" because of their upside-down crescent shape; the Viet Cong guerrillas called them "Angle Worms."[21] They were the namesake of the Shawnee people, who before the American Revolution sacrificed their blood battling for their hunting grounds in what is now Kentucky and then through the Ohio Valley in the mid-1700s, during the French and Indian Wars. After the Revolution the Shawnees, led by Tecumseh, tried to form a confederation of all the tribes from north to south in the Mississippi Valley that would be given their own lands by the whites.[22] Instead, the Shawnees became almost refugees in the face of overwhelming white advances for about a century, until today they are settled mainly on lands reserved for them in Oklahoma.

At the ceremony I interviewed Lt. Col. Robert Dillard, an aircraft company commander who was on his second tour to Vietnam. In 1961, as commander of the Fifty-seventh Helicopter Company, he had flown the first helicopter off the U.S. aircraft carrier *Core*, and now he was flying the same helicopter, numbered O-49, for the last time. He relished talking about the first moment of this unique U.S.-Vietnamese encounter. "The streets around the ship were roped off," he recalled. "But thousands of people were backed up for blocks. They had never seen helicopters before and didn't think they could fly. But when the choppers did fly, they all applauded like mad." After O-49's maiden flight, U.S. helicopters would go on to fly an amazing number of over thirty-six million flights over South Vietnam and North Vietnam.[23]

The Shawnees were being replaced by the faster, sleeker turbojet-powered HU-1 Iroquois, often called "Hueys" and the namesake of the peoples encountering the first Europeans to arrive along the upper East Coast. I rode in one of the first Iroquois to arrive. Skimming jungle treetops north of Saigon, it suddenly lost power because of a malfunction and pancaked to the ground in a surprise but soft landing that crimped its skids accordion style. No one was hurt, but I was shaken up. Some HU-1 Iroquois carried troops or cargo, defended only by crewmembers' weapons. But others arrived in Vietnam armed with 7.62 mm mini-guns mounted beside their cargo doors that could fire six barrels at six thousand rounds per minute — or one hundred rounds per second.[24]

Soon more specialized helicopters began arriving to perform a wide variety of functions, ranging from observation to lifting and carrying howitzers. These new arrivals had one feature in common: they had been given names of American Indian tribes or chiefs by the U.S. military. These names included the *Sioux* for the bubble-nosed scout; the *Chickasaw* for the fat-bellied utility vehicle used for carrying cargo or ten troops; the *Choctaw* used for transporting cargo or eighteen personnel; the *Kiowa* used for observation; the sling-carrying *Mohave* used for lifting heavy cargo under its belly; the *Tarhe*, a twin-engine, heavy-lift Skycrane that could implant an artillery piece on a hilltop;[25] and the *Chinook*, a 16.5-ton transport named after tribes encountered in 1805 by the Lewis and Clark Expedition along the Columbia River.[26]

By bequeathing Indian names to numerous helicopter models, scholars observe, the American generals saw "helicopter development as somehow a natural extension of Indian Wars."[27] Accounts of the Vietnam War are "replete with comparisons to the American West," a British historian notes, and this association was "abetted, even sponsored, by the official policy of naming helicopters after Indian tribes, evoking the Indian wars," and adding to "the mythic American style of war."[28]

The most flamboyant example evoking the Indian War association was the army's creation of the "mystique of the Air Cavalry," which arrived in Vietnam in September 1965 emblazoned in elements of the First Air Cavalry (Airmobile) Division.

The First Air Cav carried "the name, horse-head insignia, colours, history and crossed-sabre props clearly considered the symbolically appropriate heritage" for it.[29] The patch of the Ninth Cavalry's two reconnaissance units depicted an Indian in a war bonnet brandishing a rifle in one hand and with the other hand reining a flying horse with all fours skimming off the ground. The patch of the Tenth Cav pictured the side view of a grumpy-faced, humped buffalo floating above a banner exhorting: "Ready and Forward."[30]

"An Unwitting Admission of Counterinsurgency Failure"

On my visit to Soc Trang in early 1962 I was not able to interview Capt. David G. Marr, the only Vietnamese-speaking American assigned to the marine helicopter squadron. I wish I had talked with this intelligence officer because he early on saw the pitfalls of the U.S. helicopter war. I would then have included his astute observations in my 1964 dispatch to the *New York Herald Tribune* that focused only on the advantages of mobility that helicopters brought to the allied efforts.[31] Marr foresaw disadvantages because helicopters enabled the government forces to ignore the roads and canals used by most villagers and permitted the Viet Cong to expand their organization along them so they could gradually surround district and provincial towns. In that sense, he reasoned, helicopters represented "an unwitting admission of counterinsurgency failure."

A Dartmouth graduate, Marr had studied Vietnamese at the Monterey Army Language School and arrived in Vietnam in 1959. By 1962 he was becoming disgruntled about how the war was being waged. The political aspect of the war needed allied focus, he reasoned, rather than launching search-and-destroy operations against an elusive enemy. Marr foresaw Vietnam's apocalyptic future: when helicopters failed to stop the enemy, U.S. military strategists would "escalate the technology with fighter-bombers, gunships, and — eventually — B-52s, that penultimate weapon of mass, indiscriminate terror."[32]

4

The Rise and Fall of Frontier Forts

I am reminded of our own Revolution. It took eight years
to get through our Revolution, and then we ran into some
of the toughest guerrillas that we ever want to run into any
place—the American Indians.

Gen. Paul D. Harkins to President Johnson, 1964

Indian country (in'dē en kun'trē) n. [U.S. mil. slang] 1.
term used by American soldiers during Vietnam conflict
(1961–75) to designate territory under enemy control or any
terrain considered hostile and dangerous.

Journalist and writer Philip Caputo, 1987

I thought I was seeing the filming of a cowboys-and-Indians movie. As
the helicopter circled, I saw below me a bit of the old frontier days of
the American Wild West. The large wooden fort with gun ports and log
cabins were not, however, in Hollywood.

It was April 1962, and these structures at Kham Duc were for real, in
the deep jungles of South Vietnam, on cleared jungle land only thirteen
miles from the Laotian border. These structures protected South Vietnamese soldiers from their enemy—the pro-Communist-led forces—who

used hide-and-seek guerrilla tactics like the American Indians had a century earlier in the U.S. heartland. But instead of the Indians' bows and arrows, the pro-Communist warriors brandished automatic rifles. Once completed, the fort was designed to enable South Vietnamese soldiers to monitor infiltration of their enemy from Laos and to launch border surveillance patrols.

I called the fort at Kham Duc the "new frontier for South Vietnamese president Ngo Dinh Diem," who in turn was echoing President John F. Kennedy's "New Frontier" approach seeking to counter communism. Being constructed from scratch, Kham Duc was one of Vietnam's largest and most isolated resettlement schemes, an ambitious part of Diem's Strategic Hamlet Program. The making of Kham Duc involved clearing 3,166 acres of jungle to build a resettlement village — a protected fortress — for three thousand or so isolated Vietnamese and Montagnard ("hill people" in French) tribesmen. After being resettled, each family was to receive two acres of cleared land on the outskirts of the village.

I visited the Kham Duc fort in a helicopter used to ferry troops or cargo over lofty mountains, fifty miles from Danang, a major seaport south of the 17th parallel separating North and South Vietnam. The banana-shaped Shawnee was loaded with TNT, needed for blasting hillsides. Bundled in a heavy bulletproof vest, I sat on an emergency survival kit, a wooden box containing medicine, purified water, food, and a machete. Skimming the clouds, the H-21 Shawnee flew through the passes of mist-covered mountains, which Vietnamese call "Truong Son" (Long Mountains), and over small rivulets snaking down crevices. The helicopter followed Highway 14, a red clay road hugging the hillsides to their end near Laos.

"That's one of the most ambushed roads in the country," the helicopter pilot radioed me through the headset. The roaring helicopter landed on a small circular area cleared from the maze of hilly jungle. A one-mile-long airstrip was nearly finished, but remaining was three months' more work to level hundred-foot trees and mountaintops.

14. In 1962 I visited the resettlement village of Kham Duc, near the Laotian border, while it was being constructed from hewed-out jungle logs and was like an old Wild West fort. Six years later, in May 1968, it would be evacuated and abandoned. (AP Photo)

Kham Duc: The Making of a Jungle Fort

Terraced along the hillsides were log cabins with grass on top and a government center. On an opposite hillside was the five-sided fort built with a row of logs packed with clay two feet thick at the top and five foot thick at the bottom. I was told in a reassuring tone, "That fort will stop almost any kind of bullet."

Steel helmets, used as washbasins, and potted flowers decorated the porches of living quarters. Steps hewn out of hardened clay led to the office of a representative of the Vietnamese province chief (comparable to a U.S. governor but wielding both military and civilian government authority).

"Phase I in Kham Duc consists of building a market, school, church, pagoda, and medical and social services in the village for military and administrative personnel," the young Vietnamese officer told me. The second phase was to build houses and shops, he explained, and the third phase was to relocate Vietnamese and Montagnards from the hills to secure them in the fortified area and to train them to watch for and fight the Communist-led forces.

Kham Duc gave me a close-up view of the twenty forts then scattered throughout the jungled mountains dominating the northwestern portion of South Vietnam. At their peak more than one hundred such forts would serve as home base for fifty thousand Vietnamese Civilian Irregular Defense Guards organized and funded by the U.S. Central Intelligence Agency and advised by elite Special Forces. President Kennedy touted these green-bereted warriors — and the introduction of helicopters — as his two New Frontier initiatives to counter Communist-led wars of national liberation.

The Green Berets were training and leading the Montagnards. Their seminomadic population numbered an estimated seven hundred thousand from some thirty distinct ethnic groups. Their ethnic extraction and lifestyle differed markedly from that of the Vietnamese, who called them *moi* (savages), an animosity described by a U.S officer as being "much like the relationship between the American Indians and the early American colonists."[1] Montagnards held to their separate culture of longhouses built on stilts and other practices that reminded me of the walnut-hued tribesmen I had interviewed in Borneo in 1961. I later visited several Montagnard clusters of longhouses, mingled with the inhabitants, and rode one of their majestic elephants, which freely roamed the jungles until they came to be exterminated by the war.

These hill people were largely unschooled, coming from an oral tradition, but were quite intelligent. "In our camp they learn English and Vietnamese on their own," M.Sgt. William S. Burke of Baltimore told

15. I talk with highlander women in 1962. (AP Photo)

me when I visited Mang Buc outpost in November 1962. "Once they learn something, they never forget it. They rely on memory like we rely on pencil and papers." Some could count in English from one to one hundred, which was important for reporting accurate information. "Before when we asked them how deep a stream was, they'd answer 'two elephants deep,'" Burke explained. Until the American soldiers arrived, as one of them told me, the Montagnards were "people who were born, died — and nobody knew or cared."

The Green Berets were training and equipping Montagnards for small-unit reconnaissance patrols, surveillance missions, and secret forays across the Laotian border. Most of these forts were positioned along South Vietnam's three-hundred-mile border with Laos, where thousands of pro-Communist propaganda agents, soldiers, and supplies and equipment filtered under the multilayered jungle along the vital infiltration route known as the Ho Chi Minh Trail. The Trail was a honeycomb of footpaths and animal tracks flowing for miles from North Vietnam through Laos or the Demilitarized Zone (DMZ) and then into South Vietnam.

"The Trail undeniably lay at the heart of the war," a military historian states, and is "a fulcrum that turned the balance in the Vietnam War."[2] The Communists increasingly needed it when U.S.-Saigon forces more effectively blockaded their sea routes and marines after 1965 defended the Demilitarized Zone separating North and South Vietnam. At its peak nearly one hundred thousand Vietnamese and Laotians worked on the Trail,[3] which by mid-1967 carried more than 98 percent of all equipment reaching South Vietnam.[4]

For the infiltrators death could await them in many forms, including hungry black bears, tigers, and poisonous snakes or fatal diseases.[5] "The Ho Chi Minh Trail is a one-way street," a Hungarian diplomat based in Hanoi explained. "People who were sent down the pike fight till they die or are just left down there. Nobody ever comes back."[6]

The making of the Ho Chi Minh Trail touched off a ferocious debate in Hanoi about strategy. The go-slow, pro-Moscow wing of the Vietnamese Communists advocated retaining the Trail to handle only foot soldiers and bicycles carrying essential supplies for the South. The pro-Chinese advocates sought to expand the Trail up to nine yards in width so it could handle Chinese or Russian trucks, but doing so necessitated building stronger bridges, ferries, fuel dumps, and antiaircraft positions. The pro-Chinese leaders won the debate.[7]

Facing "Indian Country"

Besides building frontier forts, American military from GIs to generals subconsciously associated their enemy in Vietnam with earlier wars waged by their predecessors against American Indians. I was somewhat taken aback upon hearing this historical connection made in early 1963 by the head of the U.S. advisory effort in Vietnam, Maj. Gen. Charles Timmes. The U.S. military usually trained for a conventional war or for a "big atomic war," he told me in an interview, but "here we're fighting 'a cowboy-and-Indians' type of fighting" against the Viet Cong. For a counterstrategy, Timmes told me, "civic action is just as important if not more important that killing the VC. . . . You must win the hearts and minds of the people."[8]

Agreeing later with the general was Leroy TeCube, a Jicarilla Apache assigned to the Americal Division. The unconventional nature of the Vietnam War "was similar to the Indian Wars of a hundred years ago," he observes. "I realize that my ancestors fought the same type of war against the United States."[9]

This image of "cowboy-and-Indians" type of fighting occurred in what GIs in Vietnam called "Indian country," and it soon took on the more sinister connotation of the uncharted, menacing territory outside the barbed wire perimeters of forts where enemy fighters lurked. Taking offense at such language and imagery was an unnamed soldier from the Seneca tribe, saying: "When I got to the bush, my platoon sergeant tells me and the guys I came in with that we were surrounded. He said: 'The gooks are all out there and we're here. This is Fort Apache, boys, and out there is Indian country.' Can you fuckin' believe that? To me? I should have shot him right then and there. Made me wonder who the real enemy was."[10]

In the highest echelons of the U.S. military and political establishment the negative comparison of enemy territory with Indian country was also unconsciously made. One scholar notes that in 1965, when North Vietnam refused to buckle under his reprisal bombing, President Johnson "evoked the heroic legacy of the frontier racial war of American myth" and exhorted his top national security bureaucrats to war, imploring, "You gotta get some Indians."[11]

Scholar Michael Yellow Bird, a citizen of the Sahnish and Hidatsa Nations, castigates such pervasive attitudes, asserting, "White domination is so complete that even American Indian children want to be cowboys." He concludes, "It's as if Jewish children wanted to play Nazis."[12]

Would *Newsweek* Hire a Woman Correspondent?

The Associated Press distributed my Kham Duc dispatch, which was published in several newspapers.[13] At Kham Duc I also gleaned significant insights that I soon used to investigate another frontier fort when my journalistic career took a lucky turn. Unexpectedly, in September 1962, seven months after my arrival in Saigon, I was hired by *Newsweek*, and my freelancing days were over.

On September 4 the Diem government suddenly expelled *Newsweek*'s stringer, Frenchman François Sully, a seventeen-year resident of Vietnam, for an issue that displeased Madame Ngo Dinh Nhu, the beautiful, razor-tongued sister-in-law of the president. She soon worsened the already strained government-press relations by declaring Western correspondents in Vietnam were worse than Communists because they believe whatever the Communists say and speak for them — but in a Western tone. "That is why it is worse." No U.S. official in Saigon or Washington countered her explosive remarks.[14]

To find a replacement for Sully, *Newsweek* dispatched to Saigon its Far East correspondent from Tokyo, Rafael Steinberg. I hunted down Steinberg. In his midforties, with wavy black hair and a polished demeanor, he explained that he was still looking for a Saigon stringer, who would receive a regular retainer to cover events in Vietnam, answer queries, and fulfill other requests while being paid extra for published articles or photographs but would receive no medical or other benefits usually

16. Madame Ngo Dinh Nhu reviews the paramilitary women's youth corps she initiated. (Courtesy of the Republic of Vietnam, 1962)

accorded staff correspondents. Steinberg said he had an experienced newsman in Tokyo ready to come to Saigon, but he did not know French, the language of the Vietnamese elite.

I quickly gave Steinberg my sales pitch. I emphasized that I had received top grades in French at the University of Nebraska and had earned a master's degree with honors from Columbia University's Graduate School of Journalism. Also useful, I told Steinberg, was the background I had developed in Asian Studies, my freelancer's reporting and writing that honed critical thinking skills, a penchant for generating ideas for stories, and the stick-to-it-ness to overcome obstacles to news gathering.

He seemed satisfied but said he did not know how New York would react to having a woman represent *Newsweek* in Vietnam. I was startled.

Not having worked for long in a traditional newsroom, I was blissfully unaware that the sexism practiced in male-dominated journalism in the United States was so virulent that a managing editor of the *Washington Star* declared in 1966, "Decrying even the presence of a female in the newsroom has been an editor's prerogative so long that some of us tend to regard it as part of the Bill of Rights."[15]

I felt sure that if *Newsweek* checked my references at Columbia's Journalism School, I would get a good recommendation from my professor John Hohenberg. He had appreciated my work in his international reporting course, visiting the United Nations to interview diplomats. On September 16, 1962, I received word from New York: "Deepe collect privileges have been established cablewise." I could now cable.

As a stringer for the weekly, I was almost as free to travel as when I was freelancing. But I had to be in Saigon on Saturdays to answer queries and to send suggestions by air express to New York, and I began attending more regularly the daily press briefings. Journalists dubbed them the "Five O'clock Follies" because officials often dispensed such overly optimistic, vague, or even inaccurate information. These briefings by U.S. or Vietnamese officials provided a roundup of countrywide developments about which they often held almost exclusive knowledge and as such were newsworthy for reporters meeting daily deadlines. The resulting articles led some scholars to exaggerate that journalists in Vietnam served basically as megaphones for amplifying the official line.[16]

Working for *Newsweek* became a lot more demanding than freelancing. I was besieged by so many administrative requests that my work became all consuming. My number one priority each week was to check whether the government-licensed importer was being allowed to release *Newsweek* for sale in Vietnam. Checking with the importer, I learned that the government had banned the September 24 issue, a fact I mentioned casually to *Times* man David Halberstam. He included a comment attributed to me in his 203-word news story detailing a more stringent government clampdown on reporters and on circulation of some publications, in which *Newsweek* was being singled out. Halberstam's twenty-word sentence about me drew a sharp reprimand in senior editor Arnaud de

Borchgrave's cable, reminding me of *Newsweek*'s policy that correspondents did not speak for the newsmagazine without clearance.[17] Actually, I had not been told about that policy.

Diem's government clamped down on foreign correspondents in other ways. In early 1963 it announced a 70 percent tax on all cable costs and telephone calls, driving up the already expensive costs of transmitting news through Saigon's unreliable and antiquated telegraph system. This increase led me, as well as other journalists, to begin saving cable fees by spelling *Vietnam* as one word; Vietnamese write each word separately, *Viet Nam*. Diem's government also unofficially barred correspondents from riding into the southern region in U.S. troop-carrying helicopters being operated by U.S. crews. Although fifty helicopters and two hundred Americans were in combat on Thanksgiving Day in 1962 in one of the largest known helicopter missions to date, no firsthand coverage was allowed, and government news releases on it were irritably scant. As a veteran correspondent groused about this new censorship-at-the-source: "We have to use guerrilla tactics to get the news."[18]

Ashau: A Log Cabin near Laos

Three weeks after taking over Vietnam coverage for *Newsweek*, I cabled New York and proposed flying to another frontier fort. I wanted to eyewitness whether North Vietnamese troops were flooding into South Vietnam instead of withdrawing to North Vietnam from Laos, as required under a new international agreement. A conference of the United States and thirteen other nations, again held in Geneva, agreed to support a Declaration and Protocol on Neutrality of Laos. It was finalized on July 21, 1962 — the same date on which eight years earlier the 1954 Geneva Accords had ended the French Indochina War but failed to bring peace to Laos.[19]

The declaration about neutrality for Laos had set a deadline of October 6 calling for the fourteen signatories, including Communist China, North Vietnam, the Soviet Union, and the United States, to support a three-way neutralist coalition government, to be headed by Prime Minister Souvanna Phouma, to end the fighting in that country and to withdraw all foreign military forces except a maximum of 1,500 French military instructors requested by the Laotian government.[20] This settlement increased prospects that pro-Communist forces would use Laos to step up military pressure on South Vietnam and that the credibility of the United States would plummet by its abandoning Eisenhower's hard, anti-Communist policy and shifting to support a neutralist, coalition government.

With the approach of the October 6 troop withdrawal deadline and *Newsweek*'s approval, I prepared to travel to a Vietnamese government outpost near the Laotian border just before all foreign troops were to withdraw from Laos. The biggest question in Southeast Asia was whether the estimated ten thousand North Vietnamese troops in Laos would infiltrate into South Vietnam, I had told New York. Noting the high-stakes consequences of North Vietnamese forces moving into South Vietnam, I quoted in shortcut cablese language an apprehensive American advisor: "If they come across, will redface Kennedy administration."

To view the possible North Vietnamese infiltration from Laos, I selected an isolated outpost in the 20-mile-long, 4-mile-wide Ashau Valley, 360 miles north and west of Saigon. It was nicknamed "Shotgun Alley" by helicopter pilots because several months earlier, on a flight of five helicopters, four had been hit. Other light aircraft on scheduled Monday-Wednesday-Friday "milk runs" bringing in food, beer, and mail to the outpost were regularly shot at. My destination, Ashau outpost, was described to me as a "Vietnamese outpost so close to the Laotian border some engineers think it's on the Laotian side."

Getting to Ashau outpost was tricky. From Danang I cajoled my way onto a Piper Cub–like military aircraft that carried me inland toward the mountains, landing in a swirl of dust on a makeshift runway and depositing me in the midday heat at the outpost nestled below three-thousand-foot mountainous peaks covered with heavy jungle growths.

Inside the triangular-shaped outpost stood a frontier-style log cabin, filled with ammunition. Vietnamese soldiers of the Third Regiment, First Infantry Division, had fashioned a sort of living room out of the thick mud and log walls of the fort; they and the U.S. advisors lived in nearby grass-thatched huts. Outside the perimeter were beds of thousands of landmines and a front gate protected by huge balls of razor-sharp concertina wire. "Everyone outside the front barbed wire gates must be considered an enemy," Maj. Benjamin Rush III of Philadelphia, commander of the U.S. advisors, emphasized.

I told him I had come to eyewitness whether the Communist-led forces that were supposed to withdraw from Laos were in fact infiltrating into South Vietnam, rather than returning to North Vietnam. Rush and the handful of other advisors were astonished at my mission. They did not know — in fact, could not know — the answer, they said, because the dense jungle would prevent anyone from seeing any withdrawal of Communist-led forces into South Vietnam.

Rush pointed to the thick, triple-canopied jungle beginning right outside the encampment. I peered upward at the tall trees, barely seeing the top of them reaching to five hundred feet; then came a second layer of lower trees, which combined with the first to form a natural canopy preventing effective air reconnaissance and air strikes; and then came the lowest layer of ferns, bushes, shrubs, and bushy-tailed, razor-sharp grass. Wild animals and Montagnard tribesmen had burrowed trails and tunnels through the dense undergrowth — and so had infiltrators. The jungle was so lush that, as one GI told me, "Hollywood would love to import it for a set."

A faint whine of an airplane sounded far overhead, and Major Rush ran outside. "Too high," he said, "to tell whose. . . . It's probably one of ours operating in Laos. We know the Communists are infiltrating from Laos now — we've captured prisoners and documents. If they come across in big groups, we fight. If they come in small groups, we try to find them. If they move into those hills south of us," he waved, "there isn't a damned thing we can do."

Rush told me that the outpost had originally been built as part of a necklace of three outposts winding up the Ashau Valley to monitor Communist-led infiltration from Laos. Nine miles to the north lay the lonelier outpost of Tabat, and five miles farther north lay Aluoi. A red clay road connecting the three posts had been completed several months earlier, but because of the fear of ambushes, it was rarely used. Instead, live pigs were airdropped in wicker baskets, and mail was parachuted in.

As he talked, I pulled out my reporter's notebook from my GI fatigues and started taking notes. In short order I had gotten the gist of the Ashau Valley story. I could not see and he did not know whether North Vietnamese troops had left Laos for South Vietnam. I stayed overnight, sleeping on a cot tucked into a private corner for me. Rush placed his .45-caliber pistol near his pillow.

I hurried back to Saigon to meet *Newsweek*'s deadline and typed out an eight-page dispatch. But it had lost its newsworthiness and was not published because neither Washington nor the border watchers could pinpoint where the North Vietnamese had gone. I was disheartened that my dispatch was not published after all of my finagling to get to that remote, risky area. But two weeks later, to my surprise, *Newsweek* published nearly verbatim excerpts of my Ashau dispatch for more than a full column, giving readers a close-up of the infiltration aspects of the war on the South Vietnamese side of the border and naming me in the article — my first notice in a national newsmagazine.[21]

The Other Side of the Border: Whither Laos?

As Major Rush and I had speculated, the inside story affecting Vietnam's frontier forts was unfolding across the border in Laos. Seven months after the October 6 deadline for foreign troop withdrawals from Laos, fighting again erupted there, and Kennedy's agreement seeking peace within a neutralist government was unraveling. The fighting began to make visible the answer to the mystery of where most of the North Vietnamese troops in Laos had gone: they had gone nowhere. By the end of 1962 the CIA was secretly estimating that six thousand of nine thousand North Vietnamese military personnel had remained illegally in Laos, although this information was not revealed until 1995.[22]

On April 3, 1963, I was surprised by a cable from New York telling me to proceed to Laos, although that country had not even been mentioned when I became a *Newsweek* stringer. Laos was an Idaho-sized kingdom founded in 1353 by a powerful warrior who became King of Lan Xan, or the Kingdom of a Million Elephants. The kingdom survived in name when French colonialists in 1893 made it a protectorate,[23] and it continued after the 1954 Geneva Accords ended French rule. The kingdom was landlocked but shared strategic borders with Communist China, North and South Vietnam, as well as Thailand, Cambodia, and Burma. On March 23, 1961, Kennedy had warned, "Laos is far from America, but the world is small, . . . the security of all Southeast Asia will be endangered if Laos loses its neutral independence."[24]

I soon learned about the crisis that prompted *Newsweek* to rush me to Laos. Two days earlier Quinim Pholsena, the influential foreign minister, had been assassinated, jeopardizing the Kennedy-backed neutrality agreement. *Newsweek*'s cable instructed me to get to Laos and within days "to give us sense of 'wither [*sic*] laos? And don't spare color and quotes and personalities." If I could not get to Laos, I was given the nearly impossible assignment of covering the story by radio![25]

Newsweek told me I would be staying in Laos about a week, so I packed only a half dozen dresses and other essentials. When I arrived in the capital of Vientiane, however, the Laotians were celebrating Py My Lao, the Laotian New Year, according to the Buddhist calendar, when carefree residents celebrated for three days by dousing anyone in sight with buckets of water in order to wash away sins. A soundly drenched Russian diplomat in Vientiane told me with a growl, "They're fighting on the Plain of Jars, and all these people are doing is throwing water. They are not serious." Those drenchings included me as I traveled in a man-pedaled cyclo down deeply rutted streets, and within days I had exhausted my supply of dry dresses. Instead of a week, I ended up staying a month.

The answer to *Newsweek*'s "whither Laos" question was apparent when I arrived in the kingdom's capital of Vientiane. The Kennedy-backed support for an independent, neutralist government was being shattered by heavy fighting against the Laotian government's main armed forces, led by Gen. Kong Le. I first met the five-foot general midafternoon on April 15, 1963, and found him dressed in sky-blue jeans and a matching basketball jacket. With a closely shaven crew cut, he looked like an undernourished American teenager.

Born in 1934 of rural peasant stock, he had attended an American-supported Ranger training school outside Manila. The soft-spoken five-footer was acknowledged as a man of the people, the nearest thing to a widely popular leader that Laos had produced, I told *Newsweek*, hoping to satisfy its request for personality information. In August 1960 Kong Le led a coup d'état against U.S.-supported general Phoumi Nosavan that touched off a civil war and international flurry and caused President Eisenhower to describe Kong Le as a "lost soul and wholly irretrievable."[26] During this period, Kong Le told me, he had been feted in Beijing and Moscow, where he had been honored with caviar, presented a stovepipe-like shako hat, and given a slick newspaper printed in French showing Premier Khrushchev addressing a conference. It was being recycled as toilet tissue in the headquarters' tin outhouse.

But under the Kennedy-endorsed agreement Kong Le was the man of the moment, the only hope of the West for maintaining a strong, neutralist center to separate the rightwing forces of Gen. Phoumi Nosavan and the pro-Communist Pathet Lao. When I arrived, the Communist-backed Pathet Lao were driving Kong Le's neutralist forces from their only stronghold area on the Plain of Jars, a triangular blob only 18 miles long and 12 miles wide about 115 miles north of Vientiane. Its lush savanna was strewn with six-foot ceramic pots once used to store rice wine.

I succeeded in reaching the Plain of Jars just as Kong Le's outmanned and outgunned army was in full retreat, fleeing toward the pine-covered hills and touching off another international crisis. Three British journalists and I left for the plain from Vientiane in a four-passenger, U.S.-supplied Beaver of the Royal Lao Air Force. It flew for one hour over peaceful, heavily forested Laotian hills and over occasional circles of trenches and gun positions. Water buffalo, horses, and the crunched-up skeletons of an American C-123 and a Russian Dakota-type plane littered the area. We were forced to land at an emergency Muong Phanh grassy airstrip because Kong Le's regular airport five miles away was under heavy attack. I was warned an estimated 5,000 pro-Communists were preparing to attack Kong Le's 1,200 troops.

Touching down on the steel-planked runway, I heard the crump of mortars and rattle of artillery exploding from the pine-covered hills. I entered Kong Le's headquarters command post, a rough-timbered tin roof shack, which he had evacuated only hours earlier. One staff officer and three sentries guarded the shack while frantically stuffing canvas seabags full of papers. Behind a dirty, knotted curtain, Kong Le's dark room was empty, except for his two bewildered pet hamsters. On the blanket-covered table were stacks of tattered magazines and rock 'n' roll records, including one titled *Walk, Don't Run*.

Outside heavy firing created gray puffballs of smoke that faded into a murky haze blanketing the sweltering plain. At the grassy airstrip Kong Le's wounded lay waiting for evacuation. A teenage boy in a blue bathing suit, his legs wrapped in gauze, was carried piggyback into a plane, followed by a crusty soldier in French paratroop pants and a blue sweatshirt. Around the airstrip wives and children of neutralist fighters prepared to flee from tragedy to uncertainty. Some women, in tattered dresses with towels wrapped around their heads, carried babies at their breasts. A crescendo of tinny rattles of artillery and the concern of a tall colonel forced me to climb into a truck with the last soldiers departing the plain and a French military instructor, who prophesized: "C'est terminé pour Kong Le" (It is the end for Kong Le).[27] His words would accurately predict the death of the Kennedy-backed peace agreement for Laos.[28]

From the emergency airstrip I returned to Vientiane in the back of a Russian-made truck over tank gouges and dusty tracks of numerous other trucks, through riverbeds, and up treacherous slopes, tightly gripping side panels all the way. I found the streets of Vientiane bustling with activity. Fearing a rightwing coup d'état, baggy-suited Pathet Lao soldiers bought stocks of food and clothing in preparation for leaving for Sam Neua, their stronghold on the North Vietnamese border. Police under rightwing general Phoumi Nosavan tossed Communist literature out of the Ministry of Information. Bangkok papers were sold with stories on Laos being razored or grease-penciled out. "Pathet Lao will move slowly because U.S. is hot-tempered," a Vientiane businessman told me. "When the United States' temper cools, Pathet Lao will move again. But they will win."

In April 1963, a month after I departed the plain, the United States began intensified secret military and CIA operations without the knowledge of the American public, the Congress, and sometimes even the ruling Laotian government of Prime Minister Souvanna Phouma.[29] His government became increasingly fragile; the Plain of Jars shifted back and forth between rival forces; Kong Le traveled abroad either as an exile or as an ailing, powerless commander; and truces and cease-fires were talked about, agreed to, and broken before they went into effect.

In December 1964, unable to block pro-Communist advances on the ground, the United States began massive bombing in southern Laos. A year later, on December 10, 1965, the first B-52s, twenty-four of them, bombed a pro-Communist base, and for the first time in Southeast Asia they released cluster bombs.[30] Despite saturation bombing by B-52s, the Communist-led and aided forces regained complete control of the Plain of Jars in March 1970.[31]

In what became a holocaust from on high, U.S. fliers dropped more than 1.6 million tons of bombs over Laos from 1965 to 1971, or more than 17 tons for every one of the kingdom's ninety-one thousand square miles.[32] Over the decade beginning in 1961, the number of displaced civilians was estimated to be seven hundred thousand persons, or about one-quarter of Laos's total population, with allied bombing causing at least 75 percent of them to become refugees.[33]

A Laotian peasant from the Plain of Jars described the "lake of blood and destruction" caused by U.S. bombing raids. "Every day and every night the planes came to drop bombs on us," he recounted, as their sounds thundered in the sky and the hills. "We lived in holes to protect our lives." He saw his cousin die on a "field of death." He witnessed the life and death of many because of the warplanes, "until there were no houses at all. And the cows and buffalo were dead. Until everything was leveled and you could see only the red, red ground."[34]

The Fall of Vietnam's Frontier Forts

Ominously, the frontier forts I had visited began to fall like a row of wobbly dominoes within South Vietnam. Their collapse signaled a buildup in the numbers and prowess of forces infiltrating from North Vietnam. Mang Buc, which I had visited shortly after it was opened in May 1962, was closed after training Katang tribesmen for fifteen months. On March 10, 1966, three years after my visit, Ashau outpost fell. Months earlier its tiny northern encampments of Tabat and Aluoi had been closed,[35] leaving Ashau sitting alone near three major Communist infiltration routes leading east from Laos into the valleys that meandered northeastward for twenty miles toward Hue.[36]

The fall of Ashau was more harrowing than any story line that Hollywood could script, I learned. After midnight on March 8, 1966, the first North Vietnamese attacked when typically heavy cloud cover and early morning fog blanketed the eight-thousand-foot-high peaks that towered over the outpost. For the next thirty-six hours the outpost was under siege, as 434 Vietnamese and U.S. Special Forces defenders fought off — sometimes in hand-to-hand combat — an attack by 2,000 regulars of the North Vietnamese 325th Division.[37]

Within two days the outpost was so close to being overrun that U.S. commanders ordered it evacuated by helicopters, but heavy gunfire permitted only 69 people to be rescued. As darkness set in, survivors abandoned the camp, many of them straggling by themselves through the rugged mountains. Of the 434 originally in the camp, 42 percent, or 186, returned, including 101 wounded; the remaining 58 percent were missing in action; an estimated 121 weapons were lost;[38] 3 U.S. airmen were killed, 5 were missing; and 2 airplanes and 1 helicopter were destroyed. Then B-52 bombers pounded the fallen fort. The North Vietnamese had gained a sensational victory in what *Time* magazine described as "the fall of a fortress."[39]

After Ashau outpost fell, Kham Duc was the last border surveillance base camp in the five northern provinces and the last used by mobile strike forces for launching secret patrols into Laos. Then, on May 12, 1968, Kham Duc fell. Two days later I received a play-by-play account of the harrowing allied retreat given to me by a U.S. briefing officer in Danang; he justified the loss by saying that Kham Duc had by then served its purpose: destroying the enemy and surveilling the border along the

Ho Chi Minh Trail,[40] which had become a three-lane-wide dirt road.[41]

For two days beginning May 10, 1968, I was told, the fort was under attack by two regiments of North Vietnamese regulars holding the high ground in the surrounding mountains. For two days fifty-four B-52 Stratofortresses bombarded them with hundreds of tons of bombs. But as an air force report shows, the bombardments did little to reduce the ferocity of the North Vietnamese attacks.[42] Throughout the day of May 12 large cargo planes and U.S. helicopters evacuated most of the 1,760 American and Vietnamese camp defenders and their families. One helicopter gunship pilot reported the area resembled a World War II movie, with "burning airplanes all over hell."[43] Then the North Vietnamese crashed through the barbed wire perimeter.

The North Vietnamese capture of Kham Duc came six years after I had journeyed there, when the Wild West–type fort was being built on hillsides from scratch in lockstep with JFK's "New Frontier."

U.S.-sponsored Montagnard tribesmen, often accompanied by their families, largely shouldered the defense of these ill-fated forts. By the time U.S. troops withdrew in 1973, at least two hundred thousand highland people in Vietnam had died, and 85 percent of their villages had been abandoned or destroyed. As a veteran anthropologist sums up: "The North Vietnamese, South Vietnamese, Viet Cong, and the Americans had brought vast death and destruction to the mountain country."[44]

5

Two Ill-Fated Presidents

Day of Wrath!
O day of mourning

Communion received by Presidents Diem
and Kennedy, November 1–2, 1963

My trip to Laos in April 1963 was eventful in an unexpected way — my eyes and skin turned jaundiced from infectious hepatitis, probably caused by consuming contaminated food or water. Just after returning from the deserted Plain of Jars, I cabled *Newsweek*'s senior editor that I was "two shades lighter than a lemon." Back in Saigon a civilian secretary found me exhausted on my sofa and rushed me to a hospital on May 27.

Coming to visit me in the hospital was Nick Turner, Reuters' slight-framed bureau chief. He told me about Buddhist protests in the one-time imperial capital of Hue. At first I thought these were routine, but I soon changed my mind as the details of bloodshed surfaced. On May 8, Buddha's birthday and the occasion of Buddhist festivities, Buddhist followers began flying flags in Hue just as the Diem government began enforcing a long ignored ban on displaying religious flags outside of religious institutions. After the crowd heard a charismatic bonze accuse the government of religious oppression, a melee broke out; several explosions erupted, and the deputy province chief, who was Catholic, ordered troops to fire. At least eight people were killed, including children; some

17. President Ngo Dinh Diem (*second from right*), his brother Archbishop Ngo Dinh Thuc, and the Ngo Dinh Nhu family pose in traditional Vietnamese dress. (Courtesy of the Republic of Vietnam, 1962)

were crushed by armored vehicles.[1] The next day ten thousand–plus demonstrators in Hue protested the killings. The Buddhist leadership then transmitted a manifesto to Diem listing five demands: freedom to fly their flag, legal equality with the Catholic Church, an end to arrests, freedom to practice their religion, and indemnification of victims with punishment for perpetrators. Diem's government blamed the Viet Cong for the bloodshed but appointed a committee to resolve the issues.

Buddhist grievances had begun rising in early May when the Catholic hierarchy in Vietnam, headed by President Diem's brother, Archbishop Ngo Dinh Thuc, hoisted yellow-and-white Vatican flags while celebrating countrywide the twenty-fifth anniversary of Thuc's ordination as bishop. Undergirding the Buddhist grievances more fundamentally was the French-imposed Decree No. 10, which Diem had retained, labeling Buddhism as an association rather than a religion, rendering its followers as second-class and limiting their authority, power, and rights compared to those of Catholics.[2] Hue was the headquarters for the archbishop and another of Diem's brothers, Ngo Dinh Can, who had no official title but dominated in money-grabbing ways the northern third of the country bordering North Vietnam and Laos. A center for Buddhist learning, Hue straddled the Perfume River fifty miles south of the 17th parallel dividing Vietnam. This one-time imperial capital exuded for me a fairytale-like quality, with its vermilion citadels that miniaturized Beijing's Forbidden City.

Nick alerted me that this religious strife was so serious that it could bring down Diem's government, undermining the war effort. Diem was a Roman Catholic leading a nation in which up to 80 percent of its fifteen million or so population adhered at least nominally to Buddhism that had become intertwined with Confucian-based ancestral worship.[3] Catholics had become the core support for Diem; he often favored them as administrators and leaders because they were anti-Communist and were better educated.[4] Diem's government espoused freedom of religion and included non-Catholics as top leaders. Five out of eighteen of Diem's cabinet ministers at the time of the Buddhist crisis were Catholic, as were three of his nineteen top generals, with others being Confucianist, Taoist, or Buddhist.[5]

Nick's warning would prove prophetic. During the next five months of the sultry monsoon season, I found myself working furiously to keep pace with events that thrust Vietnam onto the world stage with a sweeping drama more bizarre and tragic than any spy thriller. The Buddhist protests shifted the focus of Saigon and Washington — and me — to the streets of the urban centers from the insurgency in the rice paddies and the forts surveilling infiltration from North Vietnam or Laos. These grievances provoked suspense-filled, high-risk controversies for both Catholic presidents, Kennedy as well as Diem, who needed popular support, respectively, to be reelected to office in 1964 or to counter a bloody war.

Diem: The Man, the Mandarin, the Enigma

I never met Diem, but I saw and photographed him at numerous public events. He usually dressed in a toothpaste white, double-breasted, Western-style sharkskin suit that bulged over his Santa Claus tummy. He led an ascetic life, sleeping with a bamboo pillow on a wooden bed without a mattress.[6] A bachelor, Diem escaped the playboy image of his imperial predecessor, Emperor Bao Dao. One Vietnamese general who was then often in and out of the palace, Gen. Hoang Lac, described Diem as the hardest-working person within the government, explaining, "He worked seven days a week, each day from dawn to midnight." Yet rather than creating a systematic administration, Diem personally decided on minutiae that enabled him to keep a tight grip on all three branches of government by assigning the key positions only to his loyal followers.[7] Diem also escaped being tarred by corruption and criticism that often denigrated some in his regime and family.

At work in the palace, Diem donned a cotton robe in the style of the Confucian mandarins who once administered China and Vietnam.[8] Diem's father had become a mandarin, those elite administrators who passed the rigid examinations based on Confucian classics. Diem served as a mandarin in 1933 but after two months resigned in protest against French colonial rule.[9] Diem as a mandarin "held as a model the Confucian ruler governing by virtue, not consensus, and who achieved legitimacy, the so-called mandate of heaven, by success," Henry Kissinger observes. "Diem recoiled instinctively from the concept of a legitimate opposition."[10] But Diem embraced the term: "I know that some Americans try to tarnish me by calling me a mandarin. . . . But I am proud of being a mandarin. . . . It may not be similar to anything that you Americans have experienced — this mandarin-Confucian system. But it has its merits and its own inner democracy."[11]

Diem often baffled U.S. officials. "Diem was an enigma to me," Secretary of Defense Robert S. McNamara observed, "and to every American who met him. . . . He appeared autocratic, suspicious, secretive, and insulated from his people."[12] I sensed that because U.S. officials did not understand Confucianism,[13] they could not fathom Diem's mandarin mind-set.

Ironically, South Vietnam, including Diem, "was a creation of the United States," the *Pentagon Papers* state.[14] The Eisenhower administration's maneuvering giving rise to Diem began at the Geneva conference ending the French Indochina War in 1954, which followed the Korean War, the Soviet's atomic weapon explosion, and the Communists takeover of China.[15] Unwilling to support either a Communist takeover of Vietnam or continued French colonial rule, Eisenhower vigorously supported Diem as a third force. Diem was passionately anti-Communist, having been arrested and detained for six months by Communist-led anti-French guerrillas, who also had a role in assassinating his older brother — a province official named Ngo Dinh Khoi — and Khoi's only son; both were buried alive.[16] With Eisenhower's backing, Diem became premier of South Vietnam in 1954,[17] and the next year he held and won a referendum by such an outlandish margin that his critics argued the balloting was rigged. Days later, on October 26, 1955, Diem was proclaimed president of the Republic of Vietnam in the South.[18] This balloting meant Diem, with Eisenhower's nod, refused to hold the 1956 nationwide elections called for in the Geneva Accords. If elections had been held in 1956, Eisenhower is quoted as saying that 80 percent of the Vietnamese people would have voted for Ho Chi Minh, a national hero.[19]

Diem began to consolidate his power by rooting out dissents, especially anti-French guerrillas who had remained in South Vietnam after 1954, but his repressions gave rise to the Viet Cong's armed struggle. By 1961 wags in Saigon dubbed Diem's one-man rule as "Diemocracy," defining it as "the government's make-believe guarantees of civil liberties and fair elections."[20] During the Buddhist crisis Diem's former booster and renowned scholar wrote, "Diem fights the Buddhists not because he is a Catholic, but because he is a dictator."[21]

Last Interview of Buddhist Bonze before His Fiery Suicide

Upon leaving the hospital, I found peaceful demonstrations of several hundred saffron-robed Buddhist bonzes (priests) occurring in Saigon under the noses of Diem's security police. Buddhists had also been diligently holding press conferences, hunger strikes, and mass meetings. Rumors were circulating in Saigon that several Buddhist bonzes had offered to commit suicide by self-immolation to spotlight Buddhist demands. I considered these rumors too fantastic to be taken seriously, especially coming from a religion such as Buddhism, which preaches compassion.

To stay on top of this fast-paced news story, I developed a routine of checking on developments at Saigon's pagodas. On many evenings, as the sun was dropping in the sky, I visited pagodas by hiring a cyclo when the workday traffic had eased. A refreshing breeze cooled my face and rustled the tamarind trees as we moseyed down the streets. I first visited the An Quang Pagoda, a smallish, concrete structure off Phan Dinh Phung Street, to see if all was quiet and would then circle a few blocks more to the Xa Loi Pagoda, the Buddhists' main temple dominating the old French quarter. The tinkling of brass bells floated through the air, and a pungent aroma wafted from incense burning from chocolate-colored joss sticks stuck in altar bowls.

I requested an interview with the first bonze who had volunteered to sacrifice himself, the seventy-three-year-old Thich (Venerable) Quang Duc. I was then filing stories for *Newsweek* and for the *London Daily Express* and *London Sunday Express*. London needed a resident journalist who could provide on-the-spot daily coverage of events becoming increasingly bizarre beyond belief—the kind savored by these two newspapers, which had captured their nation's largest circulations. I regularly received cables from London urging in capital letters: CANST UPDATE BUDDHIST TROUBLES SATURDAY PLEASE STOP THANKS YOUR WINDOW ON VIETNAM. Often these cables were flagged with a tangerine-colored label reading KHAN, meaning "Urgent."

My requested interview with Thich Quang Duc was granted for Saturday evening, June 8, at An Quang Pagoda. With another bonze serving as interpreter, the venerable priest told me he was happily awaiting the moment he would strike a match to his baggy brown robe and burn himself alive. The elder had first offered himself as a human bonfire a week earlier, on May 30, when four hundred bonzes and three hundred bonzesses began a forty-eight-hour fast to petition the Diem government to meet their demands.

"I want to sacrifice myself — I will die — but many generations after me will freely practice Buddhism," the bonze told me in a soft voice. "I am very happy to kill myself if President Diem does not agree with our five requests," he said. He had been a monk for sixty-seven years — since he was six years old. "To die is the only thing I want because the government is indirectly destroying the civilization of the Vietnamese people, which depends on Buddhist culture — it grows very deeply in our hearts."

He wound around his bony fingers a yellow tasseled string of fifty-four holy oak tree seeds used in counting the number of times he muttered the sacred phrase "nam mo amita Buddha" (return to eternal Buddha). He estimated that in his lifetime he had repeated this phrase more than ten billion times, an act he thought assured him a heavenly place in the afterlife.

As I prepared to bid farewell, he repeated his desire to sacrifice himself in flames. Then he bowed and left to say a few thousand more "nam mo amita Buddha"s. I rushed to cable a two-page dispatch to the *London Sunday Express*'s foreign editor, Thomas Jenkins, who had accepted my proposal for the interview. Three days later the elderly bonze did set himself afire, committing a shocking suicide reported by AP's Malcolm Browne.

About 9:20 a.m. on June 11, 1963, several hundred monks and nuns marched along a dusty street leading to the An Quang Pagoda and then formed a circle. A gray sedan stopped, and one monk got out, opened the hood, and pulled out a five-gallon can filled with gasoline. Another monk placed a brown cushion on the pavement, Mal recounts, "and a second monk in the center sat down on it, crossing his legs in the traditional position of Buddhist meditation known as the 'lotus position.'" Two monks poured contents from the gasoline container over the diminutive monk. Then Thich Quang Duc moved his hands in his lap and struck a match. "In a flash, he was sitting in the center of a column of flame, which engulfed his entire body," Mal elaborates. "A wail of horror rose from the monks and nuns." Quang Duc fell backward, with "his blackened legs kicking convulsively for a minute or two," Mal recalls. "Then he was still."[22]

Upon hearing the news, I was stunned. I hastened to cable foreign

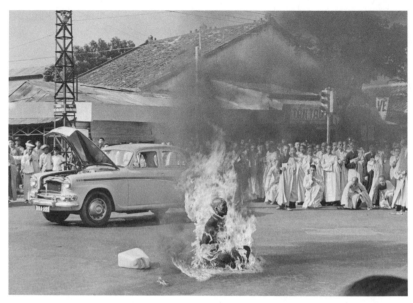

18. Three days after my exclusive interview with him for the *London Sunday Express*, Quang Duc, a Buddhist monk, burns himself to death on a Saigon street on June 11, 1963, to protest alleged persecution of Buddhists by the South Vietnamese government. (AP Photo/Malcolm Browne)

editor Jenkins to ask whether the *Sunday Express* had published my exclusive interview because the bonze had just burned himself alive. Jenkins's reply came on June 12: "We didn't use incendiary monk which proves what an idiot I am."

Mal's burning-bonze photograph electrified the world. Upon first seeing the photograph, President Kennedy, on the phone with his brother, the attorney general, exclaimed, "Jesus Christ!" He observed, "No news picture in history has generated so much emotion around the world as that one."[23]

The Second Bonze Suicide and My Taxi Ride to Phan Thiet

Sixteen days after that fiery suicide, in what I considered to be a move toward the U.S. abandonment of Diem, Kennedy announced the departure of Ambassador Frederick Nolting, a strong Diem supporter, and the appointment of a new ambassador, Henry Cabot Lodge, effective in September. Days later, on July 2, Kennedy visited the Vatican and received a forty-eight-minute private audience with Pope Paul VI.

Kennedy's visit to the Vatican — and the ovations he received on his earlier swing through Ireland — would endear him to U.S. Catholics, who had provided him in the 1960 election with the tiny advantage he needed to win by the narrowest margins in U.S. history. Catholics who had given Eisenhower 49 percent of their votes in 1956 gave Kennedy 78 percent four years later.[24] But Kennedy's vulnerability for reelection grew as Buddhist protests and religious grievances against Vietnam's Catholic president accelerated — and were being televised nationally.

After Thich Quang Duc six Buddhist bonzes and one bonzesse committed suicide by fire throughout the summer of 1963. I cabled *Newsweek* and the London newspapers about most of them. Four occurred in Saigon, at the central market,[25] on a corner facing the main cathedral as worshippers arrived for mass, and two in locked-up pagodas. Two more occurred in coastal cities.

To investigate the spread of Buddhist grievances in the provinces, I hired a blue-and-crème Renault taxi in early August to drive me to the province capital of Phan Thiet, population sixty thousand, nestled on the South China Sea 120 miles northeast of Saigon. There the second Buddhist monk in fifty-four days had a week earlier, on August 5, committed suicide by self-immolation.[26] The antiquated taxi pirouetted around the potholes rutting the asphalt of Highway 1 as we putt-putted past French-owned rubber plantations and lush jungles controlled during the nighttime by Viet Cong guerrillas. In an exclusive interview Nguyen Hong, a driver and pedal pumper of a three-wheel cyclo, told me how he grew sick after witnessing the suicide of Huynh Van Le, a twenty-four-year-old Buddhist priest who had ignited himself about noon in the town's public square. Hong was standing eleven yards from the burning priest and wanted to scream, he recounted, "but I could not utter a sound to anyone."

I photographed several dramatic scenes that were published to capture the somber mood: Buddhist nuns staging a sit-down strike, young girls kneeling in prayer,[27] and soldiers intermingled with bonzes standing behind barbed wire. I detailed the sweep of Buddhist discontent extending to the ten critical provinces edging the South China Sea northward from Saigon four hundred miles to Hue. An eighteen-year-old Buddhist student told me he would rather go to jail than be drafted into the military. "There's no purpose in fighting the VC," he muttered. "It's only to keep a privileged group in power."[28]

A Royal Bonzesse and Disowned Son

Throughout the summer I was working round-the-clock to send dispatches about a self-perpetuating chain reaction of events. Fiery bonze suicides led to student protests and walkouts. They, in turn, led to a general strike by shopkeepers, hunger strikes, numerous Buddhist ceremonial rites, government-sponsored counterdemonstrations of wounded veterans brandishing their crutches, and then counters to the counterdemonstrations.

I arrived early to cover one Buddhist memorial service, with its undertow of a strong anti-Diem message, held to commemorate the end of the initial phase of mourning on the forty-ninth day after Thich Quang Duc's blazing suicide. When I entered Xa Loi Pagoda for the 8 a.m. service, about five thousand persons were jamming the prayer hall, pagoda yard, and surrounding streets. Elderly women with red teeth from chewing betel nuts and peasant girls in black pajama-styled garb stood or kneeled on the street. The crowd chanted for two hours in heat so intense a U.S. TV journalist fainted, fell off a six-foot wall, and broke a rib.

Amid the chanting I noticed a frail nun peering over the balcony of her sunless room. Her name was Dieu Hue — which means "Holy Flower" — and she had vowed to become the third Buddhist to self-immolate. I photographed her in a yellow ceremonial robe she said she would wear for self-immolation. She was related to the royal family that once ruled Vietnam, but I did not then know that she was the great-granddaughter of Emperor Minh Mang, who governed from 1820 to 1841. He firmly believed in Confucianism, which considered both Catholics and Buddhists "heterodox doctrines" that subverted the "orthodox way" of Confucianism, which valued maintaining Vietnam as a "closed country" to keep out "barbarians."[29] His anti-Catholic policy provoked military retaliation and led to seventy-one years of French rule.

Diem summoned Dieu Hue's son, Prince Buu Hoi, to Vietnam to dissuade her self-immolation. An eminent cancer researcher and ambassador to several African countries, the prince arrived, and I waited outside the pagoda doors as the royal mother-son conversation was held for one hour and ten minutes. But instead of being dissuaded, Dieu Hue renounced her son. I read her letter crafted in her jerky handwriting. "Before Vietnam and the world, and my country," she emphasized, "I formally declare that Buu Hoi is no longer my son." While reading her note, I was struck by the depth of her emotion: "My shame and dishonor are beyond words because my son Buu Hoi has betrayed me, has betrayed Buddhism, his religion, and has betrayed the truth he has witnessed in Vietnam." As the conference broke up, Prince Buu Hoi hurried away. Christmas tree–like lights outlined the delicate curved roofs of the pagoda against the dark city sky. I rushed to cable the *Daily Express*.

Besides covering such momentous news events, I found myself swamped by so many other demands that I often fell months behind in filing my expenses for badly needed reimbursement. Time-consuming tasks that gave me little recognition — or pay — included cabling advisories suggesting future coverage, coordinating visits of editors and columnists, tracking down photographers to snap color shots requested for potential magazine covers, and writing letters requesting interviews, including one to Diem's brother, Nhu.

Throughout the summer I sent to New York undeveloped rolls of film I snapped of Diem, Buddhist leaders at news conferences, and the riveting events unfolding in the pagodas and on the streets. To get my packet of dispatches and film to *Newsweek*, I routinely took a late-night taxi to Tan Son Nhut Airport, hand-carrying my materials to be air-expressed and then cabling editors the details needed for pick up in New York. As tensions mounted between the U.S. and the Diem governments, I air-expressed maps showing cities where Buddhist troubles were most intense and biographical material on key Vietnamese who might try to overthrow Diem.

Martial Law and Crackdown on "Yellow-Robed Reds"

Before the scheduled September arrival of Kennedy's new ambassador, Diem's government made two startling moves to counter the Buddhist protests. Engineered by Diem's brother, Nhu, and his secret police force and troops, the government declared martial law and cracked down on the Buddhist pagodas and bonzes. One English-language, pro-government newspaper headlined the Buddhist protestors as "yellow-robed reds."

Shortly after midnight on August 21–22, with Diem's agreement, combat police and special units loyal to Nhu swarmed into Buddhist pagodas throughout the country. The sweeping attacks resulted in the wounding of about thirty monks, the arrest of more than 1,400 Buddhists, and the damaging, looting, and closing of the pagodas.[30] In Saigon combat police and troopers had staked out pagodas and then stormed them. At Xa Loi's canary-colored headquarters hundreds of these forces scaled the barbed wire fence and spear-tipped black gate that I had seen Buddhists erect weeks earlier to defend themselves. Then, in a fell swoop, they nabbed the core Buddhist leadership. I watched in amazement as jeeps full of steel-helmeted troops with bayoneted M-1 rifles patrolled Saigon's streets.[31]

To study Diem's martial law proclamation, I taxied to a street corner where a copy of it was pasted on a bulletin board that was by then surrounded by cyclo drivers, hawkers, shopkeepers, and students. "The government is strongly determined not to tolerate: the exploitation of religion for political purposes; the turning of pagodas . . . into quarters for agitation and propaganda."[32] As my translator and I finished reading, a blue-uniformed trooper scattered us and the crowd, barking: "You have no right of assembly."

For Western journalists martial law meant that our dispatches about the pagoda raids and mass arrests transmitted through the government's antiquated telegraph system were subject to censorship and were delayed. I searched out willing travelers to hand-carry to Manila some dispatches and rolls of undeveloped film. Western correspondents found that reporting on the Buddhist events was becoming increasingly risky. On July 7, for the first time, government police scuffled with foreign correspondents and damaged their cameras while they were covering a Buddhist ceremony at the entrance of a pagoda. In another move that seriously hampered my inexpensive flow of materials to New York, I, as well as other journalists, was warned by the government information office that I needed to get permission to air-express photo and text materials out of the country. I joined the Foreign Correspondents' Association in writing a protest letter to the Vietnamese Ministry of Interior. When the U.S. Embassy declined to protest to Diem's government, we cabled Kennedy.

Arrival of Henry Cabot Lodge, an American Mandarin

Upon hearing of Diem's martial law and the surprise crackdown on the Buddhists, the incoming American ambassador rushed to Vietnam on August 22, although he had originally been scheduled to arrive in September. The London Sunday Express wanted much copy about Kennedy's naming as ambassador such a prestigious but unusual choice, Henry Cabot Lodge. A Republican, he had been the vice presidential running mate of Richard Nixon in the 1960 election that Kennedy and Johnson narrowly won. Earlier, in 1952, Lodge had lost to Kennedy in the race for the U.S. Senate seat in Massachusetts that catapulted Kennedy into the national spotlight and ultimately the presidency. In the 1950s, as Eisenhower's ambassador to the UN, Lodge was confronted with the Soviet's shoe-slamming Nikita Khrushchev during an official session. I told London that Lodge's job in Vietnam might demand a different diplomatic finesse, noting what one U.S. official had told me: "The problem with Vietnam is working with a hostile friendly country."

Answering London's request, I described the sixty-one-year-old ambassador as an American mandarin, being bred of elite stock not unlike the Confucian-schooled intelligentsia who once administered for Vietnam's emperors. Lodge inherited a more distinguished lineage than the third-generation, Irish-Catholic Kennedy possessed. It was commonly accepted about Boston's upper crust: "The Lowells speak only to the Lodges and the Lodges speak only to God." My dispatch did not mention that Lodge was the grandson and namesake of a Republican leader who had advocated for American Manifest Destiny and the Spanish-American War and whose other forebears had dined with George Washington.[33]

By appointing Lodge, Kennedy enhanced the bipartisanship for his Vietnam policy and protected himself from any future charge that he had lost Vietnam as Democrats under Truman had lost China.[34] A newspaper reporter as a young man, Lodge had begun writing for the *New York Herald Tribune* in 1925, being paid fifty dollars a week, the same amount I regularly received thirty-eight years later as *Newsweek's* special correspondent in Vietnam. In 1928, as a twenty-six-year-old, he began a round-the-world trip with a portable typewriter and letters of introduction from newspaper editors, not unlike the voyage to Asia I began in 1961 at the same age with my Olivetti and letters of introduction. Lodge had developed a knack for image making and the charm needed to excel at it. As he arrived at Tan Son Nhut Airport, I sensed that he had made up his mind that Diem must go. My hunch would be confirmed when a week after his arrival, the *Pentagon Papers* reveal, Lodge cabled Secretary of State Dean Rusk: "We are launched on a course from which there is no respectable turning back: the overthrow of the Diem government."[35] At Tan Son Nhut, Lodge appeared so interested in image building that his first words were: "Where are the gentlemen of the press?"[36]

Lodge's arrival caused me a heartbreaking experience. *Newsweek* had requested that I arrange for a photograph to be taken with Lodge and a typical Vietnamese, and I asked a Vietnamese schoolgirl riding her bicycle in her flowing snow-white *ao dai*. Ly Thi Lien-Huong agreed. She waited with me until Lodge emerged from the posh Caravelle Hotel and posed with him. Lodge left. When the sixteen-year-old departed, she was arrested by Vietnamese police, who changed her name, called her a twenty-two-year-old bargirl, and charged her with passing secret documents to Lodge. I went to her home address — a Catholic orphanage and school. She was the daughter of a female employee there. Frantic to find her, I went to Precinct Station No. 1, where the police denied she was there and showed me cells where dozens of bargirl-type women and two young girls were held — a terrible place. She was not there but was released the next day. When I saw her a few hours later, she was upset, her lips quivering and her eyes red from crying. I expressed profound apologies and asked whether I could do anything. She snapped while sobbing, "Don't come here anymore. You bring me more unluckies!"[37]

During his first days Lodge rejected the usual meetings with heads of U.S. agencies to learn about the local scene and instead quickly sought the views of Monsignor Salvatore Asta, the apostolic delegate to Indochina, with whom Kennedy had instructed Lodge to keep in close contact. Lodge knew Asta personally from earlier European assignments.[38] For Lodge that instruction meant that "every action Kennedy took in relation to the Diem regime had the approval of Asta, and therefore of the Vatican."[39] As an Australian historian notes, Kennedy "had planned ahead to avoid a Catholic electoral backlash at home in the event of the U.S. dissociating its policies from Diem."[40]

The United States officially repudiated the anti-Buddhist crackdown moves and blamed Nhu for them. Widely considered to be the brains and the iron fist Diem relied on, Nhu controlled his own private CIA-funded and trained Special Forces troops and secret police, which had conducted the raids. Before the raids Nhu had cut the telephone lines to the embassy and to top U.S. officials, catching Americans by surprise. How the Americans had become "detached from the realities of the political situation in Saigon in August 1963" exemplified what the *Pentagon Papers* would describe as "among the most ironic and tragic of our entire involvement in Vietnam."[41]

Nhu became increasingly irked at U.S. demands when Kennedy appointed the standoffish Lodge as ambassador. In an interview with a French writer, he voiced scorching remarks: "Lodge never stopped working against us, with the cocksureness that a representative of a colonial power might have evinced, thirty years ago, toward a protectorate." Nhu continued: "Do you know that Lodge had the cheek to request my wife's departure and my own? Just as if our Vietnamese Ambassador in Washington had requested President Kennedy to order his brother Robert and his sister-in-law to leave the United States."[42]

Throughout the summer Nhu and his wife ridiculed the Buddhist bonzes with a running stream of incendiary, often shocking statements. Madame Nhu exacerbated tensions by describing Buddhist protestors as "crypto-Communists" and asserting that all the Buddhists had done was to "barbecue" a bonze and that "they had to use imported gasoline to do that."[43] Echoing Diem's fears of losing some Vietnamese sovereignty, the razor-tongued woman publicly said U.S. advisors treated the Vietnamese like lackeys and prostitutes.[44]

Alluding to Madame Nhu, Lodge lamented privately in August 1963: "The United States can get along with corrupt dictators who manage to stay out of newspapers. But an inefficient Hitlerism, the leaders of which make fantastic statements to the press, is the hardest thing on earth for the U.S. Government to support."[45] Yet as a State Department staffer told the White House, the problem with Madame Nhu was "press magnification of quotable comments by a lady who is unfortunately too beautiful to ignore."[46]

Martial law and the pagoda raids did not faze the saffron-robed bonzes. They denounced Madame Nhu and targeted Kennedy. Diem began making the conciliatory moves Washington was prodding him to do. Madame Nhu and Archbishop Thuc left for extended trips, and Nhu promised to leave the palace. On September 16 the Vietnamese government announced an end to martial law countrywide and the release of all Buddhist priests, nuns, and laity arrested in the August 21 sweep of Buddhist pagodas.

On October 7 I photographed Diem as he addressed the National Assembly and air-expressed my undeveloped film to *Newsweek*. But for the real news of the day I had to answer a tangerine-tipped cable — an urgent one — from the *Daily Express* wanting "the CIA–*Times of Vietnam* story." Trumpeted on page 1, the pro-government, English-language *Times of Viet Nam* alleged that a coup d'état financed by the U.S. Central Intelligence Agency with up to twenty-four million dollars had been planned to overthrow the Diem government on August 28, 1963. This "Mis-Coup" would later be confirmed in the *Pentagon Papers*. In a banner headline the *Times of Viet Nam* also disclosed that the United States had suspended part of its economic aid program. *Newsweek* quoted my dispatch by name, saying that the aid cuts were not creating much of a stir. I was wrong; as the *Pentagon Papers* reveal, the aid suspension was the secret signal that the coup makers asked of the United States to ensure that it supported their coup plans.

On October 24, in another move toward conciliation, Diem invited Lodge to join him at the government's resort mansions in Dalat, where, the *Pentagon Papers* note, they engaged on Sunday, October 27, in "a day-long conversation that produces little results."[47] Yet Diem had already set in motion even bigger conciliatory moves that Washington had long wanted. He had instructed senior Vietnamese diplomat Tran Van Dinh to hold a press conference in Washington on November 1 to announce new reforms, including changes in personnel and policies to produce a better administrative structure — changes Kennedy had sought as early as 1961.[48] Then, on November 1, during a twenty-minute conversation around 10 a.m., as the minutes ticked away on the future of his government, the *Pentagon Papers* reveal, Diem signaled that he was "ready to talk to Lodge about what the U.S. wants him to do."[49] In his cable to the State Department Lodge reported on his last face-to-face talk, in which Diem told him, "Tell us what you want and we'll do it." Lodge's cable arrived in Washington while the coup was well under way.[50]

The Fall and Murder of Diem and Nhu

On November 1 the summer-long rumors of an anti-Diem coup d'état fast-forwarded into reality.[51] At 1:15 p.m., when many in Saigon were still dozing in their midday siesta, U.S.-trained Vietnamese marines seized the central police station and sealed off Saigon's Chinese section, while an army unit took over pro-Diem naval headquarters along the Saigon River. Forty-five minutes later Diem's guards strung barbed wire around the Gia Long Palace compound. At 3:30 Diem's tanks raked the central avenues with gunfire. Pedestrians scattered indoors; women cried hysterically; I saw one bicycle rider dive into the gutter, as the branches of trees fell all around him, then get up and pedal away. Soon I heard throughout the city the staccato rhythms of *ack-ack*: two rocket-firing T-28 fighter-bombers swooped down on the palace and were met with

20 mm shells from rooftops and naval guns from the river. Mortar fire reverberated throughout the city.

At 4:30 in the steamy afternoon the anti-Diemists brought up heavy artillery. They were clearly winning, seizing the radio station and broadcasting. "The day the people have been waiting for has come," exulted the announcer, quoting coup leader Maj. Gen. Duong Van Minh. At 5 p.m. General Minh called Diem, gave him five minutes to surrender, and offered safe conduct to him and Nhu. Diem hung up on him.[52]

As dusk set in, I left my apartment-office a half dozen blocks from the palace and watched from the rooftop of the Hotel Caravelle, which provided the best vantage point of the city. During the night I heard heavy firing reverberate throughout the city, but it was too distant to frighten me. At 4 a.m., as the cathedral's bells tolled, the siege of the palace began. Sixteen anti-Diem tanks churned up streets radiating from Gia Long Palace and lobbed shots into it.

On the edge of dawn, around 6 a.m., a white flag was raised over the palace, and the population went wild. I ran as fast as I could to the palace. People were screaming, "Freedom" and "Long Live the Junta." Buddhists flocked to pagodas. Others climbed aboard tanks to hug troops. Crowds raced through the streets, looting stores and ransacking offices of pro-government newspapers, including the English-language *Times of Viet Nam*.

I entered the palace shortly after the troops, through a hole shot in a six-inch-thick wall. I found it eerie and in shambles. "It was a long day," a young trooper told me, "but it finally came." Inside the darkened reception rooms, filled with plastic-covered, silk-embossed chairs and crystal chandeliers, soldiers searched by candlelight. Thick dust of gunpowder and plaster crumblings hung in the crisp morning air.

Off in the wings were the dingy and damp quarters of the Ngo family. Madame Nhu's three-room suite was cluttered with letters, family photo albums, and files of her old speeches. In her wardrobe I saw eighteen silk-embroidered *ao dais* hung next to one of her husband's battle jackets. French perfume bottles and spray net were strewn around her bathroom, replete with pink tub and black marble washbasin. Diem's room was disorganized and littered with men's magazines. A double-breasted white sharkskin suit jacket hung casually over a rocking chair. On the desk, in a final ironic touch, lay a book titled *Ils Arrivent* (They're Coming).

The military junta of sixteen generals dissolved the national legislative body, suspended "at present temporarily" the national constitution, and announced, "The armed forces have only one platform: to fight communism." On the morning of the coup the CIA paid forty-two thousand dollars in immediate funds to the coup plotters, but the amounts of other funds are unknown; Lodge had proposed making funds available to the anti-Diem generals, "with which to buy off potential opposition."[53]

Diem and Nhu were resolute. In his last conversation with Lodge, Diem declared icily over the telephone: "Mr. Ambassador, do you realize who you are talking to? I would like you to know that you are talking to a president of an independent and sovereign nation. . . . The U.S. must take full responsibility before the world in this miserable matter."[54]

Diem and Nhu fled the palace during the night. The *Pentagon Papers* indicate they used "one of the secret underground exits connected to the sewer system."[55] In the Chinese section Diem and Nhu received Communion at Saint Francis Xavier Church on Friday, the day commemorating what the Vietnamese call the Feast of the Dead. An M-113 armored personnel carrier clanked up to the church, Diem and Nhu were ordered into it, and en route to meet the generals at the Joint General Staff headquarters, they were killed. At the White House, after learning about the coup, Kennedy left a staff meeting to attend mass in Georgetown.[56]

While the coup was occurring around me, Vietnamese troops took control of Saigon's telegraph office. On November 1, late at night, I sent my first cable via the U.S. military communication network to Bangkok, which relayed it to *Newsweek* in New York. The next day my urgent cables to *Newsweek* had to be submitted to Vietnamese military censors seated at makeshift tables in a dusty courtyard. In the sweltering heat I inched my way to the table and, when I got there, was relieved to see that one of my favorite Vietnamese officers-cum-sources was a censor, smiling jovially in his army uniform. Because *Newsweek* had early on served as the lightning rod for anti-Diem coverage, the jubilant officer took my copy and gave me a peck on the cheek. I was startled. It was my first kiss from a censor!

New York was happy with my dispatches and background materials on the coup makers. One tangerine-tipped urgent cable arrived for me from the number one *Newsweek* editor, Osborn Elliott: "Warmest thanks and congratulations for magnificent reporting job on this weeks cover."

I was exhausted. I realized I had witnessed a pivotal event in Vietnamese and American history. The end of Diem and his government, I sensed, meant that the United States had self-destructed its grand experiment of defeating communism by exporting to South Vietnam such democratic institutions as constitutional government and free elections of sorts. In effect the United States had snuffed out its own beacon illuminating a new frontier. But I could not foresee the coming cataclysm.

The coup and the murders of Diem and Nhu horrified me — and the world. North Vietnamese President Ho exclaimed, "I could scarcely believe that the Americans would be so stupid."[57] Richard Nixon, asserting that the coup "had a disastrous effect upon U.S. repute throughout Asia," said the murders of Diem and Nhu were "one of the blackest moments in the history of American diplomacy."[58] Belatedly, thirty-two years and forty-nine days later, Robert McNamara, who was secretary of defense at the time, wrote at the end of a little-noticed ten-paragraph letter to a newspaper editor: "I believe that the United States support of the overthrow of President Diem was a mistake."[59] Lyndon Johnson, who was then vice president, later called the coup "the worst mistake we ever made."[60] Madame Nhu blamed the United States for the treacherous killing of Diem and Nhu, adding, "If you have the Kennedy Administration for an ally, you don't need an enemy."[61]

The Backstory of Kennedy's Last Meeting on the Coup

While in Vietnam, I — like the rest of the public — did not, and could not, know the amazing, then secret backstory of the enormity of U.S. involvement in the anti-Diem coup. U.S. officials had consistently sought to portray it as an all-Vietnamese affair. But eight years after the fact the *Pentagon Papers* revealed: "For the military coup d'état against Ngo Dinh

Diem, the U.S. must accept its full share of responsibility. Beginning in August of 1963 we variously authorized, sanctioned and encouraged the coup efforts of the Vietnamese generals and offered full support for a successor government."[62]

These stunning revelations were compounded in 2003 with the release of a transcript of the audiotaped recording made of the last meeting for President Kennedy and his National Security Council to decide whether to approve the anti-Diem coup or to try to stop it.[63] These audiotapes of the White House meeting on October 29, 1963, empowered for the first time the general public to eavesdrop on how and why Kennedy had approved the coup. The meeting began at 4:20 p.m. and ran to 6 p.m. with a ten-minute break. It was being held about twenty-four to thirty-six hours before U.S. officials expected the coup in Saigon and some twelve hours before Lodge was scheduled to return to Washington for consultation. The importance of the meeting was fully recognized when the president said that if the coup failed, "we could lose overnight our position in Southeast Asia."[64]

The CIA's William Colby began the meeting with an intelligence briefing on his agency's latest estimates of which Vietnamese units would try to overthrow Diem and which would remain loyal to him. When I read about the meeting, I sensed that Colby was simply updating an article I had written for the Washington Post in mid-August 1963. In it I listed as pro-Diem an armored unit consisting of tanks and M-113 armored personnel carriers; the elite, black-bereted Presidential Guard numbering one thousand–plus; and one hundred red-capped gendarmes who patrolled around the palace.[65] Pointing to a map, Colby began his unit-by-unit analysis by tallying as pro-Diem these same units and then sizing up that the pro-Diem and anti-Diem forces were "about the same" in numbers, with about 9,800 forces pro-Diem and 9,800 anti-Diem, plus an unknown number of neutrals. My August dispatch was pegged on a no-coup news angle, but Colby was now saying that the lineup of the key units came out as an "even match." Without pause he added, "That's enough, in other words, to have a good fight. On both sides."

Some officials expressed surprise. They discussed at length what could result from a botched coup, with the NSC's McGeorge Bundy conjuring up "a mish-mash of a three-day war in Saigon." The agenda before the policy makers was labeled "Meeting in the White House with National Security Council on the Question of Supporting a Military Coup in South Vietnam."[66] But this open-ended question — whether to support the coup or not — was not on the focus of the meeting; instead, the discussion turned to whether the United States should support a coup that had a fifty-fifty chance of *failing*.[67]

The president calculated that the lineup of forces looked "pretty well balanced." But Gen. Maxwell D. Taylor interjected, "It is unrealistic to line this up as if it were a football game. Because it all depends on a few key people." Ignoring Taylor, Kennedy continued his scorecarding until being interrupted by Secretary McNamara, pleading to clarify who would be in charge of the U.S. Mission's coordination of the coup planning and execution if Lodge departed Saigon. McNamara fretted about putting the top U.S. general in charge because, he explained, "up to this point, as far as I know, Harkins has not even been informed of any coup plan," and "it's gonna be very difficult, therefore, for Lodge to get Harkins in, and discuss this with him."[68]

Responding that Lodge was for a coup because it "looks to be his ass" and other reasons, the president read from Harkins's last telegram opposing the coup: "I have seen no batting order proposed by any of the coup groups. I think we should take a hard look at any proposed list before we make any decisions." Robert Kennedy interjected, "I just don't see that this makes any sense on the face of it," adding, "We're putting the whole future of the country and, really Southeast Asia, in the hands of somebody we don't know very well," and if the coup fails, "we risked such a hell of a lot, with the war."[69]

General Taylor jumped in: "I would be willing to step farther in saying that even a successful coup, I think that you'd help the Viet [Cong] war. First because you'll have a completely inexperienced government, and secondly, because the provincial chiefs, who are so essential to the conduct of the war, will all be changed." Following directly, Director John McCone announced that the CIA thought "an unsuccessful coup would be disastrous. A successful coup, . . . would create a period of political confusion . . . and would seriously affect the war for a period of time which is not possible to estimate. It might, uh, it might be disastrous."[70] Vice President Johnson made no audible comments at the meeting;[71] twenty-two days later he would become president.[72]

President Kennedy summed up Colby's report, saying it indicated "there is a substantial possibility that they'll be a lot of fighting." In the recording of the meeting an unidentified speaker added, "Or even defeat." Then Kennedy said it: "Or even defeat." He indicated that unless Lodge or the coup makers could produce information that the balance of forces was "easily on the side" of the anti-Diem forces, then Lodge should not move forward on the coup, adding, "[If] we miscalculate we could lose overnight our position in Southeast Asia."[73]

Crucial arguments for the United States trying to avert the coup had been forcefully made by three powerful advisors — Robert Kennedy, General Taylor, and the CIA's Director McCone — but they were not given the focused consideration that the agenda heading suggested they might be. The NSC bypassed Harkins and cabled only to Lodge, leaving it up to him to decide whether he should depart Saigon and whether a coup evidenced "clearly a high prospect of success," and if it did not, to stop it.[74]

I was doubly shocked as I read the forty-three-page transcript. My first shock came from reading the disjointed, unstructured — almost chaotic — drift of discussion that had lasted for about two hours. The meeting was so unfocused that important ideas, incomplete sentences, and unfinished thoughts were bounced around like Ping-Pong balls. The transcript also confirmed the enormous communication gap between Lodge and Harkins.

My second shock was what was *not* discussed. There was no mention of the conciliatory moves Diem had taken to cozy up to the aloof Lodge. Nor was there any discussion about the impact of a coup on the Vietnamese people and on American ideals, principles, or credibility that might result from encouraging the overthrow of a democratically elected government headed by a heretofore much-touted ally. Nor was there even any questioning of the right of the United States to participate in toppling another government. The most immediate question of who would succeed Diem had been raised in General Harkins's cable and by Robert Kennedy but was left unaddressed and unanswered.[75] I sensed all of these factors had created one of the most monumental man-made communication failures in recent U.S. government history.

Ending the meeting was a somber thought offered by Governor Averell Harriman, senior statesman and undersecretary of the State Department. "There's just one thing that troubles me a little bit," he reflected. Referring to Lodge by his middle name, Harriman elaborated: "Cabot is totally inexperienced out there. He's been there just over sixty days. I don't think he'd ever been there before." President Kennedy interjected, "Been there as a young reporter once." That was thirty-five years before Lodge became ambassador, when he was twenty-six years old.[76] Harriman finished his thought: "Maybe. As a young reporter."

Kennedy, Another Fallen New Frontiersman

I learned of the assassination of President Kennedy when I was awakened in the early morning hours of November 22 by the simultaneous delivery of four urgent, tangerine-tipped cables from *Newsweek*. They were in jumbled order and made no sense to me, adding to my disbelief that Kennedy had been shot. I filed heavily. Not a line of my dispatch was printed.

Most of Saigon received the news through the early morning broadcast from the American radio station for GIs. One GI told me, "I was shaving in my pajama bottoms and the radio mentioned something about a president. But I thought it was the president of some South American country where they are always shooting themselves up." The astonishing news got virtually no play in Vietnamese-language newspapers because Kennedy's assassination reminded Vietnamese of the murders of Diem and Nhu, grisly events that put the new government in a bad light.

Kennedy was genuinely popular. A sixty-two-year-old mandarin type told me, "Kennedy was not Vietnamese; he was a stranger to me; it is none of my concern. But I feel so sad about that." In jumbled English a

Vietnamese telephone operator exclaimed, "The United States same as Vietnam — much trouble." Pointing to imaginary holes in her head, she told me, "Now Kennedy is same as Diem."

Her views linking the assassinations in Saigon and Dallas were echoed by Kennedy's successor. The day after Kennedy's funeral, and before moving into the White House, Lyndon Johnson moved down the hallway of his home and, pointing to the wall where a portrait of Ngo Dinh Diem hung, told his visitor: "We had a hand in killing him. Now it's happening here."[77]

6

"The United States Will Lose Southeast Asia"

The Congress approves and supports the determination of the President, as Commander-in-Chief, to take all necessary measures to repel any armed attack against the forces of the United States and to prevent further aggression.

Tonkin Gulf Resolution passed by Congress, August 7, 1964

The coup d'état that toppled the Diem government trickled down to affect me personally and professionally. After filing my dispatches to *Newsweek*, I rushed to my apartment-office, only blocks from the battered Gia Long Palace, and spotted Vietnamese coming down the stairs toting stuff from my place. Upon reaching the second floor, I found the door of my apartment open, my place ransacked, with looters having filched my passport, my maid's clothing, and gold-tipped Laotian sarongs from Vientiane. Shards of a wall-size mirror had been pierced by flying bullets and were splattered about, one of them prophetically nicking a scholarly 1961 book titled *Problems of Freedom: South Vietnam since Independence*. Soon I learned that worse than living in a shot-up apartment was having no apartment at all. I was evicted.

Professionally, too, bad news. François Sully, whom I had replaced for *Newsweek* when he was expelled by Diem, returned within weeks after the November 1 coup. In March 1964 *Newsweek* notified me that it no longer needed coverage by me, thanked me for what it called my commendable services, and gave me a termination bonus. But I lost my monthly retainer plus extra monies for stories and photos. Although still writing for two London papers, I saw my bank account dwindle.

Security around Saigon was getting so scary that I had packed most of my clothes and books in a metal footlocker, fearing I might have to flee the country in a hurry. Politically, for the first time, a fog of uncertainty hovered over whether U.S. and Saigon leaders would or should investigate a neutralist solution for Vietnam as advocated by French leader Charles de Gaulle and some Vietnamese Buddhists — but secretly rejected by President Johnson.[1]

A New Place, New News Outlet, New Associates

Renewing my search for work, I contacted again the *New York Herald Tribune*. I had written *Trib* editors shortly after I arrived in Saigon in 1962 but received no response. It was the number two newspaper in New York City, competing with the *Times* for highbrow readers, and it had no regular correspondent covering the Far East. One of the nation's flagship pro-Republican dailies, the *Trib* had just adopted a new approach for lively journalism that featured world-famous writers and distinguished it from the lackluster layouts and smaller headlines published in the *Times*. On my second try, in 1964, I received a letter from associate editor Richard C. Wald on March 11, saying that the newspaper wanted "background and interpretive reports mainly for the Sunday paper at first." For filing cables collect, he sent me a credit card. "If the world breaks loose, use it. Otherwise, don't." In most cases, he added, air express would do, confirming what insiders had told me: the *Trib* expected its overseas correspondents to get an exclusive story and send it by airmail.

This budget-minded approach meant that I would not be expected to report the day-to-day stories covered by the wire services and could focus on a wide array of other kinds of stories that critics often said were lacking in coverage of the Vietnam War. But, an editor warned me, "none of this Ernie Pyle stuff," referring to the World War II correspondent who masterfully described GIs' battlefield lives and deaths. Unlike *Newsweek*, the *Trib* would not cut my dispatches and often displayed them with eye-grabbing headlines and graphics. I was elated. Having studied and worked in New York, I thought that city was the center of the communications world, and my work for the *Trib* immediately began consuming virtually all of my energy and intellect.

By mid-1964 coup rumors and Buddhist-cum-student demonstrations became so rampant that my air-expressed articles would no longer be timely. So I telephoned the New York editor, telling him I needed to cable more articles and to work more regularly. He agreed and formalized my status as a special correspondent; unlike being a staff member, I received no employee benefits, health insurance, or Social Security or unemployment contributions. I also talked him into letting me hire Pham Xuan An for three hundred dollars a month to work as a stringer to help with oral and written translations. Out of my own funds I also paid another assistant, whom An considered an "older brother," Nguyen Hung Vuong. He was even more emaciated than An, with sunken-in cheeks drooping beneath his eyes. Both were fluent in English and French, and Vuong also knew Chinese.

An found for me a new home office at 64A Hong Thap Tu, only two blocks from the Vietnamese telegraph office, where I often walked after midnight to file my dispatches. A storybook house, it was half of a duplex made of walnut-colored logs set amid a postage-stamp yard filled with sweetly perfumed frangipani trees. It served as my living quarters and the *Trib's* office, with the newspaper paying half of the six-hundred-dollar-a-month rent. Inside, the floors glistened with chocolate-colored wood throughout the furnished living-dining room downstairs and two bedrooms upstairs. In the back were a kitchen and a room for the live-in maid. The one bedroom that I turned into the office opened onto an airy porch with heavy, wooden shutters that I cranked down during slashing monsoon downpours. An ordered a brass plaque with coal-colored letters etching out NEW YORK HERALD TRIBUNE, and we hung it on the front gate just beyond the frangipani.

Associate editor Wald cabled me that he needed a thousand words by Saturday, 11 a.m., for the Sunday edition on how Secretary of Defense Robert McNamara had gathered his information during his trip to Vietnam beginning March 8, 1964. Unfortunately, I did not receive the cable until the day after the story was due. I wrote and air-expressed the article anyhow, and it was published the following Sunday.[2]

That dispatch included an amazing vignette that I had gleaned from covering McNamara's earlier trip on December 18–20, 1963. Then I learned McNamara had stayed an hour beyond his scheduled time in An Xuyen Province at Vietnam's southernmost tip, a Viet Cong stronghold of mostly brackish water and mangrove swamps surrounding a few mostly Catholic hamlets. I immediately flew there to find out what had so interested McNamara and was told that for the scheduled one-hour briefing Vietnamese and U.S. top brass had given him such a "general and glossy version" of the local situation that, as a low-ranking officer reported, "we were in tears." When the briefers could not answer specific questions, McNamara broke his rule on punctuality, stayed an extra hour to hear lower-echelon field officers tell him, while the Saigon commanders glared, that Viet Cong strength was increasing, the war was going badly, the Strategic Hamlet Program was failing, and the Viet Cong had so much support from the population "they were running out of recruiting forms." Then in the anteroom of the restroom McNamara motioned a young officer aside so they could talk privately, leading a brusque sergeant to exclaim to me, "When the secretary of defense has to get his information in the latrine, something's wrong with the system."

Unlike his earlier trips, McNamara in March 1964 was doing more important work than just fact-finding. He and the chairman of the Joint Chiefs of Staff, Gen. Maxwell D. Taylor, had to demonstrate U.S. support for a new South Vietnamese leader, Maj. Gen. Nguyen Khanh, and to bolster his image, as President Johnson had instructed. Khanh on January 30, 1964, had launched a bloodless, internal coup against the military

19. Gen. Nguyen Khanh gave me exclusive interviews for the *New York Herald Tribune* in 1964 that touched off a dust-up with U.S. officials. (B. Deepe Collection)

junta that just eighty-nine days earlier had overthrown Diem and his government. Khanh arrested the five top anti-Diem generals, ousted the civilian cabinet that they had installed, and empowered himself as prime minister and military strongman.

Jaunty in a paratrooper's red beret, with a wispy goatee and short height that reached only to the chins of McNamara and Taylor, Khanh, thirty-six, had been trained in France as a parachutist, had served in the emperor's armed forces, was schooled by the United States at Fort Leavenworth, and went on to become a division commander and then commander of one of Vietnam's four military corps.[3]

President Johnson had "said he wanted to see Khanh on the front pages of the world press with McNamara and Taylor holding up his arms." And so McNamara stood on one side of Khanh with Taylor on the other side and, like victorious prizefighters, made the victory sign, holding with outstretched arms those of the much shorter Vietnamese. As Taylor would later recount, that victory sign with Khanh in front of tumultuous crowds from the Mekong Delta to the northern provinces was repeatedly staged for the benefit of correspondents. Using a description that signifies insensitivity and subordinate status, Taylor concluded that the resulting photographs demonstrated without doubt that Khanh was the "American boy, at least for the time being."[4]

Twinned Revolving-Door Leadership

Immediately after that image-making trip, McNamara wrote a grim assessment about Vietnam in his secret report to Johnson. Dated March 16, 1964, the report described the rapid deterioration in South Vietnam in the three months following the Diem coup. Then most chiefs of the forty-one provinces had been replaced at least once (one having been replaced four times), major military commanders had been replaced twice, and "the political structure extending from Saigon down into the hamlets disappeared."[5]

The next day Johnson agreed with McNamara's pessimistic assessment that the Saigon government could not prevail over the Viet Cong and set in motion contingency preparations for stepped-up overt and covert military actions outside of South Vietnam. He issued National Security Action Memorandum 288 (NSAM 288). It established U.S. policy "to prepare immediately to be in a position on 72 hours' notice to initiate the full range of Laotian and Cambodian 'Border Control actions' . . . 'Retaliatory Actions' against North Vietnam, and to be in a position on 30 days' notice to initiate the program of 'Graduated Overt Military Pressure' against North Vietnam."[6] Two months later aides prepared a draft resolution that Johnson wanted Congress to approve, giving him wide-ranging powers to wage war;[7] ultimately, Congress largely did so by passing the Tonkin Gulf Resolution.

Also sizing up the profound deterioration in South Vietnam was the top leader of the pro-Communist National Liberation Front (NLF), President Nguyen Huu Tho. About Diem's overthrow and Khanh's two-month-old coup, Tho said, "They were gifts from heaven for us."[8]

Paralleling the drastic changeovers in South Vietnam's personnel was the profound shakeup of the U.S. bureaucracy in Saigon. I was abruptly reminded of the magnitude of this shakeup when an urgent cable arrived from the *London Daily Express*: "Rush story Johnson announcing Cabot Lodge resigning as ambassador." Lodge did resign in June 1964, and many key officials heading U.S. agencies in Saigon also left within a few weeks of each other.[9] General Taylor replaced Lodge on July 7; three weeks earlier Gen. William C. Westmoreland had replaced General Harkins as commander of U.S. forces in Vietnam.

The staged photographs of McNamara, Taylor, and their "American boy" that were made in March soon appeared inadequate to buoy Khanh above the political turmoil that began swirling around him. A month after the Khanh-Do barnstorming, I interviewed Saigon's reliable sources, who were predicting the inevitability of a follow-on coup. Even Khanh confessed to foreign correspondents that he took threats of a coup seriously enough to sleep in a different house each night and to arrange for his family to reside 350 miles from Saigon. I was then viewing Vietnam's political scene as one of habitual intrigue, plots and subplots, betrayal and counter-betrayal. A Western diplomat lamented to me, "We may be able to save the Vietnamese from the Viet Cong, but can we save them from themselves?"[10]

As Lodge was departing his ambassadorship, he was worried that coup plotting had become the "national pastime." Taylor would later observe, "This activity was so general that our people in Saigon were unable to keep track of the plotters and offered no hope of being able either to detect preparations for a coup or to prevent it if detected."[11] After only a month and three days on the job, Taylor told Washington, "Khanh has a 50-50 chance of lasting out the year."[12]

Three months later Taylor would be explaining to top officials in Washington that "the Viet-Cong units have the recuperative powers of the phoenix" and that their ability "continuously to rebuild their units and to make good their losses is one of the mysteries of this guerrilla war."[13] Listing eleven instances in which the U.S. establishment in the Khanh period was "in the dark," the *Pentagon Papers* sum up that the first six months of Taylor's ambassadorship grew to "comic opera proportions."[14]

Vuong, An, and I were working furiously to cover coups and quasi-coups, Buddhists fighting Catholics, with both of them alternatively fighting what became revolving-door governments of six major changes of leadership, two failed coup attempts, and chaos erupting in the streets.[15]

Exclusive Khanh Interview: Invasion of North Vietnamese Units

To escape the political turbulences in Saigon, Khanh journeyed to Dalat, and to interview him, I also flew to that city two hundred miles northeast of Saigon where his mother had once owned a bar serving rowdy French soldiers.[16] Unlike any other city in Vietnam, Dalat reminded me of an alpine village filled with facsimiles of Swiss chalets or European grand hotels amid fog-enshrouded mountains. I had flown to Dalat seven months earlier, on November 1, 1963, when *Newsweek* editors assigned me to investigate the atomic research reactor they were astonished to see that the United States was opening there under an agreement signed in 1959 by Eisenhower's Atoms-for-Peace Program. I cabled New York a ho-hum dispatch — but Vietnamese officials had not told me one incredible fact: at the reactor site was stored 2.82 ounces of plutonium, a deadly ingredient that could be used for making nuclear weapons and that remains radioactive for a half million years. (On Easter Sunday 1975, when Communist forces were blitzing through the jungled highlands toward Saigon, two pro-American volunteers unsuccessfully attempted to retrieve the plutonium, but it fell into Communist hands, a fact that remained classified by the United States until 1997.)[17]

In the Dalat interview Khanh told me that a Communist North Vietnamese regiment had "invaded" South Vietnam, that the Chinese Communists had moved a regiment of troops into North Vietnam, and that "large quantities" of Czech and Chinese Communist weapons had been found in his country near its border with Laos. "This is overt aggression — though not like Korea," he emphasized. "It changes the problem completely."

"Before we had the problem of infiltration and subversion," he elaborated in English, while relaxing in gray slacks and a sweater in his French-styled villa. "Now we have whole units coming in from North Vietnam."

He estimated that three six-hundred-man North Vietnamese army battalions had infiltrated into the South.

In the past the Communists took soldiers from South Vietnam, trained them, and then sent them back to fight in the South, Khanh continued; "now we find for the first time we caught prisoners who were born in North Vietnam." *Trib* editors merged my Khanh interview with my earlier dispatch written from Danang about the first-ever sizable numbers of North Vietnamese combat troops infiltrating into South Vietnam, based on my interviews with U.S. field advisors and the top Vietnamese commander, Gen. Nguyen Chanh Thi. But the same day my merged story was published,[18] a top U.S. military spokesman in Washington called a special press conference and handed reporters a statement saying, "There are no indications of the presence of PAVN (People's Army of North Viet Nam) units on South Vietnamese soil."[19] Two days later, on July 16, McNamara made a similar, no-troops statement.[20]

These denials of my dispatch prompted the *Trib* to question whether Washington was managing the news, given that the Republicans were holding their national convention and the Johnson administration was trying to downplay the need to take action against North Vietnam. In Saigon a diplomat told me that American policy was "to back every status quo in sight" while trying to "hold the lid on Vietnam until after the election."[21]

In a rebuttal article I countered the Washington statements by indicating that for my Danang dispatch about the presence of North Vietnamese units I had interviewed the top Vietnamese general, his intelligence officers, and a North Vietnamese prisoner. I had also read South Vietnamese intelligence reports about two North Vietnamese prisoners, in which one had confirmed that every member of his ninety-man unit spoke with a North Vietnamese dialect and had been trained with him in the North. The *Trib* gave my rebuttal story a big play.[22] As the *Pentagon Papers* document, in 1964 U.S. officials suppressed for months the release of statistics to the public showing the increase of North Vietnamese infiltration until well after the lifting of election year pressures.[23] Six months after the *Trib* published my article and after the election, the *New York Times*,

20. I interviewed North Vietnamese private Le Phan Hung, the "Heroic One," in Hue in 1964 to report exclusively for the *New York Herald Tribune* that North Vietnamese units were infiltrating into U.S.-backed South Vietnam; the Pentagon denied my reports. (B. Deepe Collection)

echoing the Johnson administration's attempt to prepare the U.S. and world public for an expansion of the war, headlined "Infiltration from North Vietnam Now Held Bigger."[24]

Exclusive Interview with North Vietnamese Private

Upon ending my interview with Khanh, I said that to make his assertions more credible to readers, I needed to interview at least one new captive because the U.S. government had for years been accusing North Vietnam of infiltration but had yet to produce prisoners for journalists to interview. Khanh facilitated this interview. Vuong, An, and I flew to Hue in late July and talked with a twenty-three-year-old North Vietnamese private, Le Phan Hung, whose name means the "Heroic One."

The minute the prisoner began to speak, Vuong, a northerner who was translating for me, knew from the accent that the private had been born and raised in the North. One of the first North Vietnamese soldiers to be captured in South Vietnam, Hung spoke freely during our exclusive interview, accepting an American cigarette and often stopping to massage his wounded knee or tug at his gray pajama-like uniform.

For a two-part series Hung provided a first-person glimpse into a North Vietnamese farm family's life in the closed society in which he stood at the bottom of the pyramid. He was the son of a fifty-four-year-old farmer. In 1955 — before the agrarian reform — his family had twelve-plus acres of land, two houses, and five water buffalo. But in 1956, after land reforms, the government took away most of the best land, leaving the family only a little of the worst land, one house, and three buffalo. Because he was not classified as being from the poor peasant class, Hung could not apply for officer training. Before finishing his ten years of schooling, he was drafted, causing his mother to cry: "I've raised my son up to twenty years of age; I've sent him up to the ninth class; now the government takes him from me."

After one year of training, Hung was transported for about forty minutes into Laos in one of two black, Russian-made helicopters piloted by Vietnamese. All of the 180 men he went to Laos with spoke North Vietnamese. From Laos his unit marched all day for ten days, and then one southern-born Viet Cong with a different accent that was difficult for him to understand guided them into South Vietnam. After a five-day march, his platoon of twenty-two soldiers came to a village that they were supposed to attack about 7 p.m. But he and three others got lost; two were killed, one escaped, and he was captured. He was uncertain about what would happen to him next.[25]

My Unpublished News on Tonkin Gulf Shoot-Outs

NSAM 288, Johnson's National Security Action Memo in March that initiated U.S. planning for "Retaliatory Actions" against North Vietnam, unleashed a momentous chain reaction of events that began on August 2, 1964. Then Sunday morning television and radio audiences in the United States were startled by Washington's announcement that earlier during the daylight hours in the Gulf of Tonkin the USS *Maddox* "underwent an unprovoked attack" by three torpedo boats as it patrolled in international waters. The U.S. destroyer escaped unscathed; the navy returned fired and damaged three North Vietnamese vessels. Hanoi was silent.[26]

At 10:30 the next morning, however, in their first telephone conversation about the Tonkin Gulf incident, McNamara told Johnson of the allied provocation that had occurred just hours before the attack on the *Maddox*. South Vietnamese commandos had inflicted considerable damage on two targets along the North Vietnamese coast as part of a covert U.S.-Saigon raiding program code-named Operation Plan 34A. McNamara told Johnson that the two of them should explain this provocation to key congressional leaders because "there's no question" these covert operations had a bearing on the attack on the *Maddox*. And on Friday night, McNamara continued, patrol torpedo boats manned by South Vietnamese or other nationals had attacked two North Vietnamese islands and expended "a thousand rounds of ammunition of one kind or another against them. We probably shot up a radar station and a few other miscellaneous buildings." Then, twenty-four hours after that, the *Maddox*'s moving into the same area "undoubtedly led them to connect the two events."[27]

The next day, August 4, the U.S. destroyers *Maddox* and *C. Turner Joy* moved into the Gulf of Tonkin and relayed that their sound and electronic soundings indicated they were being attacked in international waters. Gunfire was exchanged; at least two North Vietnamese torpedo boats were sunk. The U.S. commander on the scene quickly backtracked, voicing doubts that any attack had occurred.[28] But by then Johnson had decided to issue a "positive reply," consulted with congressional leaders, and shortly before midnight announced the bombing of North Vietnam. It was the Retaliatory Action called for in NSAM 288. Hanoi at the time called the second attack "sheer fabrication." (Thirty years later McNamara would agree that it had never happened.)[29] Most Americans — and the U.S. press — applauded the air strikes at the time.[30]

In three days Congress almost unanimously passed the Tonkin Gulf Resolution, which was largely based on the draft Johnson's aides had written three months earlier and would come to serve as the legal justification for the U.S. war in North and South Vietnam.[31]

After the two attacks I talked in Saigon with Western diplomatic sources who voiced skepticism about Washington's repeated denials of unprovoked attacks on U.S. ships and described Hanoi's account as "more convincing." "Maybe U.S. destroyers were guarding and protecting other ships or whatever was going on on those islands," a Western diplomat told me. "But Hanoi does not fabricate attacks on islands just like that." Other sources told me that Vietnamese Special Forces commandos had been used clandestinely in North Vietnam and that Hanoi's accounts of their captivity and court trials appeared factual. Hanoi had held spy trials of South Vietnamese commandos "for a long time and results are pretty much as reported," the diplomat continued. Without explanation the *Trib* editors decided against publishing my dispatch; their editorials on August 6 and 7 applauded Johnson's prompt use of force and the congressional resolution.[32]

I had also reported at this time on a "spy trial" described in Hanoi's radio broadcasts and newspapers in which a Communist military court convicted a group of seven "spy-commandos" of the United States and "its stooges" who had been airdropped into a mountainous province of North Vietnam to carry out intelligence work, sabotaging activities, and psychological warfare. Hanoi's report included the names, ages, military duties, and sentences of those convicted in this April 1964 trial, the fourteenth of the past eleven months.

The casualties for these commandos were so high that the wife of one Vietnamese Special Forces soldier described each clandestine mission as an "express train to death." I also described the U.S. Central Intelligence Agency's cancellation in mid-July 1964 of its part of a multimillion-dollar contract with a private American aviation company that had the undercover mission of airlifting Special Forces guerrillas, saboteurs, and supplies into North Vietnam and Communist-held sections of Laos. I had gathered the explosive information during this sensitive time from a U.S. officer who knew American civilians working for the aviation firm.[33] Clandestine operations against North Vietnam and Laos under Johnson were but an intensification of those ordered by President Kennedy on May 11, 1961,[34] but kept secret from the public for a decade until they were revealed in the *Pentagon Papers*.

On the same day that Congress passed the Tonkin Gulf Resolution, Khanh declared a state of full emergency throughout South Vietnam — a sort of modified martial law.[35] Then nine days later, on August 16, Khanh tried to consolidate his power in a U.S.-approved government shakeup that made him a strong president under a new constitution. Within days Buddhists and pro-Buddhist students called the shakeup dictatorial and staged a series of coordinated anti-American and antigovernment protests in cities nationwide. A mob of two thousand hurled rocks at a U.S. billet in Danang. Buddhists and Catholics started fighting one another in the streets.

Heavily armed paratroopers turned high-pressure hoses on rioting teenagers, who hurled bricks, spears, and crowbars and set up a four-block barricade near Saigon's central market. A block from the U.S. Embassy building I saw a white-shirted teenager shouting, "Throw the rocks!" Hundreds of pro-Buddhist youths picked up saucer-sized rocks and hurled them at paratroopers armed with fixed-bayonet rifles. I heard an American observer exclaim, "The air was black with rocks."

I ran for several blocks beside one youthful, shaven-headed monk and watched as he jumped into the air like a college cheerleader urging others to run faster. They reached the U.S. Embassy at 1:30 p.m., and illustrious American spectators, including Westmoreland and Taylor, watched from the fifth-floor balcony. I had to climb a lamppost in front of the embassy to photograph the chaos in the streets, where Vietnamese paratroopers in bulletproof flak jackets were hurling tear gas grenades to disperse more than four hundred saffron-robed monks and nuns.

A block away Buddhist youth and laymen staged running street fights with government riot police and steel-helmeted paratroopers, who counterattacked by tossing teargas grenades. Like a swarm of giant golden butterflies, the Buddhist priests and nuns, their saffron-colored robes gracefully fluttering in the breeze, raced wildly through Saigon's downtown streets during the lunch hour. They passed kiosks of gladiolas and roses and fled by sedate coffee shops where astonished businessmen were eating. Paratroopers and riot police then encircled the embassy area with barbed wire and wooden barricades and drove multitudes into alleyways.[36]

After Buddhist and student demonstrators mobbed his office, Khanh suddenly resigned on August 25. He flew to Dalat, and the government was placed temporarily in the hands of acting prime minister Nguyen Xuan Oanh, a former Harvard University lecturer. On August 29 I covered Oanh's news conference at which he said Khanh had gone to Dalat because he was "mentally ill." "Khanh is quite ill," the cherub-faced Oanh told reporters in a clipped Bostonian accent. "It's mainly mentally more than physical. He was under very strenuous efforts during the past ten days. . . . There would be a long period of mental treatment."

Hearing Oanh's startling medical assessment prompted me to try to interview Khanh, so I flew to Dalat the next day by Air Viet Nam and took a taxi to Khanh's house. I was confronted by a fierce-looking guard with a red cummerbund and submachine gun. He called the house and was told the general would return at 3 p.m. While waiting, I sauntered around a rose garden with Mrs. Khanh and her sixteen-year-old daughter.

At three I received permission to interview Khanh, probably for only twenty minutes, because he was expecting to meet Ambassador Taylor and Deputy Ambassador U. Alexis Johnson at four. Khanh appeared dressed in a suit to receive the ambassadors. I took almost verbatim notes as he spoke in English to voice his frustrations about working with the U.S. establishment in Saigon. What Khanh told me was his suspicion that Taylor favored his political rival, Maj. Gen. Duong Van Minh, whom Khanh feared would become "a puppet for the neutralists."[37] His words created a bombshell when they were published in the *Trib* and, through its subscriber news service, the *Washington Post* because the Johnson administration was supposedly strongly backing Khanh in hopes of securing a stable and respectable anti-Communist government.

Explaining his difficulties, Khanh elaborated, "I had so many things to do, but I do not know what the Americans — I mean the American Embassy [in Saigon] and Washington — I do not know what they want." I asked about his health. Khanh laughed off the words that he was "mentally ill," as Acting Prime Minister Oanh had claimed the day before. Khanh retorted, "I am not at that stage yet."

It was past four o'clock when the hour-long interview ended. Khanh's appointment with the two top American officials was postponed because of bad weather. But I was able to fly to Saigon, where I promptly cabled my dispatch. In an advisory memo I told New York that the Khanh interview "caused a monstrous flap here but no one is denying it" and "I've almost verbatim shorthand notes under lock and key."

Coup Coverage: In a Taxi, with Stargazers

The frequency of rumors of coups often prompted me to grab my Olivetti and head straight to the Vietnamese telegraph office, which was the first building that wannabe coup makers typically tried to shutter to prevent news from being transmitted outside of Saigon. On September 13, 1964, I did just that and sent an advisory to the London Daily Express about the pending coup — without even knowing who the coup makers were. Instead of waiting for my delayed dispatch about who was doing what, the London paper published my first-person advisory under the headline: "Off to Coup No. 3 by Taxi." I found armored cars roaring among Saigon's churchgoers. Tanks surrounded Saigon's radio station. Soldiers lounged in the shade. People in the streets hardly noticed the fracas engineered by Maj. Gen. Duong Van Duc. A Ranger captain in a tank explained to me: "This is a little coup. We're not going to shoot anybody."[38]

I saw that the U.S. bombing of North Vietnam did little to stave off political turmoil or attract enough attention to raise the morale of Saigonese. Although some reports said American military forces were supposed to be on a new special alert, I noticed that the streets of Saigon were even more crowded than usual, as families were preparing for the upcoming celebration of the annual moon festival. Hanoi broadcasts were reiterating that Washington had concocted the Gulf of Tonkin incident "to secure more political assets to cope with the Republican party in the present Presidential campaign."[39]

Interested in how U.S. families were holding up under such chaotic conditions, I interviewed several American housewives. Some had to learn quickly. On August 5 — during the Tonkin Gulf crisis — Mrs. Joe Williams and her navy commander husband were playing golf in Norfolk, Virginia, when they were informed they were being rushed to Vietnam. "I nearly fell off my golf cart," she gasped to me. Three weeks later, "still in a state of shock," she arrived in Vietnam just as student demonstrators forced Khanh to step down as prime minister. Undaunted, she went shopping the first day, returning to find her house had been on fire. Later, on a calm Sunday morning, she and her husband went to the telegraph office to telephone relatives in Tennessee when "a man came running upstairs and asked why all the troops were outside the gates." Her husband explained to me in a southern drawl: "The rebel troops had taken over, and we did not even know it. The guard made us sneak out the back ally to avoid them." She taxied through a calm section of the city, and as she got out of the car, armored vehicles rolled by. "That's when it really hit her," her husband explained.

U.S. dependents had been warned to keep an evacuation kit packed. One housewife pointed to a brown attaché case with "every letter my husband has written me in ten years of marriage," she told me, vowing, "I am not going to leave them behind." She looked around her air-conditioned study and lamented, "but I have to leave my wedding pictures and my mother's sterling silver candelabra."[40] Three months later all U.S. civilian and military dependents were evacuated.

An, Vuong, and I developed unorthodox but thoroughly Vietnamese ways of checking out the possibility of a coup. One way was to visit and chat with friendly, talkative Vietnamese generals at their homes after dinner. Another way was to consult astrologers, who often advised generals and politicians on the verge of making big decisions; we also wanted to hear their latest predictions, using their information only as tips for more news gathering. Most worked in small homes decorated with elaborate shrines dedicated to their favorite genies. As the smell of incense and joss sticks from the altars floated through the air, they consulted their books of Chinese dates on the movement of the stars. Vietnamese commanders in the field regularly consulted fortune-tellers to determine the best hour and day to attack. Some Communists also consulted fortune-tellers, even though the Party officially disavowed these "superstitions."[41]

Exclusive Khanh-Taylor Crossfires in December 1964

November 1, 1964. For the first anniversary of the overthrow and murder of President Ngo Dinh Diem, I wrote a seven-part retrospective assessing the nature of the conflict and the stratagems, myths, and miscalculations that shaped it. For it I interviewed a wide range of sources. One was a snobbish American who was lamenting: "Communism in Viet Nam is a nineteenth-century philosophy preached to people with a thirteenth-century mentality. We're simply too far advanced for them."

In another interview a Western expert told me that the key lesson from Vietnam is that "the only good counterinsurgency is the one that is never fought because it is never allowed to start." A diplomat described Vietnam as a "predictable type of war in the future." To sum up the year after Diem, I noted a dire prophecy he had made a month before his downfall, quoting a famous French saying: "Après moi, le deluge" (After me, the deluge).[42]

The deluge he predicted was highlighted within hours of my article being published on November 1, when Communist-led guerrillas marked the anniversary by mortaring the Bien Hoa air base fifteen miles northeast of Saigon in the deadliest anti-American attack to date. I hailed a taxi to Bien Hoa and described the destruction that killed four Americans and two South Vietnamese and crippled twenty-one U.S. B-57 jet bombers, three Vietnamese fighter-bombers, and four U.S. helicopters. Eyewitnesses described the horror of the devastating attack, with a B-57 pilot telling me, "I felt sooner or later this would come, and sure enough it has."[43]

A month later I watched more student and Buddhist demonstrators stage protests against the two-month-old civilian government. Disregarding Taylor's no-more-coups ultimatum, on December 20 Khanh and a handful of "Young Turk" generals overthrew one of the three pillars of the civilian Saigon government — the High National Council, whose nine active members served as the U.S.-backed legal foundation of the tottering political structure. These generals also forcibly retired forty-one other officers, arrested ten troublesome leaders of political parties and student organizations, and warned religious leaders that further acts leading to political instability would not be tolerated.[44] Dismayed by the forcible reentrance of the South Vietnamese army into politics, the *Pentagon Papers* report, Taylor read the generals the "riot act" and fumed, "I told you all clearly at General Westmoreland's dinner we Americans are tired of coups. Apparently I wasted my words." The next day Taylor told Khanh, whom he had nine months earlier tried to anoint as the American boy, to resign and leave Vietnam.[45] In turn Khanh threatened to declare Taylor persona non grata.[46]

Instead of leaving Vietnam, however, on December 22 Khanh gave me an exclusive interview; I had applied for an interview three weeks earlier. Speaking in English as his wife rearranged patio furniture in Saigon, Khanh, as Vietnam's current strongman and commander of its armed forces, said that if Taylor "does not act more intelligently, the United States will lose Southeast Asia and we will lose our freedom."

Khanh criticized Taylor for engaging in "activities beyond imagination" during U.S. efforts to obtain restoration of the High National Council and the release of those arrested. "You must be more practical and not have a dream of having Viet Nam be an image of the United States," he told me, "because the way of life and the people are entirely different."

"Mostly one should not impose on the Vietnamese people and Vietnamese Army those leaders they do not want," he continued in the half-hour interview, making the harshest anti-Taylor comments voiced publicly by a non-Communist leader. The *Trib* published my exclusive two days before Christmas at the top of the page under a headline reading: "Khanh Assails Gen. Taylor."[47] *Time* magazine highlighted my article in a report saying that Khanh's "attack on U.S. Ambassador Max Taylor rated headline reaction all over the U.S." The interview was "so fantastic," I told *Time*, that "I didn't think anyone would believe it until it was in print."[48]

Taylor quickly retaliated behind the scenes. He summoned eight U.S. newsmen to a special background briefing. For unexplained reasons I was the only resident correspondent excluded from this session, as I had been from past backgrounders, and was also excluded from the usual poker game and drinks that followed for handpicked insiders.[49]

But being excluded from Taylor's backgrounder meant I was not bound by the restrictive ground rules that the insider information he divulged could not be attributed to him personally or to U.S. officials. I was able to get a detailed rundown of Taylor's remarks and attribute directly to him his sensational comments saying that some Vietnamese generals "are bordering on being nuts," that Khanh was the center of an anti-American camp of generals, and that South Vietnam was facing the most serious political crisis since he had arrived five months earlier. He said the current crisis resulting from the recent purge coup was being fought out on four fronts: the generals versus the government, the Buddhists versus the ambassador, the generals versus the ambassador (himself), and the generals versus the Viet Cong. My page l story led the *Trib* on Christmas Day under a five-column headline: "Viet Press Expose Taylor Rips Mask off Khanh."

Time referred to my confrontation with the U.S. Embassy as a "dustup," but I felt I was being caught in a crossfire of history-making words between Khanh and Taylor.[50] The magazine called my interview with Khanh "a singular achievement for a girl who has yet to be accepted as a regular in Saigon's corps of foreign correspondents and who had been a *Tribune* correspondent for only two months." Noting that I was the only U.S. reporter not regularly invited to U.S. briefings, *Time* included my reference to American Embassy personnel: "They don't like me because I won't say what they want me to say. They accuse me of giving the Vietnamese line, when in fact what I do is listen to them and then go out and find out for myself."

Time indicated, however, "By now, she has developed resources and contacts that largely obviate the need for getting along with the embassy, or even with Saigon's somewhat clubby and introspective press corps." Indicating that I was simply trying to hold my own amid the mostly male press corps and officialdom, I told *Time*, "Men are a luxury I can't afford." I added, "I'm a woman journalist, and I'm competing with men."[51]

My *Trib* editor was elated. Writing to me on Christmas Eve 1964, Associate editor Wald described my interview with Khanh as "absolutely great." He added, "It delighted me and everyone else on the paper; it rattled the State Department, and I think it put you on the map."

Christmas Eve Bomb: The War Comes to Saigon

I had barely filed Taylor's harsh words about Khanh in my dispatch to New York when war pierced the heart of Saigon. I was dressing for a Christmas Eve celebration when an explosion about six blocks away shook the city. I forgot the party and ran toward the billowing black cloud. I gathered on-the-scene information and again hastily cabled New York because I knew the paper was on deadline.

For a second at sunset, at exactly six o'clock, Saigon stood still. Everyone knew it was a black Christmas. Four American nurses in silk cocktail dresses waited for an elevator in the lobby of the American officers' billet, where they had gone to eat Christmas Eve dinner. Suddenly they stopped, turned around, and soon began treating a flow of wounded. Their brocades became bloodied; they never ate dinner.

A powerful terrorist bomb had ripped through a U.S. billet in the center of Saigon. At least 2 Americans were killed, and 107 were injured, the most casualties inflicted in any single terrorist incident in the capital. Fire roared through the first three stories of the seven-story bachelors' quarters, called "Hotel Brink." Windows within a half-mile area were shattered, terrifying many of Saigon's Roman Catholics, who were finishing up their Christmas shopping. Children, gashed by flying glass, were screaming.

"I was in a printer's shop," a U.S. sergeant recounted to me. "Just as the foreman pushed a button to signal the workers to go home, we heard this crackling explosion. I rushed into the street and saw this mushroom cloud. It was pink." He laughed at the incongruity. "It was the same color as the sunset. Then the pink cloud became black."

My dispatch arrived in New York in time to be published as the second lead story on page 1, right underneath my bigger article about Taylor having denigrated Khanh.[52] I later showed AP's Peter Arnett my two bylined stories on page 1 on the same day in New York. "Better save that paper," he said, chuckling. "That doesn't happen very often."

My two Christmas time articles served as bloody bookends for a year that began with a coup on January 30, followed by the attempt by McNamara and Taylor in March to transform General Khanh into the American boy, followed then by months of rioting, demonstrations, political turbulence, terrorist bombings, and U.S. air raids against North Vietnam in retaliation for the Tonkin Gulf shoot-out. By the end of 1964 the black-and-pink clouds billowing above the rooftop of the Hotel Brink signaled the epitaph for the Vietnamese phase of the war, when 23,000 U.S. military had been assigned there and 267 had been killed, with 1,531 wounded in action.[53]

The wafting clouds also signaled more political instability in South Vietnam. After 390 days of serving as the American boy, Khanh was ousted from office by other Vietnamese generals and on February 24, 1965, was exiled abroad. Six days later, on March 2, 123 U.S. and South Vietnamese planes bombed North Vietnam to begin the "Graduated Overt Military Pressure" that the United States had started planning in NSAM 288, immediately after McNamara's barnstorming with Khanh.[54] And in another six days, on March 8, a U.S. Marine Corps brigade marched ashore in a South Vietnamese province near the Demilitarized Zone. The American phase of the war on the ground and in the air in both North and South Vietnam was momentously under way.

7

Americanizing the War

Killing the enemy was not the problem; it was identifying
him. Killing him was easy once you found him and
identified him. In fact, sometimes it was much easier to do
the killing first and the identifying afterwards. Where no
answers were possible, no questions were necessary.

101st Airborne sergeant Micheal Clodfelter, 1965–66

Oh, God, I don't want to die. Mother, I don't want to die.
Oh, God, don't let me die.

Last words of army medic Sp/4 Richard
A. Carlson, twenty, May 24, 1968

I visited the provincial capital and military headquarters at Pleiku shortly
after Communists forces had unleashed a three-pronged attack along
nearby Route 19, 250 miles north of Saigon. Fierce fighting ensued for
five hours before allied forces beat back the onslaught. "This is the closest thing to Korea I've ever seen," a U.S. advisor told me in spring 1965.

When I arrived, I saw dozens of Communist dead strewn along Route
19 and photographed a truck loaded with corpses. Sitting only twenty
miles from the Cambodian border and not far from the fingerlike roadlets
forming the Ho Chi Minh Trail, Pleiku sat on a high plateau surrounded
by mountains and served as a strategic hub for the dusty, twenty-mile

stretch of Highway 19 that ran eastward to the South China Sea. Along that cinnamon-colored highway eleven years earlier 3,500 French troops equipped with tanks and artillery were practically annihilated in a series of Communist ambushes launched so regularly that the foreign fighters labeled it the "War of the Wide Open Spaces."

Now Americans were calling it the "War of the Prairies."[1] The advisor told me that more Communist units, better equipped and led, were infiltrating, with command posts in the rear using telephones to their frontline troops. Most units were composed of teenaged northerners, like the private I had reported on eight months earlier but the Pentagon had denied. "These are regular units using regular infantry tactics," the advisor summed up. "We aren't fighting guerrillas anymore."

Even amid these ghosts of old and new Communist prowess, I considered Pleiku to be an unlikely place to provoke such a historic escalation of the United States' war into North Vietnam. But on February 7, 1965, Communists launched a coordinated attack near Pleiku on the U.S. helicopter base and the U.S. advisors' barracks, killing nine Americans, wounding more than one hundred, and demolishing or damaging fifteen aircraft. The brazen attacks prompted President Johnson to order U.S. warplanes, joined by South Vietnamese ones, to retaliate with the opening salvo of a bombing raid on North Vietnam.[2]

I noted a week later that observers in Saigon believed the United States used the attack at Pleiku as a pretext — not a reason — for bombing North Vietnam and that the bombing plans had been decided upon at least a year earlier.[3] President Johnson dramatically put into action NSAM 288, which he had ordered drawn up in March 1964, immediately after McNamara's Khanh-Do barnstorming trip.

Three days later Johnson ordered a much more deadly punishment. Sustained air attacks steadily intensified against North Vietnam. More than reprisals or retaliation, these air strikes were justified as a response to aggression from the North, but, as the *Pentagon Papers* point out, they were launched "as gradually and imperceptibly as possible."[4] So imperceptibly, I observed in Danang, because U.S. information policy had changed; on the fifth raid over North Vietnam, officials would no longer disclose the number of American aircraft when they were flying jointly with South Vietnamese fighter-bombers, the bases from which accompanying U.S. jets were launched, or the amount of ordnance expended. The new information policy was issued by the Pentagon, necessitated for military security reasons, a U.S. Embassy spokesman in Saigon said, "which I myself do not understand."[5]

Guided Missiles versus the Guerrillas

Responding immediately to the Pleiku attacks, Secretary of Defense Robert McNamara announced at a news conference on February 7, 1965, that a U.S. Marine HAWK antiaircraft missile battalion would be rushed to the Danang airbase to improve its defense against air attacks because of its new strategic importance as a site to be used for U.S. bombing of North Vietnam.[6] The Communists lacked military attack aircraft then — and throughout the war in the South — and used no antiaircraft weapons in the Danang area.

Struck by the incongruity of the deployment of the HAWK guided missiles, I observed they were "perhaps one of the most ludicrous sights and eerie paradoxes in this country waging a guerrilla war." The silvery, needle-tipped missiles symbolized the most advanced American technology, but they also signaled an admission that the United States had neither the political nor military means to win the guerrilla war — but only the means to make it more expensive for the Communists to win it. The move represented U.S. policy makers' attempt to super-conventionalize the guerrilla war, I observed, while the Communists had been semi-conventionalizing their guerrilla war by attacking with bigger and better-armed units.

In this guided missile versus guerrilla confrontation, I noted, the odds were still in favor of the guerrilla. The Communists could choose their enemies and locate and selectively target them at times of their choosing. But the U.S. guided missiles could not distinguish friend from foe on the ground and could not consistently help to find foes where they were hiding. Moreover, citing historical reasons, I noted, "Any assumption that bombing North Vietnam would force Hanoi to downgrade the war in the south appears unsound." (Hanoi would remain resolute, even when two years later B-52 strategic bombers would be dropping 625 tons of bombs, the most powerful combat raids since the atomic bombing of Nagasaki twenty-one years earlier.)[7]

Eight days after my article was published in New York, the Pentagon, also recognizing that guided missiles could not protect the Danang airbase from guerrilla attacks, ordered 2,000 men of a U.S. Marine amphibious brigade to swarm ashore near Danang. While the remainder of the 3,500-man marine brigade was landing, I reported that up to 10,000 more marines were soon expected in Vietnam. To my surprise, on March 10 editors conspicuously published my dispatch on page 1, in part because Washington was then denying that more troops were bound for Vietnam.[8] Although I was congratulated on the story, I was also embarrassed that my figure of 10,000 was so low because the number of U.S. troops began to soar from 20,000 for advising and support roles to 184,314 in combat by the end of 1965.[9]

I later learned that introducing U.S. combat units sparked a bitter debate within the U.S. establishment. Ambassador Maxwell Taylor, a retired general, was strongly opposed, arguing in a secret cable: "The 'white-faced' soldier cannot be assimilated by the population, he cannot distinguish between friendly and unfriendly Vietnamese; the Marines are not armed, trained or equipped for jungle guerrilla war." The United States — like France — would fail to adapt to such conditions, Taylor prophesied.[10] He was overruled. In two weeks the U.S. Marines landed. These troop landings were "a watershed event in the history of U.S. involvement in Vietnam," the *Pentagon Papers* observe, but they represented a decision made "without much fanfare — and without much planning."[11]

Hanoi: "The Deeper the Grave" for Americans

Rather than buckling under the relentless pounding by U.S. warplanes, Hanoi remained steadfast. After ten months of bombing, I interviewed Hanoi watchers in Saigon and travelers from North Vietnam to report that the Communist country was preparing for a long, hard war. By the end of 1965 its people were digging trenches, holding air raid alerts, and camouflaging vehicles, including bicycles. Some schoolchildren carried camouflage on their briefcases, and those who had been evacuated to the countryside were returning to the city. Bomb shelters were constructed for foreigners in Hanoi at a cost of four thousand dollars each, but as one explained, "They aren't worth that much money — they aren't substantial enough to save anyone." Morale remained high, with many Vietnamese repeating with a singsong lilt: "The more Americans keep coming, the deeper the grave."[12]

U.S. bombing was galvanizing the North Vietnamese like the stealth attack on Pearl Harbor had the United States in World War II. My article would be echoed two years later in a secret Pentagon study. In May 1967 it found that Communist-led forces were sufficiently replacing their losses so that the United States would need at least ten years to defeat them.[13] That same month McNamara sketched out for Johnson the impact of U.S. bombing of the North: "The picture of the world's greatest superpower killing or seriously injuring 1,000 noncombatants a week, while trying to pound a tiny backward nation into submission on an issue whose merits are hotly disputed, is not a pretty one."[14]

By launching its destructive bombing campaign against North Vietnam, the United States was trying to rescue South Vietnam. But the U.S. combat units and increased firepower were no substitute for a legitimate, stable government worthy of popular support within the United States and South Vietnam. Americanizing the war in the South occurred just twelve days after the Saigon government's strongman, Gen. Nguyen Khanh, had been exiled from his own country (which in turn occurred just twenty-nine days after he had ousted a civilian government) and a new civilian premier, Phan Huy Quat, had been installed (which lasted only three and a half months, until June 12, 1965). Nor was this immense U.S. military might able to placate the Buddhist protestors on the streets or Buddhist leaders who were repeating their pleas for withdrawal of U.S. forces from the South, disbanding of Communist guerrillas, cessation of U.S. attacks on North Vietnam, and starting North-South talks on reunification. Within months, McNamara was lamenting, "the U.S. presence rested on a bowl of jelly."[15]

Two months after the marines landed near the Demilitarized Zone, the army's 173rd Airborne Brigade moved in to the environs of Saigon. (These paratroopers would usher in a dramatic escalation until March 29, 1969, when U.S. military strength in South Vietnam peaked at 543,400.)[16]

I waited in the steamy midday heat early in 1965 with youthful paratroopers of the 173rd Airborne Brigade as they perched their packs against the stumps of chopped-off rubber plantation trees. Unlike the marines who were assigned a defensive mission around Danang, I was joining the paratroopers for the first U.S. offensive combat operation in South Vietnam as part of a 2,800-man force supported by 120 to 150 helicopters and raids by Guam-based B-52 bombers designed to carry nuclear weapons. This operation signaled that for the first time since the Korean War a U.S. combat unit was officially being used in an offensive ground operation against Communist forces, breaching a major imperative of U.S. foreign policy — to avoid a land war on the Asian continent.[17]

As we waited, a battered truck came down the road, kicking up throat-choking puffs of dust. In the back of the truck was a Vietnamese rubber plantation worker. "He's making a fast count," one private ventured. "Then he goes behind a bush and calls Charley," the paratroopers' jargon for their enemy. Probably without realizing it, the private had prophetically put his finger on the fundamental problem he and the thousands of U.S. troops following him would face during the Americanization of the war — distinguishing friendlies from foes. I noticed that the most distinctive feature of these paratroopers was their youth; most had not yet reached their twentieth birthdays. Hanoi radio-labeled them the "teenage brigade." Even officers leading them were in their late twenties or early thirties. Combat experience resided in senior sergeants, mostly Korean War veterans.

The paratroopers were amazed to find a woman in their midst. I explained that as a journalist, unlike them, I was not drafted and could leave at any time. Dressed in military fatigues and boots, I was traveling light, not wanting anyone to have to carry my load. I wore a helmet and

21. Called the "teenage brigade" by Radio Hanoi, young U.S. draftees like these ask me what I am doing amid the Vietnam War. (B. Deepe Collection)

fisherman's jacket that Mom had sent me for packing my poncho, light blanket, camera, film, insect repellant, and C rations; a waistline belt anchored my canteen of water.

Soon the sky became dotted with helicopters that would heli-lift us into battle in D-Zone, covering parts of six provinces thirty miles north of Saigon. We had been told an estimated two thousand Viet Cong already knew we were coming. At 1:30 p.m. from the Bien Hoa airbase, the paratroopers and I loaded into helicopters, which took off as a sheet of rain and fog engulfed us, and within a half hour we were eased down into a large plain filled with waist-high elephant grass. It was rimmed on one side by charred skeletons of houses that had once been a strategic hamlet but were deserted months ago, signaling how much territory and population the Saigon government had lost in two years. Some small arms fire and mortar shots filled the air without inflicting any casualties. By 5 p.m. most paratroopers were finding the spot where they would camp overnight. "This is a real Hollywood war," one soldier groused. "So far, nothing serious has happened." Suddenly a sniper shot rang out. The soldier shut up and cocked his weapon.

Even if this operation had been made for Hollywood, the soldier probably was unaware that it was also made for the history books. Besides being a first since the Korean War, it also inaugurated the search-and-destroy kind of operation that General Westmoreland was to make the most visible and fateful signature of the Americanized war. Unlike the marines' static defense of the Danang airbase, search-and-destroy meant U.S. troops had moved beyond advising the Vietnamese and defending installations; it meant taking an offensive fight to their enemy, finding him and killing him, and disrupting his base areas and supply depots.

By 7:30 p.m. it was dark, and the platoons fanned out into their defensive positions. We had all eaten; some erected flimsy, miniature tents by spreading waterproof ponchos to tree limbs. I sought some isolated underbrush to serve as an impromptu potty and spread my poncho and blanket on the claylike soil for an almost sleepless night.

Before dawn troops were scurrying about. We ate cold C rations, beefsteak with sticky juices. We were scheduled to leave at 8:30 a.m. but at 9:15 an officer explained, "We are still here, and are going to be here a long time yet." The headquarters company for one of the two battalions was lost somewhere in the jungle. Helicopters hovered above to spot it. "That headquarters company had better stay lost," one soldier mused. "I'd hate to be him if he's ever found." (It was found, got lost again, and was then located again.)

Two hours behind schedule, the company commander was ordered, and in turn ordered his platoons, to move toward and search the next objective six hundred yards or so southwest. As the company moved in the sweltering heat through the thick undergrowth, the first sergeant barked: "Keep looking to the left and right. There's no sense looking like we own this jungle." By 1 p.m. the company had secured the objective and then swept through more underbrush for six hundred yards. At 3:20, as the rain poured, we moved about 1,500 yards ahead to another one-time strategic hamlet perched on a hilltop across abandoned rice paddies. Laboring through waist-deep paddies, we passed the wooden fence that had once protected the hamlet. The shells of four burned-out huts loomed ahead. "Okay, this is it," the first sergeant instructed. "You have two hours to get dry." Troops checked for leeches and lounged in the "green hell."

As had happened often in the past with South Vietnamese soldiers and their U.S. advisors, the Communist-led guerrillas had faded away. The results: one U.S. killed and twenty-two wounded; one guerrilla confirmed dead and seventeen wounded and three hundred tons of rice seized — in U.S. surplus food sacks. This big sweep reminded me of the "fabulous fizzle" of Operation Morning Star, which I covered in 1962. Now the U.S. military was following in the footsteps of the U.S.-trained Vietnamese armed forces. This big sweep would become a microcosm of many U.S. search-and-destroy operations that netted some resources but few guerrillas.

After this first operation the 173rd Airborne conducted at least thirty-seven search-and-destroy missions up to 1970, often producing similar paltry results.[18] U.S. officials described one of their operations as an outstanding success for destroying a secure base only twenty miles or so northwest of Saigon that the Viet Cong had held for twenty years. But less than a month later, from February 22 through March 17, 1966, the three-week-long Operation Junction City moved through basically the same area with modest results.[19]

One unique operation I covered was code-named "Rolling Stone." I watched in amazement in February 1966 as U.S. military engineers used king-sized bulldozers to clear and repair a road, laced with mines and booby traps, that the Viet Cong had held for years only thirty-five miles northeast of Saigon.[20] Called "Rome Plows," these bulldozers with mighty, tree-cutting blades in front looked like enlarged versions of those that I had seen years earlier used to terrace Dad's hilly farmland.

I wish I had asked the engineers why these machines were not used to clear jungled, flat areas like D-Zone and prepare it for distribution as part of an innovative land development program that could have populated the area, enhanced the popularity and prestige of the Saigon government, and eliminated the need for repeated search-and-destroy operations through these long-held Viet Cong bases. The U.S. government had done just that in 1954 when it cleared land in nonpopulated areas for resettlement of some of the nine hundred thousand Vietnamese who migrated from North Vietnam to the South in what became one of the most successful programs of the U.S.-backed Saigon government.[21] But in the mid-1960s no American or Saigon government initiative transformed for Vietnam's peasantry the 388,852 acres (or about 350,000 football fields) cleared by about 180 Rome Plows that would be operated by special U.S. engineering units through October 1969.[22] U.S. strategists forgot that a century earlier it was not the U.S. military that had subdued the American Indians and dispossessed them of their lands so much as sod-busting settlers with their aggressive technologies such as railroads and primitive plows.[23]

"Armored Wagons" versus "Indians in the Old West"

Unlike the 173rd Airborne's Hollywood war, I discovered six weeks later just how bloody some of Westmoreland's search-and-destroy operations could be when Communist-led forces chose to stand and fight. In mid-August 1965, as the blistering sun beat down on the man-tall bramblebush, I trudged beside a marine patrol sent to recover the dead from Hotel and India companies. These companies were part of Operation Starlight, the first marine search-and-destroy offensive since their landing. A land-sea-air pincer operation, it was conducted on the Van Tuong peninsula about sixty miles south of Danang.

Although most of the five thousand U.S. ground troops never saw their enemy, for the hundreds of marines in Hotel and India companies, it was a different story. On August 18 marines from Hotel company were heli-lifted to a landing zone and were almost immediately pinned down by such heavy fire pouring in from camouflaged tunnels and blockhouses that all eighteen helicopters were hit. Coming to Hotel company's rescue were India company's five armored, amphibious tractors, called "amtracs," but these hulking, thirty-five-ton square boxes got mired in the squishy rice paddies. They began drawing such withering weapons fire that Tank A-34 was demolished, abandoned by its crew, and left to dominate the landscape as a skeleton of charred rice paddy rubble. India company's amtracs soon morphed into what one marine called "swimming coffins." Marines in both companies were pinned down for a day and a night in a thousand-yard ring of intense fighting near a Communist-held hamlet nestled amid thick hedgerows and soggy rice land. A band of thirty marines was encircled and shelled for more than twenty-four hours by an estimated one hundred hard-core fighters. As one U.S. officer explained to me, "It was a natural tank trap, and we fell into it."

A veteran marine sergeant described the fighting differently. "It was like the Indians in the Old West surrounding and attacking a covered wagon convoy, except we were in armored wagons," he explained. "I was in the invasion of Okinawa — but I have never seen anything like this. I thought this was the end of us all." Of seventeen tanks and amtracs sent for relief, ten became trapped, two were burned out, and three became lost in the hedgerows for thirty-plus hours.

Sitting on the dusty red-clay air pad, watching helicopters ferry out the dead and wounded, a fuzz-cheeked lance corporal said that the Viet Cong had taken over one abandoned amtrac, used it as a shelter only fifteen yards from him, and "played peek-a-boo" with him all night. Sitting under his buttoned-down hatch, he said, "I took out my rosary and started praying." The dead being loaded up were encased in red dust. One had died with a knife clutched in his hand; another had been disemboweled. One survivor, a young black private, watched, wailing in horror, with tears rolling down his cheeks.

Later we approached the longtime Viet Cong–controlled hamlet of Ap Tho No. 2, where some of the bloodiest fighting had occurred. We moved past a dead pig, a dead calf, and a dead woman in a tunnel. Just beyond the first house I was even more stunned by what I saw. At first I thought it was a doll; it was puffed up like an inflated carnival toy. It was a toddler, near naked, swollen from the heat and humidity and swarming with flies. Decades later its pathetic form remains etched in my memory, evoking a gush of anguish and regret.

Marines called Operation Starlight a huge victory, describing it as reminiscent of the World War II battles of Iwo Jima and Okinawa. News stories echoed their triumph that 552 Communists had been killed and

1,000 wounded. The marines sustained the highest U.S. casualties from a single action in the Vietnam War up to that time, but restrictions on news coverage required losses to be described only as "light."

I was skeptical of the Marine Corps' exuberance. In an advisory to New York I called it "The Victory That Wasn't." Officers at the regimental level who were to verify the body count told me ground forces had barely swept the area. The marine commander in the Pacific, who had visited the battle scene, announced the marines had no right to make the estimate in the first place.[24] The Communists were also claiming victory; Gen. Vo Nguyen Giap predicted that Starlight "foreshadowed the tactical failure" of the U.S. military.[25]

U.S Firepower and Political Hatred

U.S. combat units brought with them tremendous technologies of firepower and airpower that increased the level of violence and destruction in the South. I found the cumulative impact and magnitude of allied artillery shellings and air bombardments hard to report to readers because they occurred in so many different places over sporadic stretches of time, and no official announcements about them were made.

I spotted the ruinous devastation to the countryside when I accompanied military operations. I saw, for example, numerous gaping craters created by massive B-52s bombardments often used to soften up areas before ground troops were heli-lifted into inhospitable territory. Giant craters dotted the dense jungle when I joined ten thousand Australian, U.S., and South Vietnamese troops on Operation Mastiff in February 1966. Enduring ninety-plus-degree heat that produced a sweaty lather on us, we were scouring the hundred-square-mile jungled stronghold and a French rubber plantation known as Ho Bo Woods, which one GI dubbed the "Dogpatch of the Viet Cong."

On that operation I witnessed the prodigious U.S. firepower that was available each night to protect the periphery of the ground troops but also bringing risk to noncombatants who might not have been forewarned. Throughout the night American artillery rounds swished over our heads and then, with a resounding slam, plunged into supposedly Viet Cong territory. Helicopters joined by transport aircraft dropped thirty-second flares, which brighten the skies "like someone turned on an electric light," one private explained. The light aided artillery in the rear so it could be automatically calibrated to fire just outside the U.S. defensive positions.

Even U.S. troops were wary of the accuracy of these lethal explosives. As a noncommissioned officer explained to me: "One problem is the ground troops don't know how to read maps well. They give a map location and when the artillery comes, it's not where they think they called for it." The maps were not always up-to-date. ("Up to 15 percent of U.S. deaths in Indochina — 8,700 — might have been from friendly fire.")[26]

Still, during the first night of the operation U.S. units received incoming Communist mortar and recoilless rifle fire. It prompted an officer to complain to me, "Even with all these mechanical means, we're still always one or two days behind the Viet Cong."

For villagers on the other end of the bombardments and shellings, the results were often harrowing. A one-time guerrilla described how the countryside was being ravaged in Dinh Tuong Province in the Mekong Delta in 1967. The war has destroyed houses, orchards, and crops, he said. Big holes caused by bombs in the rice fields have made farming impossible. Eighty percent of the villagers had evacuated to government areas, and 75 percent of the cattle had been killed. "Actually," he summed up, "everyone in the rural areas is ruined."[27]

Another example of the "death zone" strategy that I first wrote about in 1962 occurred in a magnified version five years later and in the very same province. I did not accompany the 25,000 soldiers, including the 173rd Airborne paratroopers, on that operation, in which U.S. forces suffered a record number of deaths in one week, 144, along with 1,044 wounded and 6 missing.[28] But I was taken aback when I read remarks about it made by the top U.S. general. U.S. planners for Operation Cedar Falls expected "that uprooting the natives of these villages would evoke resentment, and it did," Lt. Gen. Bernard Rogers, a high-ranking participating officer, recounted. He added, "The sight of the natives of Ben Suc with their carts, chickens, hogs, rice, and all else" was "pathetic and pitiful." The uprooted Vietnamese were shuttled to a parched field where no facilities or provisions had been readied for them because the province chief had not been consulted or informed about the operation. With the inhabitants gone, U.S. soldiers torched the villagers' huts. Bulldozers razed the remaining structures. Then, like my observations from Operation Sunrise in 1962, U.S. Air Force jets pulverized this death zone. As General Rogers concluded, "The village of Ben Suc no longer existed."[29]

For the six years from the Americanization of the war in 1965 through 1970, the U.S., South Vietnamese, and allied forces would expend 12.22 million tons of explosives. During one month alone in Vietnam, when the U.S. expenditure of munitions peaked in 1970, the 128,000 tons of air and ground explosives equated to the explosive force of 8.5 Hiroshima-size A-bombs, without the resulting long-lived radioactivity.[30] Yet these explosives told very little about the outcome of the war, a researcher writes, noting that U.S. policy makers sought to substitute firepower for manpower, but "overwhelming firepower cannot compensate for bad strategy." U.S. troops sweeping target areas found little impact on their enemy; usually no efforts were even made to confirm targets.[31]

Within months of the combat troops' arrival, I was warned that the indiscriminate or mistaken use of this impersonally delivered American power risked jeopardizing the political war in the South. "You can carry a military program so far that it will create political hatreds," I quoted an American source in October 1965. "You could win the war, then hold a referendum and lose."[32]

"Keeping Your Rear Covered" in a War without Front Lines

One alternative to Westmoreland's search-and-destroy operations was developed by the marines in the northernmost provinces shortly after they landed in March 1965. My interest in their alternative was sparked when I learned at a news briefing that during his week-long trip to Vietnam beginning July 14, 1965, Secretary McNamara had been briefed on the marines' pilot pacification effort.

The marines' mission "to secure enclaves in the northern region of Vietnam" included the strategic Danang airbase and the six hundred square miles surrounding it, inhabited by 411,000 people. The marines' area was included in the five northernmost provinces in South Vietnam, an area of about ten thousand square miles, where about 2.5 million lived. These provinces were critical; on the north side lay the Demilitarized Zone with North Vietnam, and on the west stretched rugged highlands along the ill-defined Laotian border. Instead of search-and-destroy operations into the highlands, the marines were seeking to concentrate on clear-and-hold operations along the coast — and within the range of U.S. naval gunfire — where Vietnamese grew rice on a ribbon of rich soil skimming the South China Sea.[33]

Shortly after landing, the marines found themselves facing a suicide attack and other problems of an "unprecedented nature," right outside the gates of the sprawling Danang airbase, the *Pentagon Papers* note, and they became over time "the most vocal advocates within the Armed Forces for emphasizing pacification more, and search and destroy less." Trying to provide security on a continuing basis for friendly villagers, marines turned to armed small-unit and medical civic action patrols in the surrounding hamlets. They tried to improve the local Popular Forces militia and to integrate with them to form Combined Action Platoons (CAPs). As the CAP marines prepared to live amid what they envisioned as a sea of hostile villagers, they whispered to themselves, "We are all alone in Indian country."[34]

I traveled to one isolated CAP outpost near Nam-O village, population six thousand, to talk with the eleven marines who were integrated with twenty-five Vietnamese Popular Forces. These were part-time citizen-soldiers, paid the equivalent of eighteen dollars a month — barely enough to buy rice for their families — and they suffered heavier casualties than the regular Vietnamese or U.S. forces. Nam-O outpost was close enough to the Danang airbase that we saw flaming puffballs pierce the darkness as Viet Cong lobbed mortars and rockets onto it. In 1967 nearly one hundred CAPs were operating in the northern provinces, often making night patrols that were like walking the edge of a knife.

"It's the eeriest thing," L.Cpl. Rick Foreman said as he described the difficulties of figuring out who was his enemy. "After 8 p.m. no villagers are supposed to be out of their houses. So you hear a sound in the bushes. . . .

Do you order your patrol to fire? Maybe it's a water buffalo. If you kill it, the Marine Corps has to pay twenty or thirty dollars for damages. Maybe it's an old grandma out on some errand. If you kill her, you could be court-martialed, but if you don't fire, maybe your patrol will be wiped out."

Foreman, a cherub-faced extrovert from Johnstown, Pennsylvania, introduced me to Sgt. Garry Smith, the twenty-six-year-old commander of the Nam-O unit. Handing me hot coffee in a C ration tin, Smith explained the CAP mission was "to instruct and go on patrol with twenty-five Vietnamese PFs so they can take over when we leave Vietnam or move inland toward the mountains." He said that a lot of progress had been made since he took command three and a half months earlier. "The PFs would refuse to go on patrols that looked a little shaky. They'd just sit down and wouldn't budge," he continued. "Now they go anywhere with us." The marines do a lot of people-to-people work, he said, ticking off treating the sick and building a junior high school that could hold 250 kids who before that had no education past the sixth grade.

We finished talking at the top of a three-tiered guard tower. Two decks below us, *Combat* flicked onto the television screen. "How can you look at *Combat* when they're trying to kill you out there?" I asked in amazement. Foreman answered: "You fight against Charlie 24 hours a day out here. . . . Sometimes you like to see someone else doing the fighting." Popular Forces in sandals and motley uniforms sat fixated as three U.S. GIs killed scores of World War II Nazis.[35]

The marines' emphasis on pacification became a war within a war within the U.S. establishment from Washington down to the battlefield, often pitting the marines versus the army and even causing disagreements within each service. In August 1965, shortly after the marines had landed, An, Vuong, and I flew to Danang and spent considerable time interviewing marines, Vietnamese and U.S. officials, villagers, townspeople, religious leaders, and a North Vietnamese prisoner. After our work in the field each day, I typed up pages of single-spaced notes, accumulated a six-inch stack of materials and writing tablets, and collected numerous documents. We stayed at the marine-operated Press Center, where, more than in Saigon, we socialized with journalists — plus some U.S. intelligence agents.

I noted that five months after the marines arrived in Vietnam, they were predicting, "We'll be in Hoi An by New Year's Day 1966." Hoi An lay only fifteen miles south of the Danang airbase, but the marines encountered stiff resistance as they maneuvered toward the picturesque province capital dotted with houses built in the fifteenth and sixteenth centuries by Japanese, Chinese, Portuguese, and French traders when it was a thriving port. Suddenly the marines were forced to change their estimate and figured getting to Hoi An would not happen for two more years — New Year's 1968. "We could easily have fought our way to Hoi An," one marine told me. "But then, we would have had to fight our way back. The essential problem of this war is not moving your front lines forward. It is keeping your rear covered."[36]

The Communists' 3-D and Underground War

The marines concentrated on securing villages surrounding the airbase until Vietnamese military and civilian units could win the support — or at least the neutrality — of the local population. "In a conventional war progress is measured by an advancing front line," one U.S. official explained to me. "But in this war . . . progress must be measured in a third dimension. We must go down into the population and dig out the Viet Cong infrastructure and then rebuild the local anti-Communist government."

The result of this coordinated U.S.-Vietnamese effort was the Five Mountain Villages Campaign, less than ten miles southwest of Danang and fifteen miles from Hoi An. It was the marines' principal pacification project and a pilot case for the future. The five villages in the campaign were subdivided into nineteen hamlets, covering a 7.72-square-mile area, home for forty-two thousand people, of whom 7 percent were believed to be related to Viet Cong. Villages in the lush rice land were surrounded by five peaks of mountains containing gray and salmon-colored marble. "These marble mountains would make a great tourist attraction," one marine observed, "but you'd be killed going out there." Unknown to the marines, the Viet Cong had dug tunnels or caves inside the mountains to set up a Viet Cong hospital; some caves housed Buddhist shrines that were declared off-limits to marines out of respect for the religion.[37]

"The role of the U.S. Marines is like an egg," one official told me. "Our front lines, on the rim of the area, are the shell — but like a shell, the lines can be broken. The vital installation — the Danang airbase — is the yolk, and we also defend that. The white is the countryside, which we are trying to pacify and solidify."

In the pacification campaign — or what the marines called the "people-to-people program" — U.S. Marines patrolled the outer limits of the area, Vietnamese paramilitary troops maintained security in the villages, and Vietnamese civilian teams distributed goods, waged psychological warfare, took censuses, and attempted to undo the Viet Cong's existing political-cum-military grip so as to lure villagers to the government side. The marines began civic action teams that within a year would give medical treatment to 773,574 and dental treatment to 21,362 and would distribute 1.19 million tons of clothing, food, and soap.[38]

Vietnamese government forces moved behind the marines' patrols to begin their civilian and paramilitary campaign on October 18, 1965. Five Vietnamese People's Action Teams (PATs) of ten persons each were responsible for census taking and other activities. These PATs were equipped, paid, and trained for political activity and intelligence work by an arm of the U.S. CIA.

As the marines fanned out to secure hamlets even five miles beyond the airbase perimeter, they found that much of the Vietnamese countryside had gone underground. Beside each house, one marine told me, was a large, earth-covered bunker into which the family jumped during fighting or bombing raids. Some bunkers led into a labyrinth of tunnels used by the Viet Cong for coming or going into the hamlet or into a river from which they could swim away from danger. One marine exclaimed to me, "Some tunnels are even split-level."[39]

"If this plan doesn't succeed here, it's not going to succeed anywhere else in the country," an official told me. "We'll really be in serious trouble then."

The plan was already running into serious trouble. During the third week of the campaign a fifty-man Viet Cong platoon broke through the marines' blocking position, killing five Regional Force troopers and several cadres. "Until that time we were just beginning to get the confidence of the people," the official continued, "but after that, the people clammed up and wouldn't tell us anything."

The attack also hurt the morale of the Vietnamese government's civilians. "One whole eleven-man team took off — but the district chief talked them into coming back," the official went on. Then, four nights later, the same Viet Cong platoon hit again, killing several civilian cadre and kidnapping two women working with a drama unit. "We haven't seen the women since." One marine saw the action from fifty yards away, but he could not open up with his machine gun or he would have killed more friendlies than enemies. "Of course, the marines can't stop all small-unit infiltration," he explained. "It would take marines shoulder to shoulder to do that. And once you had that, the Viet Cong would mortar them from across the river, which they've already started doing."

The biggest headache was that Vietnamese troops and cadre could not be moved out of this twenty-square-kilometer collection of hamlets until villagers could defend the area, the official explained. But there was not one young man who could be recruited; one side or the other had already drafted them. "We've lost the middle generation," he said, "and no one has begun to find an answer to that problem." Nor would the answer be satisfactorily found during the United States' years of the war.

Other problems were also surfacing in the city. Within seven months after the first marines landed, U.S. officials had a "grave concern" about the number of refugees who could not be housed in government centers — more than six thousand in Danang city alone and twenty-two thousand in the province around it. By November 1965 resentment against the United States had grown after bombing errors by aircraft killed twenty-one Vietnamese in a community south of the Demilitarized Zone. Anger by civil servants and villagers increased over the newfound affluence of cyclo drivers and bar girls in businesses sprouting up near marine establishments. Danang's cyclo drivers refused to pick up the local population and instead waited for marines, who paid exorbitant prices, a practice that created a serious problem in a city without a local bus system or taxis.[40]

A Special Escort Officer

When An, Vuong, and I arrived in Danang, the marines assigned their civic action officer, Maj. Chuck Keever, to escort us to the villages where their people-to-people program, which had interested McNamara, was being conducted. In Keever's jeep we rode about six miles south of Danang to Duong Son 1 (Sun Hill), where eighty families were nestled among small plots bounded by bamboo thickets, hedgerows, canals, and footpaths. It had been one of Diem's strategic hamlets, but in 1964 the government presence vanished. Only weeks before our visit, the Ninth Marine Regiment had swept through Duong Son 1 and found it saturated with Viet Cong trench systems, foot traps, and tunnels.

Although the marines sensed the villagers were becoming more friendly,[41] in my interviews with them, with An and Vuong translating, they were quick to voice grievances. A midget Vietnamese boy in a floppy Marine Corps cap standing in the middle of a thatched hut blurted out about the Americans, "When we're not looking, they go ahead and steal ducks." A woman chewing blood-red betel nuts chimed in: "We can't buy enough rice and shrimp paste in the district market. If we do, the police confiscate it and say we are supplying the Viet Cong." A phrase she used for Viet Cong was "cac ong giai phong" (Mr. Liberator). Another term she used was interpreted by Vuong to mean that the marines were "always a stranger, like the spirits or the devils." The marines' civic action effort had a tough road ahead of it, I decided, perhaps for a long time.

Keever was later assigned to the U.S. Embassy in Saigon. We continued our friendship through his two-year assignment and then departed Vietnam together. In the evening of Valentine's Day in 1969, seven years to the day after I had arrived in Saigon, we were married in Belvidere, Nebraska, near my parents' home, sealing a storybook romance.

My field reporting from Danang with An and Vuong was incorporated in early 1966 into a four-part series. To my surprise Senator Mike Mansfield, former Asian history professor and an early and powerful supporter of Diem, inserted into the *Congressional Record* all of my series on January 20, 1966, the day after my last dispatch was published. With the headline "Vietnam, Past and Prospect," the series reviewed the history of U.S. involvement since the Tonkin Gulf incident of August 1964, the arrival of the first U.S. combat troops in March 1965 and the resulting South Vietnamese perceptions of colonialism, subversion in the Mekong Delta, and the gloomy prospects facing the U.S. Marines. In the *Record* the senator said that "Miss Deepe is eminently qualified by experience to report" on the war as it has evolved over the past year. He noted that I had written the series from the Mekong Delta, from the coastal bases, and from the highlands. "The picture which emerges from the four articles is a vivid and accurate summary of the situation which confronts us in Vietnam," he said, and makes "highly informative and highly useful reading" (see appendix 2).[42]

Falling Domino Theory: Into the "Trash Bin of History"

In April 1966 I noted that some of my sources were beginning to question the domino theory that the United States had used for decades to justify supporting South Vietnam. I described high-level military sources arguing that the Johnson administration was considering the domino theory passé by calling for elections within South Vietnam as soon as possible, failing to hold a hard line in Vietnam to achieve victory. Sources I quoted indicated this shift would signal "that the Communists have found a successful, low-cost method for seizing power in other small countries." While this shift was seen as not quite capitulation, I noted, it was far short of the victory that Johnson was publicly seeking. I observed, "The president is more interested in attempting to end the war than in attempting to win it."[43]

Less than a year later, I was amazed to learn, top U.S. officials also were publicly backing off from the domino theory that they had used since the 1950s to justify keeping communism out of Indochina through the presidencies of Eisenhower, Kennedy ("Our security may be lost piece by piece, country by country"),[44] and Johnson (losing Vietnam would force the United States to fight "on the beaches of Waikiki").[45] The United States would be the last domino.

But on January 12, 1967, Secretary of State Dean Rusk declared on national television: "Well, I myself have never subscribed to something called the domino theory, because that suggests that we're merely playing games with little wooden blocks with dots on them." Instead, he said, the problem is "the phenomenon of aggression."[46] Also debunking the domino theory in more emphatic and colorful terms was Edmund Reischauer, the Harvard professor who had served as Kennedy's ambassador to Japan. Addressing the Senate Foreign Relations Committee, Reischauer criticized Johnson's continued adherence to the domino theory, saying it was now "dropped in the trash can of history wrapped in a Chinese rug."[47]

8

Her Story as History Too

One night we got to arguing while sitting around the foxhole. Someone asked, "Would you shoot a woman if you had to?" Well, I don't know, guess it would be different if she had a weapon. I don't really know, would you?

Army captain James Landing,
to *Farm Journal*, October 1967

The women peasants were constantly on the front rank of the struggle in the countryside. When this political army temporarily stops direct struggle, it will engage in the production of foods and weapons, do afforestation work, dig trenches, make spikes, fence their fighting villages, or perform their duty as transporters, scouts, or messengers to help the armymen.

North Vietnamese general Vo Nguyen Giap, 1964

Nguyen Thi Bay saw the flames and smoke leaping skyward from her family home as she approached, paddling her sampan after visiting a relative. She ran toward the house to salvage belongings; instead, she found her elder brother with blood gushing from his head and her twelve-year-old brother with a gashed-up face. Her parents had escaped the terror because they were working in nearby rice fields of the Mekong Delta.

Several jets had circled her family's house about five times and then bombed and strafed it in April 1965, the nineteen-year-old told me. She had found her bloodied elder brother near the family bomb shelter; he had not had time to dive into it before being pummeled. "In our villages the peasants built two kinds of shelters," according to Bay, whose name translates as "Seventh Child." One kind of shelter is inside the house right under the bed, usually a highly polished wooden plank platform. "When we hear any artillery, mortars, or ground fire, we just roll out of bed into the trench," she explained to me. The second kind of shelter is usually in the yard or garden and is used when aerial bombing and strafing starts.

Even the family dog knew exactly which hole to run into because he could tell the difference between a cargo plane and a fighter. "When there was mortar or artillery shelling, he ran into the shelter under the bed," Bay continued, but he did not even run out of the house when a cargo plane passed over. Some families in her village had pretty plush bomb shelters. She recounted, "Some have put their money together to build a community shelter deep in the ground with concrete walls and floor so they can sleep there during the nighttime."

She rushed her elder brother to a medical clinic, but the doctors decided to leave the metal in his head and his face still crisscrossed with scars. "After that my parents moved into the province town to live with my uncle and aunt, and I came to Saigon to get a maid's job to help support them," she explained. She was paid one thousand piastres (ten dollars) a month, plus room and board.[1]

Working women such as Bay usually wore comfortable, cotton pajama-like trousers, and a loose fitting, long-sleeved overblouse with a rounded neckline — no garish colors but mostly black or white and almost always fastidiously clean, whether in urban retail shops and stalls or rice planting in the countryside. Their waist-length jet-black hair was usually pulled back into a ponytail or coiled atop their heads. I was impressed with their quiet, stoic resilience, tireless energy, and seeming iron-willed acceptance of a boxed-in lifestyle, but I also often commiserated with them for what I saw as a future of limited opportunities and perhaps relentless heartbreak. Although Vietnamese women played a vital role in Vietnam's economic sphere, they were culturally and socially subservient in the Confucian-molded patriarchal society that expected them unquestioningly to obey their fathers, husbands, and husbands' family. In contrast, the Communists denounced such "feudal customs and ideology" and promised equality between men and women as fundamental for "building a new society."[2]

"Surviving amidst a Savage, Never-Ending Holocaust"

I interviewed Bay in late 1965 and incorporated her story into a five-part series about Vietnamese women that would become one of my most intriguing assignments because it opened wide a window onto how the war was disrupting everyday family life. To my surprise editors gave the series a Madison Avenue touch by publishing a half-page advertisement prominently featuring my photograph of a Viet Cong peasant woman looking straight at readers as she defiantly smoked a cigarette. The headline, in huge type, read: "The Women of Viet Nam . . . What Breed Are They?" Then the ad neatly summarized the numerous topics covered: "dirt, diamonds, decadence, sabotage, soldiering, survival." The advertisement touted "this extraordinary, five-part study of women who are enduring, fighting, exploiting, or just plain surviving amidst a savage, never-ending holocaust."[3]

For the series I interviewed a number of women from all walks of life, including Saigon housewives in elegant silk *ao dais* who worried about getting their children into French-run schools, the Vietnamese major and widowed mother of four heading the government's Women's Armed Forces Corps, and sources describing the impact of the boom in bars and brothels. For the interview that fascinated me most, I traveled to a province northwest of Saigon to talk to Mrs. Nguyen Van Long about her Viet Cong wedding in the jungle. For the dusk-to-midnight wedding and celebration attended by about fifty people, the twenty-two-year-old Viet Cong bride wore the traditional black pajama-styled garb; the twenty-seven-year-old groom looked resplendent in his khaki uniform decorated with the insignia of commander of the village guerrillas. They had received permission to marry from their Viet Cong superiors and their parents, aided by a go-between village elder. Their two Viet Cong superiors orally pronounced them man and wife, and, said Long, "it was generally accepted we were married." The bride and groom exchanged photographs of each other, "but we had no money and only gave each other souvenirs." The groom's comrades gave him "best wishes," and the bride received a few handkerchiefs. The godmothers of the Liberation Army fighters served cakes, candies, and tea. At the stroke of midnight they both returned to their separate duty stations, and a week would pass before they received permission to spend the first night of their honeymoon together. Then over the next two years they received permission to visit each other only two more times — and by then their baby, Thao, was a toddler. With Thao's arrival Long decided, "We have no future with the Viet Cong." In July 1965 the threesome took a bus to the provincial capital and gave themselves up to the government.[4]

When I interviewed Miss Bay in Saigon in late 1965, little did I realize that she was on the cutting edge of what would become an enormous mass exodus from the countryside and a parallel influx into urban centers. I could hardly imagine that "death zones" were to become increasingly routine three years after I had written about allied bombing and shelling of homes and hamlets of villagers forcibly uprooted by Diem's Strategic Hamlet Program. Those remaining in the new death zones, which became sanitized in name as "free-fire zones," were presumed by allied forces to be their enemy and were regularly bombarded.

The Vietnam War has mostly been portrayed as an all-male affair. Virtually all the decisions, fighting, headlines, and TV images were made of, by, or about men. Yet more than half of Vietnam's population was women, and they, too, were increasingly swept up and torn asunder by the bloodshed and disruption. In 1963 women constituted 53.28 percent of South Vietnam's population — or 8.1 million out of an estimated 15.1 million — a result of greater longevity and the loss of males in wartime since 1946.[5]

The rapid Americanization of the war from 1965 on and the increased infiltration of North Vietnamese combat units intensified dramatically the pace, fury, and scope of the fighting, bombing, and shelling and transformed the countryside and its people. Because virtually all young men were fighting on one side or the other, those remaining in the hamlets were mostly women, children, and the elderly, and they increasingly bore the brunt of the war that swirled around them. They fled the Communist-held "liberated zones" and contested areas and built makeshift huts near government-held towns, highways, or outposts or vegetated in dismal and stifling refugee centers or, like Miss Bay, chanced an uncertain existence in the towns and cities.

Typically, most women and children were noncombatants and thus were protected under international law. Yet even as noncombatants, women often performed important and widespread unarmed support functions for both sides. An estimated 1.43 million noncombatant casualties occurred in South Vietnam during the Americanizing of the war from 1965 to 1973. Civilian deaths in the North and South represented anywhere from 28 to 45 percent of the total war dead.[6]

Women, who constituted up to 70 percent of the population in some safer hamlets, were performing the jobs of building the shelters and planting and harvesting the rice. Many women were widows, some of them remarried. In one village the widow of a Viet Cong guerrilla married a government soldier. Some women became second wives of married men who were sometimes Viet Cong cadres, although they had to keep the relationship hush-hush for fear of being reprimanded by the Party.[7]

"Degrees of Shock or Horror" from Deadly Firepower

The results of U.S. and South Vietnamese shellings and bombings were not consistently followed up on by ground sweeps. But in spring 1966 paratroopers of the U.S. 101st Airborne Division reacted with "degrees of shock or horror" when they came upon the results of American artillery bombardment and Skyraider bombings in the jungled mountains infested with the Ninety-fifth North Vietnamese Regiment and Viet Cong locals outside of Tuy Hoa, the bustling province capital I had visited in 1962. Despite the paratroopers' macho history, a nineteen-year-old airborne artilleryman, Micheal Clodfelter, described the scenes of death and mayhem he saw outside of Tuy Hoa on Operation Van Buren, which was

22. A weeping mother holds her child, killed in an air strike that preceded the recapture of Dong Xoai by South Vietnamese Rangers, June 1965. Hundreds of villagers were caught in fierce fighting after the Viet Cong swept into the village. After two days of bloody fighting, casualties were high on both sides, including many civilians. (AP Photo)

designed to protect rice harvesting but had been prepped by howitzer bombardment and airplane bombing.[8] His scenes of horror included "the bodies of a Vietnamese woman and her baby, clutched firmly to her breast in the havoc of death, lying among several other corpses. . . . Even more pitiful was the sight of a blood-spattered Vietnamese mother holding tightly her wailing four-year-old daughter whose left arm had been blown off by a grenade thrown by one of the infantryman sweeping a burned-out village."[9]

Villagers were often unprepared to survive such surprise bombardments, and the Viet Cong defended themselves by going underground in trenches and bunkers. The 173rd Airborne, in an operation during the week of March 17, 1966, was told by one captured prisoner that they had unknowingly trampled over a tunnel complex where beneath them four hundred Viet Cong were huddled. As the U.S. troops advanced, they found a Viet Cong–controlled hamlet, complete with several miles of trench lines and tunnels around it. "The commies had their own little village in the jungle," one paratrooper exclaimed to me, "with their wives, pigs, chickens, and plenty of rice to stay alive."

I obtained a captured Viet Cong diary that gave me a snapshot of life — and death — in tunnels for the guerrillas, among whom were several women buried alive after one bombardment in the 125-square-mile, heavily forested Iron Triangle 20 miles northwest of Saigon. "Have spent four days in tunnel," Tran Bang wrote shortly after two o'clock one hot afternoon. "About 8,000 to 9,000 Americans soldiers were in a sweep operation. The attack was fierce." A number of underground tunnels collapsed, and it was not known what became of sisters Ba, Bay, Hong Hanh, and Tan Ho inside these tunnels. In his last diary entry, made at 2:45 p.m. on January 11, 1966, Tran Bang described life for male and female guerrillas: "Oh! What hard days, one has to stay in a tunnel, eat cold rice with salt, and drink unboiled water! However, one is free and feels at ease."

Women on the government side were also often caught in the fierce combat. Wives and children of the Civilian Irregular Defense Forces usually lived with their husbands in precariously isolated outposts and suffered with them from Communist shellings or ground attacks. I traveled to the Special Forces' Duc Lap outpost in the jungled highlands near the Cambodian border to interview Capt. Hoang Kim Bao shortly after an estimated 3,000 North Vietnamese troops had attacked the 250 camp defenders and shot down two helicopters and a U.S. fighter jet. Captain Bao smiled broadly and conceded that his wife had helped him during the ferocious sixty-five-hour battle that raged around the embattled outpost, beginning August 23, 1968. "She helped me with the radio transmissions," he explained, "because at the beginning my headquarters had only six other men. Then four were wounded, and two were killed, and . . . so my wife took over the radio." With them were their seven children, ranging in age from twelve to seven months. "My children hid in the bunkers and waited." None of the children became a casualty, but the captain was wounded.[10]

Refugees Caused by Draining the Water from Guerrilla Fish

By March 1966 it was clear to me that a refugee crisis loomed. Then about 6 percent of Vietnam's fifteen million population were refugees, of which half were existing in the government's spartan, stifling refugee camps. The war itself — from Communist attacks to American–South Vietnamese counterattacks, bombing, and shelling raids — had created a large influx of the refugees, mostly in the northern provinces, where North Vietnamese units were based and where the war was most intense. Because of the war, roads were cut, and supplies for refugees were difficult to transport. U.S. aircraft could rush in emergency goods — but not all the essentials because ammunition had to be given top priority. (The war over time would produce about 6.5 million refugees in the South, or about 40 percent of the population.)[11]

The refugee problem was "a bucket of worms — and each worm is a different problem," a veteran American social welfare expert explained to me in 1966. "The main problem is still security, and underneath that you have a long list of others — transportation and logistics, education, medical facilities."

By 1968, when allied search-and-destroy operations were failing to wear down the Communist forces significantly enough, General West-moreland wrote a memorandum labeled "The Refugee Problem," dated January 4, 1968. In it Westmoreland alluded to and countered Mao's fish-in-the-water metaphor by suggesting the best approach was to drain the people (the water), to recapture them at another location, and thus to allow the fish (the Viet Cong) "to strangle." Within weeks a bloody Communist offensive and its aftermath caused Westmoreland to launch his draining-the-water tactics, which would prove disastrous for villag-ers by accelerating the depopulation of the countryside and increasing the number of refugees. Whether premeditated or not, according to a historian, Westmoreland's draining-the-water tactic "directed an unprec-edented level of violence at the villages," led to "a catastrophically high level of civilian casualties," "and raises questions of moral accountability for U.S. commanders."[12]

Thus, Westmoreland's war of attrition was morphing into what his severest U.S. critics described as a "strategy of annihilation."[13] In Saigon pro-Communist sympathizers and propagandists argued that the war was exterminating the Vietnamese race, implying the Americans were at fault. Some went so far as to link extermination of the Vietnamese with the earlier subjugation of the Native Americans in the American West. By December 1967 some Vietnamese told a U.S.-funded public opinion survey team that the real aim of the Americans was "the extermination of as many Vietnamese as possible." In the Mekong Delta a rumor circulated among the educated elite that the United States was deliberately prolong-ing the war in order "to provide an outlet for its surplus production."[14]

Depopulating the countryside also brought major problems for the Viet Cong. A scholar notes they lost contact with the women's associa-tions and other groups that were their foundation for mobilizing the rural population and thus "were left without a source of protection and supply, and even without a mission."[15]

Womanization amid the Made-by-Men War

Throughout the war Vietnamese women remained largely nameless, with several exceptions. One notable exception was Madame Nhu, Diem's fiery sister-in-law, who had worsened tensions by accusing the Buddhist protestors of being infiltrated by Communists and denigrating the bonzes' self-immolations, much to the disgust of Washington and much of the world.[16] Before that crisis I interviewed Madame Nhu at the palace and found her alluring in an elegant silk *ao dai* tailored snugly to fit provocatively over her bosom. She was busily organizing "Women's Day" to honor two legendary sisters, Trung Trac and Trung Nhi, who in 39 BC had called the people to revolt against the cruel Chinese governor and "within a short time captured 65 citadels and proclaimed themselves queens."[17] When they were defeated two years later, they committed suicide by drowning, thus ushering in nine hundred years of Chinese rule. I sensed that Madame Nhu was trying to lead a modern-day charge against another invasion from the North.

As I left, she handed me a sheath of black-and-white photos of her benevolent-looking family. I viewed her as the most significant female in the upper echelons of the U.S. or Saigon governments during the entire war. Later she bitterly blamed the United States for complicity in overthrowing Diem and assassinating him and her husband, which occurred while she was in Europe. She lived in Rome, dropping from the spotlight because she charged exorbitant rates for interviews. But in a 1966 interview with a French journalist she reversed her anti-Communist stand, proposed a conference with the Communists to end the Vietnam War, and bitterly criticized Americans for their "liberty of the jungle, which profits only the wealthy, only the powerful, and only the arrogant — that is to say, the Americans themselves." Since Diem's overthrow, she inveighed, the United States had built up an expeditionary force and are making "punitive expeditions, as if against the Apaches."[18]

Also attracting wide, if momentary, public attention was Mrs. Nguyen Cao Ky. I profiled her in 1966 wearing a black flight suit to match that of her husband, who was then premier and a pilot who had commanded the Vietnamese air force; they were often dubbed "Captain and Mrs. Midnight." A former Air Vietnam stewardess and beauty queen, she called herself the "Grace Kelly of Vietnam." Besides beauty, she also had a lucky horoscope that supposedly predestined her to boost her husband

23. Women played an important role in the Viet Cong, as shown in this photograph printed from a roll of film taken from a dead pro-Communist soldier in the mid-1960s. (Courtesy of James Pickerell)

into leading the country and to be protected from a Viet Cong mortar that fell fifty feet from her bedroom window in their unpretentious villa at Tan Son Nhut Airport in early 1966. Six months later she was unhurt when a Vietnamese fighter-bomber crashed one hundred yards from her front door.[19]

On the Communist side I investigated and described Mrs. Nguyen Thi Dinh, who would go on to represent the National Liberation Front at the Paris peace talks beginning in 1968. In 1966 she was the forty-five-year-old deputy commander of the Communist-led Viet Cong Armed Forces; no commander in chief had been named, so her appointment seemed designed to gain women's support. She possessed a hard-earned track record of pro-Communist activism. At ten she was carrying messages to the Communists from her elder brother. At twenty-six she helped supply weapons and ammunition to pro-Communists fighting the French colonialists. According to her official biography read over Hanoi Radio, after 1954 she was in constant hiding from government forces — at times sleeping in bushes. She says she sometimes escaped capture by donning

the garb of Buddhist nuns and hiding in secret bunkers in Buddhist pagodas in the delta. She became an international celebrity in Communist
circles for spearheading an uprising in 1960 in Ben Tre in the Mekong
Delta, where she was born.[20]

March of the "Long-Haired Troops"

As the North Vietnamese and the American accelerated their buildup
of forces and the violence and pace of the war intensified, women were
playing increasingly vital roles on both sides. Women were serving the
Viet Cong in a wide array of combat and support functions. One Viet
Cong woman who had defected told me that she had heard about one
all-female platoon made up of fighters and commanded by a woman.
"They were dressed in green fatigues and were hard-core units," she told
me. She said other women sewed uniforms and Viet Cong flags, some
served in the medical corps of women, and some worked in liaison teams
carrying messages secretly. The Viet Cong's female political cadres helped
to found the women's associations in the villages, she continued, adding,
"These female political cadres round up the women in the village, talk
to them, and help organize their elections for village leaders." They also
urged young men to join the Viet Cong. "Sometimes the women put the
secret messages on the bottom of fish sauce [*nuoc mam*] jars and simply
walk through the Saigon government check points," she continued. "How
can they be discovered?"

One singer, Nguyen Thi Nga — which means "Miss Moon" — told
me how she had been recruited by the Viet Cong when she was only
thirteen and that two of her elder brothers were serving with the Viet
Cong. She first acted as a liaison; then she applied to be a singer for a
Viet Cong village cultural group. She was taught to sing such songs as
"Victory over the American Aggressors" and "The People in the North
or in the South Are Living in the Same House." Accompanied by guitars
and mandolins, she and her theatrical group entertained villagers and
guerrillas on special occasions.

I was taken aback by the ingenious ways Viet Cong women had devised
for smuggling and sabotage. Peasant women were reported entering Saigon

with grenades inside the buns of their hairdos. Others had plastic explosives and mines in false bottoms of the wooden buckets in which they toted fresh fruit. One Vietnamese typist inside a U.S. compound was captured with poison hidden inside a packet of cigarettes, which she planned to use to kill Americans. Another Vietnamese woman entering a U.S. billet compound was captured with a plastic explosive in her girdle.[21] For decades these female insurgents were dubbed the "long-haired troops."[22] In mid-1968 I learned that pro-Communist women were also urged and directed by the Party to "foster hatred" in the cities and towns, indicating that they were to spark the next phase of Communist political attempts to incite urban disturbances and to induce government soldiers to defect.[23]

In one of their first search-and-destroy operations thirty-five miles north of Saigon, Americans with the 173rd Airborne Brigade told me of their astonishment when three Vietnamese women started lobbing white phosphorous grenades at them. "I wasn't going to shoot them," a veteran American paratrooper explained. "But when they started throwing grenades at us, they were part of the enemy. It doesn't bother me to see dead women — I saw a lot of them in Korea. But it made the young paratroopers sick to shoot women."[24]

By May 1968 I used interviews with reliable sources and a captured document made public by a U.S. agency in Saigon to report on the more intensified womanization of Viet Cong work. In Long An Province, south of Saigon, I discovered that a recent U.S. air-mobile operation had killed two female guerrillas and captured six others on the battlefield. A U.S. Army officer exclaimed to me, "One of them was toting a sixty-five-pound minigun taken from an American helicopter, can you feature that!"

If captured, women were subject to the heinous torture inflicted on male suspects by both sides. Peasant woman Le Ly Hayslip describes witnessing the torture of a naked Vietnamese woman in an early version of waterboarding, considered to be torture and thus illegal by legal authorities since at least World War II.[25] Hanging by her feet from a rope and pulley, the naked woman with her hands tied behind her back was dunked into a bucket of soapy water. "For a moment her pale body bucked and squirmed like a fish on a line, then went still and the soldier raised her up," Hayslip recounts. "She blew soapy water from her mouth and nose and shook her head, flinging water around the room." She gasped noisily but did not scream. "They simply dunked her again and again."[26]

On the government side well-educated women in flowing *ao dais* eagerly signed up to join the Women's Armed Forces Corps (WAFC, pronounced *wafsee*) — a job paying the equivalent of ten dollars a month. More than a thousand had been trained in an expanded program, to which two U.S. WAC advisors were assigned, and a stepped-up effort was under way. Members of the WAFC served as security control guards to supplement Vietnamese police or as interpreters, clerk typists, social workers to counsel the families of the war dead or wounded, and assistants in schools or in food and clothing distribution centers. They received the same pay and had the same promotion and allowance scale as men; they were eligible for allowances that almost doubled their monthly take-home pay. Widows or daughters of soldiers received priority for enlistment, which was highly coveted. As Maj. Kathleen Wilkes of Cobbtown, Georgia, advisor to the Vietnamese commander, explained, "The whole Vietnamese economy is geared for war, and this is an honorable profession for educated women from good families." After the Diem coup some peasant-class women were organized and trained by Catholic or Buddhists leaders to fight to defend their homes in scattered hamlets.[27]

The number of U.S. military women who served in Vietnam over the years ranged from 7,500 to 11,000; most were nurses.[28]

The Rich Get Richer and the Poor Get Poorer

The growing devastation and depopulation of the countryside sharpened the contrast between rural Vietnamese women and the wealthy Saigon housewife. Because women usually but quietly managed the family finances, as well as much of the retail trade in shops and market stalls, the rich Saigon housewife worried about the price of rice and milk; the rural woman had rice but was worried about how long she could hold it before being forced to use it to pay off Viet Cong or government troops. The high-class Saigon housewife fretted about getting her children into Saigon's expensive, exclusive French-run schools; the young rural mother wondered how long it would be before her spartan village school was damaged. The upper-class Saigon housewife was an expert in real estate, especially renting to Americans; the rural woman was an expert on building underground bomb shelters.

The U.S. buildup helped to buoy up a privileged class in the cities. To the wealthy housewife diamonds were her best friend. She bought them not for rings but to stash them away in a biscuit box — the literal equivalent of an American hiding money in an old sock — or as a safeguard against the rising inflation or, if necessary, to be hand-carried out of the country more quickly and easily than gold, dollars, or francs. I learned firsthand how the lives of Saigonese of all classes were being ensnared by the war. In one frightening experience I was awakened about three in the morning by police knocking on my front door and demanding to view the identification papers of the live-in maid, Sinh. She had helped me for years, doing the cooking, cleaning, and laundry, but had no papers registering her as living at my place. As she was being carted off to the police station, I insisted on tagging along, staring at the haughty police official as we went by and fuming away in a dank room until Sinh was released the next morning.

The arrival of American troops brought U.S. dollars, which accelerated the inflationary spiral in the Vietnamese economy and thus increased the worries and uncertainties for women buyers. The GI-produced spiral added to the earlier inflation caused by the Viet Cong's frequent cutting of roads and canals and strangling control of the countryside, which automatically increased the price of rice, shrimp, and other foodstuffs from the provinces. To sop up this tsunami of money, U.S. aid experts imported luxury items from electronic gear to high-priced cameras that stocked stores and the black market but led to sharpening the worlds and tensions between the haves and the have-nots. Meanwhile, I saw the streets in the towns and cities become overflowing with hungry-eyed urchins, beggar boys, and the disabled. Elderly widows, traditionally venerated and cared for by their eldest sons, pleaded for a handout near Saigon's graceful tamarind trees. Before my very eyes the war was morphing the mystique of Vietnam into a heartbreaking holocaust.

The Makings of a "Brothel Society"

The U.S. troop buildup brought an unsavory buildup of bars and brothels. Along the main streets of the urban centers, Vietnamese saw their quiet, relaxed way of life dramatically give way to GI entertainment establishments. Singers in elegant *ao dais* who had crooned melodies in French such as "Non, Je Ne Regrette Rien" (I Have No Regrets) in sedate supper clubs gave way to raucous rock 'n' roll music blaring in disco parlors. Along Saigon's main street of Tu Do (Freedom), bars and garish hotels, called "short-time brothels," mushroomed. Whirling past bars and brothels along Saigon's boulevard, a Vietnamese taxi driver sputtered in disgust: "This is not America. This is America-*caca.*" *Caca* in French baby-talk means "excrement."[29]

The almost instant opportunity for a young rural girl to earn a living or at least survive in the cities marked one of the important social transformations of Vietnamese womanhood. It meant escape from rural or low-class life, from traditional cultural values, or from the fear of death or maiming. But it was often a near-poverty, sordid existence. Like Miss Bay, young women from the provinces, who a few years earlier had come to Saigon as housemaids, began shifting to work as bar girls and waitresses in restaurants. Middle-class Saigon housewives complained they could no longer find maids, housekeepers, or babysitters.

To the U.S. and South Vietnamese governments the bars and prostitutes presented security and political problems. In 1966, when Premier Nguyen Cao Ky proposed legalizing prostitution so as to bring it under a measure of control, both Saigon intellectuals and Hanoi's radio attacked him as a "pimp for the Americans." U.S. officials also blanched at the thought of legalized prostitution because of repercussions at home, including perhaps congressional investigations. Medically, a high rate of venereal disease developed. In one random catch of forty-four bar girls in the U.S. Marine Corps enclave in Danang, twenty-one had venereal disease. (By 1969 prostitutes would total six hundred thousand; one researcher noted that they were being checked medically, but venereal disease was so epidemic that by 1972 they were inflicting far more casualties, albeit less serious ones, than were the quarter million Vietnamese Communist fighters.)[30]

A bar girl's ambition was to become a bar owner — which she called being a businesswoman. For some it was not difficult. One very successful bar girl saved one million piastres (roughly ten thousand dollars) within a two-year period. Less successful bar girls complained, however, that by the time they paid off the bar owners and the police for protection, they had less than five thousand piastres (fifty dollars) a month left. As one bar girl calculated, "It's better to be a prostitute to one American man for ten thousand piastres a month until he goes home."

Intelligence information flowed as easily as liquor. "You must know the Viet Cong have a cell in every block in town, in every bar and in every restaurant," one reliable security source told me. "The waiters or the doormen or the bar girls — someone has to be Viet Cong, or the bar would not be allowed to exist." One bar girl confided: "Oh, the Americans tell us everything. They even tell us where they'll build new installations so we can buy up the land in that section."

The U.S. image was tarnished by the flourishing trade of what the Communists called "decadence." One American official, witnessing the mad rush of drunken GIs and bar girls for cyclos and taxis at the curfew hour in Saigon, groaned: "The American image here is terrific! These poor fellows lose the war in Saigon but die to win it in the provinces."

Gradually, the resentments of the Vietnamese population were ripe to be exploited by Buddhists using nationalist and religious arguments as well as by Communists. In sharp contrast with the made-for-Americans bars and brothels, one historian notes, Vietnamese traditional culture and Communist policy in the countryside were puritanical. Communists linked the expectation in traditional culture that women should be chaste when they married to the political purity of the Party. Cadres who embarrassed their party by having mistresses or second wives or scandals involving sex were disciplined, which could include expulsion from the Party. Male cadres were expected to set a good moral example and to maintain harmonious relations with women, whom they had to count on for support and sustenance.[31]

Communist leaders sought to implement and enforce one long-standing admonition voiced to me by a Saigon intellectual: "The Vietnamese peasant is very simple. Don't steal his rice or his chickens; don't touch his wife or daughters. Once you've done that, you've lost."

By the time the U.S. troop withdrawal was under way in 1971, a stalwart anti-Communist writer, Tran Thuc Linh, would launch a critical attack in a Saigon newspaper on the "brothel society." Describing Vietnamese government officials as a "gang of prostitutes," he concluded, "No foreign power can force us to become a Brothel Society."[32]

"Cruel Fate, to Mourn All Women in Soul-Rending Strains"

I sensed that many Vietnamese women's unsung stories of death, destruction, or heartbreak could easily match Vietnam's epic poem *Tale of Kieu*, originally titled as "New Cries from a Broken Heart."[33] Written around 1800 by Nguyen Du, "the greatest Vietnamese poet of all times," Kieu's tale draws on the imagery and symbolism of classical Chinese writings and history and is so etched into Vietnam's culture that Vietnamese ranging from illiterates to Ho Chi Minh often recited some couplets by heart.

Like a fairytale, the *Tale* begins happily by describing Kieu as melancholy yet so exquisitely beautiful that "a glance or two from her, and cities rocked!" Very talented, she could paint, rhyme, sing, and play the lute and, although only sixteen years old, had already composed a tune called "Cruel Fate, to Mourn All Women in Soul-Rending Strains." In the tale she meets "a youthful scholar" carrying "half a bagful of love poems." It was love at first sight:

> Beautiful girl and talented young man —
> What their hearts felt, their eyes still dared not say.
> They stood entranced, half waking, half in dream.[34]

Then, not unlike the unannounced shellings and bombardments in death zones, Kieu is struck by "disasters that come flying on the wind."[35] The youthful lovers, who had vowed to marry, are forced to separate. When her father and brother are arrested and tortured, Kieu puts filial piety to her family above her own love and sells herself as a concubine to get money for their release. For the next fifteen years she roves "a hostile world — a duckweed cut adrift, the toy of waves." Instead of a concubine, she winds up several times in brothels, where owners sold "their painted dolls twelve months a year,"[36] then as a second wife, then as Flower the Slave, who endured thirty lashes with bamboo rods and then her own two suicidal near-deaths. Kieu was purchased from one brothel by a revolutionary warrior, whom she loved deeply, but "then he had to go and like some trash throw down his life upon the battlefield!"[37] Kieu mourned all women, including herself, who are doomed "to a life of wind and dust."

Yet the *Tale* ends happily. Kieu is miraculously located by her first love and her family. Her denigrations are erased by the primary virtue of filial piety to her family and her steadfastness to her first love. In an observation made by the *Tale*'s translator that is especially applicable to Vietnamese women in the war years of the 1960s, Kieu's epic "manages to project one stark, readily recognizable image about Vietnam — the picture of a society of victims, of people punished for crimes and sins they did not commit."[38] Also resonating during the war, a Vietnamese professor writes, "Kieu is Vietnam itself: beautiful, talented, often condemned to a 'pale fate' by external forces beyond its control or comprehension."[39]

O, cruel fate for Vietnam! As the woeful Kieu foretold: "No longer can the harm done be undone."[40]

9

"Destroy the Town to Save It"

Militarily, Vietnam is a war without a front line. Politically, the front line is everywhere. The front line is in the heart of every Vietnamese. Each Vietnamese has a crisis of conscience — should he support the anti-Communist Americans or should he support his own people, the Vietnamese, even if they are Communist.

Vietnamese intellectual whom I interviewed in mid-1967

We should expect our gains of 1967 to be increased manifold in 1968. . . . Our forces have been able to detect impending major offensives and to mount spoiling attacks.

Gen. William C. Westmoreland, January 1, 1968

In mid-1966 I trudged alongside marines conducting Operation Hastings, one of the biggest of the war up till then, as they met stiff resistance with North Vietnam's heavily armed 324B Division, which had infiltrated across the Demilitarized Zone. I was making notes and interviews for gathering non-deadline-type dispatches I wanted to file in about a week when I was told the *Herald Tribune* would settle its labor strike in New York and again begin publishing. Before Hastings ended on August 3, I called my associate An in Saigon; he told me a cable from the *Trib* stated it had ceased to publish.

I was dismayed to lose my New York news outlet. More than sending me a regular retainer, the *Trib* had given my dispatches eye-catching treatment by using splashy layouts, big photographs, and more prominent display than the teensy headlines being used by the sedate *New York Times*. A full-page advertisement, for example, previewed my six-part series in mid-1965 under the heading: "What's a Nice Girl Like Beverly Deepe Doing in a Dirty War Like This? Covering It for the *Herald Tribune*."

The ad described me as one of Saigon's best-informed Western correspondents and included a quote from a *Time* magazine article: "What she does not know she can usually get from her two Vietnamese assistants, both wise in the labyrinth ways of the country's politics." That series explained why the Viet Cong guerrillas fought so hard, how the United States was failing to use its political power, how corruption and land reform were hot issues, and how some U.S. economic aid was succeeding. The third article — on the rampant corruption in the U.S-backed Vietnamese government — was published on June 1, my thirtieth birthday, not a bad present, I thought. After the glitzy spread in the daily, the series was then republished as the first two pages of a four-page special school edition.[1] The *Trib*'s demise meant that I had come full circle, back to freelancing, where I had started four years earlier.

Déjà Vu: Eviction, Freelancing

Then another déjà vu experience hit me. I was evicted from my mahogany-hued log cabin when the French lumber company owning it ended my lease. I went to court to contest the eviction but lost. With the influx of Americans apartments were hard to find, but An succeeded in securing a second-floor walk-up in a drab concrete building at 38 Vo Tanh, a mile or so from the telegraph office, U.S. Embassy, and palace.

My kitty and I were the last to vacate my charming log cabin. The silvery Siamese and I had luxuriated in my two-story office-cum-apartment and in the tennis court of a yard of perfumed frangipani. The kitten had been given to me when it was so small it fit into the palm of my hand. It had become a delightful companion, meowing happily to greet me when I used my gigantic black key to unlock the front door. I talked to and with it all the time — and it actually meowed back. Now we were off to a less enchanting place.

My associate Vuong warned me that we would not be able to catch a taxi if the driver saw the cat, which was a bad luck omen of monstrous proportions (dogs were good luck). As the spindly Vuong flagged a taxi, I gently tucked my fuzz ball into a tote and squeezed the bag gingerly as we journeyed through traffic across town to the congested central market area. Arriving in front of the building, I was paying off the driver when No Name popped her head out from my tote like a terrified jack-in-the-box. Infuriated that my kitty would bring him bad luck, the driver swore at us. Later, when I was on a field trip, No Name mysteriously disappeared.

My new place was quite a comedown. About the size of three Ping-Pong tables, it had flimsy chairs, a twin-sized mattress on the floor, no refrigeration. My bamboo desk was sawed down so it could be squeezed in. An arranged for piles of press releases, reports, and newspapers I had accumulated to be moved in and stacked to cover one wall from the floor almost to the ceiling.

After the closure of the *Trib*, I floundered for the next year, losing a lot of time in trying to find other publications to write for. Freelancing was more difficult than it had been four years earlier because, with the buildup of U.S. troops, so many more correspondents had come to Vietnam. I was just getting nicely settled in my new home-cum-office — while surviving on an iffy income — when on December 1, 1967, I became the *Christian Science Monitor's* resident correspondent, giving me for the first time in eighteen months a regular and most welcome paycheck.

Before beginning as a special correspondent, I flew to Boston to confer with the editors of the United States' unique metropolitan newspaper. Although founded in 1908 by the Christian Science Church, it was not a religious newspaper. It had been started as a means to give readers serious news about the world, much as Adolph S. Ochs envisioned in 1896, when he launched the informational model of the *New York Times*. Often described as an international daily newspaper with, as one scholar notes, "a foreign news service that was unusually good," the *Monitor* was also published (except on Sunday) and distributed more generally nationwide than any other daily in the 1960s because of its several regional printing centers and five editions, including one in London.[2] Editors wanted air-expressed "durable" dispatches that would be timely for three days, but I could cable through Reuters within a limited word length. One editor alerted me that the newspaper did not want "a lot of chitchat from GIs" or details about gory battles because, he said, it was hard to draw any significance "from death scenes."

After these conferences I wrote an eighteen-page letter to An, saying that I was amazed at how pleased the editors were with the handful of stories I had sent them as a freelancer, especially because the articles focused on Vietnamese, rather than Americans. Managing editor Courtney Sheldon told me: "When I saw them, I couldn't wait to get my hands on them. You'd think we'd never have gotten dispatches from Saigon before. Almost all were on page 1." Overseas editor Henry Hayward chimed in: "On Page 1 with monotonous regularity."[3] As we talked, our dispatch about the war without a front line was being typeset.[4]

General Westmoreland's Wee Bit of Wishful Thinking

In November General Westmoreland had told Congress and a National Press Club audience that the Communist forces were being defeated so dramatically that U.S. troops could begin withdrawing within two years. Ambassador Ellsworth Bunker then also told a national television audience: "I think we are beginning to see light at the end of the tunnel,"[5] and Westmoreland echoed Bunker's optimism.[6] (Unknowingly, Bunker and Westmoreland were echoing French general Henri Navarre, speaking in 1953: "A year ago none of us could see victory. Now we can see it clearly, like light at the end of the tunnel."[7] A year later the garrison at Dien Bien Phu fell to Communist fighters, ending the French Indochina War.)

I considered this official U.S. optimism to be based on a wee bit of wishful thinking. Westmoreland was largely describing the reduction of Communist main force units but overlooking the more numerous local guerrillas and population-based forces that undergirded the people's war.[8]

Despite official U.S. optimism, I was getting jittery about what would happen during the approaching Vietnamese New Year of the Monkey beginning January 30, 1968. The three of us were working long hours, with An and Vuong monitoring daily and decoding arcane rhetoric of Communist pronouncements, talking with their wide networks of contacts, and studying documents captured by allied forces. As I wrote for the *Monitor*, we began picking up from Saigon sources apprehensions about street fighting, economic strikes, blackouts of electricity, violent anti-American demonstrations, air bases ablaze from rocket attacks and suicide squads, and Viet Cong shellings of Saigon and other cities. These sources feared the Communists would use political intimidation and uprisings in the urban centers as well as Soviet-made rocket fire from the suburbs. We heard that in Can Tho, a province capital in the Mekong Delta, the Viet Cong had warned housewives to stockpile nonperishable foods in preparation for an attack within three months.

More sensational, in mid-January 1968 we learned that Viet Cong financial cadres were telling their taxpayers: "This is the last year you'll have to pay taxes to us. Next year you can pay your taxes to the coalition government in Saigon." The names of those refusing to pay up were often turned over to Viet Cong assassination squads.[9] Captured Communist documents we were collecting no longer talked of "total victory" — such as militarily "pushing the Americans into the sea" — but instead pressed for a "decisive victory" that welded military attacks to a political-economic uprising coordinated for a critical moment.[10]

To facilitate the Vietnamese New Year family celebrations called "Tet," the Communists and the South Vietnamese government declared a cease-fire. The South Vietnamese government and the United States announced a thirty-six-hour cease-fire beginning January 28 through January 31, and Hanoi announced a seven-day cease-fire to begin the evening of their celebrations, on January 28.[11]

Motor Scootering into Viet Cong Country

I took advantage of the lull in fighting and undertook my gutsiest, if not imprudent, self-selected assignment. On January 29, as Saigonese were boarding up their shops, as family celebrations were beginning, and when for the first time in years firecrackers were being ignited, I was on the back of a motor scooter driven by another Western correspondent. We glided at dusk along the paved superhighway northwest of Saigon, skirting the province capital of Bien Hoa, and then skimmed onto more obscure trails, eventually passing row upon row of stately trees.

We were off to conduct a rare interview with Viet Cong political leaders and guerrillas at a French-owned rubber plantation, nestled in an oasis of serenity, a cadre told us, because the United States avoided bombing it.[12] I wanted to give readers a firsthand glimpse into the lifestyle and mind-set of Viet Cong political cadres and guerrillas, vital information because Vuong, who had grown up in China, often reminded me of the wisdom of ancient strategist Sun Tzu: "If you know neither the enemy nor yourself, you will succumb in every battle."[13]

Our visit had been cleared by a veteran Communist Party liaison who greeted us and guided us along a path between a double row of Vietnamese plantation workers' concrete homes, which resembled those of rural France but were obscured by a sea of rubber trees. With a red-checkered scarf tossed casually over his shoulder, this thirty-eight-year-old senior cadre recounted that he had joined the Communist-led forces when he was nineteen to fight against the French and after 1954 had served as a province-level cadre specializing in trade unions and plantations. As he poured tea from a canteen, he told us he was the son of a tenant farmer and was married with two children but had not seen his wife for fourteen years. He described himself as a revolutionary with a mobile lifestyle who leads a "very simple life," receiving no salary but existing on seven piastres a day for food and using hammocks for sleeping. Surprisingly, he represented both the South Vietnamese government–approved trade union and the pro-Communist National Liberation Front, evidencing that a Viet Cong supporter or sympathizer had penetrated the government's own legal labor union.

We entered a drab concrete building that was austerely furnished with tables and chairs. One small table held several kerosene lamps that shed the only light in the room. I raised my eyebrows when I spied the table decorated with a bouquet of plastic asters in a vase and eight marigolds in a Fritos chip can. Above the table hung the Viet Cong flag — red and blue horizontal stripes with a gold star in the middle — attached to a faded wall curtain depicting scenes of rural France. Around the flag, arranged in a pentagon, hung five small paper banners in pastel colors, one reading "Long Live the National Liberation Front of South Vietnam," another reading "In the New Year, we wish President Ho a Long Life," and next to it "Long Live the Lao Dong Party," North Vietnam's Communist Party.

A diverse crowd sauntered in. About twenty guerrillas in uniforms ranging from green fatigues to turquoise trousers entered, including three females dressed in black pajama-like garb and Ho Chi Minh sandals made of rubber tires. All were bearing weapons, including Soviet-made rifles nearly as big as the soldiers carrying them. The last to enter was the statuesque overseer of a plantation section, who looked majestic in his Mao-collared gown of satiny royal blue embossed with flying phoenixes and dragons. The celebration was for invited guests, including representatives and members of the Saigon government–approved plantation trade union!

We arrived in time to usher in the New Year, interestingly on Hanoi time, or one hour earlier than Saigon time. Guerrillas carried in three radios that blared a high-pitched song on the clandestine Liberation Radio and then on Radio Hanoi. As chiming clocks struck midnight in Hanoi, everyone in the room stood up. For several seconds firecrackers reverberated over the radio; the North Vietnamese national anthem was played. North Vietnamese Ho Chi Minh spoke and ended, as was customary, with a poem he had composed for the occasion, proclaiming: "This spring is different from others;/More victories are coming."

After fifteen minutes the radio was turned off, and an hour-long songfest began. An eighteen-year-old female walked to the head of the table to sing — and promptly and completely disappeared. She had fallen feet first into a bunker, deep enough to hide her head. Unhurt, she sprang up and sang about going to the market to buy material for embroidering flowers and swallows for her lover so that he would remember her. Finally, the host moved to the head of the table and announced, "This year will see victory, cost what it may." The celebration ended at 1:15 a.m., Hanoi time.

Then, during a four-hour interview, the host gave us no big news but reiterated that the Communists sought negotiations leading to a coalition government favoring them. He added that cadres and guerrillas of the National Liberation Front were moving with the population into towns and cities as refugees to escape the dangers of allied firepower. Not surprisingly, the host was critical of the allies, saying that the American fighters were called "flesh targets" because they were so big they were easy to aim at. He acknowledged U.S. troops had done much for the people — like handing out medicines, food, and candies — but lacking a uniform policy, he said, they cannot win over the population by distributing medicines here but bombing people there.

Motor scootering back to Saigon the next morning, little did I realize that as I was witnessing this slice of celebratory activity ushering in the Year of the Monkey on Hanoi time, pro-Communists forces were breaking their cease-fire in the South and unfurling their Tet Offensive for their "decisive victory."

The Shock and Awe of Tet

By the time I had returned to Saigon and was preparing to write up my supposed-to-be scoop, a far more dramatic story was unfolding at the very doorstep of Saigon journalists and U.S. officialdom. The Tet holiday called for the light and noise of firecrackers to drive out evil spirits; although banned in previous years, they were again permitted by the Saigon government and were lavishly ignited by officials at the U.S. Embassy. Viet Cong sappers and guerrillas used these firecrackers as a cover for their stealth attacks.

About three in the morning on January 31, as fireworks exploded throughout the city, a nineteen-man Viet Cong suicide squad in civilian clothes blasted through the wall surrounding the U.S. Embassy, situated near the office-residences of many journalists (except mine). The $2.6 million, snow-white U.S. Embassy, dedicated only five months earlier, was rocketed and assaulted by enough Communists to require helicoptering in a platoon of the elite 101st Airborne Division, which landed on the rooftop of the six-story building. Wire services were cabling bulletins that the Viet Cong had blasted their way into and seized the supposedly invulnerable embassy, based on information provided by U.S. guards. TV crews were shipping their dramatic footage to Tokyo, where it was transmitted unedited to New York.

I could not add facts to the wire stories — and the facts in these initial stories were denounced as being inaccurate; the Viet Cong had entered the walls surrounding the compound but not the building itself, as newsmen had reported. The embassy blast stunned Americans and the White House because of Westmoreland's and Bunker's earlier light-at-the-end-of-the-tunnel optimism. In New York a shocked Walter Cronkite at CBS read the incoming wire copy about the offensive and exclaimed: "What the hell is going on? I thought we were winning this war!"[14]

The embassy attack was but a sliver of the Communist blitz — the German word for *lightning*. I was swept along by the chaos engulfing Saigon and was working furiously to cable. Tan Son Nhut, just about the world's busiest and best-defended airport and site of the headquarters of Westmoreland's command, was subjected to pitched battles, mortar fire, sniper siege, and guerrilla raids. Communists donning government soldiers' fatigues attacked the South Vietnamese High Command.

I noted that American servicemen in Saigon were bottled up in their billets for days, ordered to remain there for fear of the grave political consequences of an anti-American incident as well as the Communist menace. For days U.S. troopers and airmen who were ordinarily frontline fighters spent their time listening to rock 'n' roll music and writing letters home. Militarily, the Communist forces could never have defeated so many U.S. servicemen at one time — but at a critical moment the fighters were politically isolated and militarily neutralized.

I soon received a cable from the *Monitor* telling me of "Reuters complete communications blackout so all copy delayed" and of the postponed arrival of its Hong Kong–based staffer John Hughes because no commercial flights were running to Saigon.[15] On February 2 I responded that we were curfewed at 7 p.m., that there was nightly small arms fire around my apartment, that no incoming cables were being received, that Saigon-bound commercial flights were blocked, which meant that former editor Roscoe Drummond would not arrive as I had been told, and that I had not had time to locate *Monitor* education editor Cynthia Parsons, who had arrived the day before.

Two days later I advised Boston I was still receiving no incoming cables, our phone lines were cut, and rifle fire around the Reuters office required me to file by the more expensive telex system. Once when I had filed late and was approaching my front door, a jittery U.S. soldier with cocked weapon and heavy body armor, unaware that I had Vietnamese government authorization to be prowling the streets after curfew, nearly pulled his weapon's trigger. Even after one week of fighting, organized Viet Cong units were still hitting police stations, warehouses, and bridges, and the longer significant military contact continued, the more demoralized the population became.[16]

The Vietnamese family on the bottom floor of my apartment building made certain every evening that the accordion-style iron gate guarding the entrance was securely bolted. When that family moved in, their toddler son was waving a U.S. flag and singing "God Bless America." But as Tet struck, the husband, a lawyer who had lived in the United States, talked of where he should take his family members if they needed to leave Saigon. Two days later, as rumors of a coalition government swirled around the city, he pondered whether he should evacuate Vietnam altogether.

The United States Losing Its First Major War in History?

I attended the daily military briefings and, like An and Vuong, talked with as many sources as possible. I was stunned to learn of the scope of the Communists' countrywide blitz, which shocked leaders and people in South Vietnam and the United States. About eighty-four thousand Communist-led forces attacked 36 of Vietnam's 44 province capitals, 5 of the 6 autonomous cities, 64 of 242 district capitals, and 50 hamlets.[17] These Communist fighters had launched countrywide their "general offensive and general uprising," or Tet Mau Than — "Tet of the Year of the Monkey."

I thought that the Communists' countrywide offensive opened up the possibility of the United States losing its first major war in history. The United States, the most powerful nation militarily in history, had

24. An Quang Pagoda, which I often visited by cyclo, is surrounded by a square block section of rubble from rockets, grenades, and fire in Saigon on February 5, 1968, after it had served as Viet Cong headquarters during fierce Tet Offensive fighting. (AP Photo)

become the underdog in this multifaceted war of politics, psychology, military battles, and xenophobia.

In a dramatic shift, I noted, the original U.S. policy choice of fighting for a battlefield victory or negotiating at the conference table had flip-flopped into the choice of either negotiating or being defeated. One reliable Vietnamese observer told me that while no one thought the Communists could push the United States into the sea for a classic military victory, the Americans could become "so politically isolated and militarily humiliated, they will be sucked out politically by Washington or else asked to leave by the Vietnamese."[18] Claims by U.S. officials that ten thousand–plus Communists had been killed brought little solace to Saigonese, who could peer out their balconies to view a government military command in flames or Vietnamese warplanes rocketing a Buddhist pagoda.

I heard about some chilling experiences of Saigon's population. One Vietnamese housewife told of hearing a noise in her kitchen during the night, and thinking it was rats, she investigated, only to see a Viet Cong sitting in a tunnel that exited near her window. Another housewife told of her fright when Viet Cong guerrillas entered her upscale neighborhood. "But the Viet Cong reassured me they wouldn't come into my house," she muttered in sobs to her neighbor. "They went into my front yard — and then an American helicopter starting firing into my house and killed three of my children."[19]

I noted that even with a half million troops, a thirteen-year presence, and a sixty-six-million-dollar-a-day war expenditure, the United States had now seen it sensationally demonstrated that hardly a city or hamlet in South Vietnam felt secure. Even a U.S. Embassy spokesman gave correspondents that assessment. U.S. generals claimed victory but warned correspondents that Communists could launch another offensive — and expected them to do so.

While the outside world was debating whether General Westmoreland's command had accurate and timely enough information about the Communist blitz, I found that the heart of the debate in Saigon was whether the U.S. military command had ever understood the nature of the entire conflict. Critics argued that Westmoreland's positioning U.S. troops in the forward or border areas was ineffective, if not disastrous, because they were fighting only the Communist main force units rather than the whole spectrum of Communist people's-war organization — guerrillas, regional forces, and political cadres. Westmoreland's strategy had assumed Vietnam was a second Korea invaded by conventional forces. I viewed the official U.S. rationale for stemming the tide of Communist aggression, at the higher policy-making level, as defensive and negative, lopsidedly in the U.S. self-interest, rather than being pro-something that would bring socioeconomic and political betterment to the lives of the vast lower classes in Vietnam.[20]

Having analyzed what I could from Saigon, I knew I needed to cover the countryside and hired a taxi for a solo journey to Bien Hoa, twenty miles northwest of Saigon.[21] Only hours earlier I had been motor scootering on this superhighway going to and returning from the Viet Cong's Tet celebration. After learning of the ferocity of the fighting near Bien Hoa, I felt lucky I had survived those road trips.

In Bien Hoa I found that more optimism was being voiced by U.S. military and civilian sources, who claimed about two thousand Communist dead after the first forty-eight hours of fighting. A senior U.S. officer who had been one of the first to helicopter over the battle zone told me that one area was covered with so many enemy dead that "you could have walked across the battlefield on the bodies, without ever touching the ground." He had witnessed Chinese Communists mass human wave assaults in the Korean War, he said, "yet I've never seen so many enemy dead in one place." A Canadian Catholic priest told me he had climbed a water tower near his church and counted 125 Communist bodies.[22]

Simultaneously at dawn on January 31, Communist forces targeted the South Vietnamese Third Corps headquarters and nearby houses for military families. To dislodge their enemy, I was told, for the next two days allied tanks, helicopters, and soldiers bombed and shelled their own installations, causing immense destruction in a four-block area in the heart of the provincial capital.

Having taken risks in the taxi ride to gather this information, I was discouraged that my dispatch was not published. I received a cable from the newspaper advising me "not to embellish and describe casualties in sensational manner but still give idea of sweat problems and general strategy involved."[23] My unpublished dispatch had also documented the more optimistic views of U.S. officers and civilians in the field. (A month later the *Washington Post* published an article datelined Bien Hoa under the headline "Reds in Saigon Area Believed Hurt.")[24] Although the press had been accused of initially reporting the Communists' Tet Offensive as an allied military defeat, failure to publish unsanitized versions of battlefield bloodshed such as mine in the first weeks may partly have led to this overly critical assessment. (One analyst found that public support for both the Korean and Vietnam Wars *did not decrease because of news coverage* but instead "dropped inexorably by 15 percentage points whenever total U.S. casualties increased by a factor of ten.")[25]

My unpublished dispatch was a tip-off that the Communists had suffered a massive defeat. During the first six months of 1968, Westmoreland wrote, the Communists had lost an estimated 120,000 men, or "over one-half of their strength at the beginning of the year — or enough men to make more than 12 Communist divisions."[26]

The U.S. Dilemma: Destroy to Save

After my Bien Hoa trip I assessed that allied bombing, rocketing, and shelling of province towns and cities created a highly explosive political backlash so significant that it risked offsetting the short-term military advantages gained by killing numerous Communist forces. "This destruction in the cities is more and more looking like Hungary in reverse," a senior Vietnamese official, normally pro-American, told me. "And neither the outside world nor the Vietnamese are likely to forget this or to forgive the Americans for it. . . . The Vietnamese government officials will only look like butchering assassins for the Americans."[27]

Unlike my solo taxi ride to Bien Hoa, handpicked journalists, which excluded me, were ferried around the country by U.S. military aircraft arranged especially for them by embassy information chief Barry Zorthian because planes were in short supply and most roads were insecure. (Zorthian's decision to ferry journalists to battered remote sites dismayed the military, one journalist explained, "because each trip produced a new wave of stories of surprise attack, inadequate defense and death, destruction and discontent in the city visited. . . . The military action of the first few days was recounted over several weeks of stories on television and in the papers at home.")[28]

On February 7, when the planeload of journalists landed in the Mekong Delta at Ben Tre, AP's feisty Peter Arnett sought out U.S. advisors and promised them confidentiality. Peter learned that the Viet Cong had surprised government forces, understrength because of Tet leaves, and by dawn controlled the city's commercial center and residential areas and soon were threatening the U.S. advisory compound and Vietnamese barracks. As a last resort, to defend their own positions, a U.S. major insisted to Arnett, the allies had called in their heaviest firepower. "The Vietnamese chief of staff had to bring in an air strike on the house of his neighbor because the Communists had occupied it," he explained. "Our own positions were threatened, the government center nearly overrun."

"It became necessary to destroy the town to save it," the major was quoted as saying. Returning to Saigon, Arnett focused his copy on that memorable quote, which, he recounted, "leaped out as a comment on the essential dilemma of the Tet Offensive. The authorities had not only to defeat the attackers, but protect the civilian population."

The next day Peter learned from AP's foreign desk that the quote had echoed around the world. Even President Johnson demanded to know the name of the major who had made that damning comment.[29] When I saw Peter, he told me that after his story was published, he was astonished to learn that the first helicopter into Ben Tre carried senior U.S. officers from Saigon — not to oversee a recovery effort but to uncover the name of that forthright major. The *New Yorker* later observed that "with unwitting, insane brilliance" in making his remarkable quote, the American major "had penetrated to the very heart of what was then the Vietnam War."[30]

Hue: Bloodshed and Ruins amid Once-Imperial Splendor

In mid-February, when the *Monitor*'s staff correspondent John Hughes arrived from Hong Kong to add coverage, the newspaper wanted on-the-scene reporting from the besieged Khe Sanh base.[31] Johnson and Westmoreland were expecting it to be assaulted by thirty thousand–plus Communists encircling six thousand marines. John and I agreed that one of us should remain in Saigon for filing. I volunteered to go to Khe Sanh — but first to the one-time imperial capital of Hue, which the Communists still controlled. Although Viet Cong attacks had largely been turned back in Saigon and the province towns, Communist units

25. After the helicopter descended through mist and gun smoke, I jumped out behind U.S. Marines like these crouching atop a tower in Hue's Citadel. A slain North Vietnamese soldier lies at the base of the tower. (AP Photo)

still controlled all or parts of Hue and would for twenty-six days, from January 31 to February 25.

I flew to the Danang airbase and caught a U.S. helicopter to Hue, the sentimental heartbeat of many Vietnamese who remembered the cultural, historical, and social role of the once-upon-a-time royal capital. I had several times viewed its fairytale-like Citadel painted in bold reds, which was constructed beginning in 1802 by Emperor Gia Long to dominate the Perfume River. A square structure, the Citadel was more accurately described as "a citadel within a citadel," protecting the emperor's Imperial Palace with its fifteen-foot-high walls covering nearly a half mile on each of its four sides.[32] Dragon-tipped curves in vermilions, jade green, and glistening gold seemed to pull the rooftops toward the heavens.[33]

Shortly after daybreak, I watched anxiously as the helicopter stealthily eased toward the ground through a soupy mix of mist, fog, and puffs of smoke from expended explosives that engulfed the Citadel's double-tiered turrets and then descended on the marines below. As the helicopter made a steep descent through the thick sky to avoid gunfire, I had a sick feeling this was the most dangerous — and foolish — assignment I had undertaken in my years of covering the war. While the helicopter was barely hovering over the ground, I jumped out near marines crouching behind Citadel walls. I ducked down with these marines, who had fought eleven days and nights, block by block, turret to turret, and house to house.

Then I kept up with them as they swept southward along the east Citadel wall, trying to retake the city from the North Vietnamese and Viet Cong units. The Communists had attacked Hue in the early morning hours of January 31 and within six hours controlled virtually the whole city, the Citadel, and the palace, except for the compound for U.S. and Australian advisors and the headquarters of the First Vietnamese Army Division inside the Citadel. Marines had rushed to rescue the U.S. military compound, helped secure it, and then fanned out in fighting so fierce that sometimes only one city block of buildings was cleared in a day. At dawn the National Liberation Front's red-and-blue striped flag with giant star fluttered over the Citadel.[34] It would fly there for twenty-four days.

I found covering the battle was a miserable job. The drizzle and misty wind pierced my poncho, fogged up my camera and glasses, and dampened my notebooks. For the next four days I ate cold C rations and slept wherever I could find space in a trench line behind a wall or in an abandoned building. With help from a Saigon-bound correspondent, I sent the *Monitor* eleven rolls of black-and-white undeveloped film. I had pointed my rain-splattered lens at a panorama of the action: the marines crouched and firing near the southwest section of the Citadel, the destruction of the bombed-out Citadel walls, the shattered shops and main street on the north side of the Perfume River.

I tramped alongside the marines as we worked our way down a pocket of uncontrolled territory to within several blocks of the east palace wall. We marched down the muddy street past burned-out buses, pig carcasses, and downed trees as the sergeants kept yelling, "Spread it out." But as an enlisted trooper remarked, there were so many marines per street, it was impossible to spread out sufficiently to avoid being a target.

Within the hour a Communist rocket hit an American tank, killing two and wounding twelve. As more mortars splattered within fifty yards of the marine position, the unit commander, Maj. Robert Thompson, radioed for a 106 mm recoilless rifle, which arrived on a wheeled flatbed. He requested permission to bombard the east wall of the palace, which he soon received. About eighty-four rounds were hurled at the wall, each whistling and swooshing past my ears into the gray exterior and red-brick interior, sending mushrooms of burnt-orange clouds upward into the mist.

I followed a group of six marines into the grounds of a masonry structure of about a half dozen rooms; most were in shambles. A heavy-weapons round had crashed through a window and an arching doorway and detonated in the living room. Table and chairs were ruined, whether by rain or looters or gunfire. During the night I heard Communist mortars sporadically hit the marine area. South Vietnamese forces captured the flagpole facing the main gate of the palace, where the gold star of the Viet Cong flag had fluttered for twenty-four days; they raised two smaller golden flags of the South Vietnamese government.

A 450-man South Vietnamese task force commanded by thirty-one-year-old Maj. Pham Van Dinh spearheaded a hectic charge through the main Imperial Palace gate. Half-amused and half-amazed, I surveyed the outfits worn by Major Dinh's troops and deemed them dressed as one of the most motley, modern-day units ever to assault such an august fortress. Some troops had dredged up their old French woolen overblouses to shield themselves from the chilling rain. Others wore women's scarves — in red, yellow, and orange — around their necks for protection against the biting winds. One carried his rifle in his right hand and his plastic-covered Sony shortwave radio in his left. An advisor pushed aside a crumped-up bicycle as the Vietnamese troops surged passed jeeps, tanks, and buses demolished by rockets. At the palace Vietnamese troopers met little resistance. Two hours later the assault ended — not with a bang but with a whimper.

A short time later Major Dinh told me the news of his own private victory. His older brother, Thi, a sergeant with the division reconnaissance company, was alive. When the North Vietnamese had attacked, he escaped by diving into a moat area near the headquarters. For more than three weeks he and a friend hid in the water under lotus pads and seaweeds in the daytime and emerged to dry out at night. They had not eaten for twenty-five days.

I joined photographers in snapping pictures of gleeful soldiers in the Throne Room. The wooden throne and matching table, painted cranberry red with gilded trim, were coated with dust, plaster, and broken glass; two dud mortar shells lay nearby. Cameramen for Vietnamese television filmed a reenactment of the troops' more Hollywood-style charge of the palace.

I accompanied Vietnamese troops as they flanked the rose-colored palace proper and entered a plaza leading to other buildings. In one building, glistening with its gold-trimmed exterior, two dozen civilians were huddled after having lived meagerly for three weeks with North Vietnamese troops. They had dug a five-foot-deep bunker and covered it with planks, potted plants, and bags of dirt. Empty L-shaped trenches zigzagged along the walls of the battered palace. Thus ended the saddest battle for Hue's Imperial Citadel in its 166-year history.

I sensed the Hue battlefield was filled with some of the most poignant and bewildering paradoxes of the war. During the first days the South Vietnamese army command was reluctant to hurl artillery against its own properties. But when South Vietnamese troops suffered high casualties, officers called in heavy firepower on their own homes and offices. Then Vietnamese troops, even in the presence of an officer, meandered around, looting and plundering the homes of their own top commanders and senior government employees. Even in front of television cameras, I saw South Vietnamese troops drive up two half-ton military trucks and load them with their war booty, including refrigerators, tables and chairs, sofas, television sets, and great bundles of clothes. Looting, vandalism, and souvenir hunting during the twenty-six-day campaign increased the battle damage of this ravaged, once-royal capital. One informed source told me, "What the fighting did not destroy in the city, the plundering did."

Politically, the South Vietnamese armed forces manifested a glaring contradiction of the war — they had helped to reconquer the city and then proceeded to damage it further by looting. Their troops had in effect nullified their prime political mission — to reestablish law and order — and instead simply added to the anarchy and destruction. The emergence of semiconventional North Vietnamese units launching such a brazenly destructive campaign also peeled away the Communists' veneer of local guerrillas waging a people's war.

The day after most of Hue was secured, South Vietnamese president Nguyen Van Thieu visited on February 25 and was told by province officials that 70 percent of the civilian homes had been destroyed, 300 South Vietnamese government officials had been killed or were missing, 113,000 of the 145,000 residents were refugees, the entire population faced food shortages, about 1,000 civilians had been killed and 3,000-plus wounded, and 2,000-plus South Vietnamese military were casualties, of whom one-quarter were listed as killed. U.S. casualties were 1,000, with about 100 of that number killed. Communist dead were more than 5,000.[35]

When the gunfire died down, I looked around at the devastation and was thunderstruck. Hue's residents had either fled the city or were holed up in makeshift refugee camps in university buildings, churches, or a hospital. With the peopleless streets Hue took on an eerie daytime appearance of one vast cemetery. At night, when illumination flares were popped for lighting, Hue took on an even more macabre, shadowy semblance of a weird science fiction world of charred homes, hit-and-run graves near cabbage patches, and bombed-out Citadel turrets.

The suffering, misery, and bloodshed gnawed at the emotions not only of me but also the most hard-bitten U.S. military men. One veteran U.S. Marine said Hue was the worst city destruction he had seen in three major wars spanning a quarter century. "The damage to Seoul in the Korean War was less than and different from that of Hue," the sergeant told me. "In Seoul armies of both sides retreated or advanced through the city but didn't fight within it like Hue." Another officer acknowledged to me, "More and more when you see the cost of this war for the Vietnamese, you wonder if it is really worth it."

I left Hue to file my dispatches and proceed to Khe Sanh. But weeks later mass graves of about 2,800 specifically targeted Vietnamese government officials, officers, other residents, and a handful of U.S. and European civilians were uncovered in what has been called the "Hue Massacre." It has been described by a researcher as "by far the worst single incident of atrocity during the war." As an eyewitness at the unearthing of one mass grave in March 1968 explained, some bodies "had bullet wounds, others had their arms bound from behind by rope or wire. Many had their mouths open, silent screams frozen on their bodies."[36]

10

From Khe Sanh to the "Virtual Equivalent of Treason"

If nothing else was gained by the Vietnam experience, at least let it be a warning not to let it ever happen again.

PFC Elwin Bacon, Twenty-sixth Marines at Khe Sanh, 1968

March 1, 1968, 12:45 p.m. I was grouped with two other journalists in the austere office of the Danang military airport, "where everyone gives us a briefing on what to do." I jotted down those words in my notebook because the Khe Sanh Combat Base was being mortared "all the time" with three or four hundred mortars a day, "and we can't do much about it." The other journalists were a Korean newsman and a photographer, Sean Flynn, a dark, handsome type like his movie star father, Errol. Later the young Flynn would be missing in Cambodia.

Just as I was preparing to leave for Khe Sanh, Robert Ellison, a twenty-four-year-old photographer shooting for *Newsweek*, was killed there when North Vietnamese gunners shot down the U.S. transport plane he was riding in. I was especially saddened to hear of his death — only ten months earlier he and I had teamed up for a photo-text magazine spread about two army nurses and two army doctors married in a double wedding in Qui Nhon, ten minutes away from wartime gunshots.[1]

26. I saw crumbled aircraft destroyed by Communist fire on the airstrip as I deplaned at the Khe Sanh base during its two-month siege; airdrops were needed for supplies. (AP Photo/Dang Van Phuoc)

The air force crew chief and loadmaster were giving us an unsettling briefing. Be sure we were buckled up tight, we were warned, otherwise we would be sucked out the tailgate when the sleds of cargo were hastily rammed out the door as the aircraft taxied down onto the metal-grating runway. Once the last of the cargo was out and just seconds before takeoff, we were to exit the tailgate and then run as fast as we could for a bunker because during this split-second of ultra-vulnerability the Communists liked to hurl in explosives. A week earlier, on February 23, 1,307 incoming rounds of artillery, rocket, and mortar fire shelled the protective hillsides and the four-square-mile combat base; those rounds would become an all-time high — averaging a shell about every minute and a half.

We were going in on a resupply run carrying a planeload of wooden ammunition boxes packed with 3.5-inch rocket explosive projectiles. If the ammunition was hit, "we autorotate," we were told, meaning "we nosedive." It would be a one-hour ride to Khe Sanh in the twin-engine C-123 Provider. Bigger, faster four-engine C-130 Hercules cargo planes were no longer going in after one of them had been shot down; we would soon see its crumbled hulk dominating the runway.

The siege of Khe Sanh was capturing just as many headlines as were the urban battles for Hue that other journalists and I had been covering.[2] On January 21, ten days before the Tet blitz into the cities and towns, Communist gunners and ground troops had begun their siege of Khe Sanh, which would last seventy-seven days, from January 21 to April 8. Westmoreland was so concerned about a tidal wave of North Vietnamese invading across the Demilitarized Zone that in January 1968 he requested and received approval from his superiors to begin contingency planning for the use of tactical nuclear weapons, I later learned.[3] Little did I imagine weeks later, as I was hunkered down at Khe Sanh, that the allied troops and I might actually have been vaporized by a preemptive nuclear strike. Westmoreland, forecasting that the Communists would escalate their strategy of annihilation at Khe Sanh, had shifted U.S. combat units there, away from populated areas.[4] President Johnson was so concerned that he regularly stalked the sandbox model of the Khe Sanh plateau that he had assembled in the situation room of the White House basement.[5]

Into Khe Sanh: Buckled Up with Crossed Fingers

Even snugly buckled up, I found that getting into Khe Sanh was a harrowing experience, one deserving crossed fingers for good luck.[6] As the C-123 descended, I spotted a junkyard of burned-out helicopters and transport aircraft strewn along the airstrip, signifying the dangers of landing and taking off. Elephant grass twenty feet high hugged one portion of the camp; as one officer would describe to me, it was "so high you can lose a battalion in there." One of the Twenty-sixth Marines would tell me that their enemies had been killed in trench lines ringing the base wearing Marine Corps flak vests and carrying gas masks.

27. U.S. Air Force bombs create a curtain of flying shrapnel and debris barely two hundred feet beyond the perimeter of South Vietnamese Ranger positions in March 1968 when I arrive at the U.S. Marine base at Khe Sanh. The photographer, South Vietnamese major Nguyen Ngoc Hanh, was badly injured when bombs fell close by on a subsequent pass by U.S. planes. (AP Photo/ARVN, Maj. Nguyen Ngoc Hanh)

By the time I arrived in Khe Sanh in early March, the district head-quarters at Khe Sanh village (population about ten thousand, mostly members of the Bru tribe) had been fiercely attacked and abandoned and its inhabitants and officials moved in with the marines. Then in early February the Special Forces camp of Lang Vei, about ten thousand yards to the southwest, was overrun by North Vietnamese using flamethrowers and for the first time tanks of Soviet Model T-34 World War II vintage.[7]

I had long heard about Khe Sanh because it served as the northwestern anchor for the necklace of Vietnamese government forts running south-ward like those along the ill-defined Laotian and Cambodian borders that I had first visited in 1962. Perched on a plateau, Khe Sanh, which translates as the "Birth-Giving Gap between Mountains," lies fourteen

28. I hopscotched along deep trenches to bunkers fortified with sandbags at the U.S. Marine base at Khe Sanh, seeking protection against daily Communist artillery and other bombardments. (AP Photo)

miles south of the Demilitarized Zone and North Vietnam in the upper left-hand corner of South Vietnam, where it joins Laos, sitting astride Route 9 as it zigzags eastward to the coast for eight miles along the DMZ. During the French Indochina War colonial forces built a fort at Khe Sanh, and decades later it was still surrounded by French-owned coffee plantations and property owners' houses, or what one American described to me as "little suburbia." In August 1962 the first U.S. forces to arrive in Khe Sanh were the "Green Beret" Special Forces, who stayed for four years then moved to Lang Vei outpost and were replaced by a U.S. Marine unit.[8]

I would learn that getting out of Khe Sanh was harder than getting in. My departure was delayed for days because incoming fire limited the number of C-123 aircraft that could safely land or that had room for lower-priority passengers like me. During that time I slept in the concrete underground bunker used by the command staff. Sounds of incoming shells punctuated the air day and night. B-52 Stratofortresses designed to carry nuclear weapons dropped loads of bombs as close as a thousand yards from the marines' perimeter — the usual margin of safety was three thousand yards[9] — shaking the camp like a next-door earthquake. Water piped in from a pump outside the camp perimeter, and flush-toilet facilities were available for my use, as were C rations. I felt safe enough in this underworld, but during daylight, when I ventured above ground, I hopscotched from one bunker to the next to gather information and capture mood.

Like other correspondents, I was allowed to visit any part of the base at my own risk to observe Communist incoming fire and to talk with any American without military escort. Never in the history of modern war reporting had Western correspondents, operating without censorship, been given this much freedom of movement and access to sources in such a tactically difficult situation. The marines had placed four requirements upon the press in Khe Sanh: a limit of fifteen members of the press at a time, because of the scarcity of facilities, and agreement by the correspondents to avoid taking aerial photos of the base, entering restricted command centers, or specifying results of Communist bombardments.

The siege around Khe Sanh evoked images for me of medieval warfare. The Communists' envelopment of this combat base defended by six thousand marines represented siege warfare in slow motion — with giant balls of barbed wire rather than castle walls protecting the allied encampment, surrounded by up to at least thirty thousand North Vietnamese forces.[10] For the North Vietnamese main force units, Khe Sanh represented their final phase of guerrilla warfare; they had reinforced the area around the base with antiaircraft weapons and, buried deep in the mountains on the Laotian side of the border six miles away, 152 mm artillery with a range of eighteen miles.

"Khe Sanh is no longer a place," one U.S. officer lamented to me. "It's a mood. It's a locked-up, penned-in . . . mood." It was that and more. The siege was not simply a one-dimensional encirclement of the camp, I observed; it was a tridimensional envelopment of it in the air, on the ground, and underground.

Firepower: Volume versus Precision, Fixed versus Mobile Targets

In the air, I noted, the Communists laid an invisible siege by monitoring almost all of the radio traffic between Khe Sanh and its higher headquarters. Then, using a .50 caliber machine gun positioned off one finger of the runway, the North Vietnamese systematically raked every low-flying aircraft making supply drops or landing on the only approach to the airstrip. U.S. air strikes, as well as artillery, continually rained throughout the mountains and valleys ringing Khe Sanh but were not effective enough to wipe out a pinpoint target — such as a lone Communist machine gunner or the Communist artillery bunkered on the reverse side of a mountain in Laos. As I was talking with air officers, Communists lobbed mortars and artillery at the airstrip throughout the day. No planes landed. Only emergency medical evacuation helicopter runs were made, and many wounded were wounded a second time by incoming fire as they were running to or being carried to the aircraft. The Communists appeared at the time to allow permissive trafficking of supplies into Khe Sanh. As one officer described to me, "The Communists want just enough to get through so the marines will not leave Khe Sanh."

U.S. commanders faced the problem that the Communists' 152-mm artillery pieces, dug into the reverse slopes of the Co Roc mountain range in Laos, were presumably protected with only a narrow aperture in which the gun piece was exposed solely during firing periods. Repeated U.S. air strikes — including massive area bombing by the B-52 Strategic Air Command bombers — had failed to dislodge the pieces. U.S. firepower was measured in volume, I noted, but Communist firepower was measured in precision. American firepower was directed at the North Vietnamese mobile, hidden targets, whereas Communist firepower was directed at the allies' fixed, known targets.[11]

"Do you get the picture?" one U.S. officer asked me. "Khe Sanh is the bull's eye for their gunners in the hills all around us." Rain, fog, or darkness do not interfere with their firing because they are already zeroed in on every target on the base, he observed. But American air and artillery needed visual sightings made by forward observers — "because we are not zeroed in on him as he is on us. So the rain, fog, and night interfere with the accuracy of our firepower . . . [and] help to conceal Charlie."

On the ground the Communist siege represented the "battle of the bunkers" to the young marine corporals and privates. A week before I arrived, the first North Vietnamese trenches started to appear, and once they were close to the barbed wire perimeter, they branched off into ones that paralleled the marines' lines; North Vietnamese assaulting troops would use these secondary trenches, which looked like long fingers reaching hungrily toward the base.[12]

Marines had been ordered to stop patrolling, except for securing the supply drop zone, so as to avoid being ambushed and possibly subjecting reinforcements to a second ambush. A wounded Vietnamese lieutenant, whose patrol was ambushed three hundred meters from his own lines, waved away reinforcing units, which would also have been ambushed — and then committed suicide. A twenty-nine-man U.S. Marine patrol that had left the combat base on February 25 was ambushed on an adjoining ridgeline, and the bodies of its twenty-five dead and wounded were not recovered for weeks until the siege was lifted.[13]

"From the tops of bunkers at night, we can see Communist trucks driving along Route 9 with their lights on," one officer told me. "It looks like a little Los Angeles freeway." Each night when the fog descended on Khe Sanh, "not like little cat's paws but in great big steps," as one marine assured me, the North Vietnamese diggers moved their trench lines closer. These trench lines "are getting so close I could hit them with a five-iron if this were a golf course," one officer exclaimed. "We're increasingly getting that hemmed-in feeling.[14]

Catacombs, Stethoscopes, Swaddled Shovels

A subterranean siege was also under way. To get a good look at the Communists' underground tunnels, I climbed a small knob within the marine perimeter. The knob rose roughly three hundred yards above the plateau of the base camp proper, and at its top lay a U.S. Marine command post, camouflaged with nets. The commander, knowing Communists had zeroed in on his post, started his marines digging out the inside of the hill. The result was an underground labyrinth, damp and lighted only with candles perched on C ration cans, reminding me of catacombs.

Occasionally, marines detected the clink of Communist shovels swaddled in burlap to minimize noise. Suspecting the North Vietnamese of digging under the hill knob at its base, every morning marines intently searched for tunnel holes but to no avail. Some officers told me of their fear that the whole Khe Sanh base sat on top of an elaborate French-made concrete tunneling system, and if connected with fresh diggings, a Communist-made volcano under them could blow up their positions.

Day and night marines armed with a doctor's stethoscope took soundings of the Communists' digging they had heard. But attempts to find the North Vietnamese tunnel, even by excavating down ten feet, had failed. Electronic sensing devices were also used but were largely unproductive.

Khe Sanh's Kaleidoscope of Death and Death Cheating

During my daytime bunker-to-bunker hopscotching, talking with marines of all ranks and colors, Khe Sanh began evoking for me a kaleidoscope of heartrending fragments, moods, and tragedy. Khe Sanh was six dirty hands grabbing into a C ration box. A Communist mortar round thumps into the center of the box, between the outstretched fingers. Six marines lay dead, like tattered rag dolls.

Khe Sanh was a white overweight corporal from Seattle, nicknamed Porky, who strolled around his tent serving donuts and coffee for his supply unit. An Air Force C-130 rolls overhead, like a giant metallic butterfly, disgorging its "bundles for Khe Sanh." One parachute failed to open; Porky was scissored in half by the pallet of heavy supplies. "Porky was only twenty-one," his buddy said. "He had twenty-four more days left in Khe Sanh, and then he was going to meet his wife in Honolulu." Khe Sanh was a black staff sergeant, the top air force noncommissioned officer here, who swan dived behind a wall of sandbags, his hand bloodied and broken from Communist mortar chunks. He strode fifty feet to the medical evacuation bunker, and while running toward the helicopter for liftoff, was wounded again — twice in two hours.

"Everyone has a Hollywood view of death in Khe Sanh," an air force officer said dryly. "But actually it's quick and simple here. A round comes in, and eight Americans are killed or wounded." Khe Sanh was the close calls, the split-second margin of luck between life and death. Almost everyone in Khe Sanh has cheated death two or three times, escaping incoming Communist shells or seeing his buddies killed by them.

Khe Sanh was lovely *Playboy* pinups, but here B.B. did not mean Brigitte Bardot — it meant body bags, the zippered, plasticized shroud of the dead. And then there were the love letters to Khe Sanh. "Bob, My Love," the staff sergeant recalled. "Those are the letters I'm wary of. My wife writes three pages of mush then tells me she bought a new Pontiac, and then three more pages of mush to build me back up. I can do without letters like that."

Khe Sanh was helmets, boots, and flak jackets, worn not as armor of war but as appendages to human bodies. Marines slept in their flak jackets and boots. One private told me he took his boots off once a month. Often a marine would scribble on his flak jackets and helmets his inner thoughts, personality, or philosophy alongside his surname, serial number, and blood type. "I love Mom and Dad" or "Alabama No. 1; Birmingham the Magic City" were mixed in with choice profanities. "God is Dead," one had penned on his helmet. But the next one countered: "My God is Alive. Sorry about yours, Charlie."

"God, send more flowers and less marines," one had scribbled under the armhole of his jacket, a thought he said he had copied from an advertising sign in the "land of the Big PX." Another youngster had painted in black letters across the full breadth of the back of his jacket, "Life divided by time equals death every time."[15]

Dead End for Westmoreland and His Strategy

While Khe Sanh was still encircled and bombarded, President Johnson announced on March 22 that General Westmoreland was being removed from Vietnam to become chief of staff of the U.S. Army in Washington. While I was in the Demilitarized Zone area, I noted that in the annals of recent Vietnam warfare the imprint of Westmoreland had most indelibly been etched at Khe Sanh. I viewed Khe Sanh as representing the dead end, the self-destruction of Westmoreland's search-and-destroy strategy — the futility of his so-called forward strategy that focused on seeking and defeating the Communists' hard hat, main force units but overlooking their support from local insurgents. Based on classical conventional war textbooks at West Point, where he once had been superintendent, Westmoreland had argued that he needed to employ this offensive strategy in the nonpopulated areas to prevent Vietnam's cities from being subjected to Communist ground attacks or shellings at his enemy's choosing,[16] or, as the *Pentagon Papers* explains, to prevent each town from becoming a Khe Sanh.[17]

Yet with Tet the ruins of Hue symbolized Westmoreland's miscalculation. There, aided by the local population and cadres, North Vietnamese units marched into Hue without a battle and held it for twenty-five days, logically symbolizing the final failure and futility of the Westmoreland search-and-destroy strategy. The Communists pinned down U.S. and Vietnamese troops at Khe Sanh and used it as a diversion so that they could shift the whole course of their war into the cities and towns.[18] The North Vietnamese had followed Mao's 1937 mandate for deception: "*Cause uproar in the East, strike in the West.*"[19]

Westmoreland's light-at-the-end-of-the-tunnel predictions made four months earlier became a bad joke.[20] Although Communist forces had suffered tremendous casualties during Tet, they succeeded in producing the "shock and awe" they desired politically to prompt Washington to begin negotiating with Hanoi. A Western diplomat explained to me:

"Westy obviously cannot command a machine he doesn't have. And he doesn't have the political-economic-military counterinsurgency machine he needs to wage this war."

I added my own insight: "At a higher level, this was not simply General Westmoreland's dilemma in Vietnam; it would be an American dilemma in other underdeveloped countries for the next decade. The current criticism of General Westmoreland here is that he never attempted to adjust, or deconventionalize, American military power." The local guerrillas and political cadre who fed, nurtured, and sustained the North Vietnamese invasion had to be countered by what I called a "people-perimeter" strategy to protect the population, but this component was initially ignored by Westmoreland, and his miscalculation was exposed at Tet.[21]

And there may have been no right allied strategy, according to General Giap, because his enemies faced a "great contradiction." "If they kept their forces scattered in order to occupy territory, it would be impossible for them to organize a strong mobile force," Giap argued, "but if they reduced their occupation forces to regroup them, our guerrillas would . . . increase their activity, their posts and garrisons would be threatened or annihilated, the local puppet authorities overthrown and the occupied zones reduced."[22] Hence, Giap was arguing, counterinsurgents militarily faced a no-win war.

My June Return: Why No North Vietnamese Ground Assault?

By the time I departed Khe Sanh, army units had begun relieving the besieged marines, and a week later, on April 8, the siege of Khe Sanh was officially lifted. But plans were already under way to abandon Khe Sanh on June 11, the day before Westmoreland departed for Washington and before he could be ensconced as army chief of staff there.[23]

Before Khe Sanh was abandoned, I returned there in June, as the *Monitor* requested, to investigate why the expected and long-agonized-over Communist ground assault had not occurred. I found two opposing views. One side argued that the Communists had planned and used Khe Sanh as a diversion before Tet to suck U.S. forces away from the urban areas and major allied installations; the second side argued that the Communists had been "bombed out of the hills" by U.S. firepower.[24]

I heard that the Communists used Khe Sanh as a diversion from U.S. Army officers involved in assessing Communist actions in the northern provinces and some sources in Saigon; years later it would be the commonly accepted view of U.S. historians and in Communist writings. A U.S. Army intelligence officer with the First Air Cavalry Division, which had been rushed in to reinforce the marines in Hue, told me North Vietnamese units put heavy pressure on Khe Sanh and then started being pulled out and transported down their "high-speed highway" in January in time to reach Hue. He told me that on February 21 army intelligence had confirmed through documents and prisoners that two units that were erroneously presumed to be attacking Khe Sanh were in fact fighting the Cavalry outside Hue.

Toppling those border forts I had earlier visited gave the Communists jungled access to build elaborate road networks throughout Laos and into the Ashau Valley, leading to Hue. These networks created a high-speed system that included some asphalt links 140 miles north of Saigon and were designed to transport heavier weaponry and bigger troop movements. I learned that Hanoi had persuaded Moscow bloc countries to support its master plan with sophisticated weaponry and supplies.[25] I also learned that allies had captured in the Ashau Valley such materials as canned Hungarian goulash, Soviet trucks, tracked vehicles, field artillery pieces, and Bulgarian medicines.

Unless Khe Sanh was an extremely easy target to take, it was diversionary for the Communists, one source explained. "But to be a credible diversionary, he had to create a real and serious threat around Khe Sanh — and there's no question but that it was a real threat there. But the enemy created that threat to draw friendly forces away from the coast. His main objective was Hue."[26]

In contrast, I received plenty of on-scene observations to buttress the theory that the Communists had been "bombed out of the hills."[27] Many agreed that Khe Sanh would have been lost without bombers, fighters, and supply aircraft, but some were more cautious about accepting Secretary of

Defense Clark Clifford's claim that airpower had actually won the battle. I interviewed these seven different levels of on-scene sources who held to the view that U.S. firepower had caused the North Vietnamese to avoid trying to overrun the base: the marine division commander during the siege, the division chief of staff, the new marine general commanding Khe Sanh, a marine battalion commander I had interviewed during the March siege, the air force commander for all the Khe Sanh flights at the central control center, the commander of a fighter squadron component, and the airlift commander. I also accompanied a pilot in his low-flying, two-seater on his forward air controller mission over Khe Sanh and flew to the nearby Seventh Fleet to interview the navy admiral and pilots supporting Khe Sanh in their two-man, subsonic, all-weather attack A-6 Intruders.

"As we flew over Khe Sanh, I couldn't believe my eyes," one veteran U.S. Army officer told me. "The bomb craters were everywhere. It looked like a moonscape."

U.S. Air Force pilots I talked with indicated that the ninety-six thousand tons of bombs that had been dropped during the seventy-seven-day siege of Khe Sanh from 2,700 sorties upon twenty-five square miles around Khe Sanh amounted to 33 percent more than all American bombs dropped on Europe during 1942 and 1943.[28] As part of Operation Arc Light eight-engine B-52 Stratofortress bombers were used for the first time on such a sustained basis for the tactical support of allied troops. "We've dropped so many bombs it is difficult for me to get an eight-digit coordinate to give my exact position on the grid system of the map," one pilot told me. Air force pilots, half-jokingly, renumbered these grids, assuming they had knocked two meters off the peaks of some hills. A military historian called the tonnage dropped on Khe Sanh "the heaviest weight to fall on any single target area in the history of air warfare."[29]

"Filthy B-52s": Apocalypse for North Vietnamese Troops

I learned from captured North Vietnamese army (NVA) documents and prisoners that life under the bombs was exhausting and disheartening for Communist soldiers. "One prisoner said his regiment replaced one that had been 90 percent wiped out by B-52s," a U.S. officer told me. In one captured letter a North Vietnamese trooper lamented, "The filthy B-52s have been striking at us again." U.S. ground troops sweeping the area found many mass graves of dead North Vietnamese. A one-time Viet Cong wrote, "The first few times I experienced a B-52 attack it seemed, as I strained to press myself into the bunker floor, that I had been caught in the Apocalypse. The terror was complete."[30]

Yet a forward air controller who had probably flown more missions over Khe Sanh than any other pilot described to me the limits of U.S. firepower on North Vietnamese soldiers. "Every day I went up there and put bombs in on the NVA — and the next day they were still in there digging trenches," Capt. Gerald L. Harrington of Sumter, South Carolina, told me. "It appeared at one time we were actually dropping bombs on them and helping them dig trenches at the same time."

Harrington explained that once he had not gone up in his two-seater observation plane for three days, but then when he did, he said, "it was unbelievable what I saw." The trails looked like thousands of troops had moved into the area, and they made no attempt at all at camouflage. "'They knew we knew — and they had so many troops they didn't care." After a B-52 raid he would have to wait thirty minutes before the dust settled enough for him to assess the bomb damage in the target area. "If you've seen the World War II pictures of London and Berlin," he said, "a B-52 gives you the same impression, except they're not in the cities."

The North Vietnamese were able to neutralize some effectiveness of U.S. firepower with sturdy shovels that were barely bigger than a child's sandbox toy, I was told by air force officers who participated directly in the Khe Sanh air war during the siege and ground officers who inspected Communist bunkers once the siege was lifted. One staff officer who had inspected the Communist trench lines ventured that "the Communists were dug in well enough at Khe Sanh to survive a tactical nuclear strike."[31]

High-Tech Intelligence Gathering and the Future

Khe Sanh provided me with a peephole into the testing and limitations of sophisticated and emerging U.S. military technology — and into the weaponry of possible future wars. I inspected clothbound, granulated land mines, resembling square, olive-green powder puffs and sunburned, triangular crackers that were seeded amid electronic sensors around Khe Sanh. Khe Sanh was a testing ground for these remote, electronic sensors that were deemed so useful they would go on to become an "operational battlefield surveillance system" routinely utilized by the United States in its future conflicts.[32]

Portable radar sets, four feet high, were staked out around Khe Sanh and monitored by ground surveillance teams. "People sniffers" were employed to detect chemicals emitted by human bodies and then electronically magnified onto measuring dials. Starlight scopes, resembling elongated, old-fashioned binoculars, were issued to low-flying air controllers in mid-March 1968; the instruments magnified moonlight so the navigators could surveil potential targets moving in the darkness below. Reconnaissance aircraft flew over Khe Sanh, some carrying metal-detecting infrared cameras, some carrying black-and-white film, and some employing color photography, which distinguished between natural jungle and day-old camouflage. From these returns a miniature Khe Sanh was built in a sandbox in Saigon, where U.S. generals deduced where the North Vietnamese were most likely to concentrate their supplies, troops, and equipment.

Yet I received mixed assessments about the value of these exotic, high-tech devices. Some, such as the portable radar sets, gave "good results" in detecting NVA movements within limited distances, one source told me. But others, including a U.S. general, believed the gadgetry was generally overrated. "Frankly, we can't get over-enthused with these gadgets," one explained. "They're all aids, but they're no substitute for eyewitnesses — either U.S. patrols or Communist prisoners." An officer who had experienced the siege told me, "Frankly, no one knew how many NVA were around Khe Sanh most of the time."[33]

At a level higher than my on-the-scenes reporting, General

Westmoreland later reflected on why he and his battlefield strategists had been so surprised by the Communists' devastating countrywide blitz. A year after Tet, in spring 1969, Westmoreland confessed that the Communists' countrywide offensive had indeed caught him and his staff by surprise. "Those of us who had been in Vietnam for a long time found it hard to believe that the enemy would expose his forces to almost certain decimation by engaging us frontally at great distances from his base areas and border sanctuaries," Westmoreland confided. "However, . . . this is exactly what he did, and in doing it he lost the cream of his army."[34] (The Communists' willingness to sustain horrific casualties had been voiced decades earlier when Ho Chi Minh warned French leaders before their Indochina war: "You can kill ten of my men for every one I kill of yours. But even at those odds, you will lose and I will win.")[35]

Westmoreland's frank admission about surprise illustrates what a Harvard researcher labels "unmotivated biases" leading to faulty analyses as the central reason for the allied forces' intelligence failure. Captured Communist documents and prisoners' interrogations had given Westmoreland warnings of a looming offensive, but he and his staff had failed to analyze them adequately because of their own blinders. The researcher stated that in one of the greatest stealth attacks sprung on the United States since December 7, 1941, the Communists' Tet Offensive "constituted an unusual incident in the history of surprise attack."[36] And it remained so until the destruction by hijacked airliners on September 11, 2001. In all three historic surprise attacks U.S. officials had held some intelligence information of an approaching menace but failed to analyze that information fast or well enough.

I left Khe Sanh just as U.S. bulldozers and explosives were demolishing the combat base so that it could be abandoned. Back in Saigon I wrote and airmailed to Boston a three-part series that was later submitted along with the *Monitor*'s forms and letters nominating me for the 1968 Pulitzer Prize for International Reporting.

Describing my June series as "unique in-depth reporting of complex and hazardous events," managing editor Courtney Sheldon in his nominating letter also summed up some of my work throughout the year: "During

1968, Miss Deepe produced no fewer than 18 series of major articles on Vietnam for the *Monitor*, plus her regular string of daily articles. Among the best examples of her work under combat conditions was a series of six articles (March 20–27) from Khe Sanh on the plight of the encircled Marines there. . . . Indeed she traced the pattern of conflict all the way from the man in the Khe Sanh dugout to General Westmoreland in Saigon and the Pentagon in Washington."[37]

Impact of Tet on U.S. Leaders and Credibility

The shock and awe of the Communists' Tet blitz was on the U.S. "leadership segment" — the press, politicians, and official Washington, according to a well-established polling firm.[38] Clark Clifford, who had replaced Robert McNamara as secretary of defense on March 1, 1968, explained, "Tet hurt the administration where it needed support most, with Congress and the American public — not because of the reporting, but because of the event itself, and what it said about the credibility of American leaders." Within Johnson's official circles the psychological shock produced by Tet was profound. "The pressure grew so intense that at times I felt the government itself might come apart at its seams," Clifford, the sixty-one-year-old confidant to several U.S. presidents, explained. There was, he said, "something approaching paralysis, and a sense of events spiraling out of control of the nation's leaders."[39]

Some linked the loss of credibility to Johnson's own mismanaged public relations campaign months earlier. "The adverse impact of Tet on the United States government and its policies would never have been as serious as it was if the Johnson Administration had not spent the better part of the preceding fall in a massive propaganda campaign to raise the level of American support by [*sic*] the war with a flood of reports and public appearances by General Westmoreland, Ambassador Bunker and others," a veteran Washington journalist explained. He reasoned, "To say that the press was responsible for the impact of the Tet offensive is to overlook the role of the government itself."[40]

On March 31, 1968, the leadership paralysis was broken when Johnson made twinned surprise announcements on nationwide television: he was declaring a bombing halt of North Vietnam except above the DMZ so as to begin peace talks, and he would not seek reelection. Perhaps prompting Johnson's decision was a draft memo from his most trusted advisors dated February 29, 1968. In it they argued against further escalation of the war by using words Peter Arnett had gathered at Ben Tre during Tet: more escalation would make it "difficult to convince critics that we are not simply destroying South Vietnam in order to 'save' it and that we genuinely want peace talks."[41] General Giap interpreted Johnson's decision to decline a reelection bid to be "the end of the period in which the American imperialists considered themselves to be a super-power, and the collapse of their role in the world."[42]

Not so much because of Tet, the year 1968 was significant because of the U.S. economic crisis caused by a run on the dollar and gold resulting from Johnson's spending on both the Vietnam War and his cherished Great Society programs, according to U.S. political economist Robert M. Collins. Collins argues that the U.S. economic crisis of 1968 "both revealed and contributed to the passing of postwar U.S. economic hegemony." He called 1968 the year "the American Century came to an end."[43]

After Johnson's stunning announcement that he would not seek reelection, Khe Sanh had lost its political significance. Officials in Saigon largely viewed the besieged base as important to the Communists only as a hinge to swing the American political nominations or elections.[44] Three days later North Vietnam agreed to preliminary peace talks, and a month later, on May 3, both Hanoi and Washington agreed to begin discussions in Paris. On August 8 Richard Nixon accepted the Republican Party's presidential nomination and promised to bring an honorable end to the war in Vietnam.

My Unpublished Election Scoop amid
"LBJ's 'X' File on Nixon's 'Treason'"

During October 1968 I was busier than usual covering the impact of a talked-about permanent bombing halt, which was Hanoi's precondition for entering into peace talks with the allies. Most of my dispatches were published on page 1, often leading the *Monitor*. I interviewed senior military commanders along the Demilitarized Zone and in Saigon,[45] secured comments from Western diplomats,[46] including one who had recently visited Hanoi,[47] and sought input from other sources who assessed troop movements in Laos.[48] At the same time I was synthesizing An's reports gleaned from sources inside and outside the palace and the Vietnamese High Command.[49]

Then, out of the blue, I learned of such outlandish rumblings that on October 28 I sent an advisory to the *Monitor's* overseas editor, "Hank" Hayward: "There's a report here that Vietnamese Ambassador to Washington Bui Diem has notified the Foreign Ministry that Nixon aides have approached him and told him the Saigon government should hold to a firm position now regarding negotiations and that once Nixon is elected, he'll back the Thieu government in their demands. If you could track it down with the Nixon camp, it would probably be a very good story."[50] I was so busy I had no chance to remember my assist eight years earlier in the NBC studios when my boss, Sam Lubell, had predicted Nixon would lose the presidency to John Kennedy. Now, Nixon was facing Democrat Vice President Hubert Humphrey, who was saddled with President Lyndon Johnson's increasingly controversial Vietnam policy. I received no response to my cable from Boston.

Three days after my advisory, on October 31, Johnson announced that he had ordered a complete end to the bombing of North Vietnam within twelve hours and that the date for the first negotiation session with Hanoi was set for November 6, the day after the U.S. presidential election. Johnson's speech was received in Saigon on November 1, which, as I reported, many Vietnamese viewed as an ill-timed insult because it was made on Vietnam's National Day and the anniversary of the Kennedy administration's support for the overthrow of President Diem.[51]

Then, just four days before the U.S. election, President Thieu surprisingly rejected Johnson's peace initiative. In a bombshell televised speech before the National Assembly on Vietnam's National Day, Thieu announced that South Vietnam would not send delegates to negotiate in Paris by November 6; he feared the Viet Cong's National Liberation Front would be seated as a legitimate coequal of his government. I reported that his speech was a direct rebuke to President Johnson. "In effect, Mr. Thieu said LBJ double-crossed him," one longtime Asia observer told me. "And Mr. Thieu is pretty nearly right."[52]

To explain Thieu's stunning announcement, I cabled Hayward on November 4: "Purported political encouragement from the Richard Nixon camp was a significant factor in the last-minute decision of President Nguyen Van Thieu's refusal to send a delegation to the Paris peace talks — at least until the American Presidential election is over." I relied mostly on "informed sources" for my scoop — an eye-opening exclusive news report — and added that "the only written report about the alleged Nixon support for the Thieu government was a cable from Bui Diem, Vietnamese ambassador to Washington," confirming what I had asked Hayward to check out days earlier.

But my momentous scoop was not published. Hayward cabled back that the *Monitor* had deleted all my references to Bui Diem and to the "purported political encouragement from the Nixon camp," which, he wrote, "seems virtual equivalent of treason."[53]

Hayward could not have known then, but his description of Nixon's "virtual equivalent of treason" was being privately echoed at the time by Johnson when he sputtered: "It would rock the world if it were known that Thieu was conniving with the Republicans. Can you imagine what people would say if it were to be known that Hanoi has met all these conditions and then Nixon's conniving with them kept us from getting it."[54]

Hayward told me within a day or so: "The alleged Nixon involvement was interesting but needed confirmation from this end — which was not forthcoming — before we could print such sweeping charges on election day. It was a good story nonetheless, and you get major credit for digging it out."[55] Knowing the time-honored journalistic tradition of fairness, I understood when Hayward told me that without such confirmation, the *Monitor* had "trimmed and softened" my lead. The *Monitor's* substitute lead simply implied that Thieu had acted on his own.[56] Upon receiving the *Monitor's* Western edition days later, however, I saw my supposed-to-be scoop relegated to page 2 with no mention of Nixon under a one-column headline. I could hardly recognize it. Yet forty-four years later I was stunned to learn that President Johnson had indeed read and agonized over my lead with his top aides. Just as this book was being readied for publication, I was queried about my scoop's Nixon-Thieu connection by veteran investigative reporter Robert Parry. On March 3, 2012, Parry published an amazing exposé on his online investigative news service headlined: "LBJ's 'X' File on Nixon's 'Treason.'"[57] Parry also included links to the telltale documents he had uncovered. Although I had already pieced together from other sources much of his story line about Nixon's maneuvering for my book,[58] I had never suspected what Parry revealed about my own unpublished scoop.

Parry had opened a manila envelope in LBJ's presidential library in Austin, Texas, labeled the "X Envelope." In it he found dozens of "secret" and "top secret" memos, transcripts of audiotapes, FBI wiretaps, and National Security Agency intercepts. Johnson had amassed the documents and, before he died on January 22, 1973, had given them to national security advisor Walter Rostow. In turn Rostow labeled the manila mailer and inserted his top secret letter instructing the LBJ Library director not to open the X Envelope for fifty years from June 6, 1973 — that is, until 2023. The librarians waited only twenty-one years, until July 22, 1994, to open the X Envelope and begin declassifying its contents.

The documents in the X Envelope reveal an even closer connection between Thieu and the Nixon camp than I had made in referring to Ambassador Bui Diem in my scoop, Parry details. That connection was Anna Chennault, the China-born widow of the U.S. general Claire Chennault, who had commanded the volunteer Flying Tigers to fight the Japanese in World War II, was chairwoman of the Republican Women for Nixon in 1968, and was a driving force in the China lobby that pushed for U.S. support for Taiwan. Known in the White House at various times as "Little Flower" or "Dragon Lady," she recalls in her autobiography how she received a cable from Nixon in spring 1967 asking her to visit him in his New York apartment, where he disclosed his plans to run for president the next year and flattered her into agreeing to help him.

With the campaign beginning, Chennault flew again to New York to see Nixon, this time with Bui Diem, where they were joined by John

Mitchell, who became what she describes as "commander in chief" of Nixon's campaign. She quotes Nixon as having told Bui Diem that she was their mutual friend so that "if you have any message for me, please give it to Anna and she will relay it to me and I will do the same in the future." He added, "If I should be elected the next President, you can rest assured I will have a meeting with your leader and find a solution to winning this war." She also traveled privately to Vietnam as a columnist for a Chinese daily "while continuing to keep Nixon and Mitchell informed about South Vietnamese attitudes vis-à-vis the peace talks" and about her "many encounters with President Thieu."[59]

Other sources note that "almost every day" in the week leading up to the election, Chennault was telephoned by Mitchell, urging her to keep Thieu from going to Paris to help the Democrats get the Paris peace talks started. She relayed that and numerous other messages to Thieu, pleading with him to "hold on" instead of going to Paris.[60]

Spookily, Johnson knew of her messages to Thieu because he had ordered the FBI to place Chennault, an American citizen, under surveillance and to install a telephone tap on the South Vietnamese Embassy, both illegal activities that the U.S. government regularly conducted but were kept secret for national security reasons.[61]

Johnson and Rostow had become alarmed that Nixon was seriously colluding with Thieu to sabotage the peace talks, Parry reports, when on October 29 they learned from "a member in the banking community" in New York who was "very close to Nixon" that Wall Street bankers were sizing up that Johnson's peace initiative would fail, that the "U.S. would have to spend a great deal more — a fact which would adversely affect the stock market and bond market."

Two days later — and just hours before his 8 p.m. televised address — Johnson began calling key senators who might warn Nixon's people to stop "messing around with both sides," explaining, "Hanoi thought they could benefit by waiting and South Vietnam's now beginning to think they could benefit by waiting." The warnings failed; FBI cables report more contacts between Chennault and Bui Diem.

Calling Republican Senate leader Everett Dirksen for the second time,

Johnson implored him to intervene again with Nixon and his aides and threatened to put the story "on the front pages" because it "would shock America." Johnson emphasized: "They're contacting a foreign power in the middle of a war. It's a damn bad mistake." He added: "They oughtn't be doing this. This is treason." Dirksen responded simply, "I know."[62]

On November 4 Johnson learned from the FBI's bugging that the *Monitor*'s seasoned Washington correspondent Saville Davis had visited Bui Diem to get a comment about "a story received from a correspondent in Saigon." The FBI's "eyes only" cable, relayed to Johnson at his ranch in Texas, reported Davis as having said that "the dispatch from Saigon contains elements of a major scandal which also involves the Vietnamese ambassador and which will affect presidential Richard Nixon if the *Monitor* publishes it." Unable to get Bui Diem either to confirm or to deny my scoop, Parry reports, Davis then visited the White House for comment and showed aides there my thirty-eight-word lead about the "purported political encouragement from the Nixon camp" to Thieu.

"The *Monitor*'s inquiry gave President Johnson one more opportunity to bring to light the Nixon campaign gambit before Election Day," Parry recounts. Before deciding what to do, Johnson consulted in a conference call with Rostow, Defense Secretary Clifford, and Secretary of State Dean Rusk. "Those three pillars of the Washington Establishment were unanimous in advising Johnson against going public, mostly out of fear that the scandalous information might reflect badly on the U.S. government," Parry explains in summing up their extended answers. Johnson agreed with his advisors. An administration spokesman told Davis: "Obviously I'm not going to get into this kind of thing in any way, shape or form." Based on these evasive responses to Davis, the *Monitor* decided against publishing my lead.

My lead gave Johnson a last-minute choice of remaining silent or going public with Nixon's ploy on the eve of the election. The scoop also crystallized a unique split-screen moment: the most decisive period of the Vietnam War, settling the conditions for ending it, was moving in parallel with a most indecisive period in the American democratic process, the U.S. presidential election.

The White House joined the *Monitor* in keeping vital information secret from Americans about to cast their ballots for president while GIs and Vietnamese were dying in a faraway war. My incriminating lead provided a hinge-of-history moment — for the American election, the future of South Vietnam, and the thousands of Americans and Vietnamese dying and about to die in Southeast Asia as the war dragged on for four more bloody years. In what Parry describes in another context, my lead zeroing in on Nixon's "treason" faded away into the United States' "lost history" — history that in this case would be written with more blood and tears.

Vice President Humphrey was also alerted by his chief speechwriter, Ted Van Dyk, that Thieu was going to hold off sending a delegation to the Paris peace talks and that "in 1968 the old China Lobby is still alive." Humphrey fumed, "I'll be God-damned if the China Lobby can decide this government."[63] Yet that is what happened. Thieu's explosive address made national headlines and cast doubts on Johnson's ability to get the peace talks going and end the war. Nixon's speechwriter, William Safire, voicing the sentiments of numerous pundits and a reputable polling firm, observed, "Nixon would probably not be president were it not for Thieu."[64]

After the election An and I gleaned a play-by-play of the final confrontations between Thieu and U.S. ambassador Ellsworth Bunker that revealed why the Vietnamese had backed out of going to Paris. A Vietnamese source close to the palace conversations shared with An and me his notes detailing what I described as "one of the most bizarre — if not scandalous — American diplomatic maneuvers in war-time history."[65]

In a nutshell the U.S. chief negotiator in Paris, Averell Harriman, made a proposal that Hanoi accepted on October 27 to begin peace negotiations starting November 6 — the day after the presidential election — for a four-power conference that would give the National Liberation Front equal status and legitimacy with the Saigon government. In Saigon, however, Ambassador Bunker had secured Thieu's agreement to go to a three-power conference, with separate delegations representing Hanoi, Saigon, and Washington but with the NLF sitting as part of

North Vietnam's delegation. "Here is Bunker getting Thieu's agreement to a three-way peace conference in Paris," a stunned diplomat told me. "But Harriman had already sold out Saigon by giving away to Hanoi the most important thing of all — representation of the National Liberation Front."

On November 5, 1968, by the narrowest of margins, Richard Nixon was elected president, winning by 499,704 votes, or 0.7 percent, over Hubert Humphrey. Upon his inauguration Nixon began a two-pronged policy of talking with the Communists in Paris and "Vietnamization" on the battlefield by withdrawing all U.S. troops. But Nixon also expanded the conflict into Laos and Cambodia, vowing in 1969, "I'm not going to be the first American President who loses a war."[66] Yet that is what he would become. He failed to end the war any better than Johnson's attempt four years earlier, and he ushered in "the peace that never was."[67]

"Turn Out the Light at the End of the Tunnel"

On June 8, 1969, Nixon announced the United States would unilaterally withdraw 25,000 troops from Vietnam. Like a giant yo-yo, U.S. numbers began a free fall, from a peak of 543,000 on March 31, 1969, until on December 31, 1973, "less than 250" U.S. military personnel were assigned in Vietnam.[68] A historian observes that the U.S. de-escalation was "like watching a film run backward."[69]

Three years later, in August 1974, Nixon resigned because of the Watergate scandal. With him went congressional approval to fund the massive support he had promised Thieu that was essential for the Saigon government to stave off North Vietnamese advances.

On April 21, 1975, as North Vietnamese forces blitzed through the northern provinces and headed toward Saigon, Thieu resigned as president and four days later was flown to a U.S. aircraft carrier. On April 30, 1975, North Vietnamese tanks and troops captured Saigon. Stunning the world were iconic images of desperate residents clawing aboard an American helicopter perched on the narrow rooftop platform of a U.S. building. Vietnamese identified with the United States were terror struck. As the last helicopter flew off, Communist propagandists were shouting, "The Americans are gone, the country is free, independent, democratic."[70]

Left behind was a sign posted at the U.S. Embassy reading, "Turn off the light at the end of the tunnel when you leave."[71] The sign represented a bitter finale for the optimism voiced by Westmoreland and Bunker in 1967 that a U.S. victory in Vietnam was near. Instead, the United States had suffered the first clear defeat in its history.

29. Pham Xuan An worked side by side with me for four years while he also served as an ace spy for North Vietnam. By mistyping Mao Tse-tung's quotation, An may have subconsciously described himself as a "darling spy." (B. Deepe Collection)

11

Two "Darling Spies" and I

Tell the truth what we can, don't tell what we can't and
never tell lies.

Pham Xuan An, my associate and a Communist spy

An army without secret agents is exactly like a man without
eyes or ears.

Sun Tzu, *The Art of War*, about 400 BCE

January 1969. It was an upbeat time when Pham Xuan An and his family waved good-bye to me as I boarded a plane to leave Vietnam. They
had given me a gorgeous, embroidered linen tablecloth as a present for
my wedding, only six weeks away. I fully expected to see An and his
family again; I never suspected this would be my final good-bye to An.
Cruel Fate! as Kieu wailed in her epic poem. It was not to be. Under
newly inaugurated President Nixon, the conflagration spread to Laos
and Cambodia and escalated to even greater destruction, bloodshed,
and heartbreak than I had witnessed in my seven years of war reporting.
By April 1975 North Vietnamese tanks and troops swooped down the
peninsula and seized Saigon.

A Double Life: Strategic Spy and Ace Reporter

The years rolled on, or as Kieu lamented so poetically, "Time fled on moon-hare's feet and sun-crow's wings." Then, "like a firebolt from mid-sky,"[1] I learned in 1990 that An had been a Communist spy for years. That firebolt was delivered to me — and the world — by American journalist Stanley Karnow's news article. "That a Vietnamese had been duplicitous did not surprise me," Karnow reflects, "since civil wars invariably test allegiances." But he was astonished that An was a Communist because he considered An a detached professional journalist who did not appear to "toe the Communist line."[2]

Like Karnow, I was thunderstruck to learn that An had been operating as a colonel in the Viet Cong when he worked with me for the *New York Herald Tribune* and then the *Christian Science Monitor*; he never carried a weapon or wore a uniform. I was doubly shocked because I never imagined I was working side by side with a hard-core, certified Communist even when I often reported on Viet Cong infiltration throughout the fabric of U.S.-backed South Vietnam. In 1967, for example, I detailed the arrest of one hundred suspected Viet Cong, including Saigon's richest industrialist, an engineer at the biggest U.S.-financed sugar mill, a Vietnamese army major who headed the government's biggest ordnance depot, the wife of a judge, several journalists and writers — in short, penetration among the middle and upper classes and intellectuals in the urban centers.[3]

Working as close colleagues for four years, ours was news reporting at the edge, exciting, exasperating, exhausting, always potentially danger-ous, whether covering coups or false coups or Buddhist demonstrations or after-dark predictions of astrologers, pacification in the provinces, or shoot-outs visible from the upstairs window of my office-apartment. But all of these hazards were tame compared to the secret, shadowy world of An's life.

The value of strategic intelligence, like that gathered, analyzed, and forwarded by An, had been recognized two thousand years earlier by Sun Tzu, credited with writing the first treatise on war making. Unlike the Americans, who locate the "essence of combat" in violence, one analyst writes, Sun Tzu locates it in foreknowledge and deception.[4] Or as the master Chinese strategist quaintly put it millennia ago: "Now the reason the enlightened prince and the wise general conquer the enemy whenever they move and their achievements surpass those of ordinary men is foreknowledge." And that cannot be elicited "from gods, nor by analogy with past events, nor from calculations. It must be obtained from men who know the enemy situation." In short, he notes, "an army without secret agents is exactly like a man without eyes or ears."[5] (But even better than deception, Sun Tzu confides, is a strategy of winning without fighting.)

Most people have only one profession, An acknowledges, "but I had two: following the revolution and working as a journalist." The two professions were both extremely opposite and extremely similar to one another. "Intelligence work involves collecting information, analyzing it, and keeping it secret, protecting it like a mother cat protects her kittens," he elaborates. "Journalists, on the other hand, collect information, analyze it, and then broadcast it to the entire world."[6]

In spring 1975, as the Communists were advancing to overrun Saigon (and Chuck was stationed overseas), An feared bloodshed in the city, so he and *Time* magazine sent his wife and four children to the United States, where they stayed with me in Washington DC until he summoned them back to Vietnam about a year later. Upon learning of his spying, I first went into denial, thinking others were trying to smear him. I tried to erase him from my memory. But like a wandering ghost, he kept reemerging as details revealed his secret life and otherworldly sleuthing.[7]

By the time of his dignified state funeral in 2006, An had been promoted to the rank of senior lieutenant general, had been awarded the prestigious title of Hero of the Viet Nam People's Army, and had received sixteen Liberation Exploit Medals, including one commemorating his half century of membership in the Communist Party. An's documents and reports throughout the course of the war were indispensable, Hanoi's top intelligence official explains, because "knowing the enemy's activities was the key to victory." Upon receiving An's documents, he continues, "Prime Minister Pham Van Dong laughed happily while General Vo

Nguyen Giap said: 'We are now in the U.S.'s war room!'" From Giap the tightly held secret documents went directly to North Vietnamese president Ho Chi Minh.[8]

An's "Straw-Fire Temper" and My New Legman

I remember clearly the first day I began working with An. He was with Reuters, and I was with *Newsweek* when Nick Turner, the bureau chief of the British wire service, was out of town, and An was responsible for sending out dispatches. I sat at the typewriter in the Reuters office to hammer out what An dictated for a soft-news piece about peasant women scraping by in the Mekong Delta. We seemed destined to hit it off. He was eight years older than I, born in 1927, the Year of the Tiger. He was a "happy choice" to associate with me, born in the Year of the Pig, because I would bring him a "sense of security," according to astrology that assured Vietnamese of some hidden order in an out-of-control world.[9]

After the Diem coup, when I was freelancing for the *New York Herald Tribune*, An quit Reuters and was free to take up my earlier offer to work for me. An told me that he quit when he was ordered to remove his birdcage from a desk. Instead, An slammed the cage down and walked out in a fit of what he described to me as a "straw-fire temper" — one that flares suddenly but dies out quickly.

When events began moving so fast that my cheapie way of airmailing copy to New York was untimely, I telephoned my editor and persuaded him to put me on a regular basis that would give me cabling privileges and to add An to the *Herald Tribune*'s payroll. With the increasing number of protests from students and Buddhists, carrying banners and issuing news statements, all in Vietnamese, I needed a trusted translator. The editor agreed.

We worked well and hard together. An started to teach me Vietnamese, but the tonal language was too much for me, especially after I heard American missionaries were spending eight-hour days to master it. I came to treat An like a brother and felt like part of his family. I got to know his wife, soft-spoken Thu Nhan, and his children; I helped pay hospital bills when the fourth child arrived. I had also taken out an insurance policy and named him, after my sister, as a beneficiary. In turn An said about me, "I loved her so much, my children and my wife still love her."[10] He had hoped that I, rather than a man, would have the chance to write his life story but added, "Unfortunately, my wish didn't come true"[11] — unfortunately for him and for me. Instead of his life story, I am self-tortured to write this short chapter about him, being sorely conflicted about how such a trusted friend could be so deceptive.

The characteristic I remember most about An was his calm demeanor, his unflappability during big news stories, his gliding into a room even during crises. "He's got a very cool temperament," I wrote my foreign editor in 1965, "and it takes more than a coup to shake him up."[12] When I asked An a question, he often gave an answer that began in history, sometimes as far back as the Nguyen Dynasty in the 1800s, a long-winded response that I found unsettling during breaking-news moments. Yet behind his nonchalance An was terrified that his spying for the Viet Cong would be discovered and would lead to his death.[13] From the beginning of his spying, An told one of his biographers, "I never relaxed for a minute. Sooner or later as a spy, you'll be captured. I had to prepare myself to be tortured. This was my likely fate."[14]

I knew that An was a southerner and a nationalist. But he did not seem to be very partisan about politics. I cannot recall any personal animosity against the United States; in fact, he reveled in telling of his good times studying in California. He seemed to view the merry-go-round of governments in Saigon as a sort of joke. No matter what happened in Vietnam, he had told me, he would stay in the country to take care of his ailing mother. I understood this obligation to his mother. He and I had attended the funeral and burial service of a dedicated Vietnamese paratrooper, killed in action, who had been one of our key sources. At the grave site the paratrooper's mother, surrounded by sobbing mourners, hurled dirt onto the casket as it was being lowered into the ground and wailed at her "ungrateful son." How could she call the son ungrateful when he was not responsible for his own death? I asked An. He explained that Vietnamese custom obliged sons to take care of their mothers as they grew old.

I was not the only correspondent who respected An and his journalistic legwork. He was likable, easygoing, and humorous. Tough veteran *Times* man Homer Bigart and Reuters's Nick Turner thought An was the best in town. CBS's Morley Safer described him as "one of the few Vietnamese reporters admitted to off-the-record briefings by the American mission. It was rumored that he was a CIA agent."[15] Some journalists even suspected An of being a triple agent, working for the South Vietnamese or other governments as well as the U.S. CIA.[16]

Many admired An, writer William Prochnau indicates, because "he could cut red tape, roust out information, and talk poetry and philosophy as well as run a story to ground on deadline." But, Prochnau explained, An, then in his midthirties, often disappeared for a few days, and it was considered "obvious to all that he had a secret love stashed somewhere."[17] No one, most of all me, had an inkling he was off to D-Zone to brief his Communist superiors.[18]

Even military information officers trusted An and valued our work. Col. Rodger Bankson, chief of information for the U.S. military command during 1966 and 1967, said, for example: "Beverly Deepe was another good news person. She had the smartest Vietnamese news assistant in Saigon. She also was smart."[19]

The Saigon government often tried to use Vietnamese journalists to gain information or favorable news coverage and sometimes pressured those working for Western news outlets. Saigon officials mimeographed and circulated selectively the text of our dispatches cabled through the national telegraph office. Thus, South Vietnamese government officials (and perhaps Viet Cong spies too) were aware of our news before our own editors. The government's threat to An was recalling the thirty-eight-year-old into the Vietnamese army or civilian service. In April 1965, for example, *Trib* editors gave An and me a joint byline on a full-page article (minus big ads) about an expected shakeup in the Saigon government (which did occur) and published it under the provocative headline "Viet Nam's Invisible War of Subversion." As a result, two jeep loads of six armed combat police searched for An on Saigon's main street, and the National Police Directorate summoned him for forty-five minutes of questioning.[20] After that, I wrote to the *Trib* editor, An preferred to forgo bylines and remain as inconspicuous as possible.[21]

An and Vuong: Decoding "Tin Pots, Might-Have-Beens, Never-Wuzzes"

During our five years of working together, An and I developed a routine. We often attended the daily press briefings and then headed to Givral, a favorite hangout for journalists and key news sources ranging from national assemblymen, businessmen, or secret police. Givral, a small restaurant and pastry shop, was one hub in the Rue Catinat, the name given to a necklace of coffeehouses and eateries where the fundamental Vietnamese ritual of "transmission, after evaluation, of rumor and gossip" takes place, according to veteran *New Yorker* writer Robert Shaplen. Givral held three daily "broadcast times," Shaplen details, the one around ten in the morning focused mainly on business affairs (which An and I skipped); one in the midafternoon and one between five and seven were held after the daily press briefings at the nearby National Press Center and focused on political and military affairs.[22] It was the last one where we lingered, often until twilight.

We were often joined by Nguyen Hung Vuong, An's best friend; I was paying Vuong a stipend out of my pocket for translation and interpretation, while the *Trib* paid An. Emaciated but willowy, Vuong, like An, was too weak and spindly to carry even a lightweight backpack of supplies needed for combat operations. Vuong's piercing eyes protruded above his hollowed-in cheeks like those of opium addicts I had pitied in Singapore.

Vuong was even more intriguing to me than An. Although both spoke English and French fluently, Vuong also spoke and wrote Chinese. He had grown up in southern China, where his father was a functionary for the French governors of Indochina. His elder brother had been a Communist—but the wrong kind, a Trotskyite—and had been assassinated. Vuong therefore knew a lot about Communist theory, history, and mind-set and often commented on and corrected An's analyses of Hanoi's strategies. Vuong assumed the role of an elder brother who protected and instructed An, and An placidly accepted this role.

What I did not then know was that Vuong worked for the CIA, with his contacts beginning when it was the Office of Strategic Services fighting the Japanese in World War II in alliance with Ho Chi Minh's forces.[23] As a lieutenant in the South Vietnamese army under Diem, Vuong had worked for the Psychological Warfare Department, and as such, in 1954–56 he and An were associated closely with important U.S. spies. One of these was the CIA's Col. Edward G. Lansdale, who had been schooled in advertising and advocated Madison Avenue–like techniques for selling a better ideology in the countryside than the Communists were marketing.[24] Unbeknownst to me at the time, I was working simultaneously with a top-notch Communist spy and a longtime CIA agent!

Both of them were what Mao called "darling spies," or "men who went over the enemy lines and discovered military secrets at great risk to themselves." I stumbled across Mao's description on an aged, ivory page in packet 119 of the 170 packets of materials that I had shipped from Saigon in 1969. I had not opened packet 119 for forty years. But when I did, I found the stack of thirty-seven double-spaced pages containing Mao's quote, which An had typed out. An's typing was not the best; the smudged carbon copy of excerpts in English that An had typed contained typos, misspelled words, and crossed-out lines. But this quote took on greater significance when I learned that An indeed qualified as a darling spy. Years later I learned that Vuong did too. I thought *darling spies* seemed like an ingenious, fitting label to describe both patriotic Vietnamese risking their lives to sleuth for foreign governments engaged on opposite sides of a cataclysm.

In drafting this chapter, I decided to track down the English-language source that An had used to locate and excerpt Mao's quote. When I finally found the source,[25] I was flabbergasted. An had mistyped Mao! Instead of praising darling spies, Mao had described "daring spies." Was the adding of the letter *l* a Freudian slip made by An because of his affection for the United States? Or was it just his erratic fingers that day? Whatever the reason, An and Vuong remain both daring and darling spies in my mind, my memory, my memoirs. They embody and exemplify to me the mystique of Vietnam.

I was amused that this duo of darling spies was aptly described by CBS's Safer as "a two-man repository of all the intrigues, petty bickering, corruption, gossip, dirt, plotting and grand designs of the little kings we created, the tin-pots we overthrew, the might-have-beens and never-wuzzes."[26]

As close as the duo was, however, An never told Vuong that he was a spy for the other side.[27] As Saigon was about to fall, An told Vuong that he would remain in Vietnam. "We have been so long in this venture," An explained. "We are nearing the end; I want to see the end." To which Vuong replied that the end would not be much of an experience, adding, "I saw the change in 1945. And in 1949 in Canton. . . . We have seen it." An retorted: "Anyway I cannot bring myself up to leave."[28] Vuong's critiquing An about Communist theory and practice seems ironic years later, when we both learned An had been a master spy for Hanoi.

The sessions at Givral were usually all-Vietnamese affairs and were my main social event. I did not socialize much with members of the U.S. press corps or embassy officials, except on special occasions like a farewell send-off or firing off a protest about journalists' problems. I swapped the latest Givral gossip while soaking in the atmosphere and savoring ice cream served in the hollowed-out half of a pineapple. Vuong's chain-smoking added to An's so that the haze inside Givral often became as thick as the fog of the war swirling outside its doors. Addicted cigarette smokers, Vuong died of cancer in 1986 in Virginia,[29] and two decades later, at age seventy-nine, An died of emphysema. An had been inhaling an evil from the West almost as long as he had fought to expel foreigners from his homeland.

An: Code-Name x6 in H63 Network

After Stanley Karnow blew An's cover, I learned much about the shadow world of An's spycraft by reading several of his biographies. A 2003 biography written by two Vietnamese biographers, Hoang Hai Van and Tan Tu, was serialized in a North Vietnamese newspaper and circulated in English on the Internet, where I downloaded it. Then I obtained the English-language version of the book released by Hanoi. These cobiographers describe An as the "ace of spies," detail his methods of spying, and provide interviews with top Hanoi officials on the crucial value of An's risky sleuthing. Hanoi followed up this official biography with a thriller movie, a newspaper series, a ten-part documentary on Ho Chi Minh Television that aired in 2007, and YouTube segments. Another movie is reportedly in the works.[30]

How An pulled off his spy mastering puzzled the Central Intelligence Agency,[31] as well as the *New Yorker* magazine, for which An had been a key source for so many of its articles written by Robert Shaplen, the magazine's longtime Asia hand. The made-in-Hanoi sketch of An's double life was largely confirmed and expanded on by two biographies later written by U.S. scholars. One biography and a *New Yorker* article were seductively titled "The Spy Who Loved Us."[32]

An's code name in the Communists' military intelligence service was X6, and his alias was Hai Trung. For twenty-three years he was the lone kingpin used to secure U.S. and South Vietnamese top secret documents and other information, which were then dangerously relayed through the elaborate, clandestine Intelligence Network H63 to Communist base headquarters only twenty-five miles from Saigon.[33]

An's work for the Communists began innocently enough. As a sixteen-year-old in 1943, he and many classmates joined the Communist-led guerrillas to fight Japanese invaders. It was the patriotic thing to do, he says. Then, "when the French came back, nothing had really changed, just the enemy." His driving principle: "I knew we had to get rid of the foreigners," An explains. "Even the foreigners I love so much."[34]

In mid-1951 the Communists assigned An to spy on the French Expeditionary staff, and two years later, in February 1953, he was admitted into the Viet Nam Communist Party.[35] He worked with U.S. military officers from 1955 until 1957. This pivotal assignment enabled him to assist numerous Vietnamese army officers in preparing to leave for training in the United States. They later served as his inside sources when they became generals to lead the Saigon government or its top military commands. This assignment also enabled An to befriend and work closely with, if not for, CIA operatives and to improve his English language skills, a necessity for his selection to study in the United States on a scholarship provided by the Asia Foundation, often considered a front for the U.S. CIA.[36]

The decision for the thirty-year-old An to study journalism was made by the founder of Hanoi's strategic intelligence network, Muoi Huong; for the first and only time the Vietnamese Communists provided much of the funding to cover expenses for An's two years of study of journalism, beginning in 1957 at Orange Coast College, a community college in Orange County, California, where he worked on the college newspaper.[37] "If you are a politician in this mess," Muoi Huong alerted An, "you will be imprisoned one day. Therefore, it is better to do journalism. To engage in journalism is to engage in politics but no one knows that you are involved in politics." As An departed for California, the Communists instructed him to learn to think and write like an American and to understand American culture and people thoroughly so that, as his Vietnamese cobiographers report, "we can learn from our opponents."

Upon returning to Vietnam in 1959, An worked for the secret service of the South Vietnamese government then moved to its official Viet News Agency. It was rumored he also worked for French intelligence and the U.S. CIA before beginning in 1960 to work for Reuters.[38] During this time he was promoted to Viet Cong colonel. In 1964 he left Reuters and began working with me for the *New York Herald Tribune* and then the *Christian Science Monitor.* After the demise of the *Trib* in 1966, An worked for *Time* magazine,[39] serving as its full-fledged staff correspondent until 1976, when he closed out its bureau after Saigon fell to the Communists.

An: "Never Tell Lies" (While Hiding the Complete Truth)

An's motto was: "Never tell lies." "He never simply fed senior leaders false information that they wanted to hear," his cobiographers note. "He did not even lie to his opponents." Nor to journalists. An told countless visitors that he was not a propagandist for the Communists, nor was he one who planted stories or spread disinformation; his bosses had given him much more strategic assignments and the U.S. education needed to perform them. So, he said, he fed the same information to both his U.S.

and Viet Cong bosses.[40] The guiding principle for his bifurcated life: "To tell the truth what we can, don't tell what we can't and never tell lies."[41]

Unbeknownst to me, however, An was providing much more valuable information to his Communist bosses than he gave journalists, and it was gleaned from far better sources than those in Saigon coffeehouses. In 1962 An sent his bosses twenty-four rolls of film of the U.S. master plan of the war, the buildup of armed forces, the support of American troops, the Strategic Hamlet Plan, the plan of reoccupying liberated zones, and the plan of consolidating Saigon's army with U.S. military equipment.

From 1960 to 1963 Hanoi's top leaders knew of allied activities mainly through An's reports, and in 1964 An told them about the new U.S. plan to introduce combat units and much more devastating weaponry. This plan unfolded a year later and earned An his second Military Exploit Medal. In 1965 he sent even more useful documents to Hanoi when U.S. combat troops were introduced. Thus, An's spying helped Hanoi to devise counterstrategies before the cumbersome bureaucracies and logistical systems of the allies could unroll their strategies on the battlefield. "We had known about all of the U.S. strategies in advance," Muoi Huong confides. "It was really a miracle."[42]

How An gathered his intelligence information was a forerunner to what U.S. investigative journalists regularly began to adopt in and after 1972 to expose the Watergate scandal. First, when possible, go for the documents, which are what his superiors in Hanoi relished. Second, protect your sources. Even in his top secret documents to Hanoi, An did not reveal who provided him valuable information, nor would he write his memoirs detailing his operations, even though he had been offered by his American friends two million dollars to do so.[43]

Over time An developed such cozy relations with key sources that he readily obtained the confidential or top secret information needed to serve both his Communist bosses and journalists. On April 21, 1968, for example, his regional Intelligence Section urgently requested An find out what revelations had been spilled two days earlier by the highest-ranking Viet Cong cadre who had defected to the Saigon side, Lt. Col. Tran Van Dac.

To fulfill this assignment, An fearlessly drove to the Gia Dinh subarea of suburban Saigon with his Communist superior, Tu Cang, in the front seat. About fifteen minutes later An managed to borrow all documents related to the defector's secrets, copied them, and returned them as promised. "The person who had lent out the documents was not a revolutionary," Tu Cang observes, "but gave up the documents because he respected An." The documents showed that the defector had indeed revealed all of the Communists' combat plans for the upcoming second phase of the Tet Offensive. As a result, U.S. forces were placed on high alert, and the top military command reportedly launched a special search to find out who had leaked the defector's revelations to the press; once Communist leaders received An's information and knew what the allies knew, they changed their combat plans. I wrote a detailed page 1 dispatch about this "most sensational turncoat known to date in the Vietnam war" and the Alfred Hitchcock plot he revealed of a plan for "a military extravaganza against Saigon even more spectacular than the surprise Tet offensive."[44]

After securing secret documents, An took them to his modest home and at night photographed them with his Canon Reflex camera,[45] often guarded by his wife, Thu Nhan, and his German shepherd, King. An also wrote reports, using a primitive invisible ink, often scratched onto a rough paper that could be read by his superiors when they applied another solution.[46]

In the early years his superiors often called An for a debriefing at their home base near Trung Lap, where I had trampled through a Viet Cong–held village in 1962. But after 1966, when a U.S. division was based nearby, such trips by An became too dangerous because, as two U.S researchers explained, that area "became the most bombed, shelled, gassed, defoliated, and generally devastated area in the history of warfare."[47]

Top Secret, No-Tech Spring Rolls

Unlike the people sniffers, electronic sensors, and other high-tech devices that I reported the United States used for gathering information on North Vietnamese soldiers besieging Khe Sanh, An used Intelligence Network H63. It was a no-tech network of little-old-lady couriers and dedicated fighters that was described by his Vietnamese biographers as the "old-fashioned way of liaison officers."

Even after overcoming the dangers of obtaining top secrets, An had the hazardous task of passing his messages to his only liaison agent in Saigon for fourteen years, Nguyen Thi Ba, a gray-haired vendor of children's toys or other goods who had taken up the revolutionary cause in 1940. She never lost any of his priceless intelligence items, nor was she ever discovered or arrested. She received no pay, but sometimes the Party gave her money to replace her worn-out clothes. Ba never visited An's house nor he hers; intelligence networks were carefully compartmentalized so that captured agents could not be forced to divulge the identities of their comrades.

An and Ba choreographed a high-risk routine. They first met on crowded streets or markets about once a month but later weekly or even more often as urgent information arose. An often handed over five to ten rolls of film that he had swaddled up like spring rolls. On top of them in a basket, Ba placed real spring rolls, some fruit, and incense. When An wrote down reports in his invisible ink, Ba used these papers to wrap items for her basket.[48]

Ba traveled by bus, passing through the government's checkpoints, to hand over An's items to another trusted courier, Nguyen Thi Anh, a middle-aged, small-goods vendor who had joined the Communists when she was nineteen.[49] She in turn smuggled the items out of the city to others, who delivered them to the network's home base camp at Cu Chi, an underground tunnel complex two hundred miles long dating back to the French Indochina War and close to where the U.S. Army's Twenty-fifth Infantry Division would erect its own installations.[50] From Cu Chi, Viet Cong from an armed communication unit drove An's items to the regional intelligence bureau. It radioed information from the documents to senior leaders and then forwarded the papers,[51] which ultimately reached General Giap and President Ho.

Years later I was stunned to learn how An had played such a significant, clandestine role in the two biggest combat stories I covered at the very beginning and the end of my seven years in Vietnam — the battle of Ap Bac and the Communists' Tet blitz.

In January 1963 I covered for *Newsweek* the Battle of Ap Bac and quoted one U.S. helicopter pilot describing the surprising Viet Cong victory as "the biggest clobbering in U.S. helicopter warfare." I was not then working with An but decades later discovered how he had played key roles not only in shaping the fighting but also in shaping the news stories about it. Those stories in turn exposed U.S. officials' overoptimism about the conduct of the war, which developed into an ever-widening credibility gap.

The backstory of Ap Bac began months before the battle when An helped Viet Cong guerrillas analyze how to counter U.S. helicopter companies and new equipment such as armored personnel carriers and to plan their victorious "stand and fight" strategy. Armed with An's counter to the U.S. game plan, Viet Cong guerrillas began weeks of practice shooting at cardboard miniatures of helicopters attached to bamboo poles and concentrating their volleys simultaneously on specified targets.[52]

When the battle began, An alerted the press and directed them to the scene. "An was the first reporter to break the news," his bureau chief for Reuters, Nick Turner, recalls. "He fed me the initial story and details that got me to write it. He told me some American helicopters had been shot down and that I should go to Ap Bac.

"America was not directly involved in the war at this point; so the fact that American helicopters were getting shot down was big news. It was the first major battle of the war."

The next morning Turner took with him Neil Sheehan, correspondent for the United Press International wire service. In a masterful case of news management, Turner observes, "the story broke in the Western press and was written exactly the way the Communists wanted it written."[53] Right after the battle, his cobiographers in Hanoi gloat, An "got on board an

American helicopter, flying around the battlefield to see our resounding victory."[54]

Far more than I could have imagined, An also played a significant role in helping the Communists plan and then assess their countrywide Tet Offensive. Three months before Tet his superiors told An about their planned offensive and assigned him to ferret out and analyze key information. To accomplish his mission, An took great risks to chauffer and guide Tu Cang, the deputy political commissar and head of the intelligence service section, who had been dispatched to Saigon for an on-site inspection. They scouted out and recommended strategic targets where Communist units and sapper teams could make the most sensational and damaging impact, such as hitting the U.S. Embassy, the Presidential Palace, the Vietnamese navy headquarters, and the government's radio station. They discussed Party affairs in fancy restaurants and snooped out journalists' offices.

But the attacks in Saigon and other urban centers proved to be a stunning defeat for the Viet Cong and North Vietnamese units. In his first reports to Hanoi, Tu Cang reflected this defeat. But being aware from incoming press reports of the shocking impact on the U.S. mainland, An tried to persuade Tu Cang to change his reporting. An took him to a colonel of the South Vietnamese government's General Staff and to talk with several American advisors. "They said that anti-war movements were on the rise in the U.S. and American prestige had gone downhill," Tu Cang recounts. "After that, I changed my mind."

Tu Cang told Hanoi that although the Communists' Tet Offensive militarily was unsuccessful, "its political and psychological negative impact on the enemy would be great." Hanoi's leaders began to echo this encouraging assessment. For his sow's-ear-into-silk magic that transformed Hanoi's military defeat into a stunning political-psychological victory, Hanoi awarded An his third Military Exploit Medal.[55]

About An: "Something Untold and Untellable"

Even in retrospect, I do not think An's double (maybe even triple) life denigrated the professionalism of my reporting. Hanoi had given him a much higher mission than being a propaganda agent. Likewise, I am confident that An did not undermine the truthfulness of our dispatches; he had broadened and deepened the content of our news reporting from and about Vietnam, opening new vistas for me. He tried to wash away some of the opaqueness of the life and culture of Vietnam and its people even while he himself was adding to that opaqueness.

There was about him a quiet mystery, an inscrutability so often used to describe Asia. He seemed almost too apolitical and aloof even in the most supercharged moments, and he joked too often and lightheartedly when dark clouds hovered about. To adapt Shaplen's descriptive and profoundly accurate phrase from another context, there was about An "something untold and untellable."[56]

An personified several key factors: the ultranationalism that partly explained why some Vietnamese so devotedly and daringly served the Communist side, the long-range foresight of the Vietnamese Communist Party in helping to fund his U.S. college education, the shortcomings of U.S. intervention in Vietnam, and his steadfast resistance to U.S. values and way of life that he had experienced and enjoyed firsthand. In Vietnam's total-war insurgency An demonstrated that an unarmed civilian, as he always was, could serve as dangerously as a combatant. But An overlooked or minimized the ruthlessness of Hanoi's dictatorial regime that many southerners then knew about.

An's spycraft opened a window on how and why, at least in part, the United States failed to win over the dominant sympathies of an English-speaking, U.S.-educated intellectual and ultimately lost the war to what President Johnson in 1964 described as a "damned little piss-ant country" and a "raggedy-ass little fourth-rate country."[57]

An also personified an unseen and unseemly part of international journalism in which correspondents' prime loyalties and duties were to government spymasters rather than the public. But he was not alone. A few U.S. journalists during this period also were known to provide a cover or helping hand for U.S. government intelligence gathering, but the double life of these agents in the mostly male media world was usually treated as hush-hush.[58] Some journalists were rumored to be spies

whether they were or not. Diem's secret police spread stories about François Sully as a "Communist spy, French agent, inveterate womanizer."[59]
Morley Safer's television footage of the marines' burning Cam Ne hamlet
electrified American viewers and infuriated President Johnson, who in
turn badgered CBS executives to fire Safer (they did not) and smeared
him by spreading the untrue word that he was an intelligence agent for
the Soviet's KGB.[60]

An: The Americans "Had No Right Here"

An was asked whether he had any regrets that his spying had played a role
in the deaths of innocent people. "No," An told his biographer Thomas
A. Bass. "I was fulfilling my obligations. I had to do it."

"So you have no regrets?" Bass replied.

"No."[61]

My own conflicted emotions about An's spying were eased by remembering that so much death, destruction, and havoc had been wrought
upon Vietnam, Laos, and Cambodia that not even one uniquely effective
non–policy maker could be held all that responsible for criminal acts.[62]

Some journalists condemned An for pretending to be a journalist
while helping to kill Americans.[63] But others did not criticize him even
after learning about his spying for Hanoi.[64] Shaplen, who had toured
the ruins of Saigon's waterfront and Cholon with An after the 1968 Tet
Offensive and could see the destruction and deaths there, continued to
express confidence in him eleven years after the Communists captured
Saigon and after he had been outed as a spy. Shaplen described An as
one of the best-informed sources in Saigon, adding, "In our conversations over the years, often lasting for hours, I discovered that the facts
and opinions he furnished about the Communists, the government, and
the many contending individuals and groups — including Buddhists and
Catholics who opposed both sides in the conflict — were more on the
mark than anything I could obtain from other sources, not excluding the
American Embassy, which often knew surprisingly little about what was
going on among the non-establishment Vietnamese."[65]

Thirty-seven years after I bid what became my final farewell to An, he died on September 20, 2006, at age seventy-nine. He was given an impressive state funeral held at the Ministry of Defense in Saigon. On display was an enlarged photo of An, unsmiling but looking magnificent in a white jacket decorated with a number of medals and a high-brimmed hat reminiscent of those worn by traffic policemen in the Saigon I remembered. A gold-rimmed black board — surrounded by an altar jar holding joss sticks of incense, some fruit, and an elaborate plaque written in Chinese characters — held row after row of his medals. Conspicuously displayed also was the coffee mug signed by the staff of the California community college newspaper where An had studied journalism to launch the unhidden half of his double life.[66]

Sixteen years before his death An was asked a pointed question about his double life, or perhaps even triple life, by CBS's Morley Safer: "Do you regret what you did, now that you've seen the results?"

"I hate that question," An began. "I have asked it of myself a thousand times. But I hate the answer more. No. No regrets. I had to do it. This peace that I fought for may be crippling this country, but the war was killing it. As much as I love the United States, it had no right here. The Americans had to be driven out of Vietnam one way or another."[67]

Appendix 1

Author's Vietnam Articles in U.S. Publications

In this table APN stands for Associated Press Newsfeatures. In 1962 this news service distributed internationally my human interest and feature articles, which were published in various newspapers on different dates. NYHT stands for *New York Herald Tribune,* and CSM stands for *Christian Science Monitor.* The table is based on printed articles in my possession from these and other publications. Most publications listed are available on microfilm in selected libraries. Most of my articles published in the *Christian Science Monitor* are also available online at http://pqasb.pqarchiver.com/csmonitor_historic/advancedsearch.html.

PUBLICATION	DATE	PAGE	HEADLINE
APN	1962	—	"Death Zone" in South Vietnam
APN	1962	—	New Frontier in Viet Nam
APN	1962	—	Girl's Eyes Give War in Viet Nam New Look
APN	1962	—	Enemy Is Disease at This Viet Nam Battleground
APN	1962	—	Wife of Captured Man Expects Missionaries to Come Back
APN	1962	—	Reporter Inspires Chivalry
Washington Post	07/09/63	14	Discontent Increasing, but Coup Is Doubtful—Troops, Secret Police Prop Diem Regime
Washington Post	08/13/63	16	Buddhist Discontent Gaining Support in Viet-Nam Provinces
NYHT	03/15/64	4	As Saigon Saw Him: Intimate Glimpse of McNamara the Man
NYHT	04/19/64	1	Time and the Man in Viet Nam
NYHT	05/24/64	9	How We Help Viet Nam Get More Men for Its Army
NYHT	05/24/64	3	"McNamara's Headache"—14 Viet Provinces [information provided by author]
NYHT	05/25/64	6	Year Later: Viet Buddhists at It Again
NYHT	07/14/64	4	N. Viet Troops Cross Border, U.S. Aides Say
NYHT	07/26/64	2	Viet—Measuring an "Invasion"
NYHT	08/09/64	3	Bottom of the Pyramid—Red Viet Prisoner's Story
NYHT	08/10/64	4	Coming of Age in Viet Nam's Jungles [2nd of 2 articles]
NYHT	08/16/64	13	The CIA's Spy-Drops into Red Viet
NYHT	08/16/64	12	General Doubts Red Chinese Would Try to Bomb South Viet
NYHT	08/17/64	1	Viet Shakeup: Fateful Days Near in War—Timetable; Tightening
NYHT	08/22/64	1	Viet Buddhist Protests . . . Why?
NYHT	08/24/64	1	Viet Rioting for 5th Day
NYHT	08/25/64	1	Khanh Yields, Students Don't

NYHT	08/28/64	1		Viet: "New" Junta and Death in the Saigon Streets—Catholics vs. Buddhists
NYHT	08/29/64	1		Khanh Fights to Keep Power—Paratroops vs. Saigon Mobs
NYHT	08/31/64	1		From the Political Jungle of Viet—What Khanh Says
NYHT	09/04/64	1		Viet Musical Chairs: Khanh in, Aid [sic] Out
NYHT	09/14/64	16		Coup Flop a Boost for Khanh
NYHT	09/16/64	7		More Trouble Likely in Viet
NYHT	09/16/64	20		Madame Nhu Was Right [letter to editor commenting on author's article]
NYHT	09/20/64	2		It's the Day of the Moon Festival—Crisis Leaves Saigon Unruffled
NYHT	09/21/64	1		U.S.-Trained Viet Tribe in Open Revolt
NYHT	09/22/64	17		In Viet—A Coup Designed to Fail [1st of 2 reports after latest coup attempt]
NYHT	09/23/64	16		In Viet—The Military Coup That Became an Army Purge [2nd of 2 reports]
NYHT	10/04/64	—		Coups Are Old Hat to U.S. Saigon Families
NYHT	10/04/64	20		In Viet Nam—Fate IS in the Stars
NYHT	10/25/64	4		Viet a Year Later—U.S. Tackling Past Mistakes in Weird War [1st of 7 articles on nature of the conflict and the stratagems and miscalculations that shaped it]
NYHT	10/26/64	8		Viet Nam a Year Later—The Shadow That Rules Most of a Nation [2nd of 7 articles]
NYHT	10/27/64	6		Viet Nam a Year Later—Story of a "Have-Not" Exploited by the Reds [3rd of 7 articles on how Viet Cong seek to win popular support]
NYHT	10/28/64	8		Viet Nam a Year Later—The Buddhists, a Crucial Third Force [4th of 7 articles]

NYHT	10/29/64	6	Viet Nam a Year Later, No. 5—We Just Don't Understand [5th of 7 articles]
NYHT	10/30/64	4	New Saigon Regime Is Believed Moribund at Birth—Viet Nam a Year Later [6th of 7 articles]
NYHT	11/01/64	14	Viet Nam a Year after Diem—His Dire Prophecy Coming True [7th of 7 articles]
NYHT	11/02/64	12	Jets to Ashes—As the Yanks Saw It
NYHT	11/02/64	1	Viet Explosion—Shockwaves; Base Security Was Criticized
NYHT	11/08/64	8	Error: Making Americans Madder
NYHT	11/25/64	2	First Charge since Diem—Viet Premier Says Students "Play Reds' Game"
NYHT	11/29/64	14	Perplexity, Persuasion and Power Play—View from Saigon
NYHT	12/06/64	14	Infighting on U.S. Aid
NYHT	12/13/64	4	Viet's Course: It Changes with Our Men
NYHT	12/20/64	3	The Choppers Prove Their Worth in War
NYHT	12/22/64	4	Coup in Two Acts
NYHT	12/23/64	1	Viet Strongman Defies U.S. on Civilian Rule—Khanh Assails Gen. Taylor
NYHT	12/24/64	1	Khanh Plays Middle vs. Both Ends; Rusk Pleads for End to Bickering; The Military Intrigue
NYHT	12/25/64	1	Viet Press Briefing Expose—Taylor Rips Mask Off Khanh
NYHT	12/25/64	1	Christmas Eve Bomb in Saigon [reprinted in Reporting Vietnam, pt. 1 (New York: Library of America, 1998), 134–37; 1st of 2 articles]
NYHT	01/04/65	6	A Dilemma: Subversion by Political Priests
NYHT	01/05/65	5	Inner War: Battle for the Masses [2nd of 2 articles]
NYHT	01/09/65	6	Khanh's de Gaulle Look
NYHT	01/17/65	20	In Viet, Bomb at U.S. Pool

NYHT	01/17/65	20	A Red Attack the Viets Had to Admire
NYHT	01/21/65	7	Generals Enter Cabinet—Viet Buddhists Start Hunger Strike against Huong
Philadelphia Inquirer	01/21/65	—	Saigon Troops Quell Riots as 5 Monks Fast
NYHT	01/22/65	2	Peking's On-Spot Men with Red Viets
NYHT	01/24/65	5	New Alarums on Viet's Infernal Triangle
NYHT	01/31/65	24	Gen. Khanh Re-Emerges as the Strong Man
NYHT	01/31/65	24	North Viet Nam Recruits Its Own for the Red War
NYHT	02/07/65	22	Kosygin in Hanoi—Viet Red Attacks Kill 8 Americans
NYHT	02/09/65	1	New U.S.-Viet Air Raid—Next Move Up to Reds—On the Battle Front
NYHT	02/09/65	4	U.S. Students Want to Stay in Viet
NYHT	02/14/65	25	The Viet Cong Clinches Grip on Countryside
NYHT	02/16/65	3	See U.S. Raids as Basis for Stable Viet
NYHT	02/23/65	7	What Khanh Says on Phone
NYHT	02/26/65	—	Ouster of Khanh as Viet Chief Seen as Shift to Neutralism
NYHT	02/28/65	9	Viet Guerrillas Have the Edge on Guided Missiles
NYHT	03/07/65	5	We Get Tough, the Viets Lean to Neutralism
NYHT	03/10/65	1	Report in Saigon: More Marines Due
NYHT	03/14/65	17	Viet's "War of the Prairies"
NYHT	03/14/65	19	Reds in Yellow Robes? Maybe Mme. Nhu Was Right?
NYHT	03/15/65	1	North Viet Bombed Again; We Clam Up on U.S. Role
NYHT	03/21/65	19	Little-Known Red General Casts Shadow across Viet
NYHT	03/21/65	17	Saigon Snafu: Security Lax, Taxes Paid to Reds

NYHT	03/28/65	15	Taylor Returns Today for Decisions on Viet
NYHT	04/04/65	23	How Are Things in Hanoi? Jittery
NYHT	04/04/65	20	Viet Gas: The Story and How It Grew
NYHT	04/11/65	18	Vietnam's Invisible War of Subversion [byline with Pham Xuan An]
NYHT	04/13/65	13	Saigon: Reds Won't Talk, They'll Fight for All-Out Victory
NYHT	04/18/65	19	He Once Saved U.S. Airmen, Now They Bomb His Nation
NYHT	04/25/65	18	"Total, Bloody Mayhem"
NYHT	04/25/65	1	Viet: New Peril Looms—Inside Saigon U.S. Is Losing a Political War
NYHT	05/28/65	8	What's a Nice Girl like Beverly Deepe Doing in a Dirty War like This? Covering It for the *Herald Tribune*—Read Beverly Deepe's Vital Series on Viet Nam Starting in Sunday's *Herald Tribune* [full-page ad]
NYHT	05/30/65	12	Viet Nam Report—I: Why Guerrillas Fight So Hard [1st of 6 reports; reprinted in *NYHT* School Ed.]
NYHT	05/30/65	12	Viet Cong's "Kill" List: U.S. Advisers at Top
NYHT	05/31/65	2	Our Girl in Viet—2; America's Frozen Policy—Vital Political Power Unused
NYHT	06/01/65	12	Our Girl in Viet—Corruption—Hottest Saigon Issue [3rd of 6 reports]
NYHT	06/02/65	8	Our Girl in Viet—IV—How the U.S. Built on the Quicksand of Asian Politics
NYHT	06/03/65	18	Our Girl in Viet—V—Land Reform: The Long Delay [reprinted in *NYHT* School Ed.]
NYHT	06/04/65	2	Our Girl in Viet—Conclusion—The Program the Reds Can't Fight [6th of 6 reports; reprinted in *NYHT* School Ed.; letter to editor "Kudos for Miss Deepe" on series, 06/16/65, p. 22]
Denver Post	06/06/65	49	Viet Nam—"Need for Political Victory"

NYHT	06/13/65	1	Viet Regime's Downfall—A Step to Losing the War—Neutralist Part of Red Plot
NYHT	06/20/65	1	New Saigon Government—Generals' Balancing Act
NYHT	07/04/65	12	When the Viet Cong Snafus Saigon's Snob Set
NYHT	07/05/65	6	Ghoulish Air of Saigon, City in Death Grip
NYHT	07/08/65	13	Textbook Assault of "Teenage Brigade"—Viet Jungle Sweep; the Surprise That Wasn't
NYHT	07/11/65	14	Using 500 M.P.H. Jets against Jungle Guerrillas
NYHT	07/30/65	4	Taylor's Farewell: Pleasure and Sadness
NYHT	08/01/65	1	For U.S.: Risks of War and Peace—Free Viet Vote—Which Way
NYHT	08/01/65	8	Viet View: Little, Late, Negative
NYHT	09/05/65	8	A Native Critic on U.S. Role
NYHT	10/03/65	4	Cong Clings to Saigon Area
NYHT	10/10/65	26	Child Raising, Hanoi Style
NYHT	10/10/65	7	Reds Aren't Sole Problem in Viet [also published as "Saigon, U.S. Clash over Tribe"]
NYHT	10/17/65	8	Reds Capture U.S. Pilot; Cong Ambush
NYHT	10/25/65	4	Cong Demands Close a French Viet Plantation
NYHT	10/27/65	2	News Perspective—Viet Bombers Sow Bitter Seeds
NYHT	11/14/65	19	Viet Cong Make like Moles
NYHT	11/21/65	8	Viet Women—Friends, Foes and Madame Nhu [1st of 5 articles on Vietnamese women]
NYHT	11/22/65	2	News Perspective—Viet Cong Wedding in the Jungle [2nd of 5 articles]
NYHT	11/23/65	2	News Perspective—Viet WACs: Too Many Volunteers [3rd of 5 articles]

NYHT	11/24/65	11	Contrasts in Vietnamese Women—Rich Get Richer and Poor Get Poorer [4th of 5 articles]
NYHT	11/25/65	2	News Perspective—Saigon's Precocious Pitfalls
NYHT	12/03/65	2	News Perspective—Conflict at Home over Viet—V [last article]
NYHT	12/12/65	21	Hanoi Set for Long War
NYHT	01/16/66	23	New Series: Viet Nam, Past and Prospect [1st of 4 articles reviewing the war during 1965 and assessing prospects for 1966]
NYHT	01/17/66	9	Viet Nam: Past and Prospect—South Viets Identify GIs with Colonialism [2nd of 4 articles]
NYHT	01/18/66	5	Viet Nam: Past and Prospect—Subversion in Mekong Delta [3rd of 4 articles]
NYHT	01/19/66	4	Viet Nam: Past and Prospect—Marines' Greatest Effort: Securing Da Nang [4th of 4 articles]
Congressional Record	01/20/66	676	Vietnam, Past and Prospect [Sen. Mansfield on author's series reviewing the war; see app. 2]
NYHT	01/27/66	—	Saigon Urges U.S. to Resume Bombing Soon
NYHT	01/30/66	14	Guerrillas Kill 159—The Red Noose around Saigon
NYHT	01/31/66	2	News Perspective—Red School: Recruit to Guerrilla
NYHT	02/02/66	1	On the Carrier as Raids Resume
NYHT	02/03/66	2	News Perspective—Pilots Fear "Vietnik" Phone Calls
NYHT	02/06/66	11	Saigon Reshuffle in the Works
NYHT	02/10/66	—	The Mission: Big Goal vs. Past Failure
NYHT	02/15/66	2	News Perspective—Red Tape Snarls Viet Farm Aid
NYHT	02/21/66	7	New GI Pattern: Opening Roads to Get to People in Cong Areas
NYHT	02/23/66	6	GIs Seize Big, Empty Cong HQ

NYHT	03/06/66	8	Dr. Do Isn't Sure of Winning a Free Viet Election
NYHT	03/06/66	8	Nab Viet Cong Spies in U.S. Military HQ
NYHT	03/07/66	1	China War Peril Impels Inquiry Now—Fulbright
NYHT	03/13/66	12	Magnetic Thi Roils Viet Politics
NYHT	03/17/66	2	News Perspective—U.S. to Buddhists: We Back Ky—World Furor over Execution
NYHT	03/24/66	2	Hanoi Unit 40 Miles from Saigon [Paris Ed.]
NYHT	04/01/66	2	News Perspective—Is Asia "Domino Theory" Passé?
NYHT	04/10/66	16	Viet's Actual Power Bloc—The Which-Way Buddhists—Reckoning in Saigon: Monks Hold Control
NYHT	04/12/66	2	Buddhist Chief Quang: Is He a Communist?
NYHT	04/13/66	1	B-52 Raid Is Biggest since '45
NYHT	04/13/66	2	News Perspective—Viet Buddhist Chief Bars Reds
NYHT	04/14/66	1	Viet Riots Siphoned Off Base Guards
NYHT	04/17/66	1	Ky Loyalists under Attack in Da Nang
San Francisco Examiner Chronicle	04/24/66	26	Buddhists—Hinge of Vietnam's Fate
San Francisco Examiner Chronicle	05/01/66	29	A Buddhist Plan—3 Vietnams
NYHT	06/06/66	8	A Dozen Cong Spies Arrested after Infiltrating Saigon HQ
Omaha World Herald	10/05/66	40	Viet Nam Postal Service Is Perilous
Parade	11/20/66	—	Madame Ky, the Charmer—She Calls Herself "The Grace Kelly of Vietnam"
Parade	01/15/67	26	Honeymooners in a War
Omaha World Herald	02/12/67	13	A Background Report—This Is Decision Year for "Which-Way War"
CSM	05/03/67	1	U.S. Patrols Cross Viet Borders

CSM	05/05/67	1	"Other War" Stalls—South Vietnam Pacification Program Seen Tottering on Brink of Collapse
CSM	05/08/67	1	Two Vietnam Fronts—Red Offensives Loom [Eastern Ed.]
CSM	05/08/67	1	Viet Reds Set "Peace" Offensive [New England Ed.]
CSM	05/10/67	1	Hanoi Grips Viet Cong Tighter [Midwestern Ed.]
CSM	05/11/67	11	Hanoi Strategy May Boomerang [New England Ed.]
CSM	05/13/67	13	U.S. Streamlining of Viet Bureaucracy Curbs Infighting
CSM	05/15/67	2	Saigon Lures Defectors with "Open-Arms" Plan
Cosmopolitan	06/06/67	104	A Girl Visits the Combat Marines in Vietnam
CSM	06/24/67	9	A War without a Front Line
CSM	07/31/67	1	U.S. Role in Vietnam Pivots on Election [1st of 3 articles on Vietnamese election]
CSM	08/01/67	2	The People—Skeptical of Viet Charter [2nd of 3 articles]
CSM	08/02/67	4	Politics—Tears, Threats, and Generals Help Shape Vietnam Ticket [3rd of 3 articles]
CSM	08/12/67	1	Counterguerrilla Forces—New Look for Saigon's Army
CSM	08/16/67	1	Saigon Says Red Spy Net Cut by Security Campaign
CSM	08/17/67	1	Viet Campaign Bares Long-Standing Problems
CSM	12/11/67	1	Westmoreland Sights Viet Victory [on U.S. view, 1st of 2 articles]
CSM	12/13/67	1	Why Reds Look for Viet Win [on Communist view, 2nd of 2 articles]
CSM	12/14/67	5	"Yes, Sir—I Mean Aye-Aye"—Vietnam's Upside-Down War Jumbles Military Traditions
CSM	12/16/67	1	When a Senator Drops In

CSM	12/20/67	4	Viet Cong Orders Propaganda Offensive
CSM	12/21/67	5	Westmoreland Phase-Out Forecast Sparks Debates
CSM	12/23/67	1	Saigon Grumbles at Johnson
CSM	12/28/67	1	Vietnam Outlook—Prospects for Peace Talks Appear Bleak in 1968 [1st of 3 articles on prospects for peace in Vietnam during 1968]
CSM	12/29/67	1	Viet Cong Seeks Political Victory [2nd of 3 articles]
CSM	01/02/68	5	U.S. Policy at Stake—Saigon Effectiveness Seen Crucial to War [3rd of 3 articles]
CSM	01/20/68	1	Hints to Peasants—Cong Presses for Coalition
CSM	01/24/68	1	Military Blocs Stymie Saigon Army Reform
CSM	01/26/68	4	Thang's Resignation Jars Saigon
CSM	01/27/68	5	Reds Hint Air-War Step-Up
CSM	01/31/68	7	U.S. Seventh Fleet Carries On as Usual in Pueblo Crisis
CSM	02/03/68	1	A View from Saigon—Blitz Erodes U.S. Position in Vietnam [reprinted in 2012 in 50 *Great Stories* in Columbia Journalism School centennial booklet, available at www.journalism.columbia.edu/centennial]
CSM	02/05/68	1	Cong Raids Take High Political Toll
CSM	02/06/68	4	Blow to Cities—South Viet Control Battered
CSM	02/07/68	1	South Vietnam Shaken—"Hardly a Hamlet Feels Safe"
CSM	02/08/68	1	"Blitz" Aftereffects—Viet Propaganda Battle Seesaws
CSM	02/09/68	1	Viet Cong in Saigon Hits and Hides
CSM	02/13/68	1	Villages around Saigon—Pacification Set Back Six Months?

CSM	02/17/68	2	Ceremonies—A Glimpse of the Viet Cong [1st of 4 delayed articles about an interview with a Viet Cong political cadre on 01/29/68. The two Western correspondents present knew nothing of the general offensive against Saigon and major provincial towns planned for the following day.]
CSM	02/19/68	5	Cong Interview—Cadre Boasts NFL [sic] Expects Decisive Victory in 1968 [2nd of 4 articles]
CSM	02/20/68	2	Interview—Cong Aide Lists Five "Musts" [3rd of 4 articles]
CSM	02/21/68	7	Viet Cong Claims Peasant Support [4th of 4 articles]
CSM	02/21/68	1	U.S. Blows Feed Viet Backlash
CSM	02/23/68	1	Cong Attacks Interfere—Thieu Mobilization Plan Crimped
CSM	02/24/68	4	Red Bases—Cambodia Dispute Flares
CSM	02/28/68	2	Hue: Battle for a Walled City [1st of 2 delayed on-the-scene reports]
CSM	02/29/68	6	Battle for Hue Palace—"Assault Ends with a Whimper" (2nd of 2 reports)
CSM	02/29/68	9	On the Ho Chi Minh Trail
CSM	03/04/68	1	Hue Struck Again—by Looting
CSM	03/05/68	2	Damage High—Victory at Hue Pondered
CSM	03/06/68	13	U.S. River Units Demoralize Cong in Mekong Wetlands [1st of 2 articles on riverine warfare]
CSM	03/07/68	6	Navy "Little Boat" Fleet patrols Viet Rivers [2nd of 2 articles]
CSM	03/13/68	6	Revival Debated—Pacification Efforts Hard Hit near Hue
CSM	03/16/68	9	Chopper Hopping VIPs—Diplomats in South Vietnam Ride the Bumptious Helicopter Circuit from City to Village to Jungle [for many villagers it is the first close-up look at American and Vietnamese officials]

CSM	03/20/68	1	Encircled Khe Sanh—How Communists Lay Tight Siege against U.S. Marine Corps Base
CSM	03/21/68	1	Khe Sanh—Cheese in U.S. "Trap"
CSM	03/22/68	1	Khe Sanh Strategy Porous?
CSM	03/23/68	1	Reds Hold Two Options in Vietnam Struggle
CSM	03/26/68	1	U.S. Military Seeks Go-Ahead—Pressure for Khe Sanh Offensive
CSM	03/27/68	1	Khe Sanh: Legacy of Westmoreland
CSM	04/01/68	7	Saigon Races Reds—Vietnam Manpower Showdown
CSM	04/02/68	16	Johnson Stuns Many in Vietnam
CSM	04/03/68	1	Thieu Vows to Continue Fighting
CSM	04/04/68	2	Thieu Tightens Grip—Military Shake-Up in Saigon
CSM	04/05/68	1	Saigon Electric—South Vietnamese Reaction Ranges from Desire for Peace to Distrust of Hanoi's Motives
CSM	04/12/68	1	Viet Drives—U.S. Regains Strategic Momentum on Battlefield
CSM	04/13/68	1	Cong Bids for Local Control
CSM	04/13/68	1	Viet Battles May Sway Peace Talks [2nd of 3 articles on looming Washington-Hanoi peace talks; 1st article of series not designated]
CSM	04/16/68	2	Khe Sanh Transition—Early Escalation Expected with Shift to Mobile Warfare
CSM	04/17/68	1	Vietnamese Juggle Peace Proposals [3rd of 3 articles on looming Washington-Hanoi peace talks]
CSM	04/24/68	1	Provincial Issues Snarl Peace Try
CSM	04/26/68	1	Target: Saigon—Cong Strengthen Command in and around Viet Capital
CSM	04/29/68	5	Conflict Debated—U.S. General Laments Effects of Viet-War Credibility Gap
CSM	05/01/68	1	Cong to Attack? Defector Details New Plan for Assault on Saigon

CSM	05/02/68	1	Saigon Says Reds Wait for U.S. Political Clues
CSM	05/04/68	2	Women Reinforce Viet Cong
CSM	05/07/68	1	Cong Seen in Climax Offensive
CSM	05/08/68	6	New Alliance Accused as Red Front—Vietnam Peace Unit Seen as Peril to Saigon Rule [1st of 2 articles on new peace group]
CSM	05/09/68	9	How Hanoi Looks at Negotiating
CSM	05/09/68	1	Saigon Frets at Bomb-Halt Rumors
CSM	05/11/68	1	Saigon Hit by Peace, War Drives
CSM	05/13/68	5	Allied Victory in Saigon Cited
CSM	05/15/68	4	Goals Unchanged?—Viet Red Strategy Seen Aimed at Neutralizing Saigon [2nd of 2 articles on new peace group]
CSM	05/16/68	2	Defector Blunts Drive—Dual Political Goals Seen in Cong Attack
CSM	05/16/68	10	Talking for Peace—Saigon's Views Pivotal
CSM	05/18/68	1	U.S. Peace Diplomacy—"Offensive" Publicity Shushed
CSM	05/22/68	1	Vise Tightens—Complex Communist Supply Grid Reaches toward Vietnam Cities
CSM	05/22/68	4	Huong's Job: To Unify Non-Reds
CSM	05/29/68	1	New Cabinet Assessed—Saigon Bridge to Peace?
CSM	06/01/68	7	Saigon Cabinet Change Analyzed—Shift toward Triumvirate Rule Seen in Saigon
CSM	06/04/68	2	Worsening Scene—Saigon Economy Shaken
CSM	06/05/68	7	Saigon Interview—Turncoat Clarifies Red Goals
CSM	06/08/68	1	Viet Cordons Net Red Prisoners
CSM	06/09/68	1	Elite Hanoi Regiments Reported in Viet War
CSM	06/12/68	1	U.S. Blames Hanoi for DMZ Escalation

CSM	06/18/68	5	Red Rocketry—Communists Improvise Launchers for Attacks on Viet Cities
CSM	06/27/68	1	Why Hasn't Khe Sanh Assault Come Off? ["Khe Sanh: Vietnam Mystery" 1]
CSM	06/28/68	1	Before the Pullout—How B-52s Protected Khe Sanh ["Khe Sanh: Vietnam Mystery" 2]
CSM	06/29/68	6	What Units Besieged Khe Sanh? ["Khe Sanh: Vietnam Mystery" 3]
CSM	07/05/68	1	Training by Hanoi Sagging?
CSM	07/06/68	1	Frictions Agitate Viet Cong Ranks
CSM	07/10/68	1	Hanoi's Goal—Reds Aim to End Viet War in 1968—on Own Terms
CSM	07/10/68	7	Raids to Come?—Viet Cong Commanders Reconnoiter Saigon and Suburbs to Spot Targets
CSM	07/11/68	1	Reds Mustered in Saigon
CSM	07/16/68	2	Document Discloses Strategy—Viet Cong Weapon: Proselytizing
CSM	07/18/68	1	Tacit Pullout or Buildup?
CSM	07/19/68	1	Deescalation?—Viet Red Moves Hard to Assess
CSM	07/20/68	6	Trend for Honolulu—Parley Hints Peace Speedup [1st of 3 articles on Honolulu conferences]
CSM	07/23/68	2	Honolulu Decisions—How Much Impact? [2nd of 3 articles]
CSM	07/26/68	1	South Viet Soldiers: More than Arms Needed?
CSM	07/27/68	2	Slow Gains Registered by Saigon [3rd of 3 articles]
CSM	07/29/68	4	Proceedings Called Undemocratic—Dzu Trial in Saigon Embarrasses American Officials
CSM	07/31/68	1	North Vietnam Troop Pullback Estimated at 50%
CSM	08/05/68	2	Viet War Political Maneuvers
CSM	08/06/68	2	Anxious Saigonese Cling to Savings

CSM	08/08/68	1	Viet War Dangles as Big Units Shun Offensive
CSM	08/09/68	4	"Split-Level" Strategy—Hanoi Counts on Viet Uprising
CSM	08/13/68	4	Reward for Red Heroes
CSM	08/14/68	4	An Era Ends—Saigon Sees Victory Hopes Dashed by Republican Choice
CSM	08/15/68	1	Saigon Ponders Peace
CSM	08/17/68	1	How Long the Lull?—U.S. Seeks Vietnam Clues
CSM	08/19/68	12	More Northern Leaders Appear—Major Shifts Indicated in Viet Cong Military Command
CSM	08/20/68	1	Viet Cong Battle Plans Captured
CSM	08/21/68	1	Cong Offensive?—U.S. Officials Uncertain Whether Attacks Will Intensify
CSM	08/24/68	1	Rocketing of Saigon Shatters Viet Lull
CSM	08/26/68	1	U.S. Candidates Assailed—Hanoi Hopes for Election Gains Dulled
CSM	08/26/68	8	Tactical Nose—"Peoplesniffer" Peers beneath Vietnam Foliage
CSM	08/27/68	11	Abrams Redirects Mission of the Big B-52's over Vietnam
CSM	08/28/68	9	Saigon Gloom—Prevailing Mood
CSM	08/29/68	2	Saigon Keeps Eye on U.S. Politics
CSM	09/03/68	7	"My Seven Children Hid in the Bunkers"
CSM	09/04/68	6	Viet Communists Train Teens as Future Cadres
CSM	09/05/68	1	Cong Crackdown—Reds Criticize Themselves in Readying New Offensive
CSM	09/06/68	5	Offensive Aimed at Saigon?
CSM	09/11/68	4	Allies Force Shift in Cong Drive
CSM	09/13/68	1	Chasing Credibility in Saigon [1st of 2 articles on credibility gaps]
CSM	09/16/68	1	Vietnam—Only Victories Can Span Cong Credibility Gap [2nd of 2 articles]

CSM	09/20/68	1	Saigon Confidence Grows—Reds Set Back—but How Much? [1st of 2 articles]
CSM	09/21/68	1	Leadership Quality Undercut—Friction within Ranks Hamper Viet Cong [2nd of 2 articles]
CSM	09/28/68	1	U.S. Refines Vietnam Encirclement Technique [1st of 2 articles on U.S. military encirclement and psychological warfare operations]
CSM	10/04/68	11	Mobilizing for Peace—South Vietnam Government Has Begun Unveiling Its Own Formula for Peace
CSM	10/05/68	2	Countryside Maneuver—Viet Reds Hold Night Elections
CSM	10/09/68	1	DMZ Odyssey Yields Cong Secrets
CSM	10/12/68	1	Sad or Glad, It's Back to Khe Sanh
CSM	10/14/68	2	"Strange Sights" at Khe Sanh
CSM	10/15/68	13	Bullhorns Help U.S. Unit Win Over Viet Cong [2nd of 2 articles on U.S. military operations]
CSM	10/16/68	1	Military Sees Bomb Halt Peril
CSM	10/17/68	1	Allies Outnumber Reds along DMZ
CSM	10/18/68	12	Helicopter Hopscotching—Marines "Mobilize" the DMZ
CSM	10/19/68	1	Red Rift in Hanoi Doubted
CSM	10/22/68	1	Bunker-Thieu Dialogue—Bomb-Halt Terms Disturb Saigon
CSM	10/23/68	1	As Abrams Sees Vietnam—U.S. Deals from Strength
CSM	10/24/68	4	Logistics Called Chink in Cong Armor
CSM	10/25/68	1	Viet Quiet—Peace Hint or Tactic?
CSM	10/26/68	10	Power Strategy in South—Viet Reds Seek Local Mandates
CSM	10/29/68	1	Hanoi Repair Priority: Roads but Not Buildings
CSM	10/29/68	7	Local Vote?—Grips of Cong Still Hazy
CSM	10/30/68	1	Viet-Withdrawal Plan Reported in Laos
CSM	10/31/68	1	Step by Step toward Peace in Vietnam

CSM	11/02/68	1	U.S. Overrules Saigon Leaders?
CSM	11/04/68	2	Saigon Uneasy over U.S. Role in Asia
CSM	11/05/68	1	Refusal Viewed as Rebuff to Johnson—Thieu Balks at Talking with Viet Cong
CSM	11/06/68	2	Saigon Waits—Will U.S. Vote Alter Viet Bid?
CSM	11/08/68	1	Saigon Short Circuit?—Diplomatic Pandemonium in South Vietnam; U.S. Accused of Bobbling Peace Package [1st of 3 articles on American–South Vietnamese official conversations regarding the U.S. bombing halt over North Vietnam and the expanded Paris peace talks]
CSM	11/09/68	1	Who Sits at Peace Table? [2nd of 3 articles]
CSM	11/12/68	6	Distrust Marked U.S.-Saigon Talks on Paris [3rd of 3 articles]
CSM	11/20/68	13	Thien Saigon's Version—"President Thieu Never Agreed . . . to Two-Side, Four-Delegation Formula" [author's summary of Vietnam government spokesman Ton That Thien's news conference]
CSM	11/29/68	2	Viet Peace Still Faces Political Ambush
CSM	12/04/68	10	Saigon Slowly Names Delegates to Paris
CSM	12/06/68	1	Viet Puzzle—Are Viet Reds Preparing Another Major Offensive?
CSM	12/07/68	1	Allied Units Brace for Cong Push
CSM	12/10/68	1	Hanoi Airs North Viet Graft
CSM	12/10/68	7	Send-off for Paris Team—Saigon in Democratic Exercise
CSM	12/19/68	1	Anti-Thieu Leftists Organize
CSM	12/21/68	9	The Elusive Headquarters
CSM	12/21/68	1	Too Many Concessions?—Saigon Approaches Peace Table Warily
CSM	12/24/68	2	PW Talks—New Road to Viet Peace?

CSM	12/24/68	1	Does Viet Cong Plan Offensive? ["Our Readers Write" letters on 01/20/69 and 02/08/69 comment for and against author's references to Cambodia]
CSM	01/02/69	1	Military Goals Elusive—Ordeals of '68 Shape Viet Peace Trend

Appendix 2

Author's 1966 *New York Herald Tribune* Series (Inserted into the *Congressional Record* by Senator Mike Mansfield)

CONGRESSIONAL RECORD — SENATE
January 20, 1966
Vietnam, Past and Prospect

Mr. MANSFIELD. Mr. President, in a series of four newspaper articles, Miss Beverly Deepe has recently reviewed the war as it has evolved in Vietnam during the past year. Miss Deepe is eminently qualified by experience to report on this critical area.

Miss Deepe writes from Vietnam, from the delat [*sic*], from Saigon, from the coastal bases, from the highlands. And the picture which emerges from the four articles is a vivid and accurate summary of the situation which confronts us in Vietnam.

These articles, Mr. President, make highly informative and highly useful reading. For the benefit of the Senate, I ask unanimous consent that the four articles which appeared in the *New York Herald Tribune*, in the issues of January 16–19 inclusive be included at this point in the RECORD.

There being no objection, the articles were ordered to be printed in the RECORD, as follows:

From the *New York Herald Tribune*, January 16, 1966
New Series: Vietnam, Past and Prospect
BY BEVERLY DEEPE

PLEIKU, SOUTH VIETNAM — Amid mortar craters and charred aircraft here on the morning of February 7, 1965, three figures in the war against the Communist in South Vietnam met in a gleaming C-123 transport. Before they emerged, the nature of the war had changed.

One was McGeorge Bundy, special assistant to President Johnson for national security affairs, who took time before the meeting to survey Pleiku's blasted airplanes and helicopters and the billets where shortly before 8 Americans had died and 125 had been wounded in a Vietcong guerrilla raid.

With Mr. Bundy was Gen. William C. Westmoreland, the American commander, who provided the C-123, called the White Whale, and the only wall-to-wall carpeted airplane in South Vietnam.

The Vietnamese commander in chief, Lt. Gen. Nguyen Khanh, had arrived earlier. Meanwhile, in Saigon U.S. Ambassador Maxwell D. Taylor conferred by telephone with the highest ranking American officials in Washington.

General Khanh, Mr. Bundy, and General Westmoreland escaped inquisitive reporters inside the White Whale. Soon, the key decision was told to General Khanh and within hours 49 U.S. planes from three 7th Fleet aircraft carriers sped north of the 17th parallel to bomb the military barracks at the North Vietnamese city of Dong Hoi.

At first, the bombing of North Vietnam was a policy of tit-for-tat — if you destroy our installations, we'll destroy yours. But it soon gave way to general retaliation, and then to regular and continual bombing. In the beginning, the policy was officially proclaimed an inducement to the north to negotiate. High ranking American officials said hopefully: "We'll be at the conference table by September."

But Hanoi did not negotiate. The new official objective was to hit the military installations and communication routes which allowed Hanoi to pour men and material into South Vietnam. By the year's end, however, official estimates said North Vietnamese infiltration had more than doubled — to 2,500 men a month.

Superficially, bombing North Vietnam failed. It did not force Hanoi to negotiate; it did not stop the infiltration. But actually, the policy half succeeded. By the end of the year, the bombing had partially paralyzed the economic capacity and manpower reserves of North Vietnam.

If the bombing did not stop Hanoi's aggression, in official eyes, it would at least make it more expensive and painful for North Vietnam to continue. Escalation was accompanied by a little noticed policy of expansion, Laos was known to be subject to American bombing raids throughout the past year. By the beginning of 1966, the air war threatened to spread to Cambodia, and then would engulf the whole Indochinese Peninsula.

Ground War

The air war over North Vietnam, however, did not abate sharp deterioration in the allied ground efforts in South Vietnam, which had been worsening since the fall of the Ngo Dinh Diem regime in November 1963. The repercussions of the coup against Diem badly damaged the Government's administrative and intelligence apparatuses. Amid Government instability in Saigon swirled whirlwind changes of officials at every level. The strategic hamlet program, formulated and nurtured by the Diem regime, collapsed as the Vietcong regained one Government hamlet after another, leaving behind their own guerrilla bands and political machinery.

With some accuracy the situation in the countryside could be measured by statistics. Before the fall of Diem, the Saigon government claimed control of 8,000 of the 12,000 hamlets in the countryside. By the end of 1965, the most optimistic estimate put the number of "pacified," or pro-government, hamlets at 2,000.

After the fall of Diem, military commanders quickly began to change their "measle" maps. Pink contested areas became red; and white "measle pox" — which once had been government controlled — became contested "pink." By the middle of 1965, government provincial capitals and district headquarters were ringed by small oases of friendly villages, but otherwise were isolated by increasing Red pressure in the countryside. Then, in July 1964, the first North Vietnamese regular troops began appearing. These units, later to be designated as People's Army of North Vietnam (PAVN), solidified the growing Red strength.

By the end of 1965, military spokesmen said nine PAVN regiments had infiltrated from North Vietnam. (American, Korean, and Australian group units by late 1965 numbered 44 battalions — or roughly 15 regiments.)

On March 8, 1965, the first 3,500 U.S. marines came ashore and were welcomed by a bevy of girls.

The American and allied buildup continued throughout the rest of the year. It came part of the 3d Marine Division, and later the whole division, a brigade of the 101st Airborne Division, elements of the 1st Marine Division, the Republic of Korea's Tiger Regiment and Marine Division, an Australian regiment, and finally the entire U.S. 1st Cavalry Airmobile Division, with its more than 400 helicopters and 15,000 troops, many of them airborne. By the end of the year, American combat military personnel numbered 130,000. The outlook for 1966; the equivalent of at least 1 division a month for 12 months, or nearly 200,000 more troops.

Marines

The 1st Marines officially were to provide "local, close-in security" for the Da Nang airbase, but soon they began what U.S. spokesmen called "offensive patrolling for defensive purposes." By mid-July, American troops went into unequivocal full combat with Communist forces for the first time since the Korean War — as the 173d Airborne Brigade went out on a search-and-destroy operation in the Red stronghold known as D-Zone.

With the new employment of ground and air forces, the U.S. role went through gradual metamorphosis. At the end of 1965 America was in a war it barely realized it had entered. The cold war had gone hot in the jungles of the Indochinese peninsula.

Beyond the ideological conflict, the war dramatized and tested two systems of power. One, the massive physical power of America; the other, the power of the Communists to manipulate the masses, incite uprisings labeled by the Chinese Communists as the "war of liberation." Washington and Peiping appeared to agree it was the "war of the future."

The essence of the war was described by a 20-year-old American private who saw the build up in Da Nang:

"I can tell you when Uncle Sam moves in, there's no goofing around," he said. "There was nothing here. Then the Marines moved in and the buildings started going up. We got word an F-100 squadron was moving in here and we had 4 days to fill 200,000 bags of dirt to sandbag mortar defenses. Even the colonels were shoveling dirt.

"Now you can look down this runway and for 2 miles there are American jets wing tip to wing tip," he said. "That's real power."

The private, who had sat 14 hours a day for 13 months in a foxhole at the edge of the Da Nang runway, turned to the other side of the war.

Intelligence

"The Vietcong know more about what's happening on this airbase than the base commander and the 20,000 American Marines around it," he said. "There are 6,000 workers who come on here daily. We know some of them are Vietcong. If the Vietnamese security officer keeps them off, he and his family will be killed.

"The Vietcong can come on this base right under our noses — we don't know who's who. We saw an old woman carrying a bucket of drain oil into the gate. When we checked her, there was only and [sic] inch of oil and the rest of the bucket was a false bottom filled with plastic explosive. We captured one of the workers drawing diagrams of all the defense structures on the base. We captured one of the drivers of an American bus taking down the tail numbers of all the American aircraft on the base," the private went on.

"Once my unit was given 5 hours of leave to go to the commissary. When we returned, more than half of the 100 American foxholes around the base had small paper bags in them. Each bag had a poisonous krait snake in it. Some worker had just walked around and dropped a snake in each foxhole."

This conflict of the two systems of power — the old woman with a bucket of explosive and the double-the-speed-of-sound Phantom jets — was the essence of America's inscrutable war, which one Western diplomat described as "the unholy trinity of terrorism, subversion, and guerrilla warfare."

America's inscrutable war in Vietnam had brush-fired into another area of the volatile, underdeveloped, uncommitted third world.

From the *New York Herald Tribune*, January 17, 1966
Vietnam: Past and Prospect—South Viets Identify GI's with Colonialism
BY BEVERLY DEEPE

SAIGON — The buildup of American combat troops in Vietnam during 1965 produced a visible buildup of anti-Americanism among the Vietnamese population.

A significant date between the February 7 bombing of North Vietnam and the March 8 arrival of the first American combat units was the February 20 mutiny against Commander-in-Chief Gen. Nguyen Khanh by his generals. The net effect of General Khanh's overthrow was to fragment the anti-Communist power in Saigon, while the Vietcong had seized partial control of the country at the village level.

As commander in chief, a more important post in wartime that that of Prime Minister, General Khanh had dominated the anti-Communist scene — and had been acclaimed by Secretary of Defense Robert S. McNamara as America's strongman for Vietnam. But by late 1964, General Khanh grew bitter toward U.S. Ambassador Maxwell D. Taylor, who demanded political stability, while General Khanh was aspiring to the presidency.

False Coup

Twelve days after the bombing of North Vietnam, a false coup was led by Col. Pham Ngoc Thao, who was openly acknowledged to be associated with the U.S. Central Intelligence Agency. The next day the generals forced General Khanh out of the country. The 600,000-man Vietnamese armed forces were turned over to a weak commander in chief. Finally, the post was abolished, leaving the armed forces virtually leaderless.

Prime Minister Phan Huy Quat ran into trouble. After 3 months in office he called for support from the Vietnamese generals, who promptly tossed him out of office. A Vietnamese military junta again took on the job of governing the country while attempting to defeat an enemy.

Amid instability on the anti-Communist side, the Reds could exploit the first American combat units — who arrived without solid political, economic, or social battle plans. The instincts of the Vietnamese, traditionally xenophobic, were to identify the American troops with the former French colonial masters. Better political and economic preparation of the American troops would have eased the situation considerably.

It was widely known in Saigon that the Vietnamese — including Prime Minister Phan Huy Quat — learned of the date of the arrival of the first Marines in March from foreign press announcements made in Saigon and Washington. The Vietnamese feared they might win the war but lose their country. Outbursts from officers, students, and intellectuals charged that "the Americans were running the whole show."

The Dollar

No sooner did the American troops land in the northern provinces than the medium of exchange became the U.S. dollar rather than the piaster. With no restrictions on the amount of available dollars, an American private had purchasing power once held only by Vietnamese generals. Cokes, beers, and wash basins were purchased in villages with nickels, dimes, and quarters. In at least one instance, a Vietnamese village chief, backed up by his popular force platoons, attempted to invade the village of another chief and to seize the villagers' American dollars at an unfair rate of exchange. Six months after the arrival of the first American units, American officials abolished the use of dollars in Vietnam. Replacing them was military scrip, which now has become another "floating currency."

The American troops quickly became the predominant possessors of one of the scarcest items in Vietnam. Women. Few Vietnamese appreciated the loss of their women — or the fact that illiterate females could earn 10 times a man's pay. Gradually, in any city or village bordering American units, drugstores, villas, and furniture stores quickly gave way to bars and brothels.

Wages

The buildup of American forces also brought demands for more housing, runways, offices, and other facilities. Wages for skilled labor, and cost of building materials and transportation brought inflation. "The Vietnamese economy is in horrific shape. This could ruin the whole campaign against the Vietcong," one Western diplomat said recently.

The Vietcong sabotage of roads had also produced inflation on items such as rice, charcoal, and fish sauce. The American economic mission reacted by importing consumer goods to sop up the excess purchasing power — and financed the emergency import of 250,000 tons of rice. While the Saigon price of rice dropped, in the provinces rich merchants continued to charge what the traffic would wear.

The Vietnamese hurt most by the inflation were not the Communists, but the government's own officials and troops, paid mostly on fixed salaries.

In the city of Da Nang, an average of three or four fistfights a week break out between GI's and teenage Vietnamese gangs, popularly known as "cowboys." One American serviceman was beaten up and lay in the back alley for 2 days. Though Vietnamese shopkeepers saw the body, they did not report it to police. The American military police finally located it.

By the beginning of 1966, it became apparent that the Buddhist bonzes, as well as the Vietcong, could easily exploit Vietnamese nationalism and anti-Americanism.

One incident used by the Buddhists occurred when the American marines fired two tank rifle rounds into a pagoda from which they claimed a sniper was firing at them. The word immediately spread among Vietnamese peasants that the marines had maliciously fired into the pagoda. The marines also were accused of having deliberately broken a Buddhist statue and strewn human excrement around the pagoda.

The Buddhists, widely considered to include neutralists and pro-Communists, previously had successfully toppled two administrations in Vietnam: President Ngo Dinh Diem in November 1963, and General Khanh in August 1964.

"If the Buddhist priests do turn anti-American, the war will change into a new dimension which we can't even yet imagine," one source said, looking forward to 1966.

At the beginning of the year, rural Vietnam was half conquered by the Vietcong, and the urban portion was in a state of semi-insurrection. As more American troops arrived, resulting anti-Americanism vastly complicated the prospects for economic and political stability.

From the *New York Herald Tribune*, January 18, 1966
Vietnam: Past and Prospect—Subversion in the Mekong Delta

SA DEC, SOUTH VIETNAM — Officially, the Mekong Delta south of Saigon — where no American combat units have yet been based — is one of the spots where the Vietnamese Government is progressing well. The simple tranquility of fishing boats passing through canals, the hectic automobile traffic on the roads, the unbroken routine of peasant life would seem to confirm the official version.

But those who live in the villages say the Vietcong have seized virtual control of this rich rice bowl.

The process is not one of violent battles, but the invisible strangulation and isolation of government authority. It is a process of subversion which might be called termite warfare. Government authority has been squeezed into small rings of villages around provincial and district capitals, and into isolated outposts along the main roads and canals.

At Sa Dec is the headquarters of the Vietnamese 9th Infantry Division. Six miles away is the village complex of Nha Man. Two of its three villages are already controlled by the Communists. The third village, Tan Nhuan Dong, is protected by one company of about 100 paramilitary troops. An additional platoon is assigned to each of the two smaller outposts — Ba Thien, 1 mile away, and Nga Ba, 2 miles off.

Encircled

The company at Tan Nhuan Dong lives in an old French fort. Its job is to protect the village and a bridge which stretches across a river flanked by several operating rice mills and brick factories.

The two outposts are encircled by Vietcong guerrillas. Last month they were totally isolated from the local population. To bring in supplies and support for these two posts, the government had to use 10 armored boats. On every voyage the boats and their complement of troops draw Communist sniper fire.

The platoons in each of the two small posts theoretically send out small, regular patrols to gather intelligence. They are called the "ears and eyes of the regular forces." But recently, a local villager described them as "blind men in a jail." For it is rare that a member of either platoon dares leave his compound, even to fetch water from the river 20 yards away.

Last week, one defender crossed the outpost's barbed wire fence for water. He was wounded by a sniper and fell on the river bank. No one dared rescue him. He died and his body was left on the same spot for three days. The commander asked headquarters for reinforcements, to pick up the body 20 yards away from his post. The request was refused.

The platoon was ordered to bury the corpse inside the post, but again the men refused to pick up the body. On repeated orders, they eventually brought in the corpse, but the outpost had no shovels, so they used knives to dig the grave. They had no lumber or nails, so they ripped wood from the walls of their outpost to make the coffin.

After the grotesque burial, morale was so low the company commander decided to transfer the platoon. The 100-man company ordered to relieve them refused to obey their transfer order and most of them defected to the Communists rather than man the Nga Ba outpost. Most returned after the province district chiefs were forced to visit the company of deserters, but the order to man the outpost was rescinded.

Isolation

The influence of the Communists goes, however, far beyond the terror built with sniper's bullets.

Last month, the Vietcong ordered peasants and businessmen working or living within a half mile of the Nga Ba outpost to move away. The word went out: No one was allowed to move inside the half mile limit. Rather than sail on the river 20 yards from the outposts, villagers' sampans were assigned to small canals.

One rice miller moved his mill brick-by-brick, machine-by-machine, to a new spot nearer government authority. One villager's reaction: "The

Vietcong were very nice to give him the permission to move his rice mill. Otherwise, he would have starved to death. No one would have brought rice to him to be polished within the half mile radius of the post."

In monthly propaganda meetings with the villagers, Vietcong political agents claim "the Americans are waging an all-out war against the Vietnamese people. The people have to make a clear-cut choice between their friends and their enemies. Those who want to fight with the Americans can go to the government-controlled area. Those who want to fight against the Americans can stay with us. There is no third choice."

In Sa Dec, refugee villagers prefer to live in their sampans moored along the riverfront. They have refused to live in refugee housing provided by the government.

Many of the wealthier landowners already have been forced to flee to government-controlled zones, producing the effect of an economic purge of the area by the Communists. Their abandoned lands, especially fruit groves along the canals, have been boobytrapped and mined by Red guerrillas. The Vietcong have warned landowners that their lands will be confiscated if they allow their sons to become government soldiers.

The Vietcong forbid landowners to hire local labor, and terrorize potential workers — drying up the labor force from both ends. Once-wealthy landed proprietors must plant and harvest their own rice — backbreaking work.

Visits Halted

Within the last month, the Vietcong have withdrawn permission to local residents to visit friends or relatives in government-controlled areas. Even the father of one of the senior generals at the Vietnamese Army headquarters in Saigon — who previously had been allowed by the Vietcong to visit his son — now is forbidden to leave the Vietcong area.

But the Vietcong efforts are not all just erosive. They have established efficient — though unofficial and terroristic — taxation. Often using children as collectors, they force millers, small factory owners and businessmen to pay regular levies.

Peasants must turn over to the Reds 40 percent of the rice they grow above their own family's consumption. Any fish or grain grown in the Red-controlled area which is sent into government territory is taxed by the Vietcong—as if they maintained a national border.

So under the noses of government officials and a major army force, the Communists have established their own government in the Mekong Delta. It has almost eroded away the authority of the anti-Communist Saigon regime, and, perhaps more significantly, has taken major steps toward replacing it with an authority of their own.

From the *New York Herald Tribune*, January 19, 1966
Vietnam: Past and Present—Marines' Great Effort: Securing Da Nang
BY BEVERLY DEEPE

DA NANG, SOUTH VIETNAM—Last fall, the battle cry of the U.S. Marines here was: "We'll be in Hoi An by New Year's Day 1966." Today, they estimate it will be New Year's 1968.

Hoi An is a provincial capital, only 15 miles south of the strategic airbase of Da Nang. The change in the marines' mood illustrates the changing role of American troops in Vietnam—and some of their problems.

"We could easily have fought our way to Hoi An," one marine said recently. "But then, we would have had to fight our way back. The essential problem of this war is not moving your front lines forward. It is keeping your rear covered."

The key problem lies in getting and keeping the support of the rural population. Without it, most authorities believe the war could go on for years.

So it was decided to halt the marines' advance until the Vietnamese could win over the local population. The decision brought dissent from within the Marine Corps ranks and sneers from Army colonels, who claimed "the marines are afraid to go out and find the Vietcong." But gradually, the marine effort outside of Da Nang, under the direction of Cmdr. Maj. Gen. Lewis Walt, began to dovetail with the work of the Vietnamese Government.

Third Dimension

"In a conventional war, progress is measured by an advancing front line," one official explained. "But in this war our outlying positions are constant. Progress must be measured in the third dimension. We must go down into the population to dig out the Vietcong infrastructure and then rebuild the local anti-Communist government."

The result of this coordinated effort was the Five Mountain Villages Campaign, less than 10 miles southwest of Da Nang and 15 miles from Hoi An. It is the principal current pacification program and pilot case for the future.

"If this plan doesn't succeed here, it's not going to succeed anywhere else in the country," an official said. "We'll really be in serious trouble then."

The project already has run into some serious trouble.

The five villages of the campaign are subdivided into 19 hamlets, covering a 20-square-kilometer area. In the complex dwell 42,000 people, of whom about 7 percent are believed to be related to Vietcong. Snuggled among lush rice paddies, the villages are surrounded by the five peaks of mountains containing gray and salmon-colored marble. "These marble mountains would make a great tourist attraction, but you'd be killed going out there," one marine said.

The pacification campaign has three components: U.S. Marines are assigned to secure the outer limits of the area, patrolling to prevent the invasion by Communist units; Vietnamese paramilitary troops maintain security in the villages; Vietnamese civilian teams distribute goods, wage psychological warfare, take censuses, and attempt to undo the Vietcong's existing political devices and to bring the villagers to the Government's side.

"The role of the U.S. Marines is like an egg," an official said. "Our front lines, on the rim of the area, are the shell — but like a shell, the lines can be broken. The vital installation — the Da Nang airbase — is the yolk, and we also defend that. The white is the countryside, which we are trying to pacify and solidify."

On October 18, the Vietnamese forces began their effort, using one headquarters company and four understrength line companies of the 59th Regional Forces Battalion. A civilian cadre of 327 persons was moved in from provincial headquarters. The Vietnamese commander put them through a 2-week retraining course. They were joined by five Vietnamese People's Action Teams (PATs), of 10 persons each, who were responsible for census taking and other activities.

To each village, the Vietnamese commander sent one Regional Forces company and one People's Action Team. In each of the 19 hamlets, he put a civilian cadre team.

"During the third week of the campaign, a 50-man Vietcong platoon broke through the marine blocking position. They were in our area shooting things up. They hit us hard," an official related.

"Five Regional Force troopers and several cadremen were killed. Each of our armed companies was understrength, so we had 15-man platoons where we should have had 35 men. Fighting against 50 Vietcong, of course, we lose against those odds.

"Until that we were just beginning to get the confidence of the people — but after that, the people clammed up and wouldn't tell us anything. And it also hurt the morale of our cadre. One whole 11-man team took off — but the district chief talked them into coming back," the official went on.

"Then, four nights later, the same Vietcong platoon hit us again. They slipped in between two Marine patrols, attacked the regional force headquarters unit of 17 men, killed several civilian cadre and kidnaped 2 women working with a drama unit. We haven't seen the women since. One of the American marines saw action from 50 yards away — but he couldn't open up with this machinegun — he would have killed more friendlies than enemies.

"Of course, the marines can't stop all small-unit infiltration. It would take marines shoulder-to-shoulder to do that. And once you had that, the Vietcong would mortar them from across the river, which they've already started doing," he said.

Since the late November action, the Vietnamese and marines have slightly reinforced the area. Now the marines are not only holding the outer perimeter by extensive patrolling, they also are responsible for the securing of the civilian cadre in 11 of the 19 hamlets. Vietnamese troops secure the remaining eight.

Try Again

By mid-December, "we started pacifying again and things were moving slow, but good," the official said. "The people began giving us good intelligence and were turning in some Vietcong. For the first time, on a Sunday afternoon, families from Da Nang would come to the villages to visit their relatives. More than 100 families moved back into the area — but none of the people were of draft age."

On one night in late December, however, the Vietcong launched four harassing attacks. They hit the central command post with mortars and struck another People's Action Team, killing several.

Gradually, the cadre force fell from 331 to 304. Besides attrition, there were substantial problems with the cadre because of inadequate training and the fact that they were not natives of the villages in which they were working.

The PATs — equipped, paid, and trained for political activity and intelligence work by an arm of the U.S. Central Intelligence Agency — had their own troubles. They were better armed than the Vietnamese troops, and the local commander wanted to use them for military security. They refused. One team defected and another had to be transferred because of local conflicts.

"The biggest headache is that we can't move our Vietnamese troops and cadre out of this 20-square-kilometer collection of hamlets until we have villagers here who can defend the area," the official said. "There's not one young man here between the ages of 10 and 38 whom we can recruit. We've lost the middle generation, and no one has begun to find an answer to that problem."

Before the Marines reach Hoi An — with their backs protected — 80 square kilometers of land must be pacified. At that, the Marine estimate of New Year's Day, 1968, is not far away.

Notes

PREFACE

My newspaper articles cited in this volume may be accessed from microfilm reels maintained by major public and research libraries. For citations to my articles in this volume, I rely on the published version now in my possession. My hard copies of the *Christian Science Monitor* sent to me in Vietnam were the London, Midwestern, New England, or Western editions. Most of my citations coincide with the headlines and abstracts now used by the *Christian Science Monitor* for its online, searchable archive, available at http://pqasb.pqarchiver.com/csmonitor_historic/advancedsearch.html. In the online "search for" box on the opening page, type in "Beverly Deepe," which will permit access to most of my articles. That online archive is searchable for free by author, headline, and single or multiple words, but a fee is required to view or print the full article. If the headline in my citation differs substantially from the online version, at the *Monitor*'s request I have included in brackets the e-version of that headline, based on my search and printout made on July 21, 2009. My articles published in the *London Daily Express* and *London Sunday Express* are not archived and retrievable.

1. First published in New York by Harper in 1952, Sam's *Future of American Politics* underwent three editions, was translated into six languages, and was used as a reader in numerous political science classes.

2. The enclosed articles were the three-part series from Khe Sanh. Sheldon's letter, dated December 31, 1968, was addressed to the Advisory Board on the Pulitzer Prizes and is in my possession.

3. The successor to a foundation started in 1935 by newspaper publisher Frank E. Gannett, the Freedom Forum describes itself as a nonpartisan foundation that champions the First Amendment as a cornerstone of democracy. It is the main funding source for the building and operations of the Newseum.

4. Quoted in *The U.S. Army/Marine Corps Counterinsurgency Field Manual*, with forewords by Gen. David H. Petraeus and Lt. Gen. James F. Amos and by Lt. Col. John A. Nagl, and with a new introduction by Sarah Sewall (Chicago: University of Chicago Press, 2007), xiv (hereafter cited as *USA/MC COIN Manual*).

5. Quoted in Ahmed Rashid, *Descent into Chaos: The United States and the Failure of National Building in Pakistan, Afghanistan, and Central Asia* (New York: Viking, 2008), lvi.

6. *USA/MC COIN Manual*, xlvi.

7. *U.S. Government Counterinsurgency Guide: Interagency Counterinsurgency Initiative*, January 13, 2009, 50, accessible also at www.state.gov/t/pm/ppa/pmppt (hereafter cited as *Interagency* COIN *Guide*); U.S. Senate Subcommittee on Public Buildings and Grounds, *Pentagon Papers: The Defense Department History of United States Decisionmaking on Vietnam*, Gravel ed. (Boston: Beacon Press, 1971), 2:6 (hereafter cited as *PP*).

8. *USA/MC COIN Manual*, 192, 202, 209.

9. *USA/MC COIN Manual*, 270–71.

10. Deepe, "Khe Sanh: Legacy of Westmoreland," *Christian Science Monitor*, March 27, 1968, 1, 14 (hereafter cited as CSM).

11. *USA/MC COIN Manual*, 14.

12. Deepe, "Khe Sanh: Legacy of Westmoreland," 1, 14.

13. *Interagency* COIN *Guide*, preface (n.p.), 8, 33.

14. I also had bound separately and labeled as "Adventures of the Saigon Press Corps" the lists I had saved of correspondents accredited by the U.S. Military Assistance Command, some directives issued by that command, and minutes of meetings of foreign correspondents who gathered to send communiqués about maltreatment of a journalist or limitations on news access to information.

15. Harvey H. Smith et al., *Area Handbook for South Vietnam* (Washington DC: U.S. Government Printing Office, 1967), 313. Research and writing was completed on April 15, 1966, by the Foreign Area Studies of American University.

16. Citing a number of historians who criticize the U.S.-centric focus of their colleagues' publications, including David W. P. Elliott, *The Vietnamese War: Revolution and Social Change in the Mekong Delta 1930–1975* (Armonk NY: M. E. Sharpe, 2003), 1:3–4; James Webb, foreword to *Vietnam's Forgotten Army: Heroism and Betrayal in the ARVN*, by Andrew Wiest (New York: New York University Press, 2008), xvi. For an opposing view, see Lewis Sorley, *A Better War: The Unexamined Victories and Final Tragedy of America's Last Years in Vietnam* (New York: Harcourt Brace & Co., 1999), xiv, xv.

17. Quoted in Sidonie Smith and Julia Watson, eds., *De/Colonizing the Subject: The Politics of Gender in Women's Autobiography* (Minneapolis: University of Minnesota Press, 1992), 300.

18. "Memoirs," in *Encyclopedia Britannica Online (Academic Edition)*, www.britannica.com/EBchecked/topic/65924/biography/51207/Memoirs-and-reminiscences (accessed June 19, 2012).

19. Leslie H. Gelb, "Letter of Transmittal," January 15, 1969, *PP*, 1:xv.

20. *PP*, 1:xi, xii. Besides this four-volume Gravel edition published in 1971, a fifth volume of the *Pentagon Papers* was published a year later containing valuable subject and name indexes and a series of critical essays, which are cited in my text by the author's name.

INTRODUCTION

1. Robert M. Utley, *The Indian Frontier of the American West, 1846–1890* (Albuquerque: University of New Mexico Press, 1984), 42.

2. Patricia Nelson Limerick, *The Legacy of Conquest: The Unbroken Past of the American West* (New York: Norton, 1987), 190.

3. Limerick, *Legacy of Conquest*, 27–28, 36. The legacy phrase is taken from the title of Limerick's book. In 1887 the Indians held 138 million acres (198–99), but within the next forty-seven years they lost nearly two-thirds of their tribal lands through government actions and sales to whites.

4. Text transcript of John F. Kennedy's Nomination Acceptance Speech, Los Angeles, July 15, 1960, www.jfklibrary.org/Asset+Tree/Asset+Viewers/ Audio+Video+Asset+Viewer.htm? (accessed October 28, 2008).

5. Timothy Egan, *The Worst Hard Time: The Untold Story of Those Who Survived the Great American Dust Bowl* (Boston: Houghton Mifflin, 2006), 190.

6. Carleton History Committee, *Carleton: Milo Center of Nebraska, 135 Years of History* (n.d.), 17, 51–52; copy available from the author.

7. A sampling of my articles for AP contained in my bound volumes: "Iban Tribesman Slowly Adopting Modern Customs," *Waterbury Sunday Republican*, February 4, 1962, 5; "Almost Inside Red China," *Erie (PA) Times-News*, September 10, 1961; teletyped text dated May 20, 1961, on "Korean comment," probably moved on the World Service Wire with Seoul dateline.

8. *PP*, 2:807.

9. Frank Ninkovich, *Modernity and Power: A History of the Domino Theory in the Twentieth Century* (Chicago: University of Chicago Press, 1994), 246.

10. Quoted in Peter Macdonald, *Giap: The Victor in Vietnam* (New York: Norton, 1993), 183.

11. Robert S. McNamara, James G. Blight, and Robert K. Brigham, with Thomas J. Biersteker and Col. Herbert Y. Schandler, *Argument without End: In Search of Answers to the Vietnam Tragedy* (New York: Public Affairs, 1999), 1.

12. Gen. Bruce Palmer Jr., *The 25-Year War: America's Military in Vietnam* (Lexington: University Press of Kentucky, 1984), vii, 17.

13. William Prochnau, *Once upon a Distant War* (New York: Times Books, 1995), photo page in center of book.

14. The other training and advisory missions were in China during World War II, in Greece during its civil war from 1947 to 1949, and in Korea during 1950–53; see Robert W. Komer, *Bureaucracy at War: U.S. Performance in the Vietnam Conflict* (Boulder: Westview Press, 1986), 122.

15. Quoting the *Pentagon Papers*, Hedrick Smith, "The Kennedy Years: 1961–1963," in *The Pentagon Papers as Published by the New York Times* (Toronto: Bantam Books, 1971), 79, 82.

16. Describing document attached to *Pentagon Papers*, Smith, "Kennedy Years," 79, 82.

17. Homer Bigart, "2 Germans in Saigon Wounded by Bomb Thrown at Americans," *New York Times*, May 19, 1962 (hereafter cited as NYT); Homer Bigart, "3 G.I.'s and 8 Vietnamese Hurt by Grenade on Street in Saigon," NYT, May 20, 1962; PP, 2:825.

18. Beverley [*sic*] Deepe, "Off to Coup No. 3 by Taxi," *London Daily Express*, September 13, 1964.

19. My yellowed clips of published AP Newsfeatures articles from Vietnam include "'Death Zone' in South Vietnam," *Manila Times*, May 24, 1962, 7-A; "New Frontier in Viet Nam," *Miami Herald*, April 15, 1962, 6-G; and also "Girl's Eyes Give War in Viet Nam New Look," *Arizona Republic*, 4-A; "Enemy Is Disease at This Viet Nam Battleground," *Sunday Omaha World Herald*, May 6, 1962, 18-E; "Wife of Captured Man Expects Missionaries to Come Back," *Lincoln (NE) Star*, June 13, 1962, 6; teletyped copy of AP Foreign Service Advance for Wednesday AMS, August 22, 1962, for an article about my traveling near the Demilitarized Zone with North Vietnam to interview three U.S. engineers working under government contract to help operate South Vietnam's only coal mine.

20. My carbon copy of the minutes of the September 5, 1962, meeting of the Association of Foreign Correspondents in Vietnam, written by secretary John Stirling, called to protest the expulsion of *Newsweek*'s François Sully, lists the following Western journalists who were then residing in South Vietnam: Malcolm Browne (AP), Jean Burfin and Simon Michau (Agence France-Presse), Merton Perry (*Time-Life*), Michel Renard (Columbia Broadcasting System), Neil Sheehan (United Press International), and John Stirling (*London Observer*). Sully had departed the previous day.

In addition, a Catholic priest and longtime resident, Father Raymond de Jaeger, was accredited to the Free Pacific Association. Jacques Nevard of the *New York Times* also attended that meeting but was not a resident; Homer Bigart was filing extensively for the *Times* during 1962 but was replaced shortly by David Halberstam. Bureau chiefs or news media staffers often flew in from Bangkok, Hong Kong, or Tokyo for special assignments or during crises.

21. Prochnau, *Once upon a Distant War*, 485.

22. Joyce Hoffmann, *On Their Own: Women Journalists and the American Experience in Vietnam* (Cambridge MA: Da Capo Press, 2008), 131.

23. Maj. Gen. Winant Sidle, "The Role of Journalists — An Army General's Perspective," in *Vietnam Reconsidered: Lessons from a War*, ed. and with an introduction by Harrison E. Salisbury (New York: Harper & Row, 1984), 110; Gen. William C. Westmoreland, *A Soldier Reports* (Garden City NY: Doubleday & Co., 1976), 510.

24. Daniel C. Hallin, *The "Uncensored War": The Media and Vietnam* (New York: Oxford University Press, 1986), 6.

25. Westmoreland, *Soldier*, 333, 469–70.

26. Donna Jones Born, "The Reporting of American Women Foreign Correspondents from the Vietnam War" (PhD diss., Michigan State University, 1987). Born includes these hard-to-find "ground rules" on 205–7.

27. Westmoreland, *Soldier*, 334.

28. Richard Harwood, "As Wrong as McNamara," *Washington Post*, April 19, 1995, 7.

29. David Halberstam, "Letter to My Daughter," in *Vietnam Voices: Perspectives on the War Years, 1941–1982*, comp. John Clark Pratt (New York: Penguin Books, 1984), 659.

30. James Boylan, "Declarations of Independence," *Columbia Journalism Review* (November–December 1986): 29–45.

31. Justice Brennan, writing the opinion of the U.S. Supreme Court, in *New York Times Co. v. Sullivan* (376 U.S. 254), decided March 9, 1964, www.bc.edu/bc_org/avp/cas/comm/free_speech/nytvsullivan.html (accessed November 8, 2008).

32. Michael X. Delli Carpini, "Vietnam and the Press," in *The Legacy: The Vietnam War in the American Imagination*, ed. D. Michael Shafer (Boston: Beacon Press, 1990), 125.

33. William M. Hammond, *Reporting Vietnam: Media and Military at War* (Lawrence: University Press of Kansas, 1998), 293.

34. See, for example, Hallin, *"Uncensored War."*

35. William M. Hammond, *Public Affairs: The Military and the Media, 1962–1968* (Washington DC: Center of Military History, U.S. Army, 1988), 388.

36. *PP*, 2:228, 231.

37. Michael Herr, *Dispatches* (New York: Knopf, 1978), 226.

38. *PP*, 3:501–2.

39. *PP*, 2:611.

40. Bui Tin, *Following Ho Chi Minh: The Memoirs of a North Vietnamese Colonel*, trans. from Vietnamese and adapted by Judy Stowe and Do Van, with an introduction by Carlyle A. Thayer (Honolulu: University of Hawaii Press, 1995), 87.

41. Born, "Reporting," 4, 179. On pages 191–98 Born lists the women correspondents, the media outlet accrediting them, and their year(s) in Vietnam. Her extensive bibliography lists numerous articles written from Vietnam by the seventy or so women correspondents she studied and interviewed in depth.

42. Born, "Reporting," 37–41, 178–81; Hoffmann, *On Their Own*, 5, 8, 10. In individual chapters nine women journalists also tell about their own experiences in Tad Bartimus, Denby Fawcett, Jurate Kazickas, Edith Lederer, Ann Bryan Mariano, Anne Morrissy Merick, Laura Palmer, Kate Webb, and Tracy Wood, *War Torn: Stories of War from the Women Reporters Who Covered Vietnam*, with an introduction by Gloria Emerson (New York: Random House, 2002); see also "Correspondents: Femininity at the Front," *Time*, October 28, 1966, 39–40.

43. Hoffmann, *On Their Own*, 97.

44. The statistic of sixty-six was accessed in 2007 from the Freedom Forum in a link now broken; thirty-three of the sixty-six were killed between 1965 and 1975, according to www.newseum.org/scripts/Journalist/countryDetail.asp?countryID=79 (accessed February 12, 2011). I omitted from the Newseum's count of thirty-four the name of Duong Hung Cuong, who is described as having died in detention in 1988.

45. Micheal Clodfelter, *Vietnam in Military Statistics: A History of the Indochina Wars, 1772–1991* (Jefferson NC: McFarland & Co., 1995), 257.

46. Quoted in Sanford Wexler, *The Vietnam War: An Eyewitness History* (New York: Facts on File, 1992), 114.

1. THE PEOPLE'S WAR

1. Quoted in Douglas Pike, *Viet Cong: The Organization and Techniques of the National Liberation Front of South Vietnam* (Cambridge MA: MIT Press, 1966), 270.

2. *PP*, 1:328. Although the term was considered erroneous, even derogatory, to some pro-Communists, *Viet Cong* had been used by the Saigon press since 1956 and later came close to becoming a household word in the United States.

3. Cong. Rec. S4673 (April 6, 1954), as quoted by www.cia.gov/library/center-for-the-study-of-intelligence/kent-csi/docs/v40i5a10p.h (accessed August 31, 2007).

4. This entire section is based on my notes about my Trung Lap patrol; the "Incident Report" of the U.S. Medical Advisory Group, Trung Lap Training Center, January 15, 1962; and an interview on January 11, 1963, with Maj. Gen. Charles Timmes, head of the U.S. Military Assistance Advisory Group.

5. Beverly Deepe, "The Woman Correspondent," in *Dateline 1966: Covering War* (New York: Overseas Press Club, 1966), 93 (article on 96–97).

6. *Aspects of China's Anti-Japanese Struggle*, "Mao Zedong (1983–1976)," www .kirjasto.sci.fi/mao.htm (accessed November 28, 2008).

7. Wilfred Burchett, *Catapult to Freedom* (London: Quartet Books, 1978), 114–19.

8. Cited in Vo Nguyen Giap, *The Military Art of People's War*, ed. and with an introduction by Russell Stetler (New York: Monthly Review Press, 1970), 32.

9. Quoted in Howard J. Langer, *The Vietnam War: An Encyclopedia of Quotations* (Westport CT: Greenwood Press, 2005), 316.

10. Burchett, *Catapult to Freedom*, 118–19.

11. Deepe, "Viet Nam Report—I: Why Guerrillas Fight So Hard," *New York Herald Tribune*, May 30, 1965, 12 (hereafter cited as *NYHT*).

12. *PP*, 3:400–401.

13. Deepe, "Viet Cong Wedding in the Jungle," *NYHT*, November 22, 1965, 2.

14. Douglas Pike, *PAVN: People's Army of Vietnam* (Novato CA: Presidio Press, 1986), 236, 238.

15. Giap, *Military Art of People's War*, 32.

16. Pike, *PAVN*, 236, 238.

17. Deepe, "Viet Nam Report—I," 12.

18. *PP*, 1:328.

19. This section detailing the interview with the elder and the "shadow" government is taken from Deepe, "A War without a Front Line," *CSM*, June 24, 1967, 9.

20. Pike, *Viet Cong*, 119–23; David W. P. Elliott, *The Vietnamese War: Revolution and Social Change in the Mekong Delta, 1930–1975* (Armonk NY: M. E. Sharpe, 2003), 524.

21. Hugo Portisch, *Eyewitness in Vietnam*, trans. from German by Michael Glenny (London: Bodley Head, 1967), 81.

22. Quoted in Jeffrey Race, *War Comes to Long An: Revolutionary Conflict in a Vietnamese Province*, updated and expanded ed. (Berkeley: University of California Press, 2010), 129–30.

23. Bui Tin, *Following Ho Chi Minh*, 27–32; *PP*, 1:246.

24. Quoted in Race, *War Comes to Long An*, 243.

25. Deepe, "Our Girl in Viet—V," *NYHT*, June 3, 1965, 18.

26. *PP*, 1:329, 332.

27. *PP*, 1:336; these are statistics reported by the South Vietnamese government to U.S. officials.

28. Pike, *Viet Cong*, 246–52.

29. Deepe, "'Total, Bloody Mayhem,'" *NYHT*, April 25, 1965, 18.

30. Race, *War Comes to Long An*, 196.

31. *PP*, 1:339–46.

32. George A. Carver Jr., "The Faceless Viet Cong," reprint from *Foreign Affairs* (April 1966): n.p.; *PP*, 1:263.

33. *PP*, 1:339.

34. *PP*, 1:344.

35. This section is based on excerpts from my twenty-one-page dispatch air-expressed to *Newsweek* New York in September 1963.

36. Jean Lacouture, *Ho Chi Minh: A Political Biography*, trans. from French by Peter Wiles, ed. and trans. Jane Clark Seitz (New York: Random House, 1968), 4, 237.

37. Lacouture, *Ho Chi Minh*, 3, 4.

38. Susan Wilson, *The Omni Parker House: A Brief History of America's Longest Continuously Operating Hotel* (Lexington MA: n.p., 2001).

39. *PP*, 1:50–51.

40. Ho Chi Minh, *Selected Works* (Hanoi: Foreign Languages Publishing House, 1961), 3:434.

41. Le Ly Hayslip, with Jay Wurts, *When Heaven and Earth Changed Places: A Vietnamese Woman's Journey from War to Peace* (New York: Doubleday, 1989), x.

42. *PP*, 1:339.

43. *PP*, 2:6.

44. Theodore C. Sorensen, *Kennedy* (New York: Bantam Books, 1966), 738–40.

45. *PP*, 2:23–25, 96; McNamara, Blight, and Brigham, *Argument without End*, 97.

46. Pike, *PAVN*, 5, 213, 220, 233, 250.

2. RICE-ROOTS REPORTING

1. In 1962 about 5.8 million out of 12.6 million of the South Vietnamese rural population lived in the delta.

2. Harry D. Latimer, *U.S. Psychological Operations in Vietnam* (Providence RI: Brown University, 1973), 79; Bernard Weintraub, "U.S. Report Finds Gloom in Vietnam," *NYT*, December 6, 1967, 1, 10.

3. *PP*, 2:144, 148.

4. In July 1962, for example, Secretary of Defense Robert McNamara described it as "the backbone of President Diem's program for countering subversion directed against his state." See *PP*, 2:149.

5. Robert Thompson, *Defeating Communist Insurgency* (New York: Praeger, 1966), 123–24.

6. Quoted in William J. Duiker, *The Communist Road to Power in Vietnam*, 2nd ed. (Boulder CO: Westview Press, 1996), 231.

7. Cited in Stephen M. Sloan, "The Dichotomy between Planning and Implementation in the Vietnam War's Strategic Hamlet Program, 1961–1963" (master's thesis, Baylor University, May 1998), 13.

8. This passage about Kien Phong Province was drawn from my typed manuscript, dated June 3, 1962.

9. *PP*, 2:144.

10. *PP*, 2:149.

11. This section is based on my on-the-scene notes made on May 10, 1962, and on my two-page typed carbon of the dispatch published in the *Manila Times*, May 24, 1962, 7-A.

12. Russell F. Weigley, *The American Way of War: A History of United States Military Strategy and Policy* (New York: Macmillan, 1973), 467.

13. This section exemplifying U.S. aid in Binh Duong and in other provinces is contained in my clippings from the mimeographed *Vietnam Press* published by the Saigon government in 1963, dated February 11, 23, and 26; March 15, 25, and 26; and May 13.

14. *PP*, 3:501.

15. Cited in Sloan, "Dichotomy," 54–55.

16. This section is based on my half-page cable to *Newsweek* in New York dated December 11, 1962; my six-page dispatch sent by air express six days later; and a twenty-one-page background article air-expressed to *Newsweek* on September 29, 1963.

17. Tran Ky Phuong, *Unique Vestiges of Cham Civilization* (Hanoi: Gioi Publishers, 2000), 7–11, 69–70.

18. Robert Trumbull, "'Mandarin' Who Rules South Vietnam," *New York Times Magazine*, January 7, 1962, n.p.

19. Race, *War Comes to Long An*, 176.

20. "A Sense of Optimism," *NYT*, July 1, 1971, 8.

21. This interview exemplified the wide range of sources I talked with in Saigon about the Strategic Hamlet Program to supplement my rice-roots reporting; I also collected armloads of government documents, including a manual for training hamlet and village workers.

22. *PP*, 2:158.

23. *PP*, 2:277.

24. *Newsweek*, December 23, 1963, 31.

25. *PP*, 2:307.

26. *PP*, 2:525.

27. Deepe, "In Viet, Bomb at U.S. Pool," *NYHT*, January 17, 1965, 20.

28. *PP*, 2:525, 516.

29. William Colby, with James McCargar, *Lost Victory: A Firsthand Account of America's Sixteen-Year Involvement in Vietnam* (Chicago: Contemporary Books, 1989), 214; Giap, *Military Art of People's War*, 87, 89.

30. *PP*, 2:594–97.

31. Deepe, "'Other War' Stalls — South Vietnam Pacification Program Seen Tottering on Brink of Collapse," *CSM*, May 5, 1967, 1.

32. *PP*, 2:615–16.

33. *PP*, 2:621.

34. Deepe, "Villages around Saigon — Pacification Set Back Six Months?" *CSM*, February 13, 1968, 1, 4.

35. U.S. Central Intelligence Agency, Directorate of Intelligence, "Intelligence Memorandum: Pacification in the Wake of the Tet Offensive in South Vietnam," March 19, 1968, stamped "secret"; declassified May 30, 1990, 1, A19.

36. Deepe, "Revival Debated — Pacification Efforts Hard Hit near Hue," *CSM*, March 13, 1968, 6.

37. Quoted in *Pentagon Papers as Published by the New York Times*, 600.

38. Chief historian Gerald K. Haines, foreword to the unclassified version of a secret study by Thomas L. Ahern Jr., *CIA and Rural Pacification in South Vietnam (U)* (Washington DC: CIA's Center for the Study of Intelligence, 2001), n.p.

39. *PP*, 3:97.

40. Race, *War Comes to Long An*, 236–37.

41. Elliott, *Vietnamese War*, 2:1162.

42. Quoted in Hoffmann, *On Their Own*, 162.

43. Elliott, *Vietnamese War*, 85.

44. Robert Thompson, *No Exit from Vietnam* (London: Chatto & Windus, 1969), 169–70; Lewis Sorley, *A Better War: The Unexamined Victories and Final Tragedy of America's Last Years in Vietnam* (New York: Harcourt Brace, 1999), 76.

45. Quoted in Robert Kodosky, "The Consequences of Truth and Propaganda: American Psychological Operations in Vietnam" (PhD diss., Temple University, 2006), 241–42.

46. Don Luce, "Tell Your Friends That We're People," *PP*, 5:95.

3. "THE WORLD'S FIRST HELICOPTER WAR"

1. Quoted in Portisch, *Eyewitness to Vietnam*, 20.

2. Deepe, "The Choppers Prove Their Worth in War," *NYHT*, December 20, 1964, 3.

3. Gavin's words were published on the cover of *Harper's*, April 1954.

4. Cited by Giap, *Military Art of People's War*, 12.

5. These Soc Trang sections are based on information gathered in April 1962 and extracted from my manuscript dated July 19, 1962.

6. Quoted in Alasdair Spark, "Flight Controls," in *Vietnam Images: War and Representation*, ed. Geoffrey Walsh and James Aulich (New York: St. Martin's, 1989), 98.

7. Bui Tin, *From Enemy to Friend: A North Vietnamese Perspective on the War*, trans. from Vietnamese by Nguven Ngoc Bich (Annapolis MD: Naval Institute Press, 2002), 102–3.

8. Hayslip, *When Heaven and Earth Changed Places*, 42–43.

9. "The New Metal Birds," *Newsweek*, October 29, 1962, 37–38; and carbon copies of my dispatch to *Newsweek* in New York.

10. Paul B. Morgan, *The Parrot's Beak: U.S. Operations in Cambodia* (Central Point OR: Hellgate Press, 2000), n.p.

11. Thompson, *No Exit from Vietnam*, 136.

12. "Vietnam: A Bloody Nose," *Newsweek*, January 14, 1963, 34.

13. *Newsweek*, January 21, 1963, 46. In the January 14 and 21 issues *Newsweek* published accounts of Ap Bac (34–36 and 46, respectively), which included some from my dispatches.

14. Quoted in Neil Sheehan, *A Bright Shining Lie: John Paul Vann and America in Vietnam* (New York: Random House, 1988), 259.

15. Prochnau, *Once upon a Distant War*, 240–41.

16. Sheehan, *Bright Shining Lie*, 205–6.

17. Elliott, *Vietnamese War*, 1:400, 434.

18. This description and these statistics are from my file cabled to *Newsweek* New York that week; the Vietnamese and Viet Cong figures are from Sheehan, *Bright Shining Lie*, 263.

19. Quoting Communist sources, Ang Cheng Guan, *The Vietnam War from the Other Side: The Vietnamese Communists' Perspective* (London: RoutledgeCurzon, 2002), 67–68.

20. David M. Toczek, *The Battle of Ap Bac, Vietnam: They Did Everything but Learn from It*, with a foreword by W. B. Rosson (Westport CT: Greenwood Press, 2001), 157.

21. Sheehan, *Bright Shining Lie*, 216.

22. John Tebbel and Keith Jennison, *The American Indian Wars* (New York: Harper & Row, 1960), 85, 155–57, 214.

23. Col. Harry G. Summers Jr., *Vietnam War Almanac* (New York: Facts on File Publications, 1985), 190, 75.

24. Shelby L. Stanton, *Vietnam Order of Battle* (Washington DC: U.S. News Books, 1981), 293.

25. Spark, "Flight Controls," 89; Philip D. Beidler, "The Last Huey," in *The Vietnam War and Postmodernity*, ed. Michael Bibby (Amherst: University of Massachusetts Press, 1999), 6; Stanton, *Vietnam Order of Battle*, 280–81, 287–91.

26. See online at www.chinooknation.org (accessed March 2, 2011).

27. Beidler, "Last Huey," 15n2.

28. Spark, "Flight Controls," 89.

29. Spark, "Flight Controls," 87, 90.

30. Stanton, *Vietnam Order*, 128–29.

31. Deepe, "Choppers Prove Their Worth," 3.

32. David G. Marr, "The Rise and Fall of 'Counter-Insurgency': 1961–1964," *PP*, 5:203–5.

4. THE RISE AND FALL OF FRONTIER FORTS

1. Summers, *Vietnam War Almanac*, 253; Deepe, Associated Press, 1962.

2. John Prados, *The Blood Road: The Ho Chi Minh Trail and the Vietnam War* (New York: John Wiley, 1999), xiii–xv.

3. Prados, *Blood Road*, xiii–xv.

4. Bui Tin, *From Enemy to Friend*, 41.

5. Bui Tin, *Following Ho Chi Minh*, 47–52.

6. Quoted in Fox Butterfield, "Turn Out the Light at the End of the Tunnel," in *Tears before the Rain*, ed. Larry Engelmann (New York: Oxford University Press, 1990), 177.

7. Bui Tin, *Following Ho Chi Minh*, 47–52.

8. From my notes of the Timmes interview, January 11, 1963.

9. Leroy TeCube, *A Year in Nam: A Native American Soldier's Story* (Lincoln: University of Nebraska Press, 1999), xviii.

10. Quoted in Tom Holm, *Strong Hearts Wounded Souls: Native American Veterans of the Vietnam War* (Austin: University of Texas Press, 1996), 129.

11. Quoted in Robert D. Dean, *Imperial Brotherhood: Gender and the Making of Cold War Foreign Policy* (Amherst: University of Massachusetts Press, 2001), 228.

12. Michael Yellow Bird, "Cowboys and Indians: Toys of Genocide, Icons of Colonialism," *Wicazo Sa Review* 19, no. 2 (Fall 2004): 33–48. Abstract at http://muse.jhu.edu/login?uri=/journals/wicazo_sa_review/v019/19.2bird.html (accessed February 2, 2009).

13. Deepe, "New Frontier in Viet Nam," 6-G.

14. *Newsweek*, September 17, 1962; my air-expressed dispatch to *Newsweek*.

15. Quoted in Norman P. Lewis, "From Cheesecake to Chief: Newspaper Editors' Slow Acceptance of Women," *American Journalism* 25, no. 2 (Spring 2008): 33–55.

16. See, for example, Hallin, *"Uncensored War."*

17. *Newsweek*'s admonishment read: "NOTICE YOU QUOTED IN NEWYORKTIMES THISMORNING AS BEING SULLYS SUCCESSOR AS NEWSWEEK CORRESPONDENT AND SAYING YOU NOT CERTAIN NEWSWEEK WOULD BE PERMITTED BACK INTO SOUTHVIETNAM STOP WISH REMIND YOU COMPANY POLICY IS THAT

CORRESPONDENTS DO NOT SPEAK FOR QUOTATION ON BEHALF OF NEWS-
WEEK WITHOUT CLEARING FIRST THROUGH NEWYORK." "Foreign Reporters
Warned by Saigon," NYT, September 26, 1962, 9; Arnaud de Borchgrave's cable
to me, September 26, 1962.

18. This section is based on my six-page unpublished article on press restrictions air-expressed to *Newsweek* on December 2, 1962. I have a copy in my bound
volumes.

19. Stanley Karnow, *Vietnam: A History*, 2nd revised and updated ed. (New
York: Penguin Books, 1997), 265.

20. Reuters, "Text of the 14-Nation Declaration and Protocol on Neutrality in
Laos," NYT, July 22, 1962, 14.

21. "The New Metal Birds," 37–38; and information from carbon copies of my
eight-page dispatch air-expressed to *Newsweek* New York.

22. Kenneth Conboy, with James Morrison, *Shadow War: The CIA's Secret War
in Laos* (Boulder CO: Paladin Press, 1995), 95–96, 102n11.

23. Conboy, *Shadow War*, viii, ix.

24. Quoted in Conboy, *Shadow War*, 47.

25. Cable to me dated April 3, 1963, and signed by my supervising editor, Arnauld
de Borchgrave.

26. *PP*, 2:637.

27. This description of the plain and my Kong Le interview is from my piece
"On the Laotian Brink," *Newsweek*, April 29, 1963, 33; and my additional unpublished cables to New York.

28. Deepe, "On the Laotian Brink."

29. Walt Haney, "The Pentagon Papers and the United States Involvement in
Laos," *PP*, 5:268–69.

30. Prados, *Blood Road*, 158.

31. Haney, "Pentagon Papers," *PP*, 5:276.

32. Haney, "Pentagon Papers," *PP*, 5:280.

33. Cited in Haney, "Pentagon Papers," *PP*, 5:277, 291.

34. Quoted in Fredrick Branfman, "Beyond the Pentagon Papers: The Pathol-
ogy of Power," *PP*, 5:298.

35. Table 5 showing U.S. Special Forces CIDG Camps Established in Vietnam,
July 1961–October 1964, www.history.army.mil/books/Vietnam/90-23/tab5.htm
(accessed February 12, 2009); Vietnam Studies, "U.S. Army Special Forces, 1961–
1971," www.army.mil/cmh-pg/BOOKS/Vietnam/90-23/90-23ac.htm (accessed
July 24, 2007); Garry Hollands and Wil Nelson, "War Trophies of the Past,"
Engineer, July–September 2007, 40.

36. www.encyclopedia.com/doc/1063-AshauValley.html (accessed February 10, 2009).

37. Kenneth Sams, "Project Checo Report: The Fall of A Shau," prepared for HQ PACAF, Tactical Evaluation Center, Project Checo, April 18, 1966, n.p.

38. An undated U.S. Special Forces after-action report titled "The Battle for A Shau," www.carrscompendiums.com/ccSEA/Documents/AD0391694/AD0391694_I15.html.

39. "The Fall of a Fortress," *Time*, March 18, 1966, www.time.com/time/magazine/article/0,9171,941936,00.html (accessed February 10, 2009).

40. My interview was held May 14, 1968, in Danang; Lt. Col. Alan L. Gropman, *Airpower and Airlift Evacuation of Kham Duc*, new imprint by Office of Air Force History (Washington DC: U.S. Air Force, 1985), 8.

41. Bui Tin, *Following Ho Chi Minh*, 47–52.

42. Cited in Gropman, *Airpower and Airlift*, 8.

43. Quoted in Gropman, *Airpower and Airlift*, 18–19.

44. Gerald C. Hickey, *Window on a War: An Anthropologist in the Vietnam Conflict* (Lubbock: Texas Tech University Press, 2002), 16.

5. TWO ILL-FATED PRESIDENTS

1. Ellen J. Hammer, *A Death in November: America in Vietnam, 1963* (New York: E. P. Dutton, 1987), 111–17; PP, 2:226.

2. Robert J. Topmiller, *The Lotus Unleashed: The Buddhist Peace Movement in South Vietnam, 1964–1966* (Lexington: University Press of Kentucky, 2002), 2, 18.

3. Topmiller, *Lotus Unleashed*, 9–10; Mark W. McLeod and Nguyen Thi Dieu, *Culture and Customs of Vietnam* (Westport CT: Greenwood Press, 2001), 56.

4. U.S. Senate Committee on Foreign Relations, *U.S. Involvement in the Overthrow of Diem, 1963: A Staff Study Based on the Pentagon Papers* (Washington DC: U.S. Government Printing Office, 1972), 28–29 (Committee Print 80–332).

5. Anthony Trawick Bouscaren, *The Last of the Mandarins: Diem of Vietnam* (Pittsburgh PA: Duquesne University Press, 1965), 89–90.

6. Hoang Lac and Ha Mai Viet, *Blind Design: Why America Lost the Vietnam War* (n.p., 1996), 127.

7. Lac and Viet, *Blind Design*, 127.

8. Lac and Viet, *Blind Design*, 127.

9. Lac and Viet, *Blind Design*, 22–23. Diem's education based on Confucian principles prompted Gen. Tran Van Don to explain, "At times he reminded me of a mandarin of a bygone era, at other times of a priest/confessor to recalcitrant sinners." See Tran Van Don, *Our Endless War: Inside Vietnam* (San Rafael CA: Presidio Press, 1978), 48.

10. Quoted in Francis X. Winters, *The Year of the Hare: America in Vietnam* (Athens: University of Georgia Press, 1997), 207.

11. Quoted in Winters, *Year of the Hare*, 156.

12. Quoted in Michael O'Brien, *John F. Kennedy: A Biography* (New York: St. Martin's Press, 2005), 619.

13. Surprisingly, in the forty-three volumes of the secret *Pentagon Papers* released to the public, Confucianism is not discussed enough among Kennedy's decision makers to warrant its being used as an index term.

14. *PP*, 2:22.

15. *PP*, 1:108–65.

16. Cited in Winters, *Year of the Hare*, 158.

17. Joseph G. Morgan, *The Vietnam Lobby: The American Friends of Vietnam, 1955–1975* (Chapel Hill: University of North Carolina Press, 1997), 1, 2.

18. Joseph Buttinger, *Vietnam: A Political History* (New York: Frederick A. Praeger, 1968), 414–15; George Herring, *America's Longest War: The United States and Vietnam, 1950–1975*, 4th ed. (Boston: McGraw-Hill, 2002), 20–21, 28, 42, 138; *PP*, 1:597.

19. *PP*, 1:246.

20. Stanley Karnow, "Diem Defeats His Own Best Troops," *Reporter*, January 19, 1961, 27.

21. Quoted in Seth Jacobs, *America's Miracle Man in Vietnam* (Durham NC: Duke University Press, 2004), 271.

22. Malcolm W. Browne, *The New Face of War* (Indianapolis: Bobbs-Merrill, 1965), 177–79.

23. Cited in Seth Jacobs, *Cold War Mandarin: Ngo Dinh Diem and the Origins of America's War in Vietnam, 1950–1963* (Lanham MD: Rowman & Littlefield, 2006), 146.

24. Nancy Gibbs, "The Catholic Conundrum — The Lessons of JFK," *Time*, June 19, 2007, http://www.time.com/time/specials/2007/article/0,28804,1635958_1635999_1634947,00.html (accessed March 22, 2009).

25. Deepe, "Another Monk Dies by Fire," *London Daily Express*, October 6, 1963.

26. This date is taken from my dispatches. Some give the date of August 3.

27. "South Vietnam: 'Beat Them,'" *Newsweek*, August 19, 1963, 46; "Vietnam's Future: 'All Bets Are Off,'" August 26, 1963, 35.

28. Deepe, "Buddhist Discontent Gaining Support in Viet-Nam Provinces," *Washington Post*, August 13, 1963, 16.

29. Mark W. McLeod, *The Vietnamese Response to French Intervention, 1862–1874* (New York: Praeger, 1991), 2, 9, 23, 24. McLeod uses the spelling *Minh-Menh*, instead of the spelling I obtained from the obituary of Prince Buu Hoi.

30. *PP*, 2:203.

31. "War in the Pagodas: Who Is the Enemy?" *Newsweek*, September 23, 1963, 35–38; *Newsweek* named me as reporting that troops executing the crackdown had three dominant characteristics: "They were Catholic, they were from Hue, and they were ruthless." This description drew an angry letter to the editor from the Rev. Francis X. Keul of Philadelphia, arguing that I could not know the troops were exclusively Catholic. He added, "From here, Beverly seems to have gone off the Deepe end." *Newsweek* stood by my description; see "Letters," September 23, 1963, 6.

32. The proclamation gave the Vietnamese military sweeping powers that included searching civilians' homes, restricting freedom of the press, and controlling the radio broadcast system, movies, and plays.

33. Anne E. Blair, *Lodge in Vietnam: A Patriot Abroad* (New Haven CT: Yale University Press, 1995), 3, 6.

34. Cited in Topmiller, *Lotus Unleashed*, 3; Colby, *Lost Victory*, 135.

35. *PP*, 2:738.

36. Cited in Francis Donald Faulkner, "Bao Chi: The American News Media in Vietnam, 1960–1975" (PhD diss., University of Massachusetts, 1981), 74.

37. Based on my advisory to *Newsweek* and United Press International, "Vietnamese Girl Held," *Lincoln Evening Journal and Nebraska State Journal*, October 30, 1963, 5.

38. Blair, *Lodge in Vietnam*, 38.

39. Cited in Blair, *Lodge in Vietnam*, 38.

40. Blair, *Lodge in Vietnam*, 38.

41. *PP*, 2:203, 228, 232–33, 234–35.

42. Quoted in Bouscaren, *Last of the Mandarins*, 148.

43. Cited in Jacobs, *Cold War Mandarin*, 154.

44. Cited in Winters, *Year of the Hare*, 27.

45. Cited in Blair, *Lodge in Vietnam*, front page.

46. Quoted in Howard Jones, *Death of a Generation: How the Assassinations of Diem and JFK Prolonged the Vietnam War* (New York: Oxford University Press, 2003), 385. Former ambassador Nolting explained that with an inadequate press office, the Ngos did not realize that "something they might say would bounce all around the world within the next six hours if it were sensational." Quoted in James C. Hasdorff, "Vietnam in Retrospect: An Interview with Ambassador Frederick E. Nolting Jr.," *Air University Review* (January–February 1974), www.airpower.maxwell.af.mil/airchronicles/aureview/1974/jan-feb/hasdorff.html (accessed September 6, 2007).

47. *PP*, 2:215, 219, 236–40, 245, 253.

48. Hammer, *Death in November*, 269.

49. *PP*, 2:220, 267.

50. Hammer, *Death in November*, 283–84; Jones, *Death of a Generation*, 420.

51. This section is drawn from carbon copies of my dispatches; on the published version headlined "The Fall of the House of Ngo" in *Newsweek*, November 11, 1963, 11, 19, 27–31; on background biographical materials I had air-expressed to New York about leading Vietnamese who might be prominent in a coup or a new government; and on "Young Tigers — and Cautious Optimism," *Newsweek*, November 18, 1963, 41–42.

52. *PP*, 2:269.

53. John Prados, "JFK and the Diem Coup," National Security Archives, posted November 5, 2003, www.gwu.edu/~nsarchiv/NSAEBB/NSAEBB101/index2.htm (accessed March 5, 2009); *PP*, 2:791.

54. Cited in Blair, *Lodge in Vietnam*, 69.

55. *PP*, 2:269.

56. Winters, *Year of the Hare*, 105–6.

57. Cited in Marguerite Higgins, *Our Vietnam Nightmare* (New York: Harper & Row, 1965), 302.

58. Cited in Bouscaren, *Last of the Mandarins*, 139.

59. Robert S. McNamara, letter to editor headlined "On Vietnam, Kennedy White House Flew Blind," *NYT*, September 14, 1995, A26.

60. Cited in Jacobs, *Cold War Mandarin*, 186.

61. Bouscaren, *Last of the Mandarins*, 139.

62. *PP*, 2:207.

63. John Prados, ed., *The White House Tapes: Eavesdropping on the President* (New York: New Press, 2003), 97–150, including forty-three pages of transcripts of the audiotapes and ten pages of drafts of cables (hereafter cited as *WHT*).

64. *WHT*, 114, 123.

65. Beverley [*sic*] Deepe, "Discontent Increasing, but Coup Is Doubtful — Troops, Secret Police Prop Diem Regime," *Washington Post*, July 9, 1963, 14. My byline is misspelled; Beverley is a male name in Britain, and so some readers were sometimes confused about my gender.

66. *WHT*, 97–98, 113.

67. This section relies on *The White House Tapes* and the National Security Archives website at www.gwu.edu/~nsarchiv/NSAEBB/NSAEBB101/index2.htm (accessed March 5, 2009; emphasis added).

68. *WHT*, 107, 109, 115.

69. *WHT*, 110, 132–33.

70. *WHT*, 111–12.

71. Some parts of the audiotape and the written transcript indicate some voices were inaudible, others could not be identified, and some parts of the tape had been deleted, presumably for security reasons such as identification of certain persons or code names.

72. Two months before the anti-Diem coup, Johnson had said in an official meeting on August 31 that he had "great reservations" about a coup because he had never seen a "genuine alternative to Diem." See *PP*, 2:743.

73. *WHT*, 113, 117, 123.

74. *PP*, 2:792–93.

75. Based on my close reading, neither the Gravel edition nor the *New York Times* edition of the *Pentagon Papers* contains discussion of a post-Diem government—its structure or composition—by U.S. officials during the last crucial week before the coup, and the CIA chief had heard no such discussion "in all the meetings on Vietnam over those many months," according to Colby, *Lost Victory*, 147.

76. William J. Miller, *Henry Cabot Lodge: A Biography by William J. Miller* (New York: James H. Heineman, 1967), 98.

77. Drawn from and quoted in Hammer, *Death in November*, 309.

6. "THE UNITED STATES WILL LOSE"

1. *PP*, 2:305.

2. Deepe, "As Saigon Saw Him: Intimate Glimpse of McNamara the Man," *NYHT*, March 15, 1964, 4.

3. Robert S. McNamara, with Brian VanDeMark, *In Retrospect: The Tragedy and Lessons of Vietnam* (New York: Times Books, 1995), 112.

4. Maxwell D. Taylor, *Swords and Plowshares* (New York: Norton, 1972), 309–10.

5. *PP*, 2:312.

6. Quoted in *Pentagon Papers as Published by the New York Times*, 283.

7. *Pentagon Papers as Published by the New York Times*, 286–88.

8. Wilfred G. Burchett, *Vietnam: Inside Story of the Guerilla War*, with a new introduction (New York: International Publishers, 1966), 216.

9. *PP*, 2:619

10. Deepe, "Time and the Man in Viet Nam," *NYHT*, April 19, 1964, 1.

11. Taylor, *Swords and Plowshares*, 309.

12. Maxwell Taylor, "Summary of Taylor's Report Sent to McNamara by Joint Chiefs," in *Pentagon Papers as Published by the New York Times*, 293.

13. Quoted in *Pentagon Papers as Published by the New York Times*, 372.

14. *PP*, 2:280–81, 292–96, 350.

15. A sampling of the *Trib*'s headlines above my 1964 political articles, most displayed on page 1, provide a panorama: August 17, "Viet Shakeup: Fateful Days Near in War"; August 24, "Viet Rioting for 5th Day"; August 25, "Khanh Yields, Students Don't"; August 28, "Viet: 'New' Junta and Death in the Saigon Streets — Catholics vs. Buddhists"; August 29, "Khanh Fights to Keep Power — Paratroops vs. Saigon Mobs"; October 30, "New Saigon Regime Is Believed Moribund at Birth"; November 25, "First Charge since Diem — Viet Premier Says Students 'Play Reds' Game.'"

16. Robert Shaplen, *The Lost Revolution: Vietnam 1945–65* (London: Andre Deutsch, 1966), 228.

17. U.S. Department of Energy Openness Press Conference Fact Sheets, January 15, 1997, https://www.osti.gov/opnnet/document/jan97/prefacts.html (accessed June 11, 2008; link broken).

18. Deepe, "N. Viet Troops Cross Border, U.S. Aids [*sic*] Say," NYHT, July 14, 1964, 4.

19. Deepe, "Viet — Measuring an 'Invasion,'" NYHT, July 26, 1964, 2.

20. Deepe, "Viet — Measuring an 'Invasion,'"; Edwin E. Moise, *Tonkin Gulf and the Escalation of the Vietnam War* (Chapel Hill: University of North Carolina Press, 1996), 46.

21. Deepe, "Viet — Measuring an 'Invasion,'"; Deepe, "Viet Nam a Year after Diem — His Dire Prophecy Coming True," NYHT, November 1, 1964, 14.

22. Deepe, "Viet — Measuring an 'Invasion,'" accompanied by a photo I had snapped with credit line. See also Robert A. Caro, *The Years of Lyndon Johnson: The Passage of Power* (New York: Knopf, 2012), xix, 534–36.

23. After the election U.S. officials refined their statistics and, more significantly, lined up arguments to defend their earlier low estimates made to Congress and the press; PP, 3:244, 255–57, 681.

24. NYT, January 27, 1965, 2.

25. Deepe, "Bottom of the Pyramid — Red Viet Prisoner's Story," NYHT, August 9, 1964, 3, and August 10, 1964, 4.

26. Eugene G. Windchy, *Tonkin Gulf* (Garden City NY: Doubleday & Co., 1971), 1–4; and the Department of Defense Press Release of August 2, 1964, contained in Windchy's appendix 1; Moise, *Tonkin Gulf*, 50–93.

27. WHT, 185, 191.

28. Moise, *Tonkin Gulf*, 143–45.

29. McNamara, Blight, and Brigham, *Argument without End*, 215.

30. Moise, *Tonkin Gulf*, 225–36.

31. Tonkin Gulf Resolution, in Windchy, *Tonkin Gulf*, 19–20.

32. A copy of this unpublished dispatch, which I relied on for this section, is contained in my bound volumes; NYHT editorial "The Right Response," August 6, 1964, 16; and "Be It Resolved . . . ," August 7, 1964, 14.

33. Deepe, "The CIA's Spy-Drops into Red Viet," NYHT, August 16, 1964, 13. I air-expressed this article to New York on August 3.

34. Cited in *Pentagon Papers as Published by the New York Times*, 82, 122–24, 127.

35. Deepe, "Viet Shakeup: Fateful Days Near in War," 1, 4.

36. Deepe, "Khanh Fights to Keep Power," 1, 4; Deepe, "Viet Buddhist Protests . . . Why?" NYHT, August 22, 1964, 1, 4; Deepe, "Viet Rioting for 5th Day," 1, 12; Deepe, "Khanh Yields, Students Don't," 1, 3; Deepe, "Viet: 'New' Junta and Death in the Saigon Streets," 1, 4.

37. Deepe, "From the Political Jungle of Viet — What Khanh Says," NYHT, August 31, 1964, 1. See also my follow-up page 1 story, "Viet Musical Chairs: Khanh In, Aid [*sic*] Out," September 4, 1964, 1, 2; and evidencing more instability, my articles "Coup Flop a Boost for Khanh," September 14, 1964, 16; "In Viet — A Coup Designed to Fail," September 22, 1964, 17; and "In Viet — The Military Coup That Became an Army Purge," September 23, 1964, 16.

38. Deepe, "Off to Coup No. 3 by Taxi," n.p.

39. This passage is excerpted from my bylined NYHT article with the overline and headline "It's the Day of the Moon Festival — Crisis Leaves Saigon Unruffled," September 20, 1964, 2.

40. Deepe, "Coups Are Old Hat to U.S. Saigon Families," NYHT, October 4, 1964. I have an original copy of this article that was not published in the NYHT's New York edition now preserved on microfilm; it must have been published in a different edition.

41. Deepe, "In Viet Nam — Fate IS in the Stars," NYHT, October 4, 1964, 20.

42. Deepe, "U.S. Tackling Past Mistakes in Weird War," NYHT, October 25, 1964, 4, 5; Deepe, "The Shadow That Rules Most of a Nation," NYHT, October 26, 1964, 8; Deepe, "Story of a 'Have-Not' Exploited by the Reds," NYHT, October 27, 1964, 6; Deepe, "The Buddhists, a Crucial Third Force," NYHT, October 28, 1964, 8; Deepe, "We Just Don't Understand," NYHT, October 29, 1964, 6; Deepe, "New Saigon Regime Is Believed Moribund at Birth," NYHT, October 30, 1964, 4; Deepe, "Viet Nam a Year after Diem — His Dire Prophecy Coming True," NYHT, November 1, 1964, 14.

43. Deepe, "Base Security Was Criticized," with larger-type overline of "Viet Explosion — Shockwaves," NYHT, November 2, 1964, 1, 12; Deepe, "Jets to Ashes — As the Yanks Saw It," NYHT, November 2, 1964, 12.

44. Deepe, "Coup in Two Acts," NYHT, December 22, 1964, 4.

45. *PP*, 2:294, 346–48.

46. *PP*, 2:348, 350.

47. Deepe, "Viet Strongman Defies U.S. on Civilian Rule — Khanh Assails Gen. Taylor," *NYHT*, December 23, 1964, 1, 4.

48. "Foreign Correspondents: Self-Reliance in Saigon," *Time*, January 8, 1965, 38; "South Vietnam: The U.S. v. the Generals," *Time*, January 1, 1965, 32–33.

49. Zalin Grant, *Facing the Phoenix: The CIA and the Political Defeat of the United States in Vietnam* (New York: Norton, 1991), 254–55.

50. "Foreign Correspondents."

51. "Foreign Correspondents."

52. Deepe, "Christmas Eve Bomb in Saigon," *NYHT*, December 25, 1964, 1, 4. Reprinted in *Reporting Vietnam*, pt. 1, *American Journalism, 1959–1969* (New York: Library of America, 1998), 134–37.

53. Cited in *Vietnam Voices*, 183.

54. *PP*, 3:277.

7. AMERICANIZING THE WAR

1. Deepe, "Viet's 'War of the Prairies,'" *NYHT*, March 14, 1965, 17.

2. Deepe, "New Series: Viet Nam, Past and Prospect," *NYHT*, January 16, 1966, 23.

3. Deepe, "See U.S. Raids as Basis for Stable Viet," *NYHT*, February 16, 1965, 3.

4. *PP*, 3:306.

5. Deepe, "North Viet Bombed Again; We Clam Up on U.S. Role," *NYHT*, March 15, 1965, 1, 7. I was cabling New York so frequently that my February bill zoomed to three thousand dollars; I was ordered to cut it.

6. *PP*, 3:400, 455.

7. Deepe, "Viet Guerrillas Have the Edge on Guided Missiles," *NYHT*, February 28, 1965, 9; Deepe, "B-52 Raid Is Biggest since '45," *NYHT*, April 13, 1966, 1.

8. Deepe, "Report in Saigon: More Marines Due," *NYHT*, March 10, 1965, 1, 11.

9. *PP*, 3:417.

10. *PP*, 3:400–401.

11. *PP*, 3:433.

12. Deepe, "Hanoi Set for Long War," *NYHT*, December 12, 1965, 21.

13. *PP*, 4:227, 461–66.

14. *PP*, 4:484; Sheehan, *Bright Shining Lie*, 685.

15. McNamara, *In Retrospect*, 222; Lewis Sorley, *Westmoreland: The General Who Lost Vietnam* (Boston: Houghton Mifflin Harcourt, 2011), 86.

16. *Vietnam Voices*, 385.

17. *PP*, 3:433.

18. David Burns Sigler, *Vietnam Battle Chronology: U.S. Army and Marine Corps Combat Operations, 1965–1973* (Jefferson NC: McFarland & Co., 1992), 153.

19. *PP*, 4:408–9, 410–20, 447–56.

20. Deepe, "GIs Seize Big, Empty Cong HQ," *NYHT*, February 23, 1966, 6; and "New GI Pattern: Opening Roads to Get to People in Cong Areas," February 21, 1966, 7. In both articles my byline is misspelled as *Beverley*.

21. Robert Scheer, "Genesis of U.S. Support for the Regime of Ngo Dinh Diem," in *Vietnam and America: The Most Comprehensive Documented History of the Vietnam War*, revised and enlarged 2nd ed., ed. Marvin E. Gettleman, Jane Franklin, Marilyn B. Young, and H. Bruce Franklin (New York: Grove Press, 1995), 121.

22. See online at www.59thlandclearing.org/pages/history.htm; and www .history.army.mil/books/vietnam/tactical/chapter7.htm (both accessed May 8, 2010).

23. Utley, *Indian Frontier*, 170.

24. My unpublished dispatch and advisory dated August 24, 1965, was air-expressed to New York because of orders to hold down cabling costs. U.S. figures later indicated 45 U.S. dead and 120 wounded; 614 guerrilla bodies and 9 prisoners. See Harry G. Summers Jr., *Historical Atlas of the Vietnam War*, with an introduction and epilogue by Stanley Karnow (Boston: Houghton Mifflin, 1995), 102.

25. Giap, *Military Art of People's War*, 270–71.

26. Clodfelter, *Vietnam in Military Statistics*, 257.

27. Quoted in Elliott, *Vietnamese War*, 2:920–21.

28. *PP*, 4:401.

29. Lt. Gen. Bernard William Rogers, "Vietnam Studies Cedar Falls–Junction City: A Turning Point," http://purl.access.gpo.gov/GPO/LPS51169 (accessed May 19, 2010); Jonathan Schell, *The Real War: The Classic Reporting on the Vietnam War* (New York: Pantheon Books, 1987).

30. Clodfelter, *Vietnam in Military Statistics*, 234–35.

31. Robert H. Scales Jr., *Firepower in Limited War* (Washington DC: National Defense University Press, 1990), 153, http://purl.access.gpo.gov/GPO/LPS51515 (accessed March 21, 2011); J. A. Menzoff, "Harassment and Interdiction (H&I) Fires," in *Encyclopedia of the Vietnam War: A Political, Social, and Military History*, ed. Spencer Tucker (New York: Oxford University Press, 2000), 161.

32. Deepe, "Viet Bombers Sow Bitter Seeds," *NYHT*, October 27, 1965, 2.

33. Third MAF, "Background for Press, October 1966," third unnumbered page.

34. See online at http://capmarine.com (accessed April 1, 2011).

35. Beverly Ann Deepe, "A Girl Visits the Combat Marines in Vietnam," *Cosmopolitan*, June 1967, 104–7.

36. This section on the marines is drawn from my "Viet Nam: Past and Prospect — Marines' Greatest Effort: Securing Da Nang," *NYHT*, January 19, 1966, 4.

37. Hayslip, *When Heaven and Earth Changed Places*, 288.

38. Third MAF, "Background for Press, October 1966," seventh unnumbered page.

39. Deepe, "Marines' Greatest Effort," 4; Deepe, "Viet Cong Make like Moles," *NYHT*, November 14, 1965, 19.

40. Marcus J. Gordon (regional director, First Corps, USOM, Danang), "USOM/ Vietnam, I Corps Regional Summary Report for November 1965," 2–4, 7.

41. Maj. J. A. Buck, "Memorandum for Commanding General: A Village Called Duong Son (1)," July 31, 1965, 1–3.

42. Cong. Rec. S, 89th Cong., 2d sess., 1966, 676–79; Deepe, "Viet Nam, Past and Prospect," *NYHT*, January 16–19, 1966.

43. Deepe, "Is Asia 'Domino Theory' Passé?" *NYHT*, April 1, 1966, 2.

44. Quoted in Ninkovich, *Modernity and Power*, 246.

45. Karnow, *Vietnam*, 264–65, 267.

46. Quoted in PP, 4:662.

47. Quoted in PP, 4:454.

8. HER STORY AS HISTORY TOO

1. Deepe, "Contrasts in Vietnamese Women — Rich Get Richer and Poor Get Poorer," *NYHT*, November 24, 1965, 11.

2. Elliott, *Vietnamese War*, 1:597, 601.

3. The advertisement was published on November 19, 1965, 25. The five-part series began two days later, on Sunday, November 21, 1965, under the headline "Viet Women — Friends, Foes and Madame Nhu." The remaining four articles followed on consecutive days, published respectively on pages 2, 2, 11, and 2. This chapter is drawn in part from this comprehensive series.

4. Deepe, "Viet Cong Wedding in the Jungle," 2.

5. Smith et al., *Area Hand Book for South Vietnam*, 59–60.

6. Clodfelter, *Vietnam in Military Statistics*, 257.

7. Elliott, *Vietnamese War*, 1:592–98.

8. PP, 4:321.

9. Micheal Clodfelter, *Mad Minutes and Vietnam Months: A Soldier's Memoir* (Jefferson NC: McFarland & Co., 1988), 46, 228.

10. Deepe, "'My Seven Children Hid in the Bunkers,'" *CSM*, September 3, 1968, 7.

11. Clodfelter, *Vietnam in Military Statistics*, 259.

12. Elliott, *Vietnamese War*, 2:1126–27, 1133–34.

13. Noam Chomsky, "The Pentagon Papers as Propaganda and as History," in *The Pentagon Papers: Critical Essays Edited by Noam Chomsky and Howard Zinn and an Index to Volumes One–Four* (Boston: Beacon Press, 1972), 5:196.

14. Bernard Weinraub, "U.S. Report Finds Gloom in Vietnam," *NYT*, December 6, 1967, 1, 10.

15. Elliott, *Vietnamese War*, 2:1119, 1126–27, 1172.

16. *PP*, 2:226–27.

17. "Presenting Vietnam," *Review Horizons* (Saigon), n.d., 7.

18. "Mrs. Nhu Now Defends Reds as 'Nationalists,'" *NYT*, July 19, 1966.

19. Deepe, "Madame Ky, the Charmer," *Parade*, November 20, 1966, n.p. Photos by James H. Pickerell.

20. Deepe, "Viet Women — Friends, Foes and Madame Nhu," *NYHT*, November 21, 1965, 8; Elliott, *Vietnamese War*, 1:236–38; Mrs. Nguyen Thi Dinh, "'No Other Road to Take': Origin of the National Liberation Front in Ben Tre," excerpted and republished in Gettleman et al., *Vietnam and America*, 165–88.

21. Deepe, "Viet Women — Friends, Foes and Madame Nhu," 8.

22. This term is used in several works; for example, Mrs. Nguyen Thi Dinh, "'No Other Road to Take,'" 185.

23. Deepe, "Women Reinforce Viet Cong" [Women Build Viet Cong Ranks], *CSM*, May 4, 1968, 2.

24. Deepe, "Viet Women — Friends, Foes and Madame Nhu," 8.

25. Gary D. Solis, *The Law of Armed Conflict: International Humanitarian Law in War* (New York: Cambridge University Press, 2010), 461–66.

26. Hayslip, *When Heaven and Earth Changed Places*, 162–63.

27. Deepe, "Viet WACs: Too Many Volunteers," *NYHT*, November 23, 1965, 2.

28. Cited in Howard J. Langer, *The Vietnam War: An Encyclopedia of Quotations* (Westport CT: Greenwood Press, 2005), 202.

29. See online at www.wordreference.com/fren/caca (accessed June 23, 2009).

30. Clodfelter, *Vietnam in Military Statistics*, 242.

31. Elliott, *Vietnamese War*, 1:592–601.

32. Cited in Elliott, *Vietnamese War*, 2:1216, 1288.

33. Tran Van Dinh, "The Tale of Kieu: Joy and Sadness in the Life of Vietnamese in the United States," in *Unwinding the Vietnam War: From War into Peace*, ed. Reese Williams (Seattle: Real Comet Press, 1987), 84.

34. Nguyen Du, *The Tale of Kieu*, trans. and annotated by Huynh Sanh Thong (New York: Random House, 1973), 34, 37–38.

35. Huynh Sanh Thong, introduction to Nguyen Du, *Tale of Kieu*, 22.

36. Nguyen Du, *Tale of Kieu*, 59, 134.

37. Nguyen Du, *Tale of Kieu*, 59, 74–75, 103, 105, 108, 118.

38. Huynh Sanh Thong, introduction to Nguyen Du, *Tale of Kieu*, 22, 20.

39. Tran Van Dinh, "Tale of Kieu," 86.

40. Nguyen Du, *Tale of Kieu*, 140.

9. "DESTROY THE TOWN TO SAVE IT"

1. The articles were published from May 30 to June 4, 1965.

2. Because of these five editions in different regions, my article in some cases might have been published on different pages or days and sometimes with different headlines.

3. Deepe, "Viet Reds Set 'Peace' Offensive," CSM, May 8, 1967, 1, 11; and "Two Vietnam Fronts — Red Offensives Loom," CSM, May 8, 1967, 1, 2; "Hanoi Grips Viet Cong Tighter," CSM, May 10, 1967, 1, 6; "Hanoi Strategy May Boomerang," CSM, May 11, 1967, 11; "U.S. Patrols Cross Viet Borders," CSM, May 3, 1967, 1; "'Other War' Stalls," 1, 6.

4. Deepe, "War without a Frontline," 9.

5. Cited and quoted in John Prados, *Vietnam: The History of an Unwinnable War, 1945–1975* (Lawrence: University Press of Kansas, 2009), 219, 221.

6. Quoted in Don Oberdorfer, *Tet* (Garden City NY: Doubleday, 1971), 106.

7. Quoted in Macdonald, *Giap*, 124.

8. Deepe, "Westmoreland Sights Viet Victory," CSM, December 11, 1967, 1, 13; Deepe, "Why Reds Look for Viet Win," CSM, December 13, 1967, 1, 15.

9. Deepe, "Hints to Peasants — Cong Presses for Coalition," CSM, January 20, 1968, 1.

10. Deepe, "Viet Cong Seeks Political Victory," CSM, December 29, 1967, 1, 2.

11. Westmoreland, *Soldier*, 381–82.

12. This section is drawn from my four-part CSM series totaling 4,230 words: "Ceremonies — A Glimpse of the Viet Cong," February 17, 1968, 2; "Cong Interview — Cadre Boasts NFL [*sic*] Expects Decisive Victory in 1968" [Cadre Says Cong Will Win in '68], February 19, 1968, 5; "Interview — Cong Aide Lists Five 'Musts'" [Cong Interview — Cadre Says U.S. Must Accept Five Points to Settle Viet War], February 20, 1968, 2; "Viet Cong Claims Peasant Support" [Interview — Cong Aide Outlines Goals], February 21, 1968, 7.

13. Sun Tzu, *The Art of War*, ed. with a foreword by James Clavell (New York: Delacorte Press, 1983), 18.

14. Clarence R. Wyatt, *Paper Soldiers: The American Press and the Vietnam War* (New York: Norton, 1993), 168.

15. Cable no. 31200 from number two overseas editor Bert Johansson.

16. Deepe, "South Vietnam Shaken — 'Hardly a Hamlet Feels Safe,'" *CSM*, February 7, 1968, 1, 13.

17. Westmoreland, *Soldier*, 399.

18. Deepe, "Cong Raids Take High Political Toll," *CSM*, February 5, 1968, 1, 4.

19. Deepe, "Cong Raids Take High Political Toll," 1, 4.

20. This Saigon section is drawn from my "South Vietnam Shaken," 1, 13; "A View from Saigon — Blitz Erodes U.S. Position in Vietnam," *CSM*, February 3, 1968, 1, 4 (reprinted in 2012 in *50 Great Stories* in Columbia Journalism School centennial booklet, available at www.journalism.columbia.edu/centennial); "Cong Raids Take High Political Toll," 1, 4; "Blow to Cities — South Viet Control Battered" [South Viet Control Battered], *CSM*, February 6, 1968, 4; "'Blitz' Aftereffects — Viet Propaganda Battle Seesaws," *CSM*, February 8, 1968, 1, 4; "Viet Cong in Saigon Hits and Hides," *CSM*, February 9, 1968, 1, 2.

21. This Bien Hoa section is based on my unpublished manuscript filed February 13, 1968, and maintained in my bound volumes of dispatches to the *Monitor*.

22. During the first eleven days of the Communist offensive in the eleven provinces comprising Third Corps, official statistics revealed 9,222 Communists killed and 112 U.S. killed and 1,298 wounded; Vietnamese government and civilian casualties were not released. Captured were 230 Communist prisoners and 1,026 weapons.

23. Cable dated February 7, 1968, from assistant overseas editor Johansson. Hank Hayward cabled the next day, however, saying that my next article of 1,475 words from Bien Hoa was "excellent frontpaged"; Deepe, "Villages around Saigon," 1, 4.

24. See Peter Braestrap [*sic*], "Reds in Saigon Area Believed Hurt," *Washington Post*, March 11, 1968, 10.

25. Cited in Hammond, *Public Affairs*, 262 (emphasis added).

26. Admiral U. S. G. Sharp and Gen. W. C. Westmoreland, *Report on the War in Vietnam (as of June 30, 1968)* (Washington DC: U.S. Government Printing Office, n.d.), 168–69.

27. Deepe, "U.S. Blows Feed Viet Backlash," *CSM*, February 21, 1968, 1, 4.

28. Oberdorfer, *Tet*, 184.

29. Peter Arnett, *Live from the Battlefield: From Vietnam to Baghdad, 35 Years in the World's War Zones* (New York: Simon & Schuster, 1994), 253–57; Peter Braestrup, *Big Story*, with an introduction by Leonard R. Sussman and a public opinion analysis by Burns W. Roper (Boulder CO: Westview Press, in cooperation with Freedom House, 1977), 254–55.

30. Quoted in Braestrup, *Big Story*, 260.

31. Cable dated February 14, 1968, from overseas editor Henry Hayward.

32. Mark W. McLeod and Nguyen Thi Dieu, *Culture and Customs of Vietnam*

(Westport CT: Greenwood Press, 2001), 24, 113; Edward F. Murphy, *Semper Fi Vietnam: From Da Nang to the DMZ; Marine Corps Campaigns, 1965–1975* (Novato CA: Presidio Press, 1997), 188.

33. This section is drawn from my "Hue: Battle for a Walled City," *CSM*, February 28, 1968, 2; "Battle for Hue Palace — 'Assault Ends with a Whimper,'" *CSM*, February 29, 1968, 6; "Hue Struck Again — by Looting," *CSM*, March 4, 1968, 1; "Damage High — Victory at Hue Pondered," *CSM*, March 5, 1968, 2.

34. James H. Willbanks, *The Tet Offensive: A Concise History* (New York: Columbia University Press, 2007), 47.

35. Stanley Millet, ed., *South Vietnam: U.S.-Communist Confrontation in Southeast Asia*, vol. 3, *1968* (New York: Facts on File, 1974), 55–56.

36. Clodfelter, *Vietnam in Military Statistics*, 235; George W. Smith, *The Siege at Hue* (Boulder CO: Lynne Rienner, 1999), ix.

10. FROM KHE SANH

1. Deepe, "Honeymooners in a War," *Parade*, January 15, 1967, 26.

2. Braestrup, *Big Story*, 337–39.

3. Cited in Hammond, *Public Affairs*, 341–43; Westmoreland, *Soldier*, 411, 500.

4. Prados, *Vietnam*, 216; Andrew F. Krepinvevich Jr., *The Army and Vietnam* (Baltimore: John Hopkins University Press, 1986), 193, 238.

5. Karnow, *Vietnam*, 554.

6. This section about my March trip to Khe Sanh is drawn from these six of my articles, all published in 1968 on page 1 in the *Christian Science Monitor* and totaling 9,205 words: "Encircled Khe Sanh — How Communists Lay Tight Siege against U.S. Marine Corps Base," March 20; "Khe Sanh — Cheese in U.S. 'Trap,'" March 21; "Khe Sanh Strategy Porous?" March 22; "Reds Hold Two Options in Vietnam Struggle," March 23; "U.S. Military Seeks Go-Ahead — Pressure for Khe Sanh Offensive," March 26; "Khe Sanh: Legacy of Westmoreland," March 27. A seventh article was unpublished, probably because editors considered it "too gory."

7. News release, Military Assistance Command Vietnam, February 7, 1968.

8. USMC Capt. Moyers S. Shore II, *The Battle for Khe Sanh* (Washington DC: U.S. Marine Corps Historical Branch, 1969), 8.

9. Clodfelter, *Vietnam in Military Statistics*, 124.

10. Deepe, "Encircled Khe Sanh," 1, 4.

11. Deepe, "Khe Sanh — Cheese in U.S. 'Trap,'" 1, 6.

12. Shore, *Battle for Khe Sanh*, 111.

13. Murphy, *Semper Fi Vietnam*, 163–64.

14. Deepe, "U.S. Military Seeks Go-Ahead," 1, 2.

15. This section is based on the unpublished dispatch I sent the *Monitor*. About my first article from Khe Sanh that was published, an editor described it in cablese as "firstrate and frontpaged Tuesday with map" but pleaded, "Try hard to down-hold length." Even more dismayed by my over-filing, the editor's next cable read: "Third Khesanh article excellent frontpager full of original hardhitting material but simply unable provide space for such length dash four thousand words exclamation regretfully broke it into two parts stop repeating urgent plea to discipline yourself to more normal newspaper lengths regardest Hank." I figured I was not in too much trouble, however, because all my articles were placed on page 1 accompanied by a multicolumn photo or map to attract readers' eyes and to help them to visualize such a faraway place. Even better, one huffy cable ended with "We love you Hank."

16. Deepe, "Khe Sanh: Legacy of Westmoreland," 1, 6.

17. *PP*, 4:587.

18. Cited in Willbanks, *Tet Offensive*, 56.

19. Mao Tse-tung, *Selected Works of Mao Tse-tung*, http://www.marxists.org/reference/archive/mao/selected-works/volume-6/mswv6_28.htm (accessed July 29, 2009).

20. Quoted in Oberdorfer, *Tet*, 106.

21. Deepe, "Khe Sanh: Legacy of Westmoreland," 1, 6.

22. Quoted in Giap, *Military Art of People's War*, 119–20.

23. Prados, *Vietnam*, 448.

24. This section on my June return is based on my three-part CSM series totaling 5,710 words, "Khe Sanh: Vietnam Mystery": "Why Hasn't Khe Sanh Assault Come Off?" [Why Didn't Battle of Khe Sanh Ever Come Off?], June 27, 1968, 1, 2; "Before the Pullout—How B-52s Protected Khe Sanh," June 28, 1968, 1, 2; "What Units Besieged Khe Sanh?" [How U.S. Intelligence Weighed Khe Sanh Opposition], June 29, 1968, 6.

25. Deepe, "What Units Besieged Khe Sanh?" 6; Ang Cheung Guan, *The Vietnam War from the Other Side: The Vietnamese Communists' Perspective* (London: RoutledgeCurzon, 2000), 123–32.

26. Deepe, "What Units Besieged Khe Sanh?" 6.

27. This often-used quote is from "What Units Besieged Khe Sanh?" 6.

28. Deepe, "Before the Pullout," 1, 2.

29. Clodfelter, *Vietnam in Military Statistics*, 124.

30. Doan Van Toai, *A Vietcong Memoir* (San Diego: Harcourt Brace Jovanovich, 1985), 167–68.

31. On the Internet at www.youtube.com, you can type in the search box: "B-52 Operation Arc Light."

32. Deepe, "What Units Besieged Khe Sanh?" 6; Anthony J. Tambini, *Wiring Vietnam: The Electronic Wall* (Lanham MD: Scarecrow Press, 2007), 21.

33. Deepe, "What Units Besieged Khe Sanh?" 6.

34. Quoted in Millet, *South Vietnam*, 3:66. Westmoreland made his statement on April 6, 1969, in an unidentified report published by the U.S. government.

35. Karnow, *Vietnam*, 549.

36. James J. Wirtz, *The Tet Offensive: Intelligence Failure in War* (Ithaca NY: Cornell University Press, 1991), 4–13, 252–75.

37. The enclosed three-part series and managing editor Courtney Sheldon's letter addressed to the Advisory Board on the Pulitzer Prizes, dated December 31, 1968, are in my possession. The prize for international reporting in 1968 was awarded to the *Washington Post*'s Alfred Friendly for Middle East coverage.

38. Burns W. Roper, "What Public Opinion Polls Said," in Braestrup, *Big Story*, 703; in the context of the entire war the impact of Tet on the U.S. public at large was to add to the slide toward an antiwar sentiment that had been developing for nearly three years — and that continued for another three years, according to Roper's detailed analysis of multiple relevant polls.

39. Quoted in Robert Mann, *A Grand Delusion: America's Descent into Vietnam* (New York: Basic Books, 2001), 575–76; Wirtz, *Tet Offensive*, 275.

40. Philip Geyelin, "Vietnam and the Press: Limited War and an Open Society," in *The Vietnam Legacy: The War, American Society and the Future of American Foreign Policy*, ed. Anthony Lake (New York: Council on Foreign Relations, 1976), 190.

41. E. W. Kenworthy, "The Tet Offensive and the Turnaround," in *The Pentagon Papers as Published by the New York Times* (Toronto: Bantam Books, 1971), 601.

42. Gen. Vo Nguyen Giap, *Viet Nam People's War Has Defeated U.S. War of Destruction* (Hanoi: Foreign Languages Publishing House, 1969), 65.

43. Robert M. Collins, "The Economic Crisis of 1968 and the Waning of the 'American Century,'" in *The Lessons and Legacies of the Vietnam War*, ed. Walter L. Hixon (New York: Garland, 2000), 18, 28.

44. Deepe, "Khe Sanh Transition — Early Escalation Expected with Shift to Mobile Warfare," CSM, April 16, 1968, 2.

45. Deepe, "Military Sees Bomb Halt Peril," CSM, October 16, 1968, 1; Deepe, "Allies Outnumber Reds along DMZ," CSM, October 17, 1968, 1; Deepe, "As Abrams Sees Vietnam — U.S. Deals from Strength," CSM, October 23, 1968, 1; "Logistics Called Chink in Cong Armor," CSM, October 24, 1968, 4.

46. Deepe, "Viet Quiet — Peace Hint or Tactic?" *CSM*, October 25, 1968, 1; Deepe, "Step by Step toward Peace in Vietnam," *CSM*, October 31, 1968, 1.

47. Deepe, "Hanoi Repair Priority: Roads but Not Buildings," *CSM*, October 29, 1968, 1.

48. Deepe, "Viet-Withdrawal Plan Reported in Laos," *CSM*, October 30, 1968, 1.

49. Deepe, "Saigon Uneasy over U.S. Role in Asia," *CSM*, November 4, 1968, 2.

50. My editorial note 1 to "Hank," October 28, 1968, transmitted through Reuters, n.p.

51. Deepe, "Saigon Short Circuit? — Diplomatic Pandemonium in South Vietnam; U.S. Accused of Bobbling Peace Package," *CSM*, November 8, 1968, 1, 17.

52. Deepe, "Refusal Viewed as Rebuff to Johnson — Thieu Balks at Talking with Viet Cong," *CSM*, November 5, 1968, 1, 4.

53. Hayward cable no. 1732, 2, to me via Reuters, n.d.

54. Quoted in Larry Berman, *No Peace, No Honor: Nixon, Kissinger, and Betrayal in Vietnam* (New York: Free Press, 2001), 34.

55. Hayward cable no. 1732.

56. Deepe, "Refusal Viewed as Rebuff to Johnson," 1; see also Deepe, "Saigon Waits — Will U.S. Vote Alter Viet Bid?" November 6, 1968, 2 [Recalcitrant Saigon Hopes for Better Deal], *CSM*, November 5, 1968, 1; Bui Diem, with David Chanoff, *In the Jaws of History* (Boston: Houghton Mifflin, 1987), 243–45.

57. To access his document-based investigative report, scroll down to that headline, "LBJ's 'X' File on Nixon's 'Treason,'" at www.consortiumnews.com (accessed April 28, 2012). This section of my chapter is largely drawn from Parry's exposé.

58. Nguyen Tien Hung and Jerrold L. Schecter, *The Palace File* (New York: Harper & Row, 1986), 23–24; Berman, *No Peace, No Honor*, 32–36; Bui Diem, *In the Jaws of History*, 243–45; Karnow, *Vietnam*, 600–603. Karnow reported that Johnson was also bugging Thieu in his palace office.

59. Anna Chennault, *The Education of Anna* (New York: Times Books, 1980), 170–85.

60. Hung, *Palace File*, 23–24; Berman, *No Peace, No Honor*, 32–36.

61. Berman, *No Peace, No Honor*, 32–35; Hung, *Palace File*, 23–44. My comment regarding national security is based on a summary of remarks made by Secretary of State Dean Rusk, quoted in Parry, "LBJ's 'X' File."

62. The LBJ Library released the audio recording of the conversations cited by Parry in late 2008 and also made transcripts of it.

63. Hung, *Palace File*, 485n31.

64. Quoted in Bui Diem, *In the Jaws of History*, 244.

65. This section is based on my cables to *CSM* and my three-part *CSM* series totaling 5,509 words: "Saigon Short Circuit?" November 8, 1968, 1; "Who Sits at Peace Table?" November 9, 1968, 1; "Distrust Marked U.S.-Saigon Talks on Paris" [Versions Conflict Rancor Mars Viet Allies Talks], November 12, 1968, 6.

At the *Monitor*'s request I also made and cabled unofficial excerpts and a summary of questions to and answers made by Vietnamese minister of information Ton That Thien at a news conference in Saigon on November 13, when he reiterated Saigon's long-standing opposition to a separate representation for the NLF. Asked whether any Nixon staffers had contacted high Vietnamese government officials, Thien replied: "I don't know. But I don't think Nixon would do that sort of thing behind President Johnson's back." See Ton That Thien, "Saigon's Version: 'President Thieu Never Agreed to Two-Sided, Four-Delegation Formula,'" CSM, November 20, 1968, 13.

For my related articles during this period, see "Viet Peace Still Faces Political Ambush" [New Phase for War Viet Talks Face Political Ambush], CSM, November 29, 1968, 2; "Saigon Slowly Names Delegates to Paris," CSM, December 4, 1968, 10; "Viet Puzzle — Are Viet Reds Preparing Another Major Offensive?" CSM, December 6, 1968, 1; "Allied Units Brace for Cong Push," CSM, December 7, 1968, 1, 9; "Send-off for Paris Team — Saigon in Democratic Exercise," CSM, December 10, 1968, 7; "Anti-Thieu Leftists Organize," CSM, December 19, 1968, 1; "Too Many Concessions? — Saigon Approaches Peace Table Warily," CSM, December 21, 1968, 1; "PW Talks — New Road to Viet Peace?" CSM, December 24, 1968, 2; "Does Viet Cong Plan Offensive?" CSM, December 24, 1968, 1; "Military Goals Elusive — Ordeals of '68 Shape Viet Peace Trend," CSM, January 2, 1969, 1.

66. Quoted in Wexler, *Vietnam War*, 208.

67. Karnow, *Vietnam*, title of chap. 16, 638–84.

68. Cited in *Vietnam Voices*, 393, 497, 581.

69. Wyatt, *Paper Soldiers*, 198–99.

70. Quoted in Olivier Todd, *Cruel April: The Fall of Saigon*, trans. from French by Stephen Becker (New York: Norton, 1990), 367–69.

71. Quoted in Berman, *No Peace, No Honor*, 271.

11. TWO "DARLING SPIES" AND I

1. Nguyen Du, *Tale of Kieu*, 74, 126.

2. Stanley Karnow, "Vietnamese Journalist's Divided Allegiance," *San Francisco Chronicle*, May 30, 1990, 9; Karnow, *Vietnam*, 39–41.

3. Deepe, "Saigon Says Red Spy Net Cut by Security Campaign," CSM, August 16, 1967, 1, 2; Deepe, "New Saigon Regime Is Believed Moribund at Birth," 4; Deepe, "Reds in Yellow Robes? Maybe Mme. Nhu Was Right?" NYHT, March 14, 1965, 19; Deepe, "A Dozen Cong Spies Arrested after Infiltrating Saigon HQ," NYHT, June 6, 1966, 8; Deepe, "China War Peril Impels Inquiry Now — Fulbright," NYHT, March 7, 1966, 1, 4

4. Manuel DeLanda, *War in the Age of Intelligent Machines* (New York: Swerve Editions, 1991), 179.

5. Sun Tzu, *Art of War*, trans. and with an introduction by Samuel B. Griffith (1963; repr., London: Oxford University Press, 1973), 144–45, 149.

6. Quoted in Larry Berman, *Perfect Spy: The Incredible Double Life of Pham Xuan An, Time Magazine Reporter and Vietnamese Communist Agent* (New York: HarperCollins/Smithsonian Books, 2007), 171.

7. After the Communist victory in 1975 many other spies surfaced in South Vietnam. In one eye-opening example the tutor who had taught Vietnamese to the top CIA official in Saigon, William Colby, confessed to being a spy for Hanoi; see Colby, *Lost Victory*, 41.

8. Quoted in Hoang Hai Van and Tan Tu, *Pham Xuan An: A General of the Secret Service* (Hanoi: Gioi Publishers, 2003), 82, 86.

9. Zhang Fang, *Animal Symbolism of the Chinese Zodiac* (Beijing: Foreign Languages Press, 2001), 122.

10. Quoted in Berman, *Perfect Spy*, 166.

11. Quoted in Thomas A. Bass, *The Spy Who Loved Us: The Vietnam War and Pham Xuan An's Dangerous Game* (New York: Public Affairs, 2009), 151.

12. My single-spaced, eighteen-page letter 6 to the *New York Herald Tribune's* Harry Rosenfeld, September 18, 1965.

13. Hoang and Tan, *Pham Xuan An*, 133–39, 169.

14. Quoted in Bass, *Spy Who Loved Us*, 66.

15. Morley Safer, *Flashbacks on Returning to Vietnam* (New York: Random House, 1990), 151.

16. Robert Shaplen, *Bitter Victory* (New York: Harper & Row, 1986), 11.

17. Prochnau, *Once upon a Distant War*, 154.

18. Safer, *Flashbacks*, 178.

19. Quoted in Hammond, *Public Affairs*, 233.

20. Pham Xuan An and Beverly Deepe, "Vietnam's Invisible War of Subversion," *NYHT*, April 11, 1965, 18; Hoang and Tan, *Pham Xuan An*, 54–55.

21. My letter 6 to Rosenfeld, September 18, 1965.

22. Robert Shaplen, "Life in Saigon: Spring 1972: We Have Always Survived," in *Reporting Vietnam*, pt. 2, *American Journalism, 1969–1975* (New York: Library of America, 1998), 327–28. Reprinted from the *New Yorker*, April 15, 1972.

23. Bass, *Spy Who Loved Us*, 69, 163; handwritten notes of an interview with Vuong by David Butler, September 8, 1983. These notes are available in the Papers of David Butler at Dartmouth College, Rauner Special Collections Library

(box 5, folder 32, n.p.). I am grateful to David Butler, one of the last journalists to leave Saigon as it fell to the Communists, for making these notes available to the library and to the special collections librarian who photocopied and mailed them to me.

24. Rufus Phillips, *Why Vietnam Matters: An Eyewitness Account of Lessons Not Learned* (Annapolis MD: Naval Institute Press, 2008), 18, 22, 78–79, 173, 320n15.

25. To track "darling spies," I found a footnote at page 144 in Francis Fuller, "Mao Tse-Tung: Military Thinker," *Military Affairs* 22, no. 3 (Autumn 1958): 139–45. That footnote eventually led me to Robert Payne, *Mao Tse-tung: Ruler of Red China* (New York: Henry Schuman, 1950), 105.

26. Safer, *Flashbacks*, 177.

27. Butler notes.

28. Butler notes.

29. Safer, *Flashbacks*, 178.

30. *Pham Xuan An: His Name Is like His Life* was the first Hanoi-sanctioned biography of An, written by North Vietnamese journalist-cum-author Nguyen Thi Ngoc Hai, but it was not published in English. Her 2002 award-winning book linked An's name to the hidden or secret half of his life that had been concealed from me and others in the South for decades.

31. Hoang and Tan, *Pham Xuan An*, 213.

32. Berman, *Perfect Spy*; Bass, *Spy Who Loved Us*.

33. Hoang and Tan, *Pham Xuan An*, 130.

34. Safer, *Flashbacks*, 178, 182; Karnow, "Vietnamese Journalist's Divided Allegiance"; Karnow, *Vietnam*, 39–41.

35. Hoang and Tan, *Pham Xuan An*, 27.

36. An became acquainted with William Colby, who headed the CIA office in Saigon in 1959 and later became CIA director in Washington, and got to know a number of intelligence officials from Britain, France, South Korea, and Taiwan; see Hoang and Tan, *Pham Xuan An*, 54.

37. Berman, *Perfect Spy*, 74; Hoang and Tan, *Pham Xuan An*, 29.

38. Quoted in Hoang and Tan, *Pham Xuan An*, 12, 17, 20–21, 25, 31–33, 196–98.

39. An is listed as being accredited to *Time-Life* News Service on April 1, 1968, and Vuong is accredited to the *New Yorker*, according to Braestrup, *Big Story*, 245, 253.

40. Karnow, "Vietnamese Journalist's Divided Allegiance"; similar comments by An are in books by Karnow and Safer.

41. Hoang and Tan, *Pham Xuan An*, 151–52; Safer, *Flashbacks*, 178.

42. Cited and quoted in Hoang and Tan, *Pham Xuan An*, 45–47, 83–86, 100, 127, 198.

43. Hoang and Tan, *Pham Xuan An*, 209, 213.

44. Quoted in Hoang and Tan, *Pham Xuan An*, 97; Deepe, "Cong to Attack? Defector Details New Plan for Assault on Saigon," CSM, May 1, 1968, 1, 15. On April 22, 1968, a 396-word Associated Press account was buried on page 15 of the NYT under the headline "Enemy Colonel Is Said to Defect; He Is Reported to Bear Plan for '2d Wave' of Attacks."

45. Bass, *Spy Who Loved Us*, 197.

46. Hoang and Tan, *Pham Xuan An*, 127–28.

47. Tom Mangold and John Penycate, *The Tunnels of Cu Chi* (New York: Berkley Books, 1986), 17, 24.

48. Hoang and Tan, *Pham Xuan An*, 61–62, 135–36, 138.

49. Hoang and Tan, *Pham Xuan An*, 161–62.

50. Mangold and Penycate, *Tunnels*.

51. Cited in Hoang and Tan, *Pham Xuan An*, 118, 123–24, 157.

52. Hoang and Tan, *Pham Xuan An*, 45–47, 101; Berman, *Perfect Spy*, 141, 143, 154, 171.

53. Quoted in Bass, *Spy Who Loved Us*, 137–38.

54. Hoang and Tan, *Pham Xuan An*, 45–46.

55. Cited and quoted in Hoang and Tan, *Pham Xuan An*, 73–74, 96, 101–2; Bass, *Spy Who Loved Us*, 277–79.

56. Shaplen, *Bitter Victory*, 13.

57. Halberstam, *Best and the Brightest*, 564, 512.

58. Bass, *Spy Who Loved Us*, 69, 160–61; Safer, *Flashbacks*, 179; Carl Bernstein, "The CIA and the Media: How America's Most Powerful News Media Worked Hand in Glove with the Central Intelligence Agency and Why the Church Committee Covered It Up," *Rolling Stone*, October 20, 1977, 55–67; Richard N. Haass, "Journalists as Spies: When the Media Is the Message," *Press/Politics* 1, no. 3 (Summer 1996): 93–97; James Aronson, "The Media and the Message," in *Pentagon Papers: Critical Essays*, 5:59n2.

59. A. J. Langguth, *Our Vietnam: The War, 1954–1975* (New York: Simon & Schuster, 2000), 172.

60. Safer, *Flashbacks*, 94–97.

61. Quoted in Bass, *Spy Who Loved Us*, 200.

62. In 1907, for the first time in a multinational treaty, Hague Regulation IV in article 29 defined a spy as a person "acting clandestinely or on false pretenses [who] obtains or endeavors to obtain information . . . with the intention of communicating it to a hostile party." See Solis, *The Law of Armed Conflict*, 55.

63. Zalin Grant, letters to the editor, *New Yorker*, July 4, 2005, 6; Berman, *Perfect Spy*, 157–58, 180, 279; Bass, *Spy Who Loved Us*, 226–27.

64. Berman, *Perfect Spy*, 180, 250, 275, 280; Bass, *Spy Who Loved Us*, 227–28.

65. Shaplen, *Bitter Victory*, 11.

66. This description is drawn from the photograph in Berman, *Perfect Spy*, 271.

67. Cited and quoted in Safer, *Flashbacks*, 174–86.

SOURCE ACKNOWLEDGMENTS

Grateful acknowledgment is made for permission granted to use copyrighted, previously published material in this volume:

Newsweek articles and excerpts of articles by Beverly Deepe © 1962, 1963, and 1964 by *Newsweek*. Reprinted by permission.

Excerpts of selected Associated Press articles by Beverly Deepe are used by permission of the Associated Press.

Excerpts of selected *New York Herald Tribune* articles by Beverly Deepe © 1964, 1965, and 1966 by the *New York Times*. All rights reserved. Used by permission and protected by the Copyright Laws of the United States. The printing, copying, redistribution, or retransmission of the Material without express written permission is prohibited.

Excerpts of a *Cosmopolitan* article by Beverly Deepe © 1967 by *Cosmopolitan* magazine. Reprinted by permission.

Excerpts of *Christian Science Monitor* articles by Beverly Deepe © 1967, 1968, and 1969 by the *Christian Science Monitor*. Reprinted by permission.

INDEX

Carey, John Franklin, 57, 58–59
Catholics, 49, 94, 95, 132
cease-fires, 187
Central Intelligence Agency (CIA),
    11, 53, 86, 240, 242; and anti-Diem
    coup, 111, 114–15, 306n75; and
    South Vietnamese military, 76, 158,
    287
Champa civilization, 47
Chapelle, Dickey, 21, 22
Chennault, Anna, 226–27
China, 8, 36, 126
Christian Science Monitor, 185–86, 243;
    Beverly Deepe's dispatches for, 185,
    216, 223–24, 316n15; and Nixon-
    Thieu story, 225–26, 228–29; Pulit-
    zer Prize nomination of Beverly
    Deepe by, x, 221–22; Tet Offensive
    coverage by, 52–53, 191–92, 200
Chuong Thien Province, 55
Civilian Irregular Defense Forces, 76,
    169–70
Cleary, Fred K., 25
Clifford, Clark, 222, 228
Clodfelter, Micheal, 167, 169
Colby, William, 113, 320n7, 321n36
Collins, Robert M., 223
Columbia University, 6
Combined Action Platoons (CAPS),
    155
Confucianism, 49, 96, 102–3, 302n9,
    303n13
Congressional Record, 160–61, 273–87
counterinsurgency, xii, 37, 72, 136
Counterinsurgency Guide, xii
covert operations, 11, 90, 131
credibility loss and gap, 84, 222, 247
Cronkite, Walter, 191

Dac, Tran Van, 244–45
Dalat, 126
Danang (airbase), 143, 154–55, 199,
    276–77, 284
Danang (city), 159, 161, 280
Dao, Bao, 96
Davis, Saville, 228
Deal, William L., 68
death zones, 46, 54, 153, 166
DeCube, Leroy, 79
Deepe, Beverly, 9, 11, 15, 63, 77; apart-
    ments of, in Vietnam, 12, 13, 119,
    121, 184–85; arrival of, in Vietnam,
    xiv, 9–10; and Associated Press,
    5–7, 80; association of, with Pham
    Xuan An, 121, 236–37, 243; child-
    hood and youth of, 1, 3–5; and
    Christian Science Monitor, x, 185, 216,
    221, 223–24, 316n15; collection of
    articles by, xiii–xiv, 253–71; combat
    operations accompanied by, 65–66,
    148–49, 152–53, 183; *Congressional
    Record* and, 160–61, 273–87; cover-
    age of Tet Offensive by, 52–53,
    191–92, 195–96, 199–203, 314n23;
    finances of, 10; as freelancer, xiv,
    14, 185, 236; gender of, 20, 26,
    138; impact of articles by, 113, 139,
    225–26; interview of Madame
    Nhu by, 172; interview of North
    Vietnamese prisoner by, 128–29;
    interviews of Buddhist protesters
    by, 98–100, 101–2; interviews of
    Nguyen Khanh by, 125, 126–27, 128,
    133–34, 137, 139; interviews of rural
    villagers by, 42–45; interviews of
    Viet Cong leaders by, 188–90; mar-
    riage of, 160; *Newsweek*'s associa-

tion with, 80–83, 98, 120, 300n17; *New York Herald Tribune*'s association with, 120–21, 184, 236; Nguyen Hung Vuong's association with, 121, 239; Pulitzer Prize nomination of, x, 221–22; and Saigon press corps, x, 10, 15–18, 138, 241; scoops by, 131, 138, 224–29; trips to Bien Hoa by, 146–48, 195; trip to CAP outpost by, 155–56; trip to Hue by, 199–203; trip to Khe Sanh by, 205–22; trip to Laos by, 87–90, 93; trip to Mekong Delta by, 57, 58–64; trip to Pleiku by, 141–42; trip to Viet Cong territory by, 187–90; world traveling by, 6–7

Deepe, Doris, 1–2, 3–4, 5

Deepe, Martin, 1, 3–4, 5

de Gaulle, Charles, 8, 120

depopulation, 45, 54, 153–54, 171, 176

Diem, Bui, 225, 226–27, 228

Diem, Ngo Dinh, *94*, 95, 96–97, 302n9; and Buddhists, 94, 103; Confucianism of, 49, 96, 302n9; coup against, 106, 107, 109–16, 275; domestic policies of, 44, 48; and military, 69; Strategic Hamlet Program of, 41, 48, 50, 74, 275, 296n4

Dien Bien Phu, 186

Dillard, Robert, 70

Dinh, Mrs. Nguyen Thi, 173–74

Dinh, Pham Van, 201

Dinh, Tran Van, 109

Dinh Tuong Province, 54, 153

Dirksen, Everett, 227–28

Doering, Anne, 14–15

domino theory, 8, 161–62

Don, Tran Van, 302n9

Dong Nhi, 39, 43

Dong Xoai, *168*

Drummond, Roscoe, 191–92

Du, Nguyen, 180; *Tale of Kieu*, 180–81, 233, 234

Duc, Duong Van, 134

Duc, Thich Quang, 98–100, *100*

Duc Lap, 170

Duong Son 1, 160

Eisenhower, Dwight D., 88, 97, 126

Elliott, Osborn, 112

Ellison, Robert, 205

espionage, 239–41, 242–49; 320n7, 322n62

Essoyan, Roy, 7

Five Mountain Villages Campaign, 157–59, 285–87

forced resettlement, 45–47, 74, 166

Foreman, Rick, 155–56

fortune telling, 135–36, 172–73

Freedom Forum, x, 289n3

free-fire zones, 46, 166. *See also* death zones

French Indochina War, 10, 36, 51, 83, 186, 209, 242. *See also* Geneva Accords (1954)

friendly fire, 153

frontier forts, 74–79, 84–86, 90–92, 208

Gavin, James, 58

Geneva Accords (1954), 10, 11, 28, 44, 83, 87, 97

Giap, Vo Nguyen, 20, 235–36, 246; on armed struggle and political struggle, 30; strategy of, 26, 29; on U.S. failure, 58, 152, 216, 223

The Good Earth (Buck), 5
Gravel, Mike, xv–xvi
Green Berets, 10, 76, 78, 209

Hai, Nguyen Thi Ngoc: Pham Xuan
    An, 321n30
Halberstam, David, 16, 82, 292n20
Harkins, Paul D., 8, 114, 115
Harriman, Averell, 116, 229–30
Harrington, Gerald L., 219
Hayslip, Le Ly, 64, 175–76
Hayward, Henry, 186, 224, 225, 314n23
Hebron Journal, 3
Hebron NE, 1, 2–3
helicopters, 57–72; in combat mis-
    sions, 63–64, 65–68, 74, 147; giving
    of American Indian names to,
    70–72; military disadvantages and
    vulnerability of, 66–70, 72; U.S.
    reliance on, 10, 66; Viet Cong and,
    66, 67–68, 247–48
Herr, Michael, 19
Ho Chi Minh Trail, 78–79, 91–92, 141
Hohenberg, John, 82
Hoi, Buu, 103
Hoi An, 157, 284, 287
Hong, Nguyen, 101
Hue, 53, 93–94, 95, 198, 199–203, 215, 217
Hue, Dieu, 102, 103
Huet, Henri, 22
Hughes, John, 191, 197
Humphrey, Hubert, 224, 229, 230
Hung, Le Phan, 128–29
Huong, Muoi, 243, 244

Indians, American, 3, 150, 291n3;
    Vietnam compared to wars with,
    50, 71–72, 74, 79–80, 151, 155

inflation, 177, 280
intelligence: of Communist forces,
    242, 243, 246, 277; journalists and,
    235, 238, 249–50; South Vietnam-
    ese, 49, 127, 158, 238, 275, 282, 287;
    strategic, 234–35; U.S. military, 217,
    220, 221. See also espionage
Iraq, xi, xii

Jaeger, Neil Glenn, 60, 61
Jaeger, Raymond de, 292n20
Jamieson, Neil, 31
Jenkins, Thomas, 100
Johnson, Lyndon B., ix, 117, 120, 123,
    197, 207; and bombing of North
    Vietnam, 142; and coup against
    Ngo Dinh Diem, 112, 115, 306n72;
    depreciation of Vietnamese by,
    249; and press, 17; refusal of, to
    run for reelection, 222–23, 224; and
    Republican undermining of peace
    talks, 225, 226, 227–28; and Tonkin
    Gulf incident, 124, 130

Karnow, Stanley, 234, 241
Keane, Jack, xi
Keever, Chuck, xiv, 160, 235
Kennedy, John F., 25, 87; appoint-
    ment of Henry Cabot Lodge by,
    100–101, 105, 106; assassination of,
    116–17; election of, as president,
    ix–x, 101, 105; New Frontier imag-
    ery of, 3, 37, 74, 92; and Ngo Dinh
    Diem, 107, 113, 114; and Vietnam
    War escalation, 7–8, 10, 37, 58,
    131
Kennedy, Robert, 114, 115, 116
Kham Duc, 73–79, 75, 91–92

Khanh, Nguyen, *123*, 132, 274; Beverly Deepe's interviews with, 125, 126–27, 128, 133–34, 137, 139; and Maxwell Taylor, 122, 123–24, 137–38, 278; ouster of, 136, 140, 145, 278; and Robert McNamara, 122–23, 140, 278

Khe Sanh, 197, 205–20, *206, 208, 209*, 245–46; Beverly Deepe's dispatches from, 221–22, 316n15; Communist diversion in, 215, 216–17; consideration of use of nuclear weapons in, 207; lifting of siege of, 216; North Vietnamese tunnels and trenches around, 212, 213, 219; U.S. air power and, 211, 217–19; and U.S. military technology, 220; war correspondents in, 210

Khoi, Ngo Dinh, 97

Khrushchev, Nikita, 105

Kien Phong Province, 39, 41, 44

Kissinger, Henry, 96

Korean War, 58, 126, 141, 175, 194, 195, 196, 203

Ky, Mrs. Nguyen Cao, 172–73

Ky, Nguyen Cao, 178

Lac, Hoang, 96

land reform and development, 33–34, 44, 149–50, 283

Landsdale, Edward G., 240

Laos, 83–90; Beverly Deepe's trip to, 87–90; history of, 86–87; neutrality declaration of, 83–84; North Vietnamese infiltration through, 78, 85, 86, 91–92; U.S. bombing of, 90, 92, 275; U.S. covert war in, 11, 90

Le, Huynh Van, 101

Le, Kong, 87–88, 89, 90

Lien-Huong, Ly Thi, 106–7

Limerick, Patricia, 3

Linh, Tran Thuc, 180

Lodge, Henry Cabot, ix, 101, 105–9, 111, 114, 115, 116, 125

London Daily Express, 98, 103, 108, 125, 134

London Sunday Express, 98, 100, 105

Long, Gia, 199

Long, Mrs. Nguyen Van, 30, 165–66

Long An Province, 175

Long Binh, 53

Lubell, Samuel, ix, 6, 224, 289n1

Mang, Minh, 102–3

Mang Buc, 91

Manila Times, 46

Mansfield, Mike, 160–61, 273

Mao Tse-tung, 8, 36, 240

Marr, David G., 72

martial law, 104–5, 108, 304n31

McCone, John, 114–15

McNamara, Robert S., 8, 46, 58, 127, 143; assessments by, 51–52, 124, 145; and Gulf of Tonkin incident, 130; and Ngo Dinh Diem, 96, 112, 114; and Nguyen Khanh, 122–23, 140, 278; and pacification program, 51–52, 154

Mekong Delta, 57, 153; population of, 40, 296n1; strategic hamlets in, 41–42; during Tet Offensive, 196–97; Viet Cong and, 40, 187, 281–84

Michau, Simon, 292n20

Military Assistance Command, 52

Minh, Duong Van, 110, 133

Minh, Ho Chi, 180, 189, 221, 246; on assassination of Ngo Dinh Diem, 112; biographical information of, 35–36; as national hero, 20, 27–28, 97
Minh, Tran Van, 46
Mitchell, John, 226–27
Montagnards, 76, 78, 85, 92

Nam-O village, 155
National Geographic, 22
National Liberation Front (NLF), 34–35, 37, 229–30. *See also* Viet Cong
National Security Action Memorandum 288, 124
Navarre, Henri, 186
Nevard, Jacques, 292n20
Newsweek, 67, 86, 87, 98, 106, 108; and anti-Diem coup, 111–12; Beverly Deepe's association with, 80–83, 98, 120, 300n17
New Yorker, 197, 242
New York Herald Tribune, 72, 127, 131, 137, 139; Beverly Deepe's association with, 120–21, 236; cessation of publication of, 183–84, 243; *Congressional Record* reprints from, 160–61, 273–87
New York Times, 16, 128
Nga, Nguyen Thi, 174
Nga Ba, 281, 282
Nha Man, 281
Nhu, Madame Ngo Dinh, 80, *81*, 108, 110, 112, 171–72
Nhu, Ngo Dinh, 50, 103, 107–8, 110, 111, 112
Nixon, Richard M., ix, 19, 223, 224, 225, 226–28, 229, 230, 233

Nolting, Frederick, 100
North Vietnam, 9, 20, 126–27, 129, 217; covert operations against, 11, 131; creation of, 8–9; debate on strategy in, 78–79; and espionage, 235–36, 246; morale and determination in, 144–45; spy trials in, 131; and Tonkin Gulf incident, 11, 129–31, 134; U.S. bombing of, 134, 140, 142–45, 274–75
North Vietnamese army, 64, 128–29, 142; infiltration into South by, 86, 126–28, 166–67, 274, 275–76, 307n23; and Khe Sanh siege, 206, 210–11, 212, 213, 216–19; road networks of, 217; taking of Saigon by, 53, 230, 233; and Tet Offensive, 199, 202; weaponry and supplies of, 217
Nosavan, Phoumi, 88, 99
nuclear weapons, 126, 207

Oanh, Nguyen Xuan, 133, 134
Ochs, Adolph S., 185
Operation Cedar Falls, 153
Operation Hastings, 183
Operation Hop Tac, 51
Operation Junction City, 149
Operation Mastiff, 152–53
Operation Morning Star, 65–66, 149
Operation Rolling Stone, 149
Operation Sea Swallow, 47–48, 49
Operation Starlight, 150–52, 310n24
Operation Sunrise, 45
Operation Van Buren, 167, 169

pacification program, 51–52, 154–55, 156, 158; and depopulation, 54; Five Mountain Villages Campaign and,

157–59, 285–87; Tet Offensive as setback for, 52–53
Palmer, Bruce, Jr., 8
Parry, Robert, 226, 227, 229
Parsons, Cynthia, 192
Pathet Lao, 88, 89
Pentagon Papers, 51, 106, 137, 155, 303n13; about, xv–xvi; on anti-Diem coup, 107, 111, 112–13; on Communist forces, 13, 35, 127; on Ngo Dinh Diem, 97, 108–9; on operations against North Vietnam, 131, 142; on press corps, 19; on U.S. Embassy and Mission, 20, 125; on U.S. military, 10–11, 144; on U.S. strategy, 45, 52, 215
people-perimeter strategy, xii, 216
People's Action Teams (PATs), 158, 286, 287
Perry, Merton, 13–14, 16, 292n20
Pham Xuan An (Hai), 321n30
Pholsena, Quinim, 87
Phouma, Souvanna, 83–84, 90
Phu Yen Province, 47, 48–49
Pike, Douglas, 37
Plain of Jars, 87, 88, 90
Pleiku, 141–42, 273–74
plutonium, 126
Portisch, Hugo, 32
press censorship, 17, 82, 83, 104–5, 210
press corps: accreditation of, 16–18, 321n39; Beverly Deepe and, x, 10, 15–18, 138, 241; daily briefings for, 82, 239; "Declarations of Independence" by, 18; intelligence work by, 235, 238, 249–50; killing of members of, 21, 22, 205, 294n44; as male-dominated, 16, 82; *Pentagon*

Papers on, 19; portrait of, 15–18; South Vietnamese restrictions on, 82–83, 104–5, 238–39; during Tet Offensive, 195–96; use of guerrilla tactics by, 83; U.S. government and military suspicion of, 16, 17, 19, 250; and U.S. information policy, 143, 152, 210; women in, 20, 22, 294n41
Prochnau, William, 238
prostitution, 178–80, 279
Pulitzer Prize, x, 221–22

Quat, Phan Huy, 145, 278, 279

refugees, 54–55, 159, 166, 170–71, 202
Reischauer, Edmund, 162
Renard, Michel, 16, 292n20
Rice, Condoleezza, xi
Rogers, Bernard, 153, 154
Rostow, Walter, 226, 227, 228
rural development programs, 44, 48–49, 149–50
Rush, Benjamin, III, 85
Rusk, Dean, 161–62, 228

Sa Dec, 281
Safer, Morley, 238, 241, 250, 251
Safire, William, 229
Saigon, 10, 14, 104, 139, 187; coup against Ngo Dinh Diem in, 109–12; fall of, 53, 230–31, 233; refugees in, 54–55; streets in, 12–13; Tet Offensive and, 52, 190–91, 194; upper class in, 176–77; U.S. Embassy in, 52, 132–33, 190–91, 231
search-and-destroy operations, 65–66, 175, 215, 276–77; Beverly Deepe's accompanying of, 148–49;

search-and-destroy operations (*cont.*)
Operation Starlight as, 150–52,
310n24; pacification as alternative
to, 156; William Westmoreland's
concentration on, xii–xiii, 148, 150,
215

September 11, 2001, x, 221

Serong, Ted, 50

Shaplen, Robert, 239, 242, 250

Sheehan, Neil, 16, 247, 292n20

Sheldon, Courtney R., x, 186, 221–22

Sidle, Winant, 16

Smith, Garry, 156

Smith, Patricia, 14

Soc Trang, 58–62

South Korea, 7

South Vietnam: anti-Americanism
in, 132, 138, 159, 187, 191, 278, 280–81;
Beverly Deepe's first trip to, 6–7;
brothels and bars in, 178–80, 279;
Buddhist protests in, 93–94, 95,
97–102, 132–33, 136, 145; cost of
living in, 177, 279–80; coup against
Ngo Dinh Diem in, 106, 107, 109–
16, 275; coups and coup plotting
in, 13–14, 122–23, 125, 134, 136–37,
145, 278; creation of, 8–9, 97; fall
of, 8, 53, 230–31, 233; fortune telling
in, 135–36, 172–73; High National
Council in, 136–37; intelligence
work by, 49, 127, 158, 238, 287; land
reform and rural development in,
44, 48–49, 149–50; martial law
in, 104–5, 108, 132, 304n31; and
peace negotiations, 224–25, 229;
political instability in, 19–20, 275;
press restrictions by, 82–83, 104–5,
238–39; refugees in, 54–55, 159, 166,
170–71, 202; rural population in,
xiv–xv, 31–33, 34, 39–40, 60; Strategic Hamlet Program of, 41, 48, 50,
74, 275, 296n4; Tet cease-fire by,
187; U.S. dollars in, 279

South Vietnamese military, xii, 68,
69; and Civilian Irregular Defense
Forces, 76, 169–70; coups and
coup plotting by, 13–14, 125, 134,
136–37, 278; frontier forts of, 73–79,
84–86, 90–92, 208; looting by,
202; in Mekong Delta, 40, 281–82;
and People's Action Teams, 158,
286, 287; Ranger units of, 25–27;
Special Forces of, 107, 131; during
Tet Offensive, 200–202; women in,
76, *81*, 169–70, 176

Soviet Union, 6, 36, 217

Steinberg, Rafael, 80–81

Steine, Joel R., 68

Stirling, John, 292n20

Stone, James, 68

Strategic Hamlet Program, *40*, 47, 122;
Diem regime and, 41, 48, 50, 74, 275,
296n4; and forced resettlement,
74, 166; hardships of peasants of,
44; problems plaguing, 49–50;
statistics on, 41, 50; Viet Cong and,
41, 42, 44–45, 50, 51, 275. *See also*
depopulation; pacification program

Strickland, E. V., Jr., 60–61, 62

Sully, François, 16, 80, 119–20, 250,
292n20

Sun Tzu, 188, 234–35

surprise element, 221

Tabat, 91

Tale of Kieu (Du), 180–81, 233, 234

U.S. military (*cont.*)
154–55, 276–77, 284; body count
emphasis of, xii, 152; casualties of,
140, 151–52, 153, 196, 202; changing
role of, 140, 145, 146, 148, 166–67,
276–77, 284; escalation of, in
Vietnam, 7–8, 10, 37, 58, 131, 144,
146, 276; failures of, xi, xii, 8, 52, 53,
66, 72, 116, 152, 215, 221; families of,
134–35; firepower of, 54, 55, 152–54,
167–69, 196, 197, 217–18; high-tech
devices of, 220; intelligence of,
217, 220, 221; news coverage policy
of, 143, 152, 210; overoptimism of,
186, 215, 231, 247; reliance of, on
helicopters, 10, 66; troop totals of,
10, 144, 230; women in, 176
USS *Maddox*, 129–30
U.S. strategy: and counterinsurgency
plans, xii, 37; deficiency of, xii, 194,
215–16; and depopulation of countryside, 45, 54, 153–54, 171, 176; and
forward positioning, 194, 215; and
pacification, 51–53, 54, 154, 156, 158,
285–87; search-and-destroy operations and, xii–xiii, 65–66, 148, 150,
156, 215

Van, Hoang Hai, 241–42
Van Dyk, Ted, 229
Vann, John Paul, 68–69
Vientiane, 87
Viet Cong, 24, 25, 173; Beverly
Deepe's interviews with, 188–90;
defections from, 28–29, 49;
denunciation of United States
by, 35, 36; depopulation of areas
controlled by, 45, 171; and intel-

ligence, 277; and land reform,
33–34, 44, 283; mantraps of, 27,
160; in Mekong Delta, 40, 196–97,
281–84; mobilization of rural
population by, 31–33; name of,
24–25; nationalism of, 27–28, 29;
and NLF formation, 34–35; origin
of, 97; and pacification campaigns,
158–59, 286–87; political appeal
of, 29–31, 32; search-and-destroy
operations against, 65–66, 149, 151;
and Strategic Hamlet Program, 41,
42, 44–45, 50, 51, 275; strategy of,
26, 37; support for, 35, 122, 283; tax
collections by, 32, 283–84; territory
controlled by, 23–24, 27–29, 31–33,
45, 46, 189, 280–81, 284; terror and
coercion by, 34, 44, 187; during
Tet Offensive, 190–91, 194, 195,
196–97, 199–200, 202, 221, 314n22;
tunnels and caves of, 157, 158, 160,
169; and U.S. helicopters, 66,
67–68, 247–48; weaponry of, 35,
51; weddings of, 165–66; women in,
173–76. *See also* National Liberation Front (NLF)
Viet Minh, 44
Vietnamese nationalism, 27–28, 29,
237, 249, 279, 280
Vietnam Press, xiv
Vietnam War: Americanization of,
140, 145, 146, 148, 166–67, 276–77;
bipartisan U.S. support for, 106;
casualties of, 140, 151–52, 153, 167,
196, 310n24; comparison of, to
American Indian wars, 50, 71–72,
74, 79–80, 151, 155; de-escalation of,
230; and domino theory, 161–62;

end of, 8, 10, 53, 230–31, 233; escalation of, 7–8, 10, 37, 58, 131, 144, 146, 276; as first U.S. defeat, 192–93, 231; as helicopter war, 10, 58, 66; initial Vietnamese phase of, 140; lessons from, xi, xii, 72, 136; and peace negotiations, 215–16, 223, 224, 229–30; press coverage of, 16–18, 19, 82–83, 104–5, 143, 152, 195–96, 210, 238–39; U.S. dilemma in, xiii, 197, 216; U.S. government assessments of, 8, 51–52, 122, 124, 216; U.S. overoptimism during, 186, 215, 231, 247; U.S. portrayal of, 7–8; "Vietnamization" of, 230

Vietnam War, battles and operations of: Ap Bac (1963), 66–70, 247–48; Ashau (1966), 91; Ben Tre (1968), 196–97; Bien Hoa (1964), 136; Duc Lap (1968), 170; Five Mountain Villages Campaign (1965), 157–59, 285–87; Hue (1968), 199–203; Kham Duc (1968), 92; Khe Sanh (1968), 205–20; Operation Hastings (1966), 183; Operation Hop Tac (1963), 51; Operation Junction City (1966), 149; Operation Mastiff (1966), 162–63; Operation Morning Star (1962), 65–66; Operation Rolling Stone (1966), 149; Operation Sea Swallow (1962), 47–48, 49; Operation Starlight (1965), 150–52, 310n24; Operation Sunrise (1962), 45; Operation Van Buren (1966), 167, 169; Pleiku (1965), 141–42, 273–74; Saigon (1968), 59, 190–91, 194

Vuong, Nguyen Hung, 125–26, 135, 185, 187; accreditation of, 321n39; as Beverly Deepe's assistant, 121; as CIA agent, 239–41; as "darling spy," 240; as translator, 128–29, 160, 239

Wald, Richard C., 120, 122, 139
Walt, Lewis, 284
Washington Post, 113, 195
waterboarding, 175–76
Watergate, 230
Watlack, Richard G., 68
Westmoreland, William C., 125, 215, 222, 274; and press, 16, 17; on Tet Offensive, 220–21; and U.S. strategy in Vietnam, xii–xiii, 148, 150, 171, 194, 215–16; wishful thinking by, 186, 215
Wilkes, Kathleen, 176
Williams, Mrs. Joe, 135
women, 163–81; and prostitution, 178–80; in South Vietnamese military, 76, *81*, 169–70, 176; subservience of Vietnamese, 164–65; torture of, 175–76; in U.S. armed forces, 176; Viet Cong and, 165, 173–76; as war correspondents, 20, 22, 294n41
Women's Armed Forces Corps (WAFC), 176

Young Women's Christian Association, 6

Zorthian, Barry, 196

STUDIES IN WAR, SOCIETY, AND THE MILITARY

To order or obtain more information on these or other University
of Nebraska Press titles, visit www.nebraskapress.unl.edu.